THE NEW AMERICAN COMMENTARY

An Exegetical and Theological
Exposition of Holy Scripture

General Editor
DAVID S. DOCKERY

Consulting Editors

L. RUSS BUSH	PAIGE PATTERSON
DUANE A. GARRETT	ROBERT B. SLOAN
KENNETH A. MATHEWS	CURTIS A. VAUGHAN
RICHARD R. MELICK, JR.	LARRY L. WALKER

Vice-President for General Publishing
JOHNNIE C. GODWIN

Vice-President for Marketing and Distribution
JIMMY D. EDWARDS

Director
THOMAS L. CLARK

THE NEW AMERICAN COMMENTARY

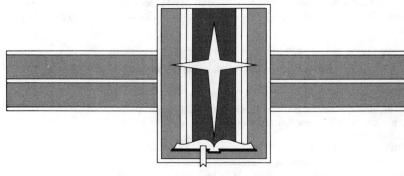

Volume
32

PHILIPPIANS
COLOSSIANS
PHILEMON

Richard R. Melick, Jr.

BROADMAN PRESS
NASHVILLE, TENNESSEE

Library of Congress Cataloging-in-Publication Data

Melick, Richard R.
   Philippians, Colossians, Philemon / Richard R. Melick.
      p. cm. — (The New American commentary ; v. 32)
   Includes index.
   ISBN 0-8054-0132-6
   1. Bible. N.T. Philippians—Commentaries. Bible. N.T.
Colossians—Commentaries.   3. Bible. N.T. Philemon—Commentaries.
I. Title. II. Series.
BS2705.3.M453   1991
227—dc20

To Shera

whose constant love has inspired the same in me,
whose life consistently reveals the Lord,
whose companionship has enriched my life, and
whose commitment to the Lord and his Word
  has been a constant source of strength.

Editors' Preface

God's Word does not change. God's world, however, changes in every generation. These changes, in addition to new findings by scholars and a new variety of challenges to the gospel message, call for the church in each generation to interpret and apply God's Word for God's people. Thus, THE NEW AMERICAN COMMENTARY is introduced to bridge the twentieth and twenty-first centuries. This new series has been designed primarily to enable pastors, teachers, and students to read the Bible with clarity and proclaim it with power.

In one sense THE NEW AMERICAN COMMENTARY is not new, for it represents the continuation of a heritage rich in biblical and theological exposition. The title of this forty-volume set points to the continuity of this series with an important commentary project published at the end of the nineteenth century called AN AMERICAN COMMENTARY, edited by Alvah Hovey. The older series included, among other significant contributions, the outstanding volume on Matthew by John A. Broadus, from whom the publisher of the new series, Broadman Press, partly derives its name. The former series was authored and edited by scholars committed to the infallibility of Scripture, making it a solid foundation for the present project. In line with this heritage, all NAC authors affirm the divine inspiration, inerrancy, complete truthfulness, and full authority of the Bible. The perspective of the NAC is unapologetically confessional and rooted in the evangelical tradition.

Since a commentary is a fundamental tool for the expositor or teacher who seeks to interpret and apply Scripture in the church or classroom, the NAC focuses on communicating the theological structure and content of each biblical book. The writers seek to illuminate both the historical meaning and the contemporary significance of Holy Scripture.

In its attempt to make a unique contribution to the Christian community, the NAC focuses on two concerns. First, the commentary emphasizes how each section of a book fits together so that the reader becomes aware of the theological unity of each book and of Scripture as a whole. The writers, however, remain aware of the Bible's inherently rich variety. Second, the NAC is produced with the conviction that the Bible primarily belongs to the church.

We believe that scholarship and the academy provide an indispensable foundation for biblical understanding and the service of Christ, but the editors and authors of this series have attempted to communicate the findings of their research in a manner that will build up the whole body of Christ. Thus, the commentary concentrates on theological exegesis, while providing practical, applicable exposition.

THE NEW AMERICAN COMMENTARY's theological focus enables the reader to see the parts as well as the whole of Scripture. The biblical books vary in content, context, literary type, and style. In addition to this rich variety, the editors and authors recognize that the doctrinal emphasis and use of the biblical books differ in various places, contexts, and cultures among God's people. These factors, as well as other concerns, have led the editors to give freedom to the writers to wrestle with the issues raised by the scholarly community surrounding each book and to determine the appropriate shape and length of the introductory materials. Moreover, each writer has developed the structure of the commentary in a way best suited for expounding the basic structure and the meaning of the biblical books for our day. Generally, discussions relating to contemporary scholarship and technical points of grammar and syntax appear in the footnotes and not in the text of the commentary. This format allows pastors and interested laypersons, scholars and teachers, and serious college and seminary students to profit from the commentary at various levels. This approach has been employed because we believe that all Christians have the privilege and responsibility to read and to seek to understand the Bible for themselves.

Consistent with the desire to produce a readable, up-to-date commentary, the editors selected the *New International Version* as the standard translation for the commentary series. The selection was made primarily because of the NIV's faithfulness to the original languages and its beautiful and readable style. The authors, however, have been given the liberty to differ at places from the NIV as they develop their own translations from the Greek and Hebrew texts.

The NAC reflects the vision and leadership of those who provide oversight for Broadman Press, who in 1987 called for a new commentary series that would evidence a commitment to the inerrancy of Scripture and a faithfulness to the classic Christian tradition. While the commentary adopts an "American" name, it should be noted that some writers represent countries outside the United States, giving the commentary an international perspective. The diverse group of writers includes scholars, teachers, and administrators from almost twenty different colleges and seminaries, as well as pastors, missionaries, and a layperson.

The editors and writers hope that THE NEW AMERICAN COMMENTARY will be helpful and instructive for pastors and teachers, scholars and students, for men and women in the churches who study and teach God's

Word in various settings. We trust that for editors, authors, and readers alike, the commentary will be used to build up the church, encourage obedience, and bring renewal to God's people. Above all, we pray that the NAC will bring glory and honor to our Lord, who has graciously redeemed us and faithfully revealed himself to us in his Holy Word.

SOLI DEO GLORIA
The Editors

Author's Preface

Commentaries are different from all other books. They are forced to deal with polarities. The agenda is set by the parameters of the biblical text, but the message of the Living Word must transcend time and find relevance in a contemporary setting. For centuries great minds have explored the meaning of the New Testament, and yet the literature on it continues to grow. New insights and technology provide vehicles for better understanding, and they bring their own unique challenges. Through all means, the commentary must illuminate the original text. After consulting a commentary, the reader should conclude that it is true to Scripture. That sense of integrity is the mark of a good work.

A biblical commentary has a higher goal as well. Christians meet their Lord through the pages of sacred Scripture. Thus a good commentary must contribute more than an interpretation of an ancient document. It must communicate a spirit about life so that it enriches the reader's thoughts, attitudes, and values. This means that the commentator must seek the mind of the original author, the Holy Spirit, since the Spirit produces a relationship with the Lord through the Word. A commentary is true to the text only when it communicates the mind of the human author and the divine author, the Holy Spirit.

Precisely this guides a theological exposition. The details of the text produce a dialogue with the thought of the author, which in turn points the reader to the Lord. The theological expositor is more than a linguistic archaeologist, as necessary as that is. The study of words and constructions in context produces a dialogue with the writer. They provide an understanding of the writer's mind and life-orientation and enable us to follow his thoughts as he communicated the word of the Lord to his generation. In seeing how that Word met the needs of the original audience, a knowledge of the dynamics of Scripture emerges. The Bible *is* the Word of God. It will remain unchanged, deriving its authority from the Lord who inspired it. The Bible must also *function* as God's Word. It always challenges human thought and life, calling its readers to a higher and better understanding of how to apply that authoritative word to contemporary life. A theological exposition exposes the thought of the writer through the pages of his text in such a way that readers understand and live better.

This commentary hopes to achieve these goals. Sometimes the commentary includes discussions of philological, syntactical, and exegetical concerns since they are the way ideas are negotiated. Most of these discussions will be found in footnotes. At other times it compares a text with the same theme in another writing by the same author. These comparisons are an attempt to understand matters of style and theology. They have been made freely but in such a way as to retain the distinctive contribution of the epistle under discussion.

The commentary makes generous use of footnoting to note alternate possibilities and to dialogue with issues which would otherwise interrupt the flow of the narrative. Many books and articles provided insight into the meaning of these biblical books. The limitations of this series, however, require a selective documentation. For that reason, extensive cross-referencing and supporting documentation have been avoided. Most of the references are to recent commentaries, and they generally note the location of supplementary information. Presumably, anyone who desires can have access to them. At the same time, several works have been extremely valuable, and these will be apparent in the number of references to them in the footnotes. I have not attempted to catalog every position, theory, or approach to the text. The target audience is the pastor and student, not the technical scholar, and I have tried to keep that in mind. Hopefully the product reflects scholarly integrity, theological accuracy, and the spirit of both the human and divine authors.

If the commentary exposes the text, it has been a success. At best, however, the ideas and words in it come from a human mind. No commentary can or should equal the importance of the New Testament. Scripture is authoritative. It will last beyond human discussions about it, and all interpretations must remain subject to it. The most that can be done is to explore its depths in the hopes that the Spirit of God will guide into the truth. This commentary is offered in that spirit. May the Holy Spirit illumine all our minds.

Many people contribute to a project such as this, and they deserve more than thanks. First, I thank the producers of the New American Commentary series for asking me to contribute this volume, as well as to serve as a consulting editor for the series. The general editors, at the beginning Mike Smith and then David Dockery, and the staff of Broadman Press provided consistent encouragement and help in many ways. Gray Allison and the administration and faculty of Mid-America Baptist Theological Seminary gave me enthusiastic support, offering their invaluable resources which enabled me to complete the writing. I am particularly indebted to Susan Brown, my secretary, who read, proofed, and verified both the English and Greek of the text. She took the project to heart as though it were her own, and I could ask no more of anyone. Many students over the years have dialogued with me on these epistles, and their thoughts have helped to focus mine.

Finally, but most importantly, I am indebted to my family. My wife, Shera, and children, Rick and Joy, Kristi, and Karen, showed their love, patience, and commitment to the project as I spent long hours of their time at the computer. They encouraged constantly, often in unconscious ways which meant so much. I pray that the Lord will reward them. They share my commitment to the Lord and his Word, and I have seen the Scripture text lived out in their lives individually and corporately.

My hope is that this commentary may help the reader (as the apostle John phrased it in another context) to "hear what the Spirit says to the churches." If anyone sees the Lord more clearly through this work, the long hours of labor have been rewarded. Both the study and the attempt to encapsulate it in writing have produced many wonderful hours of personal and private communion with the Lord. My work has been worship, and it is offered to the Lord for his glory.

Abbreviations

Bible Books

Gen	Isa	Luke
Exod	Jer	John
Lev	Lam	Acts
Num	Ezek	Rom
Deut	Dan	1,2 Cor
Josh	Hos	Gal
Judg	Joel	Eph
Ruth	Amos	Phil
1,2 Sam	Obad	Col
1,2 Kgs	Jonah	1,2 Thess
1,2 Chr	Mic	1,2 Tim
Ezra	Nah	Titus
Neh	Hab	Phlm
Esth	Zeph	Heb
Job	Hag	Jas
Ps (*pl.* Pss)	Zech	1,2 Pet
Prov	Mal	1,2,3 John
Eccl	Matt	Jude
Song of Songs	Mark	Rev

Commonly Used Reference Works

AB *Anchor Bible*
Arch *Archaeology*
BA *Biblical Archaeologist*
BAGD W. Bauer, W. F. Arndt, F. W. Gingrich, and F. Danker, *Greek-English Lexicon of The NT*
BalSt *Balkan Studies*
BBB Bonner biblische Beiträge
BBC *Broadman Bible Commentary*

BDB	F. Brown, S. R. Driver, and C. A. Briggs, *Hebrew and English Lexicon of the Old Testament*
BDF	F. Blass, A. Debrunner, and R. W. Funk, *A Greek Grammar of the New Testament*
Bib	*Biblica*
BSG	*Bible Study Guide*
BSt	*Biblische Studien*
BZNW	Beihefte zur ZNW
CBQ	*Catholic Biblical Quarterly*
CGTC	*The Cambridge Greek Testament Commentary*
CTR	*Criswell Theological Review*
DNTT	*Dictionary of New Testament Theology*
EBC	*Expositor's Bible Commentary*
EQ	*Evangelical Quarterly*
ExpTim	*Expository Times*
GTJ	*Grace Theological Journal*
HatRed	Hatch and Redpath
HDB	*Hastings' Dictionary of the Bible*
Her	*Hermeneia*
HNTC	*Harper's New Testament Commentaries*
HNT	*Handbuch zum Neuen Testament*
HTR	*Harvard Theological Review*
IB	*Interpreter's Bible*
ICC	*International Critical Commentary*
JBL	*Journal of Biblical Literature*
JTS	*Journal of Theological Studies*
JTS [NS]	*Journal of Theological Studies [New Series]*
MNTC	Moffatt NT Commentary
NBC	*New Bible Commentary*
NCB	*New Century Bible*
NClarBib	*New Clarendon Bible*
NIC	*New International Commentary*
NGT	Nestle's Greek Testament
NTC	*New Testament Commentary*
NTD	*Das Neue Testament Deutsch*
NTS	*New Testament Studies*
NTTS	New Testament Tools and Studies
NovT	*Novum Testamentum*
NovTSupp	Novum Testamentum, Supplements
RB	*Revue Biblique*
RTR	*Reformed Theological Review*
SBLDS	SBL Dissertation Series
SBLSBS	SBL Sources for Biblical Studies

SNTSMS	Society for New Testament Studies Monograph Series
TDNT	G. Kittel and G. Friedrich (eds.), *Theological Dictionary of the New Testament*
ThayLex	Thayer, *Lexicon*
TNTC	*Tyndale New Testament Commentaries*
TR	*Textus Receptus*
UBS	United Bible Societies *Greek New Testament*
UNT	*Untersuchungen zum Neuen Testament*
USQR	*Union Seminary Quarterly Review*
WBC	*Word Bible Commentary*
WEC	*The Wycliffe Exegetical Commentary*
WH	Westcott and Hort

Contents

Philippians

──────────────── **INTRODUCTION** ────────────────

Philippians, more than any other Pauline epistle, reveals insights into Paul's situation, commitments, and background. Paul spoke candidly to his strongest supporters. He explained the situation at Rome and how his imprisonment caused mixed reactions in the church. He thanked his dear friends for their financial and prayer support and urged them to continue in the faith in spite of opposition. By sharing his thoughts and actions, Paul hoped to provide a model of the truth. This incarnational principle permeates his writing in this epistle.

He found that he could even counter the false teachers by appealing to his past experiences. As a rabbi, he had lived what they taught and found it lacking.

In addition to revealing the life of Paul, the epistle contains a fresh presentation of Jesus Christ. In a lofty hymn about Jesus Christ, Paul called his readers to an examination and interpretation of the mind of Christ. Paul clearly believed his life had been transformed radically because of following Christ, and thus every portion of the epistle reveals the Lord through his servant.

The epistle reads easily. Paul's thoughts flow logically and personally, and there are few places where interpreters question the nature of the language or what it discloses. Apart from Philemon, Philippians is the most personal of all the Pauline corpus. Contemporary readers naturally and properly honor the apostle Paul. Paul, however, sought to honor his Lord, Jesus Christ. The focus on Paul can only be acceptable if it brings a clearer picture of the grace of God in Christ. This commentary, then, intends to honor that aspect of Paul's life. A goal of the commentary is to help readers see the apostle Paul in a new light, with real and vital, life-changing commitments. Another goal is that readers will feel the depth of his understanding and practical insights. The overriding goal, however, is that readers will see the Lord through the pages of the text.

1. The City and Its People

Philippi is one of the better known New Testament cities. Scholars have done extensive historical and archaeological investigation at the site of Philippi, and information is readily available. The French Archaeological School of Athens excavated the site from 1914 until 1937.[1] The Greek Archaeological Service continued the excavations after that time. Philippi's main street was the *Via Ignatia*, the main east-west Roman road of Macedonia. The present ruins include the forum, agora, streets, gymnasium, baths, library, and acropolis. In addition to what may be a 400 B.C. temple of Apollo and Artemis,[2] the site has produced numerous inscriptions and coins.

(1) Location

Philippi was located in the northeast section of the Roman province of Macedonia, between the Strymon and Nestos Rivers. Being about eight hundred miles from Rome and approximately ten miles from the seaport of Neapolis made the city strategic in ancient times. Originally the city lay on a steep hillside on the edge of an inland plain. Abundant natural resources, such

---

[1] See P. Collart, *Philippes, ville de Macedoine depuis ses origines jusqu'a la fin de l'époque romaine* (Paris: E. de Boccard, 1937).

[2] See P. Ducrey, "The Rock Reliefs of Philippi," *Arch* 30 (1977): 103ff.; St. Pelekanidis, "Excavations in Philippi," *BalSt* 8 (1967): 123; and P. Davies, "The Macedonian Scene of Paul's Journeys," *BA* 26 (1963): 95ff. An excellent master's thesis on Philippi records significant information about the city and its people: J. G. Armistead, "The Social Setting of the Early Christian Community at Philippi" (Unpublished M.A. thesis presented to the faculty of the University of Mississippi Department of Classics, 1987).

as water supplies, timber, and metals, made the city important.[3] Most importantly, the area contained extensive gold mines on the Hill of Dionysus not far from town.[4] These attracted the early settlers and prepared the city as a capital of the Greek armies.

The most imposing geographical feature was a 750-foot-high rock cliff which overlooked Philippi. Many reliefs, depicting the religious cults popular at Philippi, were sculpted on it. Everyone who entered the city was immediately confronted with the religious symbolism of the area.

(2) History

Philippi had a long, varied history. The occurrence of several name changes may be indicative of its importance. Many scholars suggest the earliest name was Tasibasta, "the place of the Thasians,"[5] and some believe the city was also called Datus.[6] All agree that the ancient name was Crenides, "fountains" or "springs," a name given because of the abundant water supply there.

The city rose to prominence when it became the capital of the Greek empire. In 359/358 B.C. Philip II of Macedon gained control of the city after the residents appealed to him for help against the neighboring Thracians. He renamed the city Philippi, the first time a city had been named for its benefactor.[7] With the resources there, especially gold and timber, Philip dreamed of uniting Greece and conquering the world. His untimely death ended his plans, but his son, Alexander, inherited his vision. At the age of nineteen, Alexander ventured from Philippi and in twelve years established a world dominion for the Greeks. Philippi became the showpiece of Greek culture, and Alexander devoted significant energies to its development.

About two hundred years later, Roman soldiers conquered Macedonia (168 B.C.). They divided the territory into four districts, each having its own legislature, and discontinued the mining operations.[8] The city's significance diminished until about 40 B.C., following the battle of Philippi.

Civil war broke out following Julius Caesar's death in 44 B.C. Antony and Octavian fought Brutus and Cassius on the plains near the city. Two battles ensued. Antony's army defeated Cassius first, and two weeks later Octavian defeated Brutus. Antony and Octavian disbanded their armies and established a colony at Philippi in 42 B.C. and in 30 B.C., respectively. The city was revived by army veterans, giving the city a predominant Italian flavor.

---

[3] See S. Casson, *Macedonia, Thrace, and Illyria* (Oxford: University Press, 1926), 3ff.

[4] Appion, *Bella Civilia*, 4:106. Quoted in Armistead, 16.

[5] Casson, *Macedonia*, 49.

[6] Ibid., 47. Others think that Datus was another place close by.

[7] N. G. L. Hammond and G. T. Griffith, *A History of Macedonia* (Oxford: Clarendon, 1972), 2:360. The plural name of the city is interesting. Perhaps it indicates that several settlements existed in the area. Further, this was the first Macedonian colony. The practice was later repeated in the advance of the Greek armies.

[8] Armistead, 19.

Additionally, Octavian conferred upon it the *ius Italicum*, giving the colonists the same privileges and rights as those who lived in Italy.[9]

Although Roman colonies emulated Rome, each enjoyed considerable self-government. Colonies elected their officials in pairs: two *duumviri* (judicial and political figures), two *aediles* (public works officials), and two *quaestores* (financial officers).[10] Each Roman colony also had a *territorium* composed of land surrounding the city. Philippi's *territorium* consisted of 730 square miles which encompassed many small villages.[11] This made the city significant to the area, but Macedonia had five other colonies. Philippi never attained the status of Thessalonica, the principal city of the province, located 100 miles away.

(3) People and Language

In the first century, Philippi contained a diverse population. Three primary ethnic groups lived there, but many others came for various reasons, including commerce. The native Thracians remained from the days when Philippi was outside of Macedonia. Many Latin inscriptions have been found that contain Thracian elements. This witnesses to the strength of the Thracian community even after Greek and Roman dominance.

The second major population group was Greek. Originally the Greeks were fourth-century B.C. colonists who shared Philip's dream of a world empire. Later, others moved to Philippi because of the commercial opportunities. Greek culture and language quickly conquered the Thracian culture, and by Paul's time any traveler with a knowledge of Greek could easily move about Philippi.

Finally, the Romans occupied the territory. From appearances, the Roman element was the strongest. Although it is impossible to know the identity of the various groups, clearly the Romans ruled every aspect of life in the city. Perhaps the double colonization of veterans after the Roman civil war gave them this prominence.

The strong Roman element suggests that Latin was the primary language of the city. The inscriptions bear this out, as do the tombstones.[12] It continued to be the primary language into the second century and survived until after the time of Constantine.[13] Greek was always spoken as well. Although anyone could make his way through the city with a knowledge of Greek, to be fully conversant with the affairs of the city, Latin was necessary. Apart from Rome, Philippi was no doubt the most Roman of all the cities Paul visited.

---

[9]Ibid., 20-22.

[10]G. H Stevenson, *Roman Provincial Administration* (New York: Strechert, 1939), 172ff.

[11]Collart, 185ff, 276ff.

[12]B. Levick, *Roman Colonies in Southern Asia Minor* (Oxford: Clarendon, 1967), 161, reported that of 421 inscriptions found in Philippi, 361 were in Latin and 60 were in Greek (some of them were pre-colonial). Collart said the number of tombstones in Latin is double the number in Greek (301).

[13]Collart, 313.

Other cultures mixed at Philippi, but there is little evidence of a Jewish population. Paul did not go to the synagogue, as was his custom, presumably because there was none in the city. Instead, he went to the river where he knew the Jews would be worshiping (Acts 16:13). Even there, those who responded were Gentile women. Since Jewish law commanded that a synagogue be established where ten male heads of household lived (a *minyan*), apparently few Jewish males lived in Philippi. Possibly the military nature of the city did not attract the Jews. More likely, the pro-Roman flavor of the colony caused the Jews to be expelled, as they were in Rome in A.D. 49 under Claudius. Paul entered the city in approximately A.D. 50-51. Certainly such a devoted Roman colony shared the same political sentiments as the mother city. This would include anti-Semitism.

(4) Religion

Most large cities of the Roman Empire had complex religious environments. Philippi was no exception. Native Thracian religions were "somewhat crude and barbaric, oftentimes involving animal-worship, human sacrifice and orgiastic rites."[14] Three outstanding Thracian gods were Liber Pater, Thracian Rider, and Bendis. Liber Pater was identified with the grape harvests and, therefore, with wine. He frequently was equated to Bacchus or Dionysus and was the great local god of Philippi. Thracian Rider was associated with hunting and represented the native hunter cult. He was always depicted on a horse. Bendis was a Thracian goddess identified with Diana and Artemis. She always was dressed in boots and short skirt and carried a spear or knife and appeared extremely athletic. Worship directed to her involved orgiastic practices.[15]

In addition to the Thracian religions, many Greek and Roman cults entered the city. The inscriptions, rock reliefs, and scriptural testimony reveal the worship of a number of these deities.[16] Paul encountered a follower of Apollo in Acts 16:16.[17] Apollo was particularly known for divination, but he was also associated with music, archery, medicine, and shepherding. A favorite Italian god was Silvanus, god of the woodland. A temple dedicated to him was completed in about A.D. 20-30.[18] One of Paul's companions had the name of this god. Paul consistently called him Silvanus; Luke always called him Silas (cf. Acts 16:19).

The archaeological finds reveal the strength of the Eastern cults as well. The

---

[14] Armistead, 47.

[15] She was not the Diana or Artemis of Ephesus who is depicted with rows of breasts. That Diana was a local goddess. Much of the information in the text comes from Armistead.

[16] They include Zeus-Jupiter, Hera-Juno, Apollo, Athena-Minerva, Aphrodite-Venus, Cupid, Ares-Mars, Hermes-Mercury, Heracles-Hercules, Dionysus-Bacchus, and Artemis-Diana. Armistead, 50.

[17] This is evidenced by the Greek text which states she had the spirit of the "python" ("who had a spirit," NIV), a tradition associated with the worship of Apollo.

[18] Davies, 101.

Egyptian cult of Isis was most popular, but many others appeared.[19] The religious climate produced more than two dozen cults at the time of Paul. Some, however, estimate that there were more than forty varieties of these cults actively carrying on their religious practices.[20]

Finally, the emperor cult was a favorite religion. In fact, the specific charge brought against Paul and his company was that he advocated customs "unlawful for us Romans to accept or practice" (Acts 16:21). The acknowledgment and worship of the emperor served Rome's political interests and distinguished Roman loyalists. Inscriptions mention Julius, Augustus, and Claudia. Rome had a relatively tolerant attitude toward religion at that time, and one could easily practice both a national religion and the imperial cult.

In that light, the Roman attitude toward religion emerges. Rome determined two classifications of religion: legal and illegal. Legal religions were affirmed by the senate, which generally accepted the ethnic, national religions of its conquered people. Some religions were unsanctioned (illegal). In general, however, if the people of the religion did not promote public discord, anti-Roman sentiments, or excessive debauchery, Rome gave significant freedom to them. At the time of Paul, Christianity had not been accepted or rejected by the Roman officials. In fact the first encounter with the Roman government occurred at Philippi. Since the first missionary leaders were Jews, it seems likely that Rome considered Christianity a sect of Judaism, and its practice was protected as a national religion. After the destruction of the temple in A.D. 70, it became increasingly clear that Christianity did not have a necessary tie to Judaism to qualify as a national religion, and the potential for persecution from the Roman government increased.

2. The Founding of the Church

The church at Philippi was founded by the apostle Paul on his second missionary journey from Antioch, Syria. The precise time of Paul's arrival is unknown, but most likely it was around A.D. 51.[21] When Paul determined to return to the churches founded on the first missionary journey, he and Barnabas differed on taking John Mark. They parted company, and Silas accompanied Paul to the churches of Lystra and Derbe. At that time Timothy joined them, and they traveled west. Forbidden by the Holy Spirit to speak in Asia (Acts 16:6-7), they journeyed northwest to Troas, a major seaport on the west coast of Asia. There Paul had a vision of a Macedonian calling for help. Subsequently, he and his team sailed to Neapolis and walked to Philippi. As was his

---

[19] These included: Harpocrates and Serapis (Egyptian), and Cybele (Anatolia).

[20] Armistead, 45-46.

[21] Although estimates vary as to the exact date, the best chronology places the second missionary journey at about A.D. 50, shortly after the Jerusalem Council. Paul was in Corinth in about A.D. 52 because he appeared before Gallio during his proconsulship there. Paul probably entered Europe in the middle of this second journey.

habit, Paul looked for a synagogue where he could initiate conversations about Christ. Apparently there was none in the city, so on the Sabbath Day Paul went to the riverside outside the city gates to meet with those who practiced the Jewish faith.

In Acts 16:11-40, Luke recorded three significant events associated with the beginning of the church. An important convert to Christianity in Europe was Lydia from the Asian city of Thyatira.[22] She probably moved to Philippi to further her import business, which consisted of selling the purple cloth so famous in Thyatira. No doubt she had considerable resources since the purple dye was quite expensive. After her conversion, she invited Paul and Silas into her home. Lydia was already a proselyte to Jewish religion, and her conversion to Christ was a natural outworking of her desire to know God. Her household followed in her decision to accept Paul's message.

A feature of the period, as Beare notes, was the proliferation of "private brotherhoods. There were cult-associations devoted to the worship of a chosen god; and there were many such groups at Philippi."[23] The groups needed some influential person to provide the resources and location for the meetings, and the church was no exception. Lydia may have become the local patroness of the church. She also may have provided a link to the Gentile population of the city and, perhaps, to the more influential business community.

The second significant event at Philippi was the exorcism of demons from a slave-girl. Though the Scriptures do not state that she became a convert to Christianity, there is every reason to assume that she did. The masters of the demon-possessed girl made considerable money from her ability to predict future events.[24] Paul encountered her, and through the gospel the demon was exorcised. The masters, realizing that they would lose their living, dragged the missionaries to court to have them silenced. This was Paul's first Roman trial. The charges included causing a disturbance and introducing a foreign religion. Paul and Silas were stripped of their clothing, beaten with rods, and thrown into a dungeon with common criminals.

The third event Luke recorded occurred while Paul and Silas were in jail. In spite of the adverse circumstances, the missionaries sang praises to God at midnight. At that late hour, an earthquake shook the prison; the cells opened so that all could escape. The jailer, assuming the prisoners had fled, feared for his own life at the hands of the Roman officials. He drew his sword to kill himself, but

---

[22]F. W. Beare suggests that Lydia "was probably not her personal name but a nickname: 'the Lydian.'" *The Epistle to the Philippians*, HNTC (San Francisco: Harper & Row, 1959), 11.

[23]Ibid., 9.

[24]The Scriptures record that she had the spirit of "the python," a phrase reflecting the worship of Apollo, who surrounded himself with the snake. The prophecies connected with the worship caused the snake to be the symbol of the phenomenon. Some suggest her ability was actually ventriloquism, such as R. Martin, *Philippians*, NCB (London: Oliphants, 1976), 8-9. That hardly explains her ability to foretell events, which brought the owners great gain.

Paul assured him that all the prisoners were in their cells. The frightened jailer fell at the feet of the missionaries, and that night he and his family were converted to Christianity. They welcomed Paul and Silas into their home, bathed and cared for them, and gladly received the gospel message.

The next morning the city officials asked Paul and Silas to leave the city. Paul sent word that it was unlawful for Roman citizens to be subject to such treatment. The officials fearfully apologized to them and sent them on their way.

Paul maintained contact with the Philippian church. The missionaries visited the city again on the third journey. The church also took advantage of several occasions to send financial support to Paul (cf. Phil 4:15; 2 Cor 11:9) and to the believers at Jerusalem (2 Cor 8:1-5). When Paul was in prison at Rome, the church sent Epaphroditus, a leader among the brethren, to minister to Paul. He responded by sending Timothy to them and planned to visit in person after his impending trial. Perhaps Luke joined Paul at Philippi since the Acts account changes from "they" to "we" during this time.

The Philippian church became a model. From its beginning, it was healthy, even though at the time of Paul's writing, it was experiencing a minor problem of disunity in the congregation (4:2-7). The New Testament evidence suggests several characteristics of this congregation.

(1) Gentiles

The first converts were Gentiles, and Gentiles predominated in the fellowship. The Gentile character of the church may be questioned from Phil 3:1-4:1, which has a Jewish flavor to it; nevertheless, the historical data supports a primarily Gentile congregation.

(2) Women

Women played an important role in the life of the church at Philippi.[25] The New Testament mentions four women: Lydia and the slave girl, the first converts, and Euodia and Syntyche, who were identified as colaborers with Paul. They were noted for their involvement in the spiritual battles of the area (4:2-7). Although they occupied a prominent place, when the disturbance between these last two occurred, Paul urged the "yokefellow" to care for it (4:3). They did not have the chief place of leadership in the congregation.

(3) Generosity

The church became an example of generosity to the other churches of Macedonia and Achaia (2 Cor 8:1ff.). It gave to Paul and to the Jerusalem saints who were in need. The church apparently was not wealthy, even though some persons of means were members. Paul said the members gave beyond themselves and out of their rock-bottom poverty (2 Cor 8:2-4). The Philippian congregation was the only one specifically mentioned as sending a financial gift to Paul. The church remains an example of genuine Christian concern.

---

[25] Luke also recorded the prominence of women at Thessalonica, the other church of Macedonia (Acts 17:1-9).

(4) Loyalty

This church stood by Paul throughout his life, as evidenced in the gifts it gave for his support and in its desire to know Paul's state in Rome. It thoughtfully and lovingly maintained contact with its founder. Caird suggests that this church "was the one which gave him [Paul] the most satisfaction and the least trouble."[26]

The church remained strong into the second century. Its location on the *Via Ignatia* made it ideally suited for hospitality to travelers. Fifty years after Paul's letter to the church, Ignatius was escorted to Rome by Roman soldiers to be tried for his faith in Christ and he was comforted by the church at Philippi on the way.

3. The Occasion

Why did Paul write the epistle when he did? Several suggestions come from the epistle. Perhaps Paul wanted to inform the believers of Timothy's approaching visit and prepare them for it (2:19). Likewise, Paul intended to visit the church in the near future, and the letter could have prepared it for his visit (2:24). Others suggest that Paul felt the need to address the problem of disunity which had surfaced in the congregation (4:2-4). None of these, however, have significant enough material devoted to them to offer a plausible answer to the question of the timing of the letter.

More likely, Paul wanted to thank the Philippians for a gift received for his support. In 4:10-20, he expressed his thanks for their gift and took advantage of the opportunity to instruct them in a theology of material resources. Clearly the church's support had significant impact on Paul for two reasons. First, no other church gave to him like it did (4:15). Second, Paul's situation in Rome probably caused him to reflect on his ministry to other cities. To receive a tangible expression of confidence no doubt lifted his spirits. Even so, there could have been other occasions for expressing his appreciation. This suggestion may have contributed to the timing, but another possibility fits the data better.

Paul's companion Epaphroditus wanted to return to his friends at Philippi. The church had sent Epaphroditus to Paul as a personal embodiment of its concern. In the meantime, Epaphroditus almost died from a prolonged sickness. The church heard of his situation, and he, in turn, heard of its concern for him. He recovered, and Paul was eager to send him back to the church (2:28). Since he almost gave his life in service to Paul for fellow believers, Paul anxiously desired that they honor him appropriately. He would be better off at home. Paul took advantage of Epaphroditus's desire to return to the church. He wrote the letter expressing two concerns: thanks for the gift and a plea for unity.[27]

---

[26]G. B. Caird, *Paul's Letters from Prison* (Oxford: University Press, 1976), 98.

[27]M. Silva suggests that Paul had to explain why he sent Epaphroditus without their beloved Timothy. He states, "Aware that the Philippians would be deeply disappointed to see Epaphroditus

If this analysis is correct, it clarifies the nature of the letter. Paul wrote a warm, friendly letter to his loyal children in the faith. A problem of Jewish false apostles who attempted to bring the church under the law, loomed on the horizon. The problem did not require an urgent reply like the situation which prompted Galatians. This letter barely mentioned the problems. It accentuated the relationships between the members and Paul.[28]

4. The Authorship

No one seriously questioned Pauline authorship until the eighteenth century, when F. C. Baur expressed his extreme view that the letter is spurious.[29] Few followed him in that since his arguments rested "on grounds which even his disciples of the Tübingen School found unconvincing."[30] At least one author selected the epistle as the standard by which to measure Pauline thought.[31] Contemporary questions relate to the integrity of the epistle, but even most of those who see two or three letters collated into one accept the Pauline authorship of the fragments. It is agreed, therefore, that the epistle is Pauline. Polycarp (ca. A.D. 135) commented on the letter of Paul to the Philippians, and the letter appears in all the lists of canonical writings. The letter claims to have been written by Paul and the external evidence for Pauline authorship is overwhelming. No serious objection to Pauline authorship exists today.

5. The Integrity

The question of authorship quickly passes to integrity. The two are distinguished in Philippians in ways that other epistles are not. Generally, the question of integrity involves multiple authorship of a given epistle. Regarding Philippians, most scholars agree that Paul wrote the entire letter. They disagree, however, on how many fragments of letters Paul composed and whether Philippians reflects one letter or more. Today, there are advocates of one letter, two letters, and three letters now contained in the one canonical letter.

Some support for the view that there are multiple letters in this epistle comes

---

rather than Timothy return Paul was faced with a serious challenge. How would he cushion this inevitable disappointment? Might Epaphroditus become the object of undeserved criticism?" *Philippians*, WEC (Chicago: Moody, 1988), 5. This reconstruction may capture the tone of 2:19-30, and it deserves consideration. Nothing in the text explicitly states that such disappointment would occur, however.

[28]This does not diminish the change of tone in 3:2-4:1, which will be addressed later. It does assume that the letter in its present form does not have the flavor of urgency. Often Paul changed tone when he turned his attention to a theological problem. He handled it appropriately as an apostle.

[29]F. C. Baur, *Paul: the Apostle of Jesus Christ*, 2 vols. (London: Williams & Norgate, 1875), 2:45-79.

[30]Caird, *Letters*, 98-99.

[31]C. L. Mitton attempts to prove that Ephesians was not written by Paul. He compares it with Philippians to prove his point. Cited in Caird, 99.

from Polycarp, who mentioned that Paul "wrote letters, by which, if you study them carefully, you will be able to edify yourselves in the faith imparted to you" (Polycarp to Philippians, 3:2).[32] Some have taken the plural words ("letters . . . them . . .") to mean there were actually letters from Paul to the Philippians. A. Harnack thinks the Thessalonian letters were included in Polycarp's plural since the two cities were in Macedonia. E. Schweizer regards 2 Thessalonians as a letter sent by Paul to the church at Philippi. A. Wikenhauser suggests that Polycarp was making a guess because of the abruptness of the canonical epistle at 3:2.[33] Perhaps J. B. Lightfoot correctly assessed the situation when he interprets the plural "letters" as referring to a letter of importance which had a plural designation because of its significance.[34]

Those who challenge the integrity of Philippians identify various fragments in the letter. The first assumed fragment is 4:10-20, where Paul thanked the church for its financial support. Advocates say that Paul hardly would have waited for months to write a note of thanks for their support, especially at this time of his life. They assume that it would have taken months for news to travel back and forth from Rome to Philippi and that Paul would have sent thanks immediately after his receiving the gift. In addition, why would he put the word of appreciation at the end of the letter rather than the beginning? Normally Paul thanked his readers at the beginning of his letters, and that would have been appropriate here as well.

The second assumed fragment begins at 3:2. At this point, the tone of the letter changes radically. No one doubts that Paul employed different writing styles, but they question whether he did so in one letter. Scholars who hold this view differ on where the fragment ends, at 4:1, 4:3, 4:9, or 4:20. Some assume that the change of tone is unusual because Paul addressed the same opponents in 3:2ff. as he did in 1:17ff. If that is true, the change is remarkable.

The third assumed fragment is 2:5-11. This section may well be pre-Pauline, but most scholars think Paul included the words himself, not that they were inserted by a later editor. This section, therefore, deserves its own treatment.

Today, scholars accept various ideas about Philippians. Those who reject one letter divide into those who accept two (3:2ff. as inserted into the original letter), and those who accept three (3:2ff. and 4:10-20 inserted into the original one). However, there is little agreement on the numbers of letter fragments, and there is even less on the precise verses which comprise each.

Fragment theories have difficulties. There must have been some reason for preserving and joining the fragments into the form in which they are preserved,

---

[32] Quoted in Martin, 11.

[33] See ibid., 11-12.

[34] J. B. Lightfoot, *St. Paul's Epistle to the Philippians*, reprint ed. (Grand Rapids: Zondervan, 1953), 142. He stated, "Whenever it occurs in prose of a single epistle, [it] seems to denote a missive of importance, such as a king's mandate or a bishop's pastoral." See also his section "Lost Epistles to the Philippians?" 138-42.

and there must be clear evidence that they do not fit into the "original" document. It is impossible to prove either of these in the case of Philippians. The most that can be said is that "it is possible," but the evidence suggests otherwise.

From the methodological perspective, several points argue for the integrity of the epistle. No external evidence exists for any other form of the epistle than the canonical one.[35]

There is no apparent motive for joining the letter fragments into one and concealing the parts. Paul's letters vary in length from the short letter of Philemon to the longer letters. There was no reason to put several together because of their length. Some suggest that the three letters were Paul's way of addressing separate problems, but in epistles like 1, 2 Corinthians multiple problems were addressed in the same letter. The theories of interpolation raise the question of the thinking of the interpolator. Why would anyone insert a document in such an awkward place as 3:2, and why would someone place the note of thanks at the end if everyone knew it should come first? Finally, why would the church be so sloppy as to lose the introductions and conclusions of the letters from one so dear to them as Paul?

The two main "fragments" reveal more in common with the epistle than is often thought. The thank-you note of 4:10-20 is placed well if two matters are considered. If Epaphroditus's sickness occurred on his way to Paul, so that the journey was completed only after Epaphroditus's recovery, the note from Paul may have been written immediately after receiving the money. Perhaps word returned to Philippi before Paul knew of the sickness, and it is conceivable that when Epaphroditus arrived at Rome with the gift a messenger from Philippi also arrived to inquire about Epaphroditus. Thus a delay of some months before sending the thanks is not the only possibility. C. J. Bahr suggested that Paul put the thanks at the end purposely so as to sign it with his own hand.[36] In that case, the thanks would have more personal significance since it came from Paul's own hand, which was customarily at the end.[37] Furthermore, there are "preparatory allusions to [the gift] in 1:5 and 2:30."[38] These considerations reveal that the "fragment" is not necessarily as disconnected as some have thought.

The second so-called fragment (3:2ff.) has also been explained reasonably. Paul often wrote with abrupt shifts in style, and it would not be surprising that

---

[35] The earliest extant form of the epistle is the Chester Beatty Papyrus (P-46) dated about A.D. 200. If the epistle existed in fragments, it did so well before that time, and there is no textual evidence to suggest such a history.

[36] C. J. Bahr, "The Subscriptions in the Pauline Letters," *JBL* 87 (1968): 27-41.

[37] Judging from Gal 6:11, two factors may be seen regarding the Pauline signatures. First, they authenticated the letters. Second, sometimes they had a personal message associated with them (Gal 6 ends some seven verses after Paul stated he signed in his own hand). Both of these factors would have relevance to the Philippian situation.

[38] Caird, 100.

he would do so in a warm, personal letter such as Philippians (see Rom 16:16-19; 1 Thess 2:13-16). The change in tone from warmth to harshness is difficult only if the opponents were the same ones as in 1:15-17. If he had addressed them earlier, the new invective would be startling. If he had not, a change in tone might be expected. Paul clearly was more soft-spoken with the opponents of 1:15-17, treating them as misguided Christians. In 3:2ff. the opponents were represented as being motivated by the things of the world and hardly could have been Christians. The hard tones do not continue throughout the entire section (3:2-21). At 3:7, the language of faith and commitment predominates. The section is not radically different from the previous portions of the epistle. Similar words and themes were used in this section.[39] The ethical admonitions of 2:12 resume in 3:2. Similarly, the issues raised in 1:28,29 and 2:14-16 also continue in 3:2; and the types of dangers were hardly compatible with each other.[40] The evidence for this segment as a fragment is not convincing.

Recently several scholars have approached the epistle from a literary perspective. The most enlightening of these approaches is by D. Garland.[41] He argues that the epistle has a solid literary unity intended to build to the point of addressing Euodia and Syntyche. The so-called harsh elements must be reevaluated in light of linguistic and semantic evidence. When this is done, the hard language is considerably softened. The biggest obstacle to disunity, the change of tone, is removed. The text has greater affinity with other passages in Philippians, and the need for a fragment hypothesis no longer exists. The details of this exegesis surface in the specific sections of the commentary as they are appropriate. The work of these scholars offers a new way of analysis which complements traditional exegesis and may provide a way beyond the seeming impasse of present analysis.[42]

After analyzing all the arguments, a conclusion may be reached. Significant evidence suggests the unity of the epistle, although some notable scholars disagree. The following reasons argue for the unity of Philippians: Definitive evidence of any kind supporting the fragment theories is absent. Those who accept a fragment theory have been unable to agree on the exact length of the fragments. Knowledge of a specific situation which called for the loss of portions

---

[39]This and the previous three arguments are well stated in G. Hawthorne, *Philippians*, WBC (Waco, Tex.: Word, 1983), xxxi. This discussion is an excellent overview of the subject.

[40]These last three points come from Martin, 15.

[41]D. Garland, "The Composition and Literary Unity of Philippians: Some Neglected Factors," *NovT* 27 (1985): 141-73. This article is very significant in the analysis of Philippians. Among the strengths in it are: a good survey of the history and current state of the problem, extensive bibliography for further reading, proper application of literary criteria in exegesis, and a new and effective way to solve the problem of the fragment theories. The direction of scholarly argument should be changed as a result of this article.

[42]The literature on this subject is extensive. An excellent summary is provided in Garland's article, and Hawthorne's commentary also provides good bibliographic data.

of the two or three letters is lacking, as is the lack of knowledge of any time when the fragments were put together. A clear motivation for joining the fragments is also lacking. The redactor, if there were one, did sloppy work when he chose to leave the epistle with such changes of tone and abrupt breaks after attempting to collate them. Good explanations exist as to how the "fragments" actually fit into the plan and purpose of Philippians. More recent literary analysis demonstrates a valid way of explaining the unity of the epistle. In short, the fragment theories do not contain compelling evidence, and there are at least two different methods of approaching the epistle which support the unity and integrity of the letter.

6. The Origin and Date

One's opinion about the date of the epistle depends in large measure on one's conclusions about the provenance of the epistle. The questions regarding these issues basically fall into two divisions: the circumstances of Paul and the theology of the epistle. These must be considered both separately and together since the theology has compelled some to look to a date that differs from the traditional.

(1) The Origin

ROME. The traditional view (i.e., the view that stems from the earliest centuries of Christianity) is that Paul wrote the epistle from Rome during his first Roman imprisonment. No other tradition survived from the second century until the eighteenth. The only external evidence available comes from the Marcionite prologue to the letter. The writer, speaking about the Philippians, stated, "The Apostle praises them, writing to them from Rome, from prison, by Epaphroditus."[43] Although it is the only history available, no one knows the origins of this prologue or what basis lay behind it.

The traditional view fits most of the details required by the text. Many factors enter into discussions regarding the origin of the epistle. Some of the more important are: Paul was in prison at the time of writing; Paul had the freedom to entertain friends, write letters, and lead a movement which was suspect in the eyes of the government; Paul faced a trial, the outcome of which was uncertain; the church engaged in extensive evangelistic work apart from Paul; Paul planned to visit Philippi, assuming he received a favorable verdict; most importantly, the interpreter must account for the number of times Paul's companions traveled to and from Philippi.[44]

Each of these easily fits into the Roman hypothesis except the travel records. The strongest objection to a Roman hypothesis is the distance between Philippi

---

[43] The Latin Marcionite prologue dated from the second century. Quoted by Beare, 24.

[44] Many sources provide extensive details regarding these matters. Helpful recent surveys from commentaries, with good bibliographies, include Martin, 36-57; Hawthorne, xxxvi-xliv; and Beare, 15-24.

and Rome. Objectors to the Roman hypothesis point out that the evidence calls for a minimum of four trips between Philippi and Rome, and perhaps as many as six would be necessary. The trips would have been: (1) news of Paul's imprisonment was sent to Philippi; (2) Epaphroditus was sent from Philippi to Rome with a gift and an offer of help (2:25); (3) news of Epaphroditus's sickness (after some time?) reached Philippi (2:26); (4) word reached Paul and Epaphroditus that the Philippians were concerned about Epaphroditus (2:26); (5) Paul hoped to send Timothy before he came himself (2:23-24); and (6) Paul possibly expected that Timothy would return and journey with him to Philippi.

The trip to Rome from Philippi was approximately 800 miles. From Rome, the traveler would follow the Appian Way to Brundisium (360 miles), take a ship across the Adriatic to Dyrrachium (2 days with favorable weather), and follow the Ignatian Way to Philippi (370 miles).[45] Sir William Ramsay estimated that a foot-traveler covered 15-20 miles per day on the Roman roads.[46] That equals 52 days by the slower rate and 39 by the faster. Imperial couriers traveled at a rate of 50 miles per day, perhaps with the help of carriages or horses.[47] That makes the travel time only 15 land travel days, 2 sea travel days, and whatever intervals were needed for rest or inclement weather. Some estimate that the travel requirements of 5 months traveling round trip, and thus 10 months total for 4 one-way trips, easily fit into 1 year of time [48] It is difficult to see how earlier commentators, such as A. Deissmann, claimed that the travel was impossible in less than 2 years.[49]

Many scholars also question the necessity of 4 to 6 trips from Rome to Philippi. Some have suggested that fewer trips were necessary. The travel could be reduced to a minimum with the following reconstruction: The Philippians heard that Paul was going to be sent (or possibly had been sent) to Rome to await trial; immediately they sent Epaphroditus with a gift for Paul's support, perhaps having heard he would have to rent housing; on the way, Epaphroditus took sick, and news of his sickness reached Philippi;[50] the church dispatched the news of their concern for him, knowing that the courier would reach him on the way to or in Rome; and Epaphroditus continued his journey upon his recovery and presented the money to Paul. This would have required two trips to Rome, which may have been undertaken simultaneously in part, although

---

[45] Beare, 18.

[46] W. Ramsay, "Roads and Travel (NT)," *HDB* 5:375-402.

[47] See Silva, 6, n 4.

[48] Beare, 19; Silva, 7.

[49] Quoted in Martin, 41.

[50] This was suggested by C. O. Buchanan, "Epaphroditus' Sickness and the Letter to the Philippians" *EQ* 36 (1964): 157-66. Martin, 42, objects to Buchanan's thesis because it contains "all manner of speculation," but nothing in Philippians states when Epaphroditus became sick. The primary speculative element is how the sickness occurred, not that it may have occurred earlier than his arrival to Rome.

there would obviously be delays for the sickness and recovery.

While this reconstruction is possible, it is hardly likely. The travel scenario is overdone. Too much may be built on unnecessary assumptions. The normal way to read the text allows for some time for Epaphroditus's sickness, and surely enough time elapsed for more than two trips from Rome to Philippi. Even if four seem likely, they could easily have been done in ten months, and Paul was imprisoned for two years. This removes the greatest obstacle to the Roman origin of the letter.

Other problems with the Roman origin have surfaced. Primarily, they are Paul's expected visit to Philippi upon his release and the nature of the content of the epistle. Paul could have changed his earlier plans to visit Rome after the relief offering was deposited in Jerusalem. Although in Rom 15:23-29 Paul spoke as though he had finished his ministry in the eastern Mediterranean, things changed. Time passed, and five years in prison could easily redirect thoughts and intentions. F. W. Beare's sentiments regarding this should be heard:

> This argument is singularly weak. When Paul wrote Romans, he was a free man, and at the height of his powers. It would not be strange if after five years in custody he would no longer have the impulse to start new work in strange territory, but would long to return to the Aegean cities to see his old friends once again.[51]

The content of the epistle is another matter. The argument is that the content of the epistle resembles Romans, Corinthians, and Thessalonians. Both the content and the apparent opponents do resemble these other books. After scrutiny, however, no compelling theological parallels demand an earlier date.[52] The epistle may have been written earlier, but nothing demands such a conclusion.

On one hand, the arguments against the traditional date do not compel the reader to forsake it. On the other hand, nothing in the epistle requires a late date, and the traditional date rests on slim evidence. The question that must be answered is, Does the evidence seem to fit better in another setting and time? If it does not fit better elsewhere, the traditional dating of Rome in A.D. 60-62 should be accepted.[53] Nevertheless, three other suggestions demand consideration.

---

[51] Beare, 19. This makes good sense.

[52] Ibid., 21, quotes Mitton's study on the subject, concluding that "'there is little evidence of passages from other letters exerting a sustained or a recurring influence in Philippians. . . . The parallels appear to be unrelated to each other.'" He continues, "Thus it appears that no light can be thrown on the date of Philippians by any conspicuous degree of similarity to one group of the other epistles. There is nothing in the style or language to deter us from affirming that it is the latest of them all."

[53] This is the conclusion of many modern scholars, including Beare, 24; Silva, 8; C. H. Dodd, *New Testament Studies* (Manchester: University Press, 1953); P. N. Harrison, "The Pastoral Epistles and Duncan's Ephesian Theory," *NTS* 2 (1955-56): 250-261.

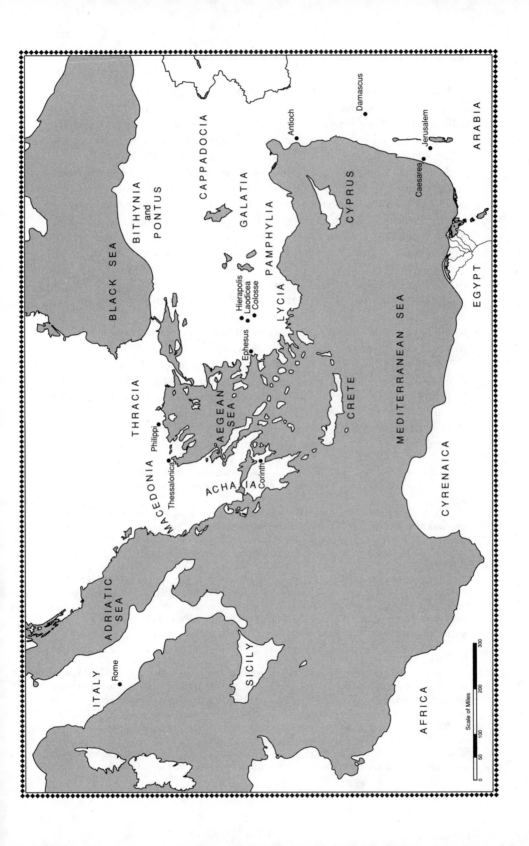

EPHESUS. The Ephesian hypothesis goes back to 1900 when H. Lisco suggested that Paul may have written from there about A.D. 54-57.[54] He has been followed by several scholars, including G. S. Duncan, who popularized the theory.[55] The theory basically assumes that the distance between Ephesus and Philippi makes the logistics more likely than from Philippi to Rome.[56]

Four considerations argue against the Ephesian hypothesis. First, it is based on conjecture. No evidence confirms Paul's imprisonment there, though such an imprisonment was possible. Second, the letter does not mention the "collection for the saints" which so occupied Paul's thoughts during this period. Further, it is unlikely that Paul would have received a gift for himself when he was so involved in fund-raising for this project.[57] Third, Paul spoke in Philippians as though he had no friends with him at the time except Timothy (2:19-21), yet Aquila and Priscilla were in Ephesus when he was (Acts 18:18-26).[58] Fourth, it does not appear that he faced death at Ephesus, especially since he had not yet appealed to Caesar. To these may be added the fact that Paul probably would not have had the freedoms described in Philippians at Ephesus since he would have been imprisoned because of a riot.[59]

The idea of the Ephesian hypothesis is attractive, but it does not fit the details as well as the Roman. If sure evidence existed that Paul was in prison there and that he had the freedoms and friendships demanded by the letter, the hypothesis could be accepted. The theory gained prominence in reaction to the Roman view and because of the problem of the distance. It offers a solution which contains more problems than what it intends to solve.[60]

---

[54] See Hawthorne, xxxviii. His discussion of all these theories is well worth reading for specific data.

[55] G. S. Duncan has written several works espousing this position. They include *St. Paul's Ephesian Ministry* (London: Hodder & Stoughton, 1929); "A New Setting for Paul's Epistle to the Philippians," *ExpTim* 43 (1931-32): 7-11; "Paul's Ministry in Asia: —The Last Phase," *NTS* 3 (1956-57): 211-18. Others have agreed with Duncan, but generally the hypothesis is associated with him.

[56] Other arguments supporting the theory are: Timothy was with Paul in Ephesus and where Philippians was written; there was a praetorium at Ephesus if it can refer to any provincial governor's residence; extensive evangelistic activity occurred at that point in Paul's ministry; Acts records great difficulty and public riot in Ephesus (19:23-41). See also 2 Cor 1:8-10 and 11:23ff.; and the language and style of the epistles of that time parallel Philippians.

[57] Hawthorne, xxxix.

[58] Ibid., xxxix.

[59] Beare graphically says, "It was not every prisoner who would be free to turn his cell into an executing office for the propagation of a religion of doubtful legality" (23). The same fact holds for Caesarea, where Paul was imprisoned because of a riot, and he had a change of venue because of the threat on his life. There he did appeal to Caesar.

[60] Martin, 56-57, gives three reasons why continental scholars hold to the Ephesian origin: the theory of Philippians being a composite document made up of several letters, the letter's affinities with 2 Corinthians, and the identity of the rival preachers in Phil 1:12-18. Those who argue these points simply seem to want to hold on to other theories which are best served by this one as well.

CAESAREA. As early as A.D. 1779 H. E. G. Paulus proposed Caesarea as the place of origin for Philippians.[61] Unlike the Ephesus hypothesis, the distance between the two cities did not prompt the development of the Caesarean hypothesis. Caesarea is further from Philippi than Rome, approximately 1200 miles over land, so other issues need to be considered besides accessibility to Philippi when deciding between Caesarea and Rome.[62] The primary reason for suggesting Caesarea is that it reconciles with Paul's travel plans after his release.[63] Paul easily could have expected to visit the church at Philippi because the overland route to Rome would take him through the Philippi. It also reconciles with his earlier intention to go to Spain.

Apart from the resolution of the supposed conflict in mission plans, little commends the Caesarean hypothesis. The primary reason for the Ephesian theory was to avoid the distance in travel. That problem is more difficult with a Caesarean origin. Unlike the Ephesian hypothesis, it can claim the support of the Book of Acts, which records a lengthy imprisonment in Caesarea. In reality, however, nothing commends the hypothesis positively to such a degree that it should replace the traditional view, and certain problems persist.

CORINTH. The final suggestion is that Paul wrote Philippians from Corinth. It too claims early support since the first suggestion occurred in 1731 by G. L. Oeder. S. Dockx revived the theory in 1973.[64] The suggestion suffers some of the same problems as the Ephesus hypothesis, but it also solves some of the same problems.[65] The hypothesis dates Philippians early, about A.D. 50-51.

Against the proposal, some major obstacles remain. First, Acts does not record an imprisonment in Corinth. The account reveals that Paul had less trouble at Corinth than other places, such as Caesarea or Ephesus. Second, at Corinth Paul had good friends surrounding him, but in Phil 2:20-21 it seems that only Timothy remained with him. Few today hold to this option. It creates more problems than the Ephesus hypothesis and has even less to commend it.

---

[61] Cited in Hawthorne, xli. Hawthorne is the most recent commentator to accept the Caesarean origin of the letter. His arguments should be consulted for a good defense of the hypothesis.

[62] Hawthorne states, "If distance from Philippi is the major objection for considering Rome as the site for the origin of Philippians (so Collange), then there exists no possibility for suggesting Caesarea in its place" (xlii).

[63] Other factors do accord with the facts as well: Luke stated that the Caesarean imprisonment was in the praetorium of Herod (Acts 23:25); the imprisonment was for two years, which allowed plenty of time for the travel; Paul had some liberty (Acts 24:23); Paul apparently already had made some defense, such as was the case at Caesarea (Phil 1:7; Acts 24:20-21); Paul's opponents in 3:2ff. seem to have been Jews, and that would fit this scenario; Paul delivered the collection for the saints and thus felt no restraint in accepting gifts. See Hawthorne, xli-xlii.

[64] See Martin, 44; S. Dockx, "Lieu et Date de l'epitre aux Philippiens," *RB* 80 (1973): 230-46.

[65] Martin, 44, gives the following support: Corinth had a proconsul, by inference, a praetorium (Acts 18:12); the geographical problem is solved; the anti-Judaizing polemic occurs in other writings of the time as well; Paul's statement in 4:10-20 that there was no opportunity for a gift fits well in the time frame.

(2) The Date

The date of the epistle depends on the origin. Those scholars who locate the writing at Corinth pick an early date, about A.D. 50-51, shortly after the founding of the church. Those who locate the writing at Ephesus date Philippians in the mid-50s, when Paul ministered at Ephesus on the third missionary journey. Those who locate the writing at Caesarea date the epistle later, about A.D. 58-60. Finally, those who affirm the traditional view, from Rome, generally date the epistle at about A.D. 60-62, during Paul's first Roman imprisonment. This is the preferred view in this commentary.

Some interpreters attempt to date the epistle even more precisely. Was it at the beginning, middle, or end of the imprisonment? There is no way of knowing this. The epistle seems to imply that when the letter was written Epaphroditus had been in Rome for a short time. Additionally, the letter reveals that repercussions of Paul's imprisonment were widespread, suggesting some time of development after his arrival. Also, it may be that Paul expected a quick trial. These factors suggest that Paul had been in Rome for some time. On the other hand, he hoped for a quick verdict and a visit to Philippi soon (2:24). The best suggestion, therefore, is that the letter was written from the middle to near the end of his stay in Rome, around A.D. 61-62.

The relationship of Philippians to the other Prison Epistles also causes some interest. Apparently Colossians, Ephesians, and Philemon belong together in time (see the notes on Colossians). It is likely that Paul would have delayed Onesimus and Epaphras if he had expected a quick release. The three of them could have traveled together.[66] In light of that factor, Paul probably wrote Philippians after the others as he saw his trial date approaching.

7. Paul's Opponents at Philippi

Who were Paul's opponents at Philippi? The question is not easily answered, though the epistle provides ample information regarding them in four basic passages: 1:15-17; 1:27-28; 3:2; 3:18-19. Scholars question whether these passages refer to the same group, two groups, or three groups.

Several observations guide the investigation. In 1:15-17 Paul referred to the opponents as preachers of Christ. He exposed them by describing their motivations, but his ultimate evaluation was joy that they preached Christ. Clearly he considered them Christian brethren, and their differences were minor. The situation changed in chpt. 3. He addressed those opponents sharply and condemned their message and activities. Could the opponents of chpt. 1 have been the same as the opponents of chpt. 3? It seems not.

In chpt. 3 Paul first addressed the opponents as "dogs, evil workers, and cutters" (v. 2). Later in the chapter the problem was libertinism, and Paul

---

[66] He obviously did expect to be free soon. He asked them to prepare for his coming (Phlm 22).

described the opponents as "enemies of the cross" (vv. 18-19). The difficulty appears to have been a mixture of legalism related to law and liberty related to foods. Were the opponents the same people with the same message? It seems not.

Another difference is worth noting. The opponents in 1:15-17 were within the Christian community at Rome; the opponents in 3:2ff. appear to have been outside the Christian community at Philippi. Did something tie together people from two different places and with different attitudes toward Christianity? Paul seems to have identified them differently. In 1:15-17 he knew well those who opposed him. Perhaps he could have called them by name. In chpt. 3, however, another group with whom he was not personally acquainted opposed his message. They loomed on the horizon, ready to invade the church from outside. Paul's attacks were general, relating to the group and its characteristics rather than specific individuals.

Finally, the interpreter must determine what Paul's opponents opposed in Paul. Paul identified his opponents' message in Phil 1:15ff. as Christ, and he handled it as though it were no problem to him. Presumably he could have preached the same message! The point of division was probably the same as Paul encountered everywhere he went. He proclaimed implications of the gospel that some could not accept. His distinctive insight was that Gentiles were included in the gospel and that they did not need to accept the Jewish social and religious obligations as a part of their salvation. The Roman church discussed the same matters (Rom 14:1-15:6), and divisions occurred as convictions formed.

The opponents in chpt. 3 opposed Paul's teaching that Gentiles were saved as Gentiles and that the law was fulfilled in them by the Spirit. It is likely, therefore, that the issue was one of degree rather than kind. The law was the issue. The early part of the epistle reflects a long-term situation in Rome and the tension between Jewish and Gentile believers. The third chapter reflects a situation like the ones at Galatia and Corinth. The opponents attacked the heart of the message; they preached another gospel. So, it appears that two different groups were addressed in the epistle. The first were those who opposed Paul in Rome (chpt. 1); the other posed the threat to the church at Philippi (chpt. 3).

The history of identifying the opponents reveals several different options for chpt. 3. Some suggest they were entirely Jewish, either Judaizers (from within the church) or Hellenistic Jews (from outside). Their preoccupation with law formed the basis of Paul's attacks. First, they displayed a legalism regarding circumcision (3:2). Paul defended his position by claiming that genuine circumcision is spiritual. Second, they had a fascination for food laws as a part of the ceremonial law. Thus in 3:19 Paul said their "god is their stomach," referring to the scrupulous manner of choosing foods carefully. In both cases, then, the opponents were Jewish missionaries who opposed Paul's mission to the Gentiles.[67]

Others have seen a Gnostic influence in the chapter. Perhaps the opponents were teachers who claimed to have membership in the Jewish-Christian-Gnostic community by virtue of their circumcision. They boasted of their own circumcision but added to it a perfectionist element. They already had been raised to a heavenly, spiritual life on earth, and moral and nutritional restraints made no difference to them.[68] For that reason, Paul countered these opponents with a revelation of his personal attitudes regarding Christian perfectionism (3:12-16). He directly dealt with their claims of freedom from any restraints on diet or morality (3:18-19).

Finally, the data have led some commentators to see two or more kinds of opponents in the chapter. These opponents generally are considered to be Judaizers who attacked the church from outside (3:2) and libertine heretics who may have come from within (3:19).

In summary, the opponents of chpt. 3 appear to have preached the Jewish law. While Gnostic influence is possible, the data may be well understood and satisfied by the position that these false teachers were Jews. It appears that they came from outside the church since Paul's words hardly referred to Christian brothers. The opponents of chpt. 3, then, called the church to accept the laws of the Old Testament, boasting in their own self-effort. The opponents of chpt. 1 preached with a view to hindering Paul's universal application of Christianity. They taught that as Christians it was necessary to keep the law.

The Jewish flavor of the argument predominates. One question remains. Why would Paul have to engage in such a Jewish dialogue with a church in a city with few Jews? If there were too few to have a synagogue and the first converts were Gentile, by what avenue did the Jewish teachers come in? The answer must be that they had a concern to oppose Paul's preaching wherever they encountered it. That is likely the tie between the opponents of 1:15ff. and 3:2ff. They both had an interest in "the Christ" and his relationship to Gentiles.

8. The Theological Structure of the Epistle

Philippians divides into four primary sections. Paul had definite concerns which he wanted to express, and he also wrote to warn of false teachers who threatened the church. Unlike many of Paul's letters, Philippians cannot be divided into theological and practical sections. Every section is incarnational. Paul's theological interests are expressed in biographical sections. Within this motif, however, certain movements occur.

---

[67] Those who hold to this view of one Jewish opponent are, among others, J. Gnilka, M. Dibelius, K. Barth, O. Michaelis, Beare, Hawthorne, and Silva. See Martin, 23-24; Hawthorne, xlv-xlvii; Silva, 9-11.

[68] See the discussion in Martin, 28-29.

First, Paul explained his situation at Rome (1:12-26). Although he was concerned about the divided Christian community there, his outlook was strengthened by the knowledge that Christ was magnified. Paul's theology of life formed the basis of his optimism. Whether he lived or died, whether he continued his service to others or went to his own rewards, or whether he was appreciated or not, he wanted Christ to be glorified. Philippians describes this commitment better than any other of Paul's epistles.

Second, Paul exhorted the church to unity (1:27-2:18). Two factors influenced him. The church at Rome was divided, and he lived with a daily reminder of the effects of disunity. Further, similar disunity threatened the Philippian church as two prominent women differed with each other. Selfishness lay at the heart of the problems at Rome and Philippi. The answer came in an incarnational vehicle. Paul reminded the believers of the humility of Jesus. If they would allow the outlook of Christ to guide their lives, harmony would be restored. The hymn to Christ dominates the epistle.

Third, Paul warned the church to beware of Jewish legalists (3:2-21). Legalistic Jewish teachers threatened to destroy the vitality of the congregation by calling it to a preoccupation with external religious matters. Paul countered the legalists with a forceful teaching about justification by faith. He chose to express his theology through his personal experience. He had lived their message and found it lacking.

Finally, Paul thanked them for their financial support. The church had sent money and a trusted servant, Epaphroditus, to care for Paul. Its generosity encouraged Paul at a time of personal need. Even here Paul took advantage of the situation to express the rewards of its giving and to teach Christian living. Again, theological instruction was occasional.

The epistle abounds with Christian models for imitation. Most obviously, the church was to imitate Jesus, but other genuine Christians also merit appreciation. Paul, Timothy, and Epaphroditus embodied the selflessness God desires in his people.

Philippians also instructs in the meaning of salvation. Salvation was provided by Christ who became obedient to death (2:6-8). It was proclaimed by a host of preachers who were anxious to advance the gospel. It was promoted through varying circumstances of life—both good and bad—so that the lives of believers became powerful witnesses. Finally, salvation would transform Christians and churches into models of spiritual life.

This little epistle provides insight into church relationships. Paul expressed his concern for unity. Christian unity came when individuals developed the mind of Christ. In more difficult situations, the church collectively solved problems through the involvement of its leadership (4:2-3). Harmony, joy, and peace characterize the church which functions as it should. Paul taught about Christian stewardship. The Philippian church had reached a maturity regarding material possessions. It knew how to give out of poverty. It knew the value of supporting the gospel and those who proclaim it, and it knew that God could provide for its needs as well. Paul also demonstrated his attitude toward material things. He could live with spiritual equilibrium in the midst of fluctuating financial circumstances. Christ was his life, and Christ's provisions were all he needed. In everything, Paul's joy was that Christ was glorified in his life.

Philippians contributes to a knowledge of genuine Christianity. Most of its themes occur elsewhere in Scripture, but the lessons impact life most powerfully in this letter. It is filled with theology, Christian commitment, and Christlikeness. Every Christian should learn these lessons well.

─────────── *OUTLINE OF THE BOOK* ───────────

—————————————— *SECTION OUTLINE* ——————————————

I. SALUTATION (1:1-2)
    1. The Writers (1:1a)
    2. The Readers (1:1b)
    3. The Greeting (1:2)

——————————————— **I. SALUTATION (1:1-2)** ———————————————

The greeting Paul sent the church resembled the greetings of other first-century letters. Commonly they contained three elements: identification of the writers, identification of the readers, and the greeting. Some differences occur, however, which reinforce the Christian nature of the letters. Paul changed from the typical greeting *charein* to *charis* ("grace"); he added "peace" and explained that "grace and peace" come from both God the Father and Christ.[1]

The greeting reveals that Paul chose to write this in a letter (epistolary) format. Epistles may be formal or informal.[2] Formal epistles tend to reflect forethought in subject matter, stylized writing, and an organized presentation. Informal letters generally contain a tone of warmth and spontaneity and, at times, reflect an intimacy regarding specific contexts that leave the modern interpreter puzzled.[3] Philippians is informal. This conversation between friends suggests two important truths. First, the letter is not systematic. This means that much of the writing simply flowed from Paul's mind. At no place in the epistle did Paul sustain a fully developed, systematic presentation. The closest to it is in Phil 2:5-11, which has the marks of more formal writing, but it illustrates another point. Second, the letter is occasional. Some specific situation(s) prompted Paul to write. The letter is "theology in street clothes." Paul answered the Philippians' specific concerns in ways that they could understand. That is the beauty of such portions of Scripture: they are applied theology. At the same time, that approach brings some frustration to modern readers, and the interpreter must always ask what lay behind the writing.

---

[1] Many point out the similarity between Paul's letters and other first-century correspondence. Hawthorne, however, suggests that in the differences between Paul and his surroundings, Paul contributed to the history of letter writing. G. Hawthorne. *Philippians*, WBC (Waco, Tex.: Word, 1983), 2.

[2] These categories need revision because of the many ways epistles are being classified, but they serve adequately the point made here.

[3] E.g., when Paul wrote in 1 Thess, "We have no need to write to you" (stated in various ways, but see 4:9; 5:1). At other times the "in house" references are not so explicit.

1. The Writers (1:1a)

¹Paul and Timothy, servants of Christ Jesus

1:1a The epistle identifies two writers: Paul and Timothy. Other New Testament books reveal significant information about both men, and no doubt the church at Philippi knew them very well. Timothy occupied a prominent place in Paul's ministry. No doubt Paul met him on the first missionary journey in the area of Lystra/Derbe. When he embarked on his second journey, Paul asked Timothy to accompany him, and Timothy became a prominent member of the ministering team. Paul mentioned him in the salutations of six epistles (2 Cor; Col; Phil; 1, 2 Thess; Phlm) and wrote two epistles to him (1, 2 Tim).[4]

Why was Timothy mentioned? Various suggestions have been made. The most obvious answer lies in the close relationship Timothy had with the Philippians. He was part of the team that founded the church (Acts 16–18), Paul intended to send Timothy to the church not long after writing the letter (Phil 2:19), and Paul had no one who better shared his outlook and burden for his ministry (2:20). M. Silva suggests that, given the prominence of Timothy in Macedonian evangelism, the surprise would have been if he were not included in Paul's letter.[5] Perhaps Silva is correct, but if that criterion is applied consistently, Timothy should also have been mentioned in 1 Corinthians.

Paul referred to himself and Timothy as "servants of Jesus Christ." He generally reserved the title *doulos* ("servant" or "slave") as a description of himself, and even then it occurs sparingly. This is the only place he referred to Timothy as a "servant" of Christ, and he only called two persons other than himself by the title. In Col 4:12, Paul called Epaphras a "servant of Christ" (*doulos Christou*), and others are called "fellow-servants" (Epaphras, Col 1:7; Tychicus, Col 4:7).[6] Thus Paul identified Timothy by a title which revealed high esteem for Timothy's commitment to Christ and his effective and humble service (see 2:20–24).

The word *doulos* occurs in only three salutations (Rom, Phil, and Titus). Elsewhere he used the term "apostle" to describe himself. Before considering

---

[4]Hawthorne lists the following in his discussion of why Timothy was called a slave: He was with Paul in his imprisonment; he was co-author of the letter; he was Paul's amanuensis; he was a co-founder of the church at Philippi; Paul wanted to be courteous to a loved associate; Paul wanted to show his humility in describing Timothy as a co-laborer (3–4). To these might be added the following reasons: Paul wanted to substantiate his testimony, and Paul intended to send him to Philippi in his place.

[5]M. Silva, *Philippians*, WEC (Chicago: Moody, 1988), 39.

[6]Hawthorne states, regarding Paul's calling Timothy a slave, that it is unique. "In describing only himself as a 'slave,' or 'apostle,' or 'prisoner' of Christ Jesus—never anyone else. . . . The fact that it *is shared* only this once demands explanation." He later asked: "Why then did the apostle dare to share, for this one time only, his otherwise carefully and jealously guarded uniqueness?" (3–4). Other commentators share Hawthorne's observation and sentiments. In fact, the point he makes is a proper one, but others are called "slaves."

the meaning of "servant," it is necessary to ask why Paul used it here and elsewhere. He had not met the Roman church personally, but neither had he met the Colossian congregation.[7] In Romans Paul used both "servant" and "apostle" (1:1). There "servant" designates his humility, and he stated that even his apostleship came by divine call. Perhaps more to the point, he did not have to assert his authority at Rome or Philippi. In Romans, Paul hoped to solve the problem of division between the Jewish and Gentile elements, but ultimately he had no personal responsibility for the church. When writing to Titus, Paul did not need to assert his apostleship. Titus knew him well and accepted his authority. Further, the problems addressed in Titus related to sub-Christian practice, not false teachers entering the Christian community.[8]

The word "servant" or "slave" has been defined in various ways. Its basic meaning is clear, but it may have implied two different ideas. The first comes from Greco-Roman culture. Slaves were common because of war, and Christian slaves probably worshiped in the churches along with their masters.[9] Everyone knew slaves. A slave had no rights or privileges, and all personal interests and ambitions had to be repressed. Everything related to the master.[10] This title did not refer to a position of honor in the first-century world. The Philippians no doubt thought it strange, if not shocking. Paul chose his words carefully, and "servant" truly characterized his life.

The second possibility comes from the Old Testament. Frequently the Septuagint used the word "slave" for one who served Yahweh (e.g., Num 12:7). Moses was the "servant" of the Lord, and from his day onward, the title became one of honor. It stood for one who was commissioned by God for a special task. That background may have influenced Paul, but he employed the word because it spoke of humility. Paul used it of himself in epistles written largely to Gentile audiences (though the Roman church was mixed Jew and Gentile), where they would not necessarily perceive the Old Testament tradition.

The term represented the Christian era. Whether it was heard with Hellenistic or Hebraistic ears, it became a Christian ideal. Paul certainly knew of its centrality to the hymn found in 2:5-11; if the term characterized the Lord, it was equally appropriate as a model for his servants.

---

[7] There was a difference in the two, however, in that the church at Colosse was Pauline. (See the introductory notes to Colossians.)

[8] This latter distinguishes the epistles to Timothy from the Epistle to Titus. The heresy at Ephesus demanded an authoritative voice, even in a personal letter. Perhaps Paul assumed that Timothy would read the letter to the congregation.

[9] See Phlm 15-16; the instructions in Eph 6:5-9, especially Col 3:22-4:1; and the greetings from "Caesar's household" in Phil 4:22.

[10] Some slaves had considerable privileges and some autonomy, but only if the master allowed it.

2. The Readers (1:1b)

To all the saints in Christ Jesus at Philippi, together with the overseers and deacons

1:1b Paul identified two groups of readers. They were the church at large and special persons within the congregation. The church was called "the saints." The term has no other New Testament meaning than Christian people, and Paul used it in place of "the church," which he had used earlier in his ministry.[11] The saints were those who were set apart by God at conversion, and they were in process of becoming like Christ. The term thus reminded the church of its special status in God's redemptive plan.

The other group consisted of bishops and deacons. This is the only time Paul used the word "bishop" outside of the Pastoral Epistles.[12] The word means "overseer," and the question here is whether it refers to an office. At that time in church history, the title "bishop" did not refer to one person who had the charge of a number of churches in a geographical area. That came in the second century.

Was there some type of office in the church this early? The text reveals several factors. They were singled out in a special way, not as simply "saints" and not as "deacons." They also were placed second in Paul's opening remarks. Perhaps this revealed his concern that they had a secondary importance. Third, the term is plural. That definitely rules out the possibility of a "one man" rule over several churches, if Philippi had only one church, which seems to be the case. On the other hand, it suggests that several had this function or office. In the only Lukan use of the term, bishops were called to service by the Holy Spirit (Acts 20:28). The term sounds much like the separation of Barnabas and Saul for the missionary task in Acts 13:1-3. Another reason for not considering the term as a designation of a church office is that it does not appear in any list of spiritual gifts or church functions outside the references identified above.

There was precedent for offices in the church. The early church probably took over the worship patterns of the synagogue, which had two chief officers. Likewise, some scholars point to a parallel in Essene communities, which had an administrative supervisor who was responsible for community leadership.[13] Finally, some suggest that the titles "bishops" and "deacons" simply reveal "the Roman penchant for organization" which "gave the Philip-

---

[11] See the note on Col 1:1.

[12] It only occurs twice there, 1 Tim 3:2 and Titus 1:7. A related word, ἐπισκοπῆς (rather than ἐπίσκοπος), occurs in 1 Tim 3:1. Peter used each word (1 Pet 2:12; 2:25). Ἐπίσκοπος also occurs in Acts 20:28.

[13] See J. Jeremias, *Jerusalem in the Time of Jesus* (Philadelphia: Fortress, 1969), 260-61. Jeremias states that the "overseer" was the same as the office in Essene communities.

pian church a regular system of office-bearers."[14] How much any church was influenced by these organizational precedents is impossible to know. Anyone could have provided the organizational pattern.

Clearly the early church was organized. The lists of leadership positions reveal at least an informal structure (Eph 4:11-13), which probably grew out of natural ability and spiritual giftedness. Similarly, in Acts 20:28, Luke recorded the presence of "overseers." In just a few years after the Epistle to the Philippians was written, the church had defined offices with qualifications clearly identified (1 Tim 3:1ff.). Since 1 Timothy may have been written only two to five years after Philippians, it seems there was an emerging or developing structure.

On the other hand, the precise function of "bishops and deacons" is not clear. In writing to the Ephesians at about the same time as Philippians, Paul did not mention "bishops and deacons," even though he listed several offices which helped the church develop (4:11-13). Ephesians has perhaps the most profound theological presentation of the church in the Pauline epistles, and the fact that bishops and deacons were not mentioned there is significant. In Phil 4:3, Paul alluded to another church leader, asking for his help in solving the misunderstanding between Euodia and Syntyche.[15]

Two other factors deserve mention. First, many commentators identify the overseers with the gift sent to Paul; perhaps they generated the gift. Since the letter is, in part at least, a thank you, their role was acknowledged.[16] The title "bishop" was common in Greek society and had a variety of uses in the LXX.[17] Perhaps it was a natural term to identify leaders within the church community. Second, if this were a description of formalized church officers, it is surprising that "elder" ("presbyter") is omitted. That title drew more on Jewish/Christian background than "bishop,"[18] although there is sufficient evidence that "bishop" and "elder" referred to the same persons.[19] The title probably related to a function rather than an office. Providing oversight in the areas of teaching

---

[14]F. W. Beare, *The Epistle to the Philippians*, HNTC (San Francisco: Harper & Row, 1959), 48. Beare does not suggest this as the most likely possibility. He prefaces the comment by "if it is not simply an indication."

[15]This person is surrounded with obscurity, and not everyone agrees as to who or what he is. What is clear is that Paul could appeal to someone in a position to address these women, apparently because he had the responsibility to do so. His function was also known well enough that all would understand Paul's cryptic reference there.

[16]J. B. Lightfoot, *St. Paul's Epistle to the Philippians*, reprint ed. (Grand Rapids: Zondervan, 1953), 82, seems to have been one of the first of modern times to make this suggestion. He said further, "It seems hardly probable that this mention was intended, as some have thought, to strengthen the hands of the presbyters and deacons, their authority being endangered."

[17]Ibid., 95-99, gives an excellent discussion of this data.

[18]See ibid., 96.

[19]See the following references where the terms are used either interchangeably, or they explain each other. Acts 20:17 with 20:28; 1 Pet 5:1-2; 1 Tim 3:1-7 with 5:17-19; Titus 1:5-7.

and administration were the primary functions of a bishop or elder.

The word "deacon" described the other group. It may have been used in a technical sense (1 Tim 3:8) to refer to an office in the church. This use probably draws its origin from Acts 6:1-6, though the word "deacon" is not used of the seven who were elected.[20] The word also occurs nontechnically in many passages. Many simply "ministered" in the name of Christ (Eph 3:7 of Paul; Col 1:7 of Epaphras). It may be difficult to suggest that the word "bishop" here could be functional in nature and the word "deacon" official. It is possible, however, that Paul identified the specific overseers of the gift collection first, out of courtesy, then mentioned the deacons. Since neither "bishops" nor "deacons" occurs elsewhere in the epistle, obviously the letter was written to the church at large, the saints.

3. The Greeting (1:2)

[2]Grace and peace to you from God our Father and the Lord Jesus Christ.

1:2 The specific greeting, "grace and peace," adds to the normal epistolary introductions.[21] Since grace always reminded Paul of God's grace in Christ, no doubt this word conveys full Christian meaning. It means "may God's grace be with you." The fact that Paul placed it before "peace" may indicate further his theological orientation that grace provided for and secured peace. "Peace" no doubt conveyed Paul's Hebrew background and the typical greeting "shalom." It had a full sense of "may all things be well with you." Both words as used by Paul imply a petition as well as a greeting.

Grace and peace come jointly from God the Father and the Lord Jesus Christ. That God sends them to believers was no surprise to anyone. Many prayed to their gods for the same qualities. The addition of "Jesus Christ" here adds a profound Christological dimension to the blessing. The church knew well that grace was embodied in Jesus (Titus 2:11-14), and peace was his gift to the believer (John 14:27; 16:33). In so combining the work of God and Jesus, Paul reflected his deep conviction about the deity of Jesus. Jesus does what God the Father does.[22]

---

[20]It is perhaps significant that the word root occurs twice in these verses, but not as a title for the seven. The Greek women were neglected in the διακονία (6:1), and the twelve had to give themselves to the διακονεῖν of the word.

[21]The word "grace" (χάρις) also differs from the typical Greek letter which begins with χαρεῖν or χαρά.

[22]The use of the title "Lord" with Jesus Christ also identified him in that way.

──────────────── *SECTION OUTLINE* ────────────────

II. EXPLANATION OF PAUL'S CONCERNS (1:3-2:30)
  1. Paul's Thanksgiving and Prayer for the Philippians (1:3-11)
    (1) Paul's Thanksgiving (1:3-8)
    (2) Paul's Prayer for the Philippians (1:9-11)
        Prayer for a Growing Love (1:9-10a)
           The Nature of a Growing Love (1:9a)
           The Environment of a Growing Love (1:9b)
           The Result of a Growing Love (1:10a)
        Prayer for Complete Character (1:10b-11)
           The Nature of Complete Character (1:10b)
           The Means to Complete Character (1:11a)
           The Purpose of Complete Character (1:11b)
  2. Paul's Joy in the Progress of the Gospel (1:12-26)
    (1) Paul's Circumstances (1:12-17)
        Paul's Imprisonment (1:12)
        Reactions to Paul's Imprisonment (1:13-17)
           The Gospel Spread Among Roman Soldiers (1:13)
           Christians Encouraged to Speak (1:14-17)
    (2) Paul's Attitude (1:18-26)
        Paul's Joy in Salvation (1:18-24)
           Paul's Salvation and Hope (1:18b-20)
           Paul's Commitment to the Philippians (1:21-24)
        Paul's Confidence of Future Ministry (1:25-26)
  3. Exhortation to Christlike Character (1:27-2:18)
    (1) A Unified Stand (1:27-30)
        The Nature of the Philippians' Stand (1:27-28)
        Christian Suffering (1:29-30)
           The Nature of Christian Suffering (1:29)
           The Pauline Model of Suffering (1:30)
    (2) A Unified Mind (2:1-4)
        The Basis of Paul's Appeal to Unity (2:1)
        The Essence of Unity (2:2a)
        The Expression of Unity (2:2b-4)
    (3) The Example of Christ (2:5-11)
        The Form of the Text
        The Function of the Text
        Analysis of the Text
           The Introduction to the Hymn (2:5)
           The Hymn to Christ (2:6-11)

———— II. EXPLANATION OF PAUL'S CONCERNS (1:3-2:30) ————

1. Paul's Thanksgiving and Prayer for the Philippians (1:3-11)

The epistle proper begins like many of Paul's epistles—with praise to God for the church and a specific petition on its behalf. The pattern occurs regularly enough that it no doubt reflects Paul's natural inclination in prayer. God's call on the Philippians' lives brought Paul joy, even though he had specific concerns about their Christian growth.

Philippians 1:3-11 forms a unit of thought in two movements. Several factors reveal the unity: the synonyms "I thank my God" (1:3) and "this is my prayer" (1:9), the general content of praise and petition, and Paul's epistolary pattern in introductions. The section divides naturally into two subsections, however. First, vv. 3-8 express praise for the Philippians. The verb translated "I thank my God" contains the idea of thanksgiving. Furthermore, all of vv. 3-8 modify that one main verb. Second, vv. 9-11 express Paul's more specific petition. He introduced his prayer with a consecutive conjunction ("and," *kai*) which both continues the previous idea and introduces another. These verses contain one long sentence in Greek, but Paul made two petitions in them.

(1) Paul's Thanksgiving (1:3-8)

³**I thank my God every time I remember you. ⁴In all my prayers for all of you, I always pray with joy ⁵because of your partnership in the gospel from the first day until now, ⁶being confident of this, that he who began a good work in you will carry it on to completion until the day of Christ Jesus.**

7It is right for me to feel this way about all of you, since I have you in my heart; for whether I am in chains or defending and confirming the gospel, all of you share in God's grace with me. 8God can testify how I long for all of you with the affection of Christ Jesus.

The format for this thanksgiving resembles others, but the content is unique. Paul remembered God's working in the believers' lives, as well as their participation in his ministry. Clearly, he did not simply recite a thanksgiving that could be true of any group of Christians. These verses are warm and personal. The best analysis is thematic. Three ideas support Paul's main statement in the opening verb: "I always pray with joy" (1:4), "being confident of this" (1:6), and "It is right for me to feel this way" (1:7).[1] Following these structural components, the text reveals that Paul's thanksgiving was joyful (1:4-5); it was confident (1:6); and it was proper (1:7-8).[2]

1:3   Paul expressed his pleasure for the church. He let the believers in on his thoughts. Two significant aspects of Paul's thanksgiving emerge in v. 3. These aspects reveal information about Paul's prayer life and his fondness for the Philippians. First, Paul was thankful for them, even though a problem of disunity threatened the fellowship of the congregation. He lived his life in response to the love of Christ (2 Cor 5:14-15), hoping to reach people everywhere. The validation of his ministry, which was his life, was that people actually did respond to the gospel he preached and that they remained true to their faith. He stated as much in 1 Thess 2:19; 3:8. Any positive response to the gospel brought Paul joy; when a church embraced the Lord and the gospel message as enthusiastically as the Philippians did, it was cause for great thanksgiving.

Second, Paul's thankfulness never wavered. It was "every time I remember you." The reasons for that are detailed in 1:4-5. Here he stressed the consistency of his memories. Paul turned each thought of them into praise for them.[3] What kind of church produced those memories? They had shared hard times which served to deepen their friendship.

1:4   The first characteristic of Paul's thanksgiving for them was that it was

---

[1] In this sense, then, this is simply an alternate form of petition so typical for Paul. He used participles in these introductory sections and sometimes followed them with clauses of one type or another. For the former see 1 Thess 1:1-5; for this type see Col 1:3-8, an almost identical structure. In Col 1:6 the καθώς clause introduces a new direction but ties this new direction to the previous statement as well.

[2] The first two of these are predicate participles which modify the main verb. Their structure is parallel. Third is a comparative clause (καθώς) which continues the sentence. The NIV makes a new paragraph with it, indicating the strength of this usually relatively minor construction. The UBS Greek text separates it with a colon. It is a strong comparison, equal in structural weight to the two participles, and the outline of the passage reflects that analysis.

[3] The Greek construction of ἐπί with the locative actually provides a basis for the thanksgiving. It therefore is conducive to temporal ideas, such as "when I remember you." The most basic idea, however, is that the remembrance provided a basis for thanksgiving.

joyful. The Greek text stresses this by placing the words "with joy" before the words "I always pray." This is the first reference to joy, a major theme in the epistle.

The grammatical and syntactical relationships in this section are quite complicated. Several questions must be answered that pertain to vv. 4-5 and their function in the sentence. Is the NIV text correct in starting a new thought at the beginning of v. 4? Does the phrase "because of your partnership in the gospel" connect with the main verb "I thank," or does it go with something else? Where does the phrase "from the first day until now" go?

Regarding the first question, how should the thoughts of v. 4 be arranged?[4] The NIV correctly interprets the sense of the passage, though there should be no major break such as it makes. This observation is based on some literary patterns which prevail. Twice the same root word for "prayer" occurs, though in different parts of speech ("In all my prayers" and "I always pray"). These two occurrences, which go together logically, also somewhat repeat and specify the word "I give thanks." Paul informed his readers that his thanksgiving was actually done in prayers.[5] Therefore, the sense of the thanksgiving was resumed in the two words for "prayer."

1:5 The resolution of the second question begins at this point. Does the phrase "because of your partnership" (*koinōnia*) go with v. 3 or v. 4? The parallelism of the text suggests that it goes with v. 4. The two terms for "prayer" belong together in sense, and the two clauses which provide a reason for the prayers conform to each other as well. The first clause, "every time I remember you," provided a reason for Paul's thankfulness. The second, "because of your partnership," provided a corollary reason for his specific joyful prayers. His remembrance was stirred by the gift they gave him. Their partnership was also the support they rendered to the apostle.[6] Here it is emphatic, not careless.[7] The new element in this verse is the statement of joy, which emphasizes the importance of the phrase "with joy."

The third question is the location of "from the first day until now." Some scholars want to place it with "I thank my God"; others, with "being confident of this"; still others, with "I always pray." Taking it with "I thank my God" makes the sentence extremely awkward and surely should be rejected. Under-

---

[4]There are three good possibilities: The entire verse begins a new thought; a new thought begins in the middle of the verse; and the entire verse is a thought unto itself. The first position is taken here.

[5]As pointed out earlier, the participles are typical structural indicators, and this one seems to carry the other form of the word for prayer with it.

[6]This reconstruction makes good sense of the structural arrangements but is somewhat awkward by its repetition of ideas. No matter what structural arrangement, there is repetition.

[7]The repetition is seen in the four words for prayer ("I thank," "I remember you," "my prayers," and "I always pray") and in the four times words for "all" are used. This analysis makes the opening clauses basically parallel as well.

standing it with "being confident of this" causes an abrupt change of direction from the emphasis on the gifts of the church to the attitudes of Paul. That, too, should be rejected. The church participated with Paul in the gospel from the first day until now. That considers the normal flow of the text and satisfies the need for consistency of subject matter.

Since the primary contribution of v. 4 is the identification of Paul's joy, the basis of Paul's joy is revealed in v. 5. The NIV correctly captures the relationships by stating "because of your partnership in the gospel."[8] The relationship between Paul and the church went deeper than human friendships. They had a tie that came from joining in the work of God in the world. Such cooperation in the spread of the gospel was something Paul appreciated very much. That fellowship was with Paul only in an intermediate sense; the ultimate contribution they made was to the spread of the gospel itself.

"Fellowship" is a major theme of the letter. The word occurs primarily in the Pauline Epistles (thirteen of nineteen times in the New Testament) and three times in Philippians. In 2:1 Paul urged, "If any fellowship with the Spirit," and in 3:10 he expressed his desire to share in the "fellowship of sharing in his sufferings." Additionally, the verbal form of the word occurs in 4:15, which the NIV translates "shared with me." This last occurrence presents a context for understanding Paul's use of the word in Philippians. It referred to the believers' involvement with Paul by sending a gift to support his work. The grammar of 1:5 confirms this primary meaning. The noun "partnership" may be followed by various cases or parts of speech. For example, in the other two occurrences of "fellowship" in Philippians, the word "of" occurs. Here the word "unto" follows.[9] In other places where the preposition "unto" follows, the people experience "fellowship" by contributing to a gift (Rom 15:26; 2 Cor 9:13). Thus when Paul thanked God for their fellowship "in [eis] the Gospel," he meant that they were contributing to the spread of the gospel in tangible ways, i.e., primarily through their support.

The gospel was not only the environment of their fellowship but also its goal. Had it not been for the gospel, they would not have met. Paul generally stated that the tie that bound Christians together was the gospel message. Here,

---

[8]The Greek construction is the preposition ἐπί followed by the locative case. Two such constructions are in these first two verses, and for reasons suggested in the text, they are complementary and somewhat repetitive.

[9]The difference is that in 1:5 the preposition εἰς follows the word κοινωνία, whereas in 2:1 and 3:10 it is followed by a genitive case noun (2:1, "fellowship of the spirit" πνεύματος; 3:10, "of his sufferings" παθημάτων). A Pauline pattern emerges: κοινωνία is either followed by the genitive case (1 Cor 1:9; 10:16; 2 Cor 8:4; 13:13; Phil 2:1; 3:10; Phlm 6) or the preposition εἰς (Rom 15:26; Phil 1:5; 2 Cor 9:13). Two times it has no modifiers. When the genitive occurs, Paul identified the tie which produced the fellowship or the entity within which fellowship occurs. When the preposition εἰς occurs, Paul described something larger than the two to which they contribute. That pattern holds in this reference.

however, the construction suggests that the advancement of the gospel united them. In their support of Paul, they contributed to the work of God in the world through the gospel. When the Philippians were converted, they were given a privilege of promoting the gospel. Through their relationship with Paul, they were true to that aspect of their faith.

Paul mentioned the gospel nine times in Philippians.[10] His other epistles reveal that he conceived of the gospel as a message of salvation based on historical, theological, and experiential evidence.[11]

In this epistle, the gospel was proclaimed (1:15-17), defended (1:16), and advanced by the lives of those who knew it (1:12; 2:22). In this text, Paul used the term to suggest that the gospel was the movement of God through history and that it was perpetuated by God's human spokespersons.

Paul's joy came as he remembered the history of the church, as well as the relationship it had with him. Immediately upon Paul's preaching, some people had responded to the gospel, and the church remained firmly committed to Paul, who had taken the gospel message to them. Paul, therefore, looked back to the beginning and appreciated its general support from the first day. Acts 16 records the early history of the Philippian church. The beginning was difficult for both believers and the apostolic band. In addition to the common difficulties faced in spreading the gospel, Paul faced imprisonment for his faith. His joy as he remembered the Philippians, therefore, was not because of his good circumstances when they believed. Rather, it was because of the firm faith of the believers in spite of their difficulties. As they grew in their Christian maturity, they also grew in their appreciation of Paul. He, in turn, prayed for them with joy.

1:6 The second characteristic of Paul's thanksgiving for the Philippian believers was that he prayed with confidence. That confidence was based on the working of God in their midst, not in his own ability or persuasiveness. Two matters emerge as significant emphases: the nature of the work in the Philippians and the time orientation involved.

God began the work in the church. Obviously if he starts something, it will reach completion. Paul easily moved between the tensions of human agency and divine initiative, accepting both in a natural way. The Philippians had a partnership with Paul, but God actually worked it in them. Both the contrasts between these two realities and Paul's comfort with each deserve attention.

What work had God begun? Referring to the immediate context only, some interpreters prefer to explain it as the support the church gave to Paul. They say

---

[10] These are 1:5,7,12,16,27 (2); 2:22; 4:3,15. The word occurs 76 times in the New Testament.

[11] The historical evidence is twofold: the life of Jesus and the resurrection (1 Cor 15; see Acts 2). The theological evidence is the continuity between the Old Testament and the New Testament (see Galatians). The gospel actually fulfilled Old Testament expectations. The experiential evidence came in the testimony of Paul and other believers who responded to the gospel message (Phil 3).

Paul meant the "sharing in the gospel."[12] The rule of context always guides the interpreter, but it is conceivable that Paul may have drawn on the wider context of Christian experience as well. The experience of God's grace always lay under the surface of Paul's words. Most likely that is true here since a reference to the support seems awkward.[13] Further, how does the reference to the "day of Christ" relate to their completion of the gift? Did Paul expect them to continue supporting him until the second coming?

Paul had a general Christian characteristic in mind when he made this statement. Even those who interpret the passage as referring to the specific financial gift normally generalize it somewhat. They refer to the spirit which produced the gift or the opportunity and responsibility of supporting the gospel.[14] It is more likely, however, that Paul saw the Philippians' generosity as evidence of the grace of God in their lives, and in this text he spoke to that grace. In 2 Cor 8:7, a passage that urged the Corinthians to be like the Philippians in giving, Paul urged the development of the grace of giving. Giving evidenced the maturity of their thought and action. The good work in 1:6 refers to what lay behind their generosity, the calling and Christian maturity of the church.

Since Paul spoke of the work beginning and ending, that he had only their initial salvation experience in mind is unlikely. He also had in mind an ongoing process of growth in the Christian's life (Phil 2:12). The whole salvation process, particularly the progressive element, is what Paul meant here. Since God began a work of Christian growth, evidenced by their giving, he would complete that growth.[15]

---

[12]So G. Hawthorne, *Philippians*, WBC (Waco, Tex.: Word, 1983), 21.

[13]First, this would be better suited to an articular expression in Greek, like "the good work," i.e., the previously mentioned participation in the gospel. The text, however, says simply "good work," leaving the precise nature of that work to the reader's understanding. Second, it is difficult to see how the work of the gift to Paul could have been unfinished, and it is equally difficult to know what would have completed it. Paul never approached his congregations with the expectation of continued support. He did just the opposite. He seemed surprised when they sent a gift for him. If each gift were a complete act, which seems likely, what was left undone?

[14]Hawthorne says, "Paul was certain that the Philippians would never waiver in their generosity, would never cease sharing their good gifts to help spread the gospel, until the Parousia" (21). He does say that other interpretations can "be right by extension" (22).

[15]This suits the need of some progressive element in this passage, as well as the fact that for Paul giving is one aspect of the Christian life which measures growth (2 Cor 8:1-7). Commentators sometimes draw attention to the fact that these words recall the LXX translation of creation. There are some parallels in Gen 1, 2. They point out the allusion to God's work in the beginning and Paul's commitment to the truth that God will consummate it. The allusion may be significant (see R. Martin, *Philippians*, NCB [London: Oliphants, 1976], 66, and Hawthorne, 21; but the linguistic correspondence is not as significant as the conceptual correspondence (the work was finished in creation), the correspondence with Genesis is incomplete, and Paul used the expression of "beginning and completion" elsewhere (2 Cor 7:1; Gal 3:3). See M. Silva, *Philippians*, WEC (Chicago: Moody, 1988), 51-52. The parallel to Genesis is vague and hardly provides the basis for understanding. It may, at best, recall the fact that God begins and ends the process.

Paul expressed the confidence that the growth would take place "until the day of Christ Jesus." He glanced backward to their salvation and forward to the completion of their character when the Lord returns. No doubt the reference to the "day of Christ Jesus" is the "day of the Lord" so common in the Old Testament (Joel 2:1; Amos 5:20). The question is why the end times were included at this point. Although Paul could have thought in terms of the imminent coming of the Lord, he also was more aware of a delay than earlier in his ministry.[16] Paul's use of the phrase "until the day" actually called to mind the consummation of the present age. It was Paul's way of making two emphases: sanctification was an ongoing process and the process would continue to the end of the age. At that time the believers would be complete in character. They needed not to fear the judgment which characterized that day.[17]

Some scholars take the confidence to be directed to the church at large, rather than to individuals within the church.[18] The plural "you" makes the text uncertain, and it could have been addressed to the church collectively. On the other hand, the distributive plural commonly occurs in the epistles. It seems better here. Paul's thankfulness came with the confidence that God would work in the individual Christians until the day of Christ. This confidence occurred for two reasons. First, Paul was confident that what God began God would complete, and his words came from a deep conviction that God worked in them. Second, Paul saw the manifestations of their right relationship with God. Their gift evidenced their Christian maturity. Since God worked in them and they responded, Paul's confidence was justified.

1:7 The third characteristic of Paul's thankful attitude was its properness. The Greek text has the word "right, just" (*dikaion*), a descriptive term expressing the sense of propriety. A structural question should be asked here: What does this clause modify? It could explain why Paul felt such confidence in God's working in the Philippians. Alternatively, it could add a reason Paul was thankful for them, expressing a thought parallel to his great joy for them.[19] The latter is better. The "even as" clause parallels the two verbal ideas found here ("I always pray" and "being confident"). Further, Paul's confidence that God would complete his work hardly rested on emotional ties with them. His thankfulness for them could.

Paul provided three reasons for his attitude of thankfulness. First, he had them in his heart. Commentators differ over the precise meaning of this

---

[16] He wrote of a delay in the Lord's return as early as 2 Thess 2:1-12, so by the time of the writing of Philippians this delay had been reinforced in his mind.

[17] A similar time orientation occurs in Phil 1:10-11 where Paul prayed that they would be filled with the fruit of righteousness at the day of Christ. Paul's use of the preposition ἄχρι parallels the use of εἰς in 1:10.

[18] Martin says, "The Philippian church will be preserved to the end time" (65).

[19] The former takes καθώς ("even as") to modify the participle πεποιθώς ("having this confidence"). The latter takes the καθώς to modify the verb εὐχαριστῶ ("I give thanks").

structure. On one hand, the Greek could read, "You have me in your heart," and the context could be interpreted to support it.[20] Paul was explaining his appreciation of their gift on his behalf. Perhaps he continued his appreciation for their financial support. On the other hand, the construction more naturally reads, "I have you in my heart."[21] Taken this way, Paul's thanksgiving was more than a response to the gift they sent and to the knowledge of God's working in their behalf. It came from a true blending of hearts. Emotional ties bound them together.

The second reason for this attitude was their fellow-service in the apostolic ministry. Paul's circumstances did not hinder their relationship. Being a prisoner could have presented an obstacle to their wholehearted support, but they took the attitude that it was their imprisonment too. No doubt this meant more to Paul because the church at Rome divided into two groups concerning him—to some, his imprisonment was part of the problem. No church was in a more patriotic setting than the Philippian church, but the chains proved to be no obstacle. Paul also mentioned his "defensing" and "confirming" the gospel. The words are legal terms. They are official language for a formal defense, and some interpret them as evidence that Paul had presented his case in court. In fact, he had presented himself and the gospel to various political officials in Palestine.[22] His presence in Rome was also a defense of the gospel. Paul stated later that the topic of conversation was "Christ" (1:13). The ordeal of his incarceration may be correctly called a "defense and confirmation." It was the ultimate opportunity for Christians to present their claims to the emperor. Thus, by life or death, Paul was committed to the gospel message. The church stood by him in it. Whether good or bad times came, Paul counted on the Philippian church.[23] Their support evidenced the fact that they were true "fellow-workers."[24] They joined with him in his apostolic calling to

---

[20]The infinitive construction in Greek has two accusatives with it. The first is με ("I"); the second is ὑμᾶς ("you").

[21]This follows a rule of thumb in such constructions, that the accusative nearest the verb is the subject. Further, if the existing subject works in a statement, it is best to retain it. Both of these rules fit well with taking "I" as the subject, in spite of the early commentary of Chrysostom to the contrary. The evidence for "I" being the object is well presented by Hawthorne, 22-24. The evidence to the contrary is well presented by Silva, 56-57, especially see note 21 with its instructive data surveys.

[22]These defenses were before the rioting crowd (Acts 22:1-29); before the Sanhedrin (Acts 23:1-10); before Felix (Acts 24:1-21); before Drusilla (Acts 24:24-27); before Festus (Acts 25:4-12); and before Agrippa and Bernice (Acts 26:1-32). Since the Caesarean imprisonment was two years duration, it is likely that the church heard of these opportunities to defend the gospel.

[23]The words "defense and confirmation" may refer to specific activity while he was in prison, or they may refer in a general sense to the fact that they stood with him whether he was free or bound. The latter seems more historically true. They supported him in the relief offering at Corinth, and now they supported him directly in his own trials.

[24]The term consists of "with" (σύν) and "fellowship" (κοινωνούς), a play on terms with "partners" of 1:5. "Fellow-workers" occurs in the accusative case along with the participle ὄντας

reach Gentiles for Christ. The partnership between them formed the strong tie which Paul addressed in the next verse.

Paul referred to his apostleship with the word "grace." The term may identify general Christian attitudes, a state of grace in which a Christian stands, or Paul's specific calling of grace.[25] The last correctly describes this reference. To understand it as depicting a general state of grace does not take the immediate context seriously. The defense and confirmation of the gospel directly relate to the grace. They are the arena in which the grace operates. Here is another reference to his apostolic function. The Philippians recognized Paul's unique place in God's economy as apostle of God's grace, and they demonstrated their support for it by participating with him as they could.

1:8 The third reason for Paul's attitude in prayer was the deep Christian tie between them. The force of this statement is demonstrated in two ways. First, the new sentence[26] is in the form of an oath, as Paul called God to the witness stand. They could not see Paul's heart for them, but God did. Second, this intense desire was distinctly Christian. Paul used two terms: "long" (*epipothō*), which expresses a strong desire, and "affection" (*splanchnois*), which identifies the "entrails" as all being involved in the emotion.[27] The "entrails" were actually those of Christ Jesus. Paul thereby expressed the fact that his feelings came from the Lord. This was a total Christian emotion that was the result of both of them being Christian and of both sharing in what God was doing in Christ.

(2) Paul's Prayer for the Philippians (1:9-11)

⁹And this is my prayer: that your love may abound more and more in knowledge and depth of insight, ¹⁰so that you may be able to discern what is best and may be pure and blameless until the day of Christ, ¹¹filled with the fruit of righteousness that comes through Jesus Christ—to the glory and praise of God.

Paul's thoughts easily moved from thanksgiving to petitioning prayer. The two were part of the same spiritual activity, but more than that, Paul acknowledged that the good done in the Philippians' lives came from God. As a part of his response in praise, he prayed that God would continue his work in them.

This prayer resembles the prayer in Colossians. The similarity goes beyond the fact that the prayer follows quickly upon thanksgiving. Similarities of words reveal a similarity of content. No doubt Paul wrote them both at a time

---

because of the accusative ὑμᾶς of 1:7. Probably there is a causal force to the participle, which then reads "because you are fellow-workers."

[25] See Rom 1:5; 12:3; 15:15; 1 Cor 3:10; Gal 2:9. These are places where Paul referred to himself or a Christian calling as a "grace."

[26] The editors of the text recognized the new energy in this verse.

[27] This strong term points to the seat of the emotion, the bowels. Hawthorne, pointed out that these were the "nobler organs," not "the entrails" (ἔντερα) or intestines (25). Either way, they were considered the center of the emotion.

when he pondered the same thoughts on Christian growth, perhaps because of his own situation in life.[28] The lexical and conceptual parallels include the following:

Phil 1:9-11	Col 1:9-11
I pray	praying
(*proseuchomai*)	(*proseuchomenoi*)
abound in knowledge	growing in knowledge of God
(*epignōsei*)	(*epignōsin*)
in all discernment	in wisdom and understanding
(*aisthesei*)	(*sophia kai synesei*)
being filled	you may be filled
(*peplērōmenoi*)	(*plērōthēte*)
fruit of righteousness	bearing fruit
(*karpon dikaiosynēs*)	(*karpophorountes*)
glory and praise of God	power of his glory
(*doxan kai epainon*)	(*kratos tēs doxēs*)
a good work	every good work
(*ergon agathon*)	(*ergō agathō*)

These parallels reveal that Paul thought consistently on the matter of Christian growth, and the fact that they are parallel emphasizes the basic themes found in his requests.[29]

The prayer contains two basic petitions. These are known by two "that" (*hina*) clauses in the Greek text. The NIV fails to pick up this distinction and even makes the second petition part of a parallel statement ("and may be pure and blameless").[30] The two petitions are: "that your love may abound . . . so that you may be able to discern what is best" (1:9-10a); and that you "may be pure and blameless . . . having been filled with the fruit of righteousness" (1:10b-11). The first looks to the time interval between the present situation and the return of the Lord. The second takes the perspective of the second coming and looks back to the preparation of the church for that event. Paul prayed for a growing love (1:9-10b) and for a complete character (1:10b-11a).[31]

---

[28] This fact is often overlooked in Colossians, where most accept the fact that the prayer was suited to the specific problem faced there. While it is true that the problem colors specific expressions, it is equally true that the concepts are shared with other letters, such as Philippians. That fact diminishes the urgency of the impact of the false teachers at Colosse.

[29] The list of parallels comes from Silva, 57-58.

[30] It is most awkward to fail to acknowledge a major conjunction like ἵνα ("that"). They have taken a purpose infinitive (εἰς τό plus infinitive) as the beginning of a new clause rather than the end of the first ἵνα clause. Of the ways to understand the relationships, this is the least likely.

[31] It is possible that the two primary clauses are consecutive so that the translation is "that your love may abound . . . in order that you may be sincere and void of offense." This takes the two ἵνα clauses in different relationships, however. The first one would be an object clause, the second a

PRAYER FOR A GROWING LOVE (1:9-10a). Love entered Paul's thoughts first. Perhaps that was because of the Philippians' love demonstrated in supporting him at such a crucial time in his life. Perhaps it was because love summarized the Ten Commandments, as presented in Deut 6:5 and Luke 10:27. Love also epitomized Christian responsibility to other Christians (John 13:35; 1 John 2:7-11).

To these rather obvious commands regarding love, Paul added his own insights. If the Philippians' love abounded, they would be well on the way to Christian maturity. Here Paul described the nature of a growing love, the environment for a growing love, and the result of a growing love.

The Nature of a Growing Love (1:9a). Some confusion always exists in discussing love. It is at the same time the universal ideal to which all should aspire and the most personal and existential of all expressions.

1:9a The definition of love is addressed in this part of v. 9. Paul used the word *agapē*. The word predominates in Scripture as the expression of love. It is sometimes difficult to distinguish *agapē* from *philos* because the two occur frequently in Scripture with seemingly interchangeable meaning. Nevertheless, *philos* does contain an element of mutuality not found in *agapē*. It is a satisfying interaction with others. What is clear is that for Paul *agapē* emphasized the self-sacrificial love of Christ. It is a selfless action to benefit someone else. The model for this love is Christ, who gave himself for the sins of the world.

As Paul prayed for the readers' love to abound, he prayed for their Christlike attitude of self-sacrifice to continue as it had been demonstrated earlier in their giving.[32] The sacrificial nature of the love is further stressed in that there is no object for the love; it is a characteristic of the "lover" regardless of the object.[33] Jesus taught that aspect in the parable of the good Samaritan (Luke 10:25-37).

The lawyer asked, "Who is my neighbor?" seeking to come to a clear understanding of his neighborhood and, thereby, of his responsibility (10:29). Jesus responded, "Which . . . was a neighbor?" informing the man that he had framed the question incorrectly (10:36). There are no boundaries to a Christian's neighborhood. Love was to follow in the wake of their living.[34]

---

purpose clause. This construction would be awkward in the same sentence. In addition, another purpose element is in the verse: εἰς τό with the infinitive. The sentence is actually quite balanced structurally, which is not uncommon in Paul's prayers. The first has a non-final conjunction (ἵνα) modified by a purpose infinitive; the second has a non-final ἵνα modified by a predicate participle.

[32] See 2 Cor 8:1-6 where Paul spoke of their "rock bottom poverty" (v. 2), of their gift exceeding their ability (v. 3), of their begging Paul to accept the gift (v. 4), and of their gift as an expression of commitment to the Lord (v. 5).

[33] It is always easier to measure love if there is a specific object who should be loved. The absence of such parameters makes love all the more the responsibility of the initiator, not the receiver.

[34] F. W. Beare, *The Epistle to the Philippians,* HNTC (San Francisco: Harper & Row, 1959), correctly sees this aspect of syntax. He states it is not only love for him or others, but "love in the most comprehensive sense as the central element of the Christian life" (54).

The dynamic growth of love is presented in two ways in this first clause. First, the verb "abound" (*perisseuē*), which means to "be present in abundance,"[35] occurs in the most dynamic of expressions possible.[36] Their love was to "keep on abounding." Second, the adverbial expression "more and more" stresses the dynamic of love. The Greek text actually has the expression "still more and more," the first part of which is omitted in the NIV. The expression builds layer upon layer to make the point. "More" would have sufficed, "more and more" was better, but "still more and more" accentuated the point being made. Although exemplary in their love, the Philippians had not yet reached perfection. There was still room for growth.

The Environment of a Growing Love (1:9b). **1:9b**　The prayerful exhortation to love came with instructions about how to implement it. The words "knowledge and depth of insight" provide the twofold environment in which love may grow.[37] They are, in fact, the most basic elements which foster love.[38] The first aspect of the environment for growing love is knowledge. The Greek word for "knowledge" (*epignōsis*) is difficult to translate into acceptable English. The root word is *gnosis*, and the preposition *epi* ("upon") is prefixed to it. Both parts of the compound need explanation.

The basic word used here (*gnōsis*) contains a slight contrast with its synonyms. Most often it is compared or contrasted with the common Greek term for "knowledge" (*oida*). This latter term generally signifies an intellectual knowledge (the product of the mind). It may convey the idea of a complete knowledge because the other terms are not well suited to the idea of completion. In contrast, *gnōsis* generally conveys the idea of an experiential knowledge (the product of experiencing by living). It easily lends itself to expressing relationships since they come from experiences. Further, since experiences provide the process of learning, *gnōsis* often stresses the process of knowing, rather than the outcome. Here Paul used the term in its full sense of real, per-

---

[35] *BAGD*, 650-51. Hawthorne points out that the word is typically Pauline (26 of 39 times in the New Testament) and that it typifies the new age brought by Christ (26). This assessment is correct and insightful.

[36] It is a present subjunctive. The progressive idea is a product of the verb root, the tense, and the context which demands it. Together they stress the dynamic nature of the love.

[37] Hawthorne seems to provide an alternate option. He states that love is to be "accompanied by knowledge and understanding," and, later, "One of the things that directs love is knowledge" (26). In actuality, he is not far from the position of this commentary, but the principle followed here is that, if the locative idea with ἐν ("in") will work, it should be employed. That is its most common and natural force, and to understand these as locatives of sphere works well in this passage.

[38] Martin suggests that these terms are common among hellenistic philosophers "in the twofold sense of an intellectual apprehension of the good in life and a moral choice which determines a man's course of action" (68). Paul probably had the philosophers in mind in this statement, but certainly the intellectual and moral combine here. The outline captions for this section reflect that understanding.

sonal knowing. It is not the product of deductive reasoning and, therefore, intellectual (*oida*). Nevertheless, it is not fully relational, indicating only relationships with persons. Paul wanted them to have a personal knowledge which, as he stated later in this prayer, would surface in practical ways as well.

The compound form heightens the definition. In Greek, prefixed prepositions may be either directive, pointing to a specific knowledge, or perfective, emphasizing an accurate knowledge. Since this context does not provide a direction, clearly Paul used the word in the perfective sense.[39] This first aspect of love, therefore, is a complete knowledge. Part of the completeness is its ability to apply what is known to the practical aspects of life.[40]

Paul added judgment, the moral environment, to knowledge. The term "depth of insight" occurs only here in the New Testament, although a form of the root word occurs in Heb 5:14. It conveys the sense of moral discretion.[41] Thus morality affects the growth of love.

Although the terms knowledge and judgment have no specific modifiers, two matters are clear. First, Paul wrote in Christian terms. The love and judgment he espoused were those seen in Christ and consistent with Scripture. While the words sometimes occur in secular contexts discussing general morality, Paul certainly rooted his prayers in Christ and the resources which come from the Holy Spirit. The Philippians would realize, therefore, that in disclosing his prayer for them, Paul called them to the highest and best of Christian qualities and growth. Second, these two terms provide a collective environment which fosters growth. If either is lacking, love will not grow. In this, Paul's expression is consistent with his Jewish-Christian ethical background. Knowing and living go hand in hand. Failure to grow in the knowledge God expects of Christians hinders love. Similarly, failure to discipline the moral life hinders love. Attention to both of these realms promotes a healthy and positive Christian life.

Like "love," the terms "knowledge" and "insight" have no expressed objects. They speak to broad, general concerns. The comprehensive knowledge includes an accurate understanding of God and the world, as well as the "lover" himself.[42] Similarly, the moral insight comes from various sources and is comprehensive in nature. It exposes the rightness and wrongness of all thoughts and actions.

---

[39] J. B. Lightfoot, *St. Paul's Epistle to the Philippians*, reprint edition (Grand Rapids: Zondervan, 1953), 86, called it an intensive preposition.

[40] Silva points out that Paul preferred the compound term in the chronologically later epistles and that there may be no significance to the form (63). Silva's observation may be partially correct. That is, Paul may well have developed such a preference, but that preference no doubt came from his insistence on real knowledge. The word became his favorite later because of its suitability to his theological outlook.

[41] *BAGD*, 25.

[42] Thus love is fostered by seeing a model (God), knowing the object (the world), and being an intimately personal expression (myself).

The Result of a Growing Love (1:10a). **1:10a**   Paul envisioned mature
Christians who had the ability to distinguish right from wrong. He directed his
prayer toward that end.[43] The NIV correctly translates what may be taken in
several ways. The word "discern" has the meaning of *test by trial,* and the term
"best" emphasizes the result of that testing. The phrase need not stress the fact
that some things are harmful and, therefore, should be avoided. It has equal
application to affirming and embracing the best of good choices, and that reading fits this text better. Since this context calls for a wisdom related to life, the
words suggest the ability to discern moral conduct and values so that life and
energy are not misdirected. A growing love, fed by proper knowledge and
moral insight, enables one to see the best way to live in light of the day of
Christ.

PRAYER FOR COMPLETE CHARACTER (1:10b-11).   Discerning what is best
develops character. A growing love provides for character development and
completion. As Paul prayed, his thoughts moved to the day of accountability.
He prayed that the Philippians would live in such a way that they would be
without blame at that time. In this second petition, therefore, Paul saw the end
of life on earth. As always, the return of the Lord and Christians' preparation
for it occupied his thoughts. Paul identified through prayer the nature of complete character, the means to it, and the purpose of it.

The Nature of Complete Character (1:10b). **1:10b**   Two words describe
Paul's concern for the Philippians: "pure and blameless." Strictly defined these
words convey two slightly different ideas. "Pure" (*eilikrinēs*) occurs only one
other time in the New Testament (2 Pet 3:1), although other words with the
same root occur (i.e., 1 Cor 5:8). The most common etymology of the term suggests that it comes from the two words "sun" (*helios*) and "to judge" (*krinō*)
and that the word meant *to hold up to sunlight for inspection.*[44] "Blameless"
(*aproskopoi*) also occurs rarely in the New Testament.[45] The term may have an
active meaning (*to cause blame*) or a passive one (*to be free from blame*).[46] The
decision is a difficult one since both have a precedent (cf. Acts 24:16; 1 Cor
10:32). The text, however, follows with a reference to the "fruit of righteousness," a term which implies character, and thus it favors the passive sense. Paul
hoped they would have a blameless life.

The Means to Complete Character (1:11a). **1:11a**   Similar to the first
petition, Paul provided a context out of which such character could come. In
the first, the environment of knowledge and morality produced a discriminat-
ing love. In this petition the fruit of righteousness produces complete character.

---

[43]The construction εἰς τό plus the infinitive shows purpose in this case as it often does when
the ἵνα clauses are non-final.

[44]Hawthorne, 28.

[45]Phil 1:10; Acts 24:16; and 1 Cor 10:32. *BAGD*, 102.

[46]Lightfoot, 87. He argues that in this context any reference to conduct toward others is out of
place. Paul spoke only of their relationship to God here.

The phrase "fruit of righteousness" also demands interpretation. The primary concern is the use of the term "righteousness."[47] Some interpret it to mean the fruit produced by their imputed righteousness.[48] Most, however, understand the phrase to mean the result of righteous activity as Christians. It refers to an ethical righteousness. The Old Testament supports this conclusion (Hos 10:12), and it fits Paul's attitude expressed in Philippians.

Here Paul used an agricultural metaphor which included the word "fruit." Some translate the word as "harvest," a translation which no doubt captures Paul's thought well. The fruit was that which Jesus Christ produced in them. It parallels Gal 5:22. For that reason, the participle is best understood as a passive idea, "having been filled" (e.g., by Christ).[49] The prayer was for them to live in such a way that Christ could work in them the harvest of morality and righteousness which would be acceptable at the day of Christ.

Righteous living would protect the church; it would be blameless. As Paul would clarify later (see 3:4-6), his concern was that blamelessness be because of Christ and his righteousness, not one's own. The passage teaches that if those who are righteous by God's grace through faith live as they should, the fruit of their lives will be true blamelessness. No one will condemn them, and they will stand the test of judgment day.

The Purpose of Complete Character (1:11b). **1:11b** Paul concluded this prayer with a reference to God's glory. The day of Christ characterized Paul's thoughts; the glory of God motivated Paul's actions. He saw the entire scope of salvation as an outworking of God's grace and as a contribution to God's glory.[50] The chief end of persons was the glory of God. He reminded the Philippians of their ultimate calling, to reflect God's character in their lives. He explained the reason for their careful living: the glory of God in their lives.

With this prayer for God's glory, Paul ended the first section of the epistle. The epistle began with appreciation for their relationship to Paul from the beginning. It called them to realize that God began a work in them and it must continue, and it reminded them of the need to prepare for the day of Christ's appearing. Paul masterfully revealed his concerns for them, introducing each of the major themes of the epistle. In a manner appropriate to friends, Paul

---

[47] The construction is actually capable of three possible translations of the genitive "righteousness": fruit which is righteousness (appositional genitive); the fruit which righteousness produces (subjective genitive); the fruit which is righteous fruit (descriptive genitive). Regarding the definition of righteousness, there are two options: forensic (imputed righteousness) or ethical (moral conduct).

[48] So Beare, 55.

[49] In contrast to Beare, who takes it as middle (produce a harvest). It is equally difficult to see how Hawthorne, 28-29, takes the participle as an adjective (attributive function) when it fits the normal structural patterns of adverbial participles (predicate forms), and the context makes good sense with this reading.

[50] This is specifically clear in Eph 1:3-14 where three sections of doxology are marked by some form of the phrase "to the praise of the glory of his grace" (1:6,12,14).

spoke first in appreciation for who they were, then urged them to continue in Christian growth. Even his prayer provided a positive approach to them. His was no disinterested concern. He prayed that they would achieve the character prized so highly for them and himself (3:8-11). The concern did not bypass the present life, however. Love was to characterize all Christians. It uniquely expressed their relationship to Christ and prepared them for meeting him at the end of life.

2. Paul's Joy in the Progress of the Gospel (1:12-26)

With v. 12, Paul began a discussion of his situation in Rome. He rarely wrote so early in an epistle about his own situation.[51] Perhaps several reasons prompted this approach. First, no doubt the church anxiously awaited this news; it had sent Epaphroditus to Paul's side, anticipating his needs. Perhaps it had heard of the potential difficulties Paul might have with the Roman government. Although at this time Christianity was not a capital crime, no one knew how the emperor would rule regarding Christians. This was the test case.

The second reason Paul discussed his circumstances so soon was that the Philippians would hear a firsthand report from Epaphroditus, and Paul needed to address their concerns quickly. Their anxiety regarding Epaphroditus would quickly turn to continued anxiety about Paul. Although Epaphroditus's report would be accurate, it could easily be filled with his impressions. Little could be done constructively to address the needs of the church if readers were waiting to hear how Paul responded to his circumstances.

Third, Paul saw firsthand how divisions affected the work of the gospel. The divided church at Rome surely grieved Paul. Although he did not complain in his letter, and he pointed out the positive aspects of the situation, obviously the disunity concerned him. An explanation of his circumstances provided a natural and easy way to encourage the Philippians in the qualities he saw lacking at Rome. Thus the description of his situation served to anticipate his point to the readers. Surely they would conduct themselves differently from the Roman church.

Finally, this section responded to the gift they had sent. They wanted to know Paul's circumstances because they were friends; because of their stewardship, they needed to know how the work progressed. At specific intervals Paul wrote autobiographically, informing the readers of his own thoughts. Three times this occurs in major sections: 1:12-26, regarding his circumstances; 3:1-14, regarding his experience of salvation; and 4:10-20, regarding the gift from the church. In each case, Paul's experiences became an effective vehicle for communicating his concerns.

---

[51] He does in 2 Cor 1:8-11, but there he summarized what happened to him in order to address their attacks against him. In Philippians Paul wrote a "free standing" disclosure of his situation and placed it at the beginning. That calls for some explanation.

A major structural question concerns the ending of the first section. It is difficult to know whether 1:27-30 concludes the first section by applying Paul's concerns regarding Rome to the church at Philippi, or whether it begins the first set of exhortations. There are thematic and conceptual ties to both sections.

The problem is to determine what criteria actually indicate a new section has begun. On one hand, Philippians has the marks of a personal letter, and informal allusions to the tie between writer and reader occur throughout. In 1:27-30 Paul made reference to his desire to hear of the Philippians' firm stand. Such a stand confirmed his apostolic ministry. In 2:1-11 Paul appealed to the common bond between himself and the church. The humility he advocated was a fulfillment of his joy. In 2:12-18 he urged them to obey and work out their salvation even if he were sacrificed. Their obedience vindicated his sufferings for them. The criterion for structural divisions may be personal allusion, but such allusions are frequent in the section. In each portion Paul appealed to their friendship. On the other hand, the criterion may be that the form changes to exhortation rather than information. Three basic commands occur in 1:27-2:18. This change of tone appears more significant, and the three no doubt form a section to themselves. The first section, therefore, ends at 1:26.[52] It divides naturally into two primary sections: Paul's circumstances (1:12-17) and Paul's attitudes (1:18-26).

(1) Paul's Circumstances (1:12-17)

[12]Now I want you to know, brothers, that what has happened to me has really served to advance the gospel. [13]As a result, it has become clear throughout the whole palace guard and to everyone else that I am in chains for Christ. [14]Because of my chains, most of the brothers in the Lord have been encouraged to speak the word of God more courageously and fearlessly. [15]It is true that some preach Christ out of envy and rivalry, but others out of goodwill. [16]The latter do so in love, knowing that I am put here for the defense of the gospel. [17]The former preach Christ out of selfish ambition, not sincerely, supposing that they can stir up trouble for me while I am in chains.

The church primarily desired to know Paul's circumstances. While his description is in some ways quite explicit, in other ways many questions remain unanswered. For one thing, Paul assumed that the church knew the details. If it did not, Epaphroditus would surely report more then Paul could write. Writing all that he felt could have jeopardized his legal situation. For another, what he wrote was one-sided, and the readers had to piece things together as best they could.

---

[52]The difficulty in determining structure points should be considered in discussions of the unity of the letter. The fabric has few clear seams since firsthand references and bases of appeal occur throughout. There are also few section indicators: 1:12, "now I want you to know, brothers"; 1:27, "only"; 3:1, "finally"; 4:8, "finally." Twice "so that" (ὥστε) occurs as well as a minor sectional marker (2:12 and 4:1).

PAUL'S IMPRISONMENT (1:12).   **1:12** Rather than detail the hardships he faced, Paul took a divine perspective. He recognized that all events could be redeemed for the Lord's sake, and he took what advantage he could to continue his mission. The primary concern was that the gospel go forward. This happened through adverse circumstances, but as long as it happened, Paul could be joyful.

Paul did not specifically mention his imprisonment. The Greek text says simply "the things to me" (*ta kat' eme*). Most likely he included all the events from his imprisonment at Jerusalem through his imprisonment at Rome. These were the riot, the two-year imprisonment at Caesarea, the appeal to Caesar, the threat on his life, the trip to Rome with its shipwreck, his house-arrest and restricted freedom, and the impending trial.[53] However, the focus is on the Roman events. As Paul described them, he spoke in terms of the effect on the soldiers and the Roman church.

The church might have expected the worse, but Paul countered that quickly. The gospel advanced. The term "advanced" (*prokopēn*) was used in the Greek-speaking world to describe blazing a trail before an army, the philosophical progress toward wisdom, and the progress of a young minister.[54] Paul, therefore, saw the events as forging new territory for the gospel. They took Paul into contact with a select group of people, soldiers and Roman officials, who otherwise would have had no relationship to him, and they also prompted a renewed evangelistic effort in the city. While others may have seen the end of missionary activity, Paul saw the new ways the gospel could advance. The events which seemed to inhibit the freedom of the gospel became its springboard. Paul did not say "in spite of" these events, but rather "through them." There is a note of sacrifice here. Paul's private concerns did not matter; the gospel did.

REACTIONS TO PAUL'S IMPRISONMENT (1:13-17).   In explaining the situation at Rome, Paul disclosed two important results of the events that had happened to him. Neither of these was expected, and thus Paul's word was news to them. At the same time, both reactions advanced the gospel; Paul made specific what he had claimed to be the case in 1:12. His statement there did not come without evidence. Even here, however, one of the reactions continued to be a mixed blessing, and it proved to be a continuing circumstance of the gospel's advance through difficulties.

The Gospel Spread Among Roman Soldiers (1:13). **1:13** In this undesirable situation, the gospel spread through the ranks of the soldiers. Basically, Paul said that they knew he was a prisoner of Christ, not just of Rome. The clarification of that fact was an encouragement since Paul would later state "to live

---

[53] A. T. Robertson, *Paul's Joy in Christ: Studies in Philippians* (Nashville: Broadman, n.d.), 41, adds all these events to the statement. It seems unlikely that Paul stressed them all.

[54] Ibid., 40-41. Interestingly he says, "The opposition to Paul in Rome had kicked the gospel upstairs."

is Christ" (1:21). Two matters deserve comment: the meaning of the phrase "manifest in Christ" (*phanerous en Christō*), which the NIV translates "become clear . . . for Christ," and the meaning of "the praetorium" (*praitōrion*), which the NIV translates "palace guard."

Paul's basic reason for encouragement was that his real imprisonment became clear. Commentators differ on the meaning of the words "in Christ." Some think they go with "chains," with the resultant meaning being something like "it became evident that I was a Christian," or "that I was a prisoner of Christ." Since Paul lived for the gospel, perhaps he stated that he was not guilty of any charge brought against him and that the soldiers knew he could be released except for his commitment to Christ. In the truest sense, he was a prisoner of Christ.[55] That prior relationship caused him to a be literal prisoner of Rome. Others, like the NIV translators, interpret the phrase to mean that the chains were manifest that they were "for Christ." Pointing out the awkwardness of the construction in Greek if any other interpretation holds, they state that Paul was really a prisoner for the sake of Christ.[56] His predicament was because of the Christian message he proclaimed.[57]

Paul actually took advantage of the situation to call to mind a deeper slavery. In Eph 3:1, he referred to himself as the prisoner of Christ. Surely he intended a similar meaning here, though neither passage is determinative. Paul did use words in such a way that they conveyed deeper meanings (not in violation of simpler meanings, however). The first interpretation fits better than the second. Paul's joy came because what he lived for (the manifestation of Christ) was actually happening. Further, the principle he held so dear was clarified to those around. They understood his slavery to Christ.

Paul said this knowledge spread in the praetorium. Considerable debate

---

[55] G. B. Caird, *Paul's Letters from Prison* (Oxford: University Press, 1976), provides a list of charges brought against Paul as found in Acts. They were sacrilege (21:28) and political agitation (24:5). He continues, "He had therefore been at pains to prove to all he met that loyalty to *Christ* was his sole offence" (110).

[56] The Greek construction puts "in Christ" after "my chains manifest." That is awkward if "chains in Christ" belong together. However, the verb "became" is also dislocated from the rest; the entire construction is unusual.

[57] K. Barth, *The Epistle to the Philippians* (Richmond: John Knox, 1962), 26-27, n.1, assumes that such interpretations were commonly accepted but fail to satisfy the text. They assume that Paul was expecting release because it became apparent that his "crime" was being a Christian. At that time, that was no crime. He argues: (1) that the positive outcome was an assumption of the interpreters and would not have been prominent in Paul's opening words; (2) that the Roman Christians would have taken courage because there was nothing to fear for being a Christian is a wrong assumption; and (3) that the Greek order argues against it. His arguments lose their weight because this is not an essential assumption to the position. In fact, regardless of the outcome of the trial, Paul lived for "Christ magnified in my body," and so would have joy regardless. Barth offers the rather strange interpretation that the bonds were "publicized in Christ," that the *fact* of his imprisonment became a problem to all concerned, and many were reached through this word. His interpretation has little to commend it.

focuses on whether the *praitōrion* (praetorium or palace guard) was a place (i.e., a barracks) or a people (i.e., an elite imperial guard). On one hand, the praetorium was a place.[58] Those who interpret it as a place assume that the place was the barracks of the imperial guard. The evidence from Acts reveals that Paul had his own leased dwelling, so he could not have been incarcerated at the praetorium (Acts 28:30). Seen this way, Paul stated that the topic of conversation in the barracks was Paul and Christ. On the other hand, the praetorium was also a group of men. The term stood for the emperor's bodyguard of nine cohorts. They were the only troops stationed in Italy after the settlement of Augustus.[59] Although Paul did not claim that people of the guard were converted, he did claim that they heard his message.[60]

Christians Encouraged to Speak (1:14-17). **1:14** The second result of Paul's circumstances involved the church at Rome. A new evangelistic effort sprang up that affected the entire Christian community. Paul saw that his situation was the catalyst for this renewed interest in outreach, and he knew it would be good news to the church at Philippi.

In actuality, the church at Rome had two different reactions. Some members were encouraged by Paul and preached out of sympathy; others hoped to get Paul into more trouble with the Roman officials. Paul focused first on the brethren who supported him. In addition, he was able to see beyond the differences in motivation and realized that Christ was proclaimed. He was comforted by this reality.

Most of the Christians took heart from Paul's situation.[61] They preached more courageously and fearlessly. Some commentators have suggested that the believers' preaching came because they knew that Paul's only crime was Christianity, and that was no crime at all. Before they had feared their own imprisonment; now that fear no longer existed. There is no evidence for that

---

[58]Lightfoot, 99-104, indicates that the word could mean the general's tent, the residence of a governor or prince, any spacious palace, the imperial residence on the Palatine, the barracks attached to the imperial palace itself, the great camp of the praetorian soldiers, a body of men, the imperial guard. His discussion provides the basic evidence of the varieties of usage.

[59]Caird, 110.

[60]This conclusion assumes that Paul wrote from Rome. If Ephesus or Caesarea were the location of writing, the term possibly could have referred to a building. The arguments for and against a building rest on some assumptions. Certainly Paul would not call the emperor's residence on Palatine Hill a "praetorium," yet some say a visitor from the east could easily call a building something it was not. The text is best satisfied if Paul had the guard in mind. Naturally, the guard needed barracks, but the stress appears to be on the people who heard and transmitted the word.

[61]Some statements reveal that Paul expected to be freed. He knew how law operated because he was a Jewish lawyer and knew where he stood with the Roman government officially. Nevertheless, Christianity was an unknown factor in the empire, and Paul was the first serious test case of the official Roman attitude. Paul's optimism resulted from his reading of the situation coupled with his spiritual insights. There is no evidence that he had an inside track on the outcome of the trial.

interpretation, however. While Paul's general tone was optimistic, he never indicated that he knew the trial would exonerate him. Paul actually stated that "the brothers in the Lord have been encouraged to speak." He emphasized their spiritual motivation, not the evidence they might have derived from Paul's circumstances.[62] Further, the context assumes their preaching was encouraged by the imprisonment, not by the expected release. As the next verses indicate, their support for Paul had given them courage to preach God's word.[63]

Paul acknowledged that they preached the word, but not all preached with proper motivations. In vv. 15-17 Paul described two groups of preachers who reacted to him. The verses fall into a literary pattern of a chiasm.[64] The literary pattern reveals three important aspects of their preaching. First, the "outside" members of the chiasm receive the emphasis. When Paul turned his thoughts to these preachers, therefore, he thought first in terms of those who opposed him.[65] Second, each group has two sets of descriptive phrases accompanying it. All of these contribute to an understanding of the motivations involved. Third, the chiasm further describes the preachers of v. 14. "Most of the brothers" included those supportive and those opposed to Paul.

The ones preaching to harm Paul are discussed in 1:15,17. The content reveals a close connection between vv. 14-15, but the translators show a separation. The only word against the preachers of 1:15 is that they had wrong motives. They were still brothers. The first portion of the chiastic unit, however, mildly changes to describing an activity unexpected of brothers. The translation "It is true that" captures the thought. Some opposed Paul, but that was a minor obstacle.

---

[62] A major concern occurs in the placement of the phrase "in the Lord." Some see the phrase as "brethren in the Lord," i.e., Christians, who were encouraged. The arguments in favor of it are: the natural reading of the text makes a prepositional phrase follow what it modifies, and normally πέποιθο ("encouraged") comes first in its clause. Others take the phrase as "encouraged in the Lord." They say the phrase "brothers in the Lord" involves a redundancy (where else would brothers be?), "in the Lord" comes first for emphasis, and other times the verb πεποίθα is followed by the preposition "in." The arguments do not clearly favor one over the other. However, similar constructions with the verb occur in Phil 2:24; 3:3-4, and the prepositional phrase follows. The better understanding, therefore, is that these are "brethren encouraged in the Lord."

[63] The UBS Greek text simply says "to be speaking the word." Some of the translations follow, including the KJV. The NIV, however, has "to speak the word of God." This translation is no doubt correct, as the variant readings affirm. The stronger external evidence supports it, and the internal evidence is undeterminative. The words "of God" were probably part of the original, but if not, the earliest interpretations worked their way into the text.

[64] A chiasm is a literary device containing two or more sets of members arranged in an ABBA pattern. In chiasms the outside members (A,A) receive the emphasis.

[65] This exegetical factor is softened further by the fact that vv. 15-17 describe v. 14. In v. 14 the preachers in general are addressed so that the pattern is general to specific. If Paul had desired to expose the preachers in a harsh way, he would have placed them first in his discussion and used a more direct means of identification.

1:15 Paul exposed their method and motivations. The method was "envy and rivalry."[66] The words always suggest relationships which have gone bad, and the terms normally occur in Paul's lists of sins to avoid. Paul used the same construction in stating that others preached "out of goodwill." Certainly their goodwill was not be directed toward the Roman authorities, and it was unlikely that it was goodwill toward the church. In fact, some would no doubt think that the best course of action for the church would have been to remain silent and allow unity and harmony to prevail.

The motivation of the opposing preachers was "selfish ambition" (cf. 1:17).[67] While they may have eyed Rome, hoping that an unfavorable judgment would come, they actually sought to elevate themselves at Paul's expense. Their insincere preaching intended to bring greater affliction to Paul. Perhaps they thought Rome provided the key to rid the church of Paul and his kind.

1:16-17 Paul also described his supporters' motivations. They preached from "goodwill" and "love." These relational terms contrast with the descriptions of the opponents. Those of goodwill directed their support toward Paul, just as the others directed their animosity toward him.

One further contrast between these groups indicates how Paul's imprisonment became the occasion for such attitudes to surface. Paul stated that his supporters knew he was "put here for the defense of the gospel" (1:16), while his antagonists hoped to "stir up trouble for me while I am in chains" (1:17). The first statement, from his friends, reveals a theological understanding of Paul's unique place in God's missionary program. The words "I am put here" translate the Greek word *keimai* ("I have been set").[68] Paul used the word (*keimai*) to express the divine purpose of his imprisonment, which was "the defense of the gospel."

Paul revealed a similar self-understanding in Gal 1:15-16. In a statement that parallels Jeremiah's experience (cf. Jer 1:5), Paul explained that God separated him from the womb, called him by grace, and sent him to preach the gospel to the Gentiles (Gal 1:15).[69] He could not foresee all of the situations he

---

[66]The Greek construction has the preposition διά with the accusative case for these. Strictly speaking, it should show the standard by which something is measured. Modern linguistics, however, has warned about pressing classical semantic and grammatical distinctions without warrant from the context. These warnings should be heeded, and the distinction made here may press the construction and the difference between it and the description of v. 17 (ἐξ ἐριθείας). Nevertheless, the shades of variation do occur, and at least a slight difference exists between the two.

[67]This construction is ἐξ ἐριθείας. Strictly, this points to the origins of an activity, rather than its means.

[68]The word κεῖμαι is "lie or recline" literally. It is built on a perfect tense paradigm and, thus, came to express an appointment. It could well be translated "I have been set" toward the end its context describes.

[69]The parallel with Jeremiah goes beyond the words and the concept of election in the womb. Perhaps Paul began to identify with Jeremiah early in his ministry (at the time of writing Galatians,

would encounter in responding daily to God's call on his life. He knew his appointment involved suffering as a regular part of his ministry,[70] and he knew God called him to defend and present the truth of the gospel to both Jews and Gentiles. His defense before Jews reached a theological climax at the Jerusalem Council when it was decided that Gentiles did not need to adopt Jewish patterns of life, worship, and service. Throughout his ministry, however, he had to live out that agreement, many times among those who did not accept it as well as the Jerusalem apostles did. Paul's presence in Rome occasioned this segment of the ongoing debate. His defense before Rome also had a long developing history. In several cities where he founded churches, Paul defended himself against Gentile attacks (cf. Acts 17:6-9; 18:12-14; 19:24-41; 26:19-20).

Paul knew from these experiences that he not only encountered Jewish opposition but also had to answer to Rome. No doubt as he walked the many miles of Roman roads, he planned how to defend the gospel should such an occasion arise. Paul's defense involved the gospel. Others may have thought about the repercussions of their preaching in relation to their own lives, but Paul lived for the gospel. For him, the opportunity to appear before Caesar provided a test case for the gospel. Would it be accepted? Perhaps there is a note of anticipation, as well as resolution. He was the apostle to the Gentiles. He struggled to bring the gospel to them, and now he would have opportunity to present the new ideology to the emperor. He knew that in a real way the task of Gentile evangelism was his, and he could finish it this way. The emperor of the world would actually hear the gospel. Opponents also saw this as the time to silence Paul. They hoped—or perhaps imagined[71]—to bring affliction to him and, perhaps, to sway the sympathies of the emperor against him.

Such a disclosure of the situation at Rome prompts the question of who these two groups were. Some have suggested they were Judaizers like those who troubled Paul at Galatia and, perhaps, in Phil 3. Paul had little sympathy for Judaizers, however. His harshest words spoke against their theology and methodology.[72] They hardly fit the accepting attitude of Paul in this text. Others suggest that they were preachers who believed martyrdom was a high ideal. They preached with an intent of bringing Paul to martyrdom, while realizing that whatever consequences he received, they would likely bear as well.[73]

---

ca. A.D. 49). Jeremiah suffered during his lifetime as a fulfillment of the divine plan. In a similar way, Paul would suffer, too. See the notes on Col 1:24ff.

[70] See Acts 9:16; Col 1:24; Phil 3:10.

[71] This may better capture the feeling of this word οἰόμενοι.

[72] See Galatians, Paul's most abrupt epistle. In Galatians, Paul did not even thank God for the believers or their Christian experience. His concern for them brought him straight to the point at hand. Even Corinth with its party spirit did not receive such harsh treatment.

[73] This suggestion fits the second century better than the first. When persecution became widespread and martyrdom became quite probable, a theology of martyrdom developed and Christians prayed for it. A form of this, however, is argued in Hawthorne, *Philippians*, 35, and in his earlier article "Phil 1:12-19 with special reference to vv. 15,16,17," *ExpTim* 62 (1950-51), 316ff.

These preachers, however, preached against Paul out of jealousy. They could hardly have hoped to bring Paul to a higher spiritual stature if they were envious of what he already had. This suggestion has little to commend it. A third possibility is that they preached against the Jews for what they did to Paul.[74] The Jewish flavor of the situation is quite likely, but preaching against the people who opposed Paul does not fit the context. Paul stated that they preached against him.

Finally, some scholars note that the opponents preached against Paul. Perhaps they did so because of his weaknesses. The fact that he was a prisoner demonstrated for them that he was not who he claimed to be. Surely he would triumph in Christ if God were with him. Instead, they said that God had *manifested* his presence through them. Paul responded by saying what was *manifest* about him.[75]

More than likely, the problem came from the dynamics of the Roman church and Paul's relationship to it. Possibly the situation resembled Corinth, where the various factions rallied around one great leader or another.[76] The situation at Rome was pluralistic. No great Christian leaders were there before Paul arrived, so there was no primary apostle. Perhaps many vied for the position or, at the least, they did not want someone from the outside claiming that status.

Rome welcomed various ethnic groups and cultural practices. Normally immigrants lived in common tenement houses by ethnic and language groups. Sometimes various groups subdivided by ideologies or places of origin. For example, the city had at least thirteen Jewish synagogues, which probably served Jews from different places in the empire.[77] How the church fit into that social and ethnic structure is difficult to discern. The issues that separated the Gentile and Jewish Christians had become more pronounced with the expulsion of all Jews from Rome in A.D. 49 and their return in A.D. 52. No doubt Gentiles dominated at least during the period of expulsion, and they probably vied for power and leadership when the Jews returned. Earlier, Paul had written to the Roman church with a major concern about unity between Jews and Gentiles. Although the letter to Rome was written five years before Philippians, the complexities of the situation surely continued until Paul arrived in Rome.[78]

---

[74] F. C. Synge, *Philippians and Colossians* (London: Torch Bible Commentaries, 1951), 24-25.

[75] This suggestion has much to commend it based on the situation at Corinth, where Paul's opponents did attack his weaknesses with a "theology of triumphalism." There is little in the epistolary context to support it except the reference to "manifest." Greater evidence may come from the historical context since Philippi was at the north end of the peninsula from Corinth. See R. Jewett, "Conflicting Movements in the Early Church as Reflected in Philippians" *NovT* 12 (1970): 362-90.

[76] Beare, 59.

[77] Caird, 111.

[78] On the situation at Rome, see the excellent though dated article by W. Wiefel, "The Jewish

The situation regarding Paul is, therefore, difficult to untangle. Tensions arose between and among the various groupings: Jews against themselves, Gentiles against Jews, Jews against Gentiles, and various Gentile factions against each other. Further, Paul entered this difficult situation with the authority of the apostle to the Gentiles but limited by the Roman government. All of the groups within the church knew him, but not all welcomed him.

Perhaps a theological tension underlay the social and economic situation. Paul championed Gentile freedom from the law. In his Roman letter, he had sided with the Gentiles in affirming that they did not need to keep the practices of Jewish culture.[79] Although the Jewish Christians would have expected that from Paul, no doubt it forced an intense debate on the matter. The debate followed Paul wherever he went, and his arrival at Rome perhaps triggered it again. Most likely it involved the law. Paul's writings and the historical data reveal that Paul had intense conflicts over the relevance of the Ten Commandments and the ceremonial aspects of Jewish law. Additionally, the argument in Phil 3 concerned these matters. There the debate intensified and broadened beyond the concerns of the preachers of Phil 1.

Significantly, Paul evaluated these preachers carefully and objectively. Three areas of concern emerge in his evaluation of others: their methods, their motives, and their message. They clearly had a correct message. Christ was proclaimed (1:14-18). Likewise, their methods caused no problem. The text reveals only one way of ministry: They preached. The point of difference was their motives. Motivations generally remain inside and quiet, but these preachers quite openly explained their motives.[80] Paul had a great concern for motives in the ministry,[81] yet he did not attack these preachers the way he did others. Apparently this was because they acted toward him, not toward the gospel or Christianity in general. He chose to look on the bright side since the message and the method furthered the truth. God alone can deal with motives!

Community in Ancient Rome and the Origins of Roman Christianity," reprinted in *The Romans Debate*, ed. Karl Donfried (Minneapolis: Augsburg, 1977), 100-19.

[79]The debate between Jews and Gentiles permeates the epistle, but the focal passage is 14:1-15:6. There the specific matters included days and diet. On the surface they sound like Jewish versus Gentile distinctions. On deeper reflection, however, they clearly were in some measure Gentile Christian issues as well. The meat issue was neither clean versus unclean nor meat offered to idols. It was over vegetarianism. These make the specific identity of the problem difficult. On the other hand, they do point out the complexities of the varieties of Christian experiences at Rome.

[80]Otherwise Paul could not have known them for sure, and it is doubtful that he would have discussed them so openly had their motives not been common knowledge. This in itself points out the arrogance of the situation—they openly and energetically opposed Paul.

[81]This is evidenced by the way he defended his own motives when he was attacked (1 Thess 1-2; 1 Cor 1-4; 2 Cor) and his warnings regarding other preachers' motives (2 Tim 3:1-9; Titus 1:10-11).

(2) Paul's Attitude (1:18-26)

[18]But what does it matter? The important thing is that in every way, whether from false motives or true, Christ is preached. And because of this I rejoice.
Yes, and I will continue to rejoice, [19]for I know that through your prayers and the help given by the Spirit of Jesus Christ, what has happened to me will turn out for my deliverance. [20]I eagerly expect and hope that I will in no way be ashamed, but will have sufficient courage so that now as always Christ will be exalted in my body, whether by life or by death. [21]For to me, to live is Christ and to die is gain. [22]If I am to go on living in the body, this will mean fruitful labor for me. Yet what shall I choose? I do not know! [23]I am torn between the two: I desire to depart and be with Christ, which is better by far; [24]but it is more necessary for you that I remain in the body. [25]Convinced of this, I know that I will remain, and I will continue with all of you for your progress and joy in the faith, [26]so that through my being with you again your joy in Christ Jesus will overflow on account of me.

Paul's situation caused deep reflection. His concerns were twofold: the outcome of his imprisonment and trial and the possibility of death. These verses reveal the tensions in Paul's life. The tribulation he endured reached their zenith as he awaited his trial. In many ways, that was his finest hour for the gospel. The commitments which drove him in his life now kept him as he contemplated his death. Even in the midst of such deep reflection, Paul was optimistic. He would be saved, Christ would be glorified one way or another, and the gospel would go forth.

Structurally, two questions arise in these verses. The first is, Where does the section begin? The second relates to the progress of thought through 1:18-26: Are there one, two, or three movements? Regardless of the number of movements, Paul's argument progresses with one discussion flowing from a previous idea. The thought of joy (1:18a) brought to mind the expectation of continued joy in the future (1:18b). In v. 20 Paul introduced the concept of death, and in 1:21-24 the themes of life and death are further developed. Finally, 1:24 ends with a desire to do what was best for the Philippians, and 1:25-26 continues the themes of remaining on earth and sacrificing for them. It is a carefully composed section that expressed Paul's emotions.

PAUL'S JOY IN SALVATION (1:18-24). **1:18a** The section begins in v. 18— all interpreters affirm that. The problem is whether it begins at the beginning of v. 18, at the middle, or at the end. The NIV translators assumed correctly that the new section began in the middle of the verse. The theme of the preachers continues until that point, and Paul ended the previous section on a note of joy. The repetition of the word "rejoice" serves as a transition, providing another reason for Paul's joy: his own anticipation of success in the trial that lay before him.[82]

---

[82]Hawthorne, *Philippians*, 39, refers to the work of M. E. Thrall, *Greek Particles in the New Testament*, NTTS 3 (Grand Rapids: Eerdmans, 1962), 11-16, to demonstrate that the construction

The second structural question relates to the three movements within the section. The question is whether they should be seen as three different ideas or two. Those who see three separate units argue that the grammar suggests them. The first unit is 1:18-20, which is one sentence in the Greek text. The second unit is 1:21-24. This contains the section about life and death and is introduced by "for" (*gar*), as is the first section. The third unit is 1:25-26, which is one sentence in Greek introduced by the expression "and having this confidence."[83]

This arrangement is quite possible, but a two-unit arrangement makes better sense in light of the parallels and the thematic structure of the passage. Two basic parallels confirm the flow of thought. The main verb of 1:18b-19 is "I know," and that same verb is repeated in 1:25. The other parallel is a conceptual tie between "I will . . . rejoice," which introduces the first "I know," and "convinced of this," which introduces the second. Paul's joy and confidence were two expressions of the same attitude: He would be able to achieve his deepest desires of glorifying Christ. The same ideas and root words occur in 1:4-6, where Paul's prayer for the Philippians was both joyful and confident. Here Paul's desire was that Christ would be magnified in his life, and his confidence was that he would remain for their edification.[84]

Paul's optimism was obvious. Why was he optimistic? Was it because he expected to be released from prison soon? Was it that he knew whatever happened, he was surely to be delivered from this evil world? Was it a joy that came from a backward glance to his conversion experience that sustained him through the difficulties of the present? These three suggestions call for careful analysis, and they are not necessarily mutually exclusive. The first section contains two parts: a description of Paul's salvation and hope (1:18b-20) and an expression of his commitment to them (1:21-24).

Paul's Salvation and Hope (1:18b-20). **1:18b-19** Paul fully expected deliverance, and these verses express that hope clearly. He wrote with a joyful note as he contemplated what that meant for him and for the Philippians. The

---

"but and" (ἀλλὰ καί) begins a new section. He translates it well: "And *in addition* I will be glad for still another reason."

[83] The NIV translates "Convinced of this." This three-unit arrangement acknowledges the two times the conjunction is γάρ and the sentence units. Further, the thematic analysis reveals the cogency of these units as "self-contained" in thought.

[84] This suggests that the "this" (τοῦτο) of v. 25 looks ahead to the "that" (ὅτι) clause that follows, though it could look backward. A forward look is somewhat unusual, but it does occur in Phil 1:6 and 1:9, the only other two occurrences of the pronoun to this point in the epistle. After 1:25 the pronoun looks ahead for its antecedent in 2:5. It does not in 2:23. The difficulty of determining the antecedent of "this" in 1:25 is that the same themes occur before and after it. In 1:21-24 Paul spoke of the necessity of remaining for their betterment, and in 1:25-26 he made that explicit. Could the antecedent be ambiguous, referring to the general concept which brought confidence? Further, the confidence is derived, not from his expected release from prison, but from his knowledge of their need of his ministry. This point will be developed later.

first question to answer in this text is about the nature and means of Paul's salvation.

Paul spoke of his salvation with a note of certainty. The verb "know" (*oida*) used here contains an air of confidence. The term may be used of a complete knowledge identified with the mind rather than the process of knowledge which comes from the experience.[85] How Paul knew this is unknown, and the many suggestions made depend on the meaning of the word "salvation."

"Salvation" has been interpreted in two primary ways. First, a common interpretation today is that Paul knew he would be delivered ("saved") from death and/or imprisonment. Since Rome had nothing against Christians at this early date, Paul had no reason to suspect anything but a positive decision at his trial. Two main lines of argumentation support this conclusion. The word "salvation" may have the sense of "deliverance from death."[86] Those who accept this interpretation, such as the NIV, invoke that meaning in this passage. Additionally, 1:25 expresses Paul certainty that he would remain on earth. This last argument is the most significant.

Against this interpretation, several factors in the context must be considered.[87] First, Paul stated that his adversity would result in his deliverance. His words indicate that the difficulty would itself have the positive results he anticipated. That hardly fits a deliverance from prison. Second, Paul entertained the possibility of death, but that did not affect his optimism. His deliverance would come in spite of imprisonment or even death. Third, Paul anticipated gaining his hope of "not being ashamed." Finally, Paul's statement in this section is similar to Job 13:13-18. Thus, while many equate the passage with an expectation of release, that interpretation does not fit all the details well.

The second interpretation of salvation takes the word in its full, eschatological sense. The completion of the salvation begun with commitment to Christ

---

[85]The differences between οἶδα and γινώσκω have been studied often with diverse conclusions. The verb was translated "knowing well" by M. R. Vincent, *Critical and Exegetical Commentary on the Epistles to the Philippians and to Philemon, ICC* (Edinburgh: T & T Clark, 1897), 23. Others disagree with a fast distinction between the two (Hawthorne, *Philippians,* 39). Whether the certainty of knowledge comes from the fact that Paul used the word οἶδα or whether it comes from the context, the term does imply a certainty and confidence. It appears that Paul chose this word because of its suitability to that meaning. Hawthorne's Pauline examples do not support the point because there is not an equivalent of the terms in the passages. Οἶδα is used in 1 Cor 8:1-3 to introduce a principle which is explained by the consistent use of γνω- root words. In 2 Thess 1:8 Paul quoted the LXX and then applied it with the word "obedience" (ὑπακούω), a moral term synonymous with πιστεύω more so than γινώσκω.

[86]The definition of the term influences interpretations significantly. *BAGD* indicates that the word means "deliverance, preservation." It is "generally of preservation in danger, deliverance fr. impending death." Further, "quite predom. *salvation*, which the true religion bestows . . . In our lit. this sense is found only in connection w. Jesus Christ as Savior. This salvation makes itself known and felt in the present, but it will be completely disclosed in the future" (801).

[87]The best presentation of these comes from Silva, 76-80.

would be the final vindication of the believer when he met Christ. Paul knew that he would arrive at that great day and see the complete salvation he so desired. This longing did not come from an unsettledness or unassured attitude toward salvation. Paul knew that perseverance through this life was one of the identifying characteristics of a Christian. Knowing he had been saved, he also anticipated the full joy of complete salvation. Several factors support this interpretation.

Paul's wording in this section clearly reflects Job 13:13-18 in the LXX text. Both the Greek wording and the circumstances parallel each other. If Paul quoted Job *in context*, as he normally did when he referred to the Old Testament, he must have consciously derived comfort from Job's course of life. Paul's life had, in fact, taken much the same course. When nothing made sense to Job and everyone opposed him, his "salvation" was that he knew he was just and that he would stand before God and be vindicated.

A significant question to answer in 1:19 is the reference to "this" ("this shall result in my salvation"). The NIV translates "what has happened to me." The pronoun must look to the mixed preaching of the Christians at Rome. In that way, many brought their accusations against Paul and his righteousness. Like Job, he would stand vindicated at last.

A second reason for this interpretation is that it deals seriously with the question of life and death (1:21-24). Paul would be "saved" regardless of his physical condition. The element of uncertainty regarding the trial did not affect his confidence inside.

Third, Paul's real joy was that Christ was proclaimed. The factor of his life-call enters this context. Paul wanted to hear "well done" when he stood before God. His task was to reach the Gentiles for Christ, and how that was accomplished was of secondary consequence. The mixed preaching at Rome actually furthered his deepest Christian desire, which was to make Christ known.

Finally, the passage contains terms that relate to spiritual deliverance: salvation and hope. Thus, the better interpretation is to see Paul's salvation in an eschatological sense—he looked forward to his entrance into heaven and vindication by the Lord himself.

In spite of Paul's confidence in his destiny, he sought the Philippians' help. His deliverance would come "through [their] prayers and the help given by the Spirit of Jesus Christ" (1:19). Paul considered these two ideas to be closely related because they both provided the means through which his goal was achieved.[88] He sought their prayers on his behalf, realizing that God answers prayer and works through it to accomplish his purposes. There was

---

[88]The grammar reinforces that. The two nouns "prayers" and "supply" are joined in a phrase introduced by the one preposition, introduced further by one article which goes with both (when in prepositional phrases no articles are actually needed and yet they occur, they are emphatic), and joined by the word "and" (καί).

no "resignation to the inevitable" here. Paul combined his foundational trust in Christ with the need for prayers on his behalf.

The "help given by the Spirit" goes along with the prayers. This phrase has been handled in different ways. Some scholars take it to be "the supply that the Spirit gives," or "the help given by the Spirit of Jesus Christ" (NIV). Others take it to mean "the help which consists of the Spirit."[89] A parallel idea occurs in Gal 3:5, where Paul asked how they had received God's Spirit, obviously meaning the gift of the Spirit himself. Most likely the NIV translation is correct. Paul expected the Holy Spirit to provide whatever he needed to meet life's demands. This would occur through their prayers as well.

1:20 The second portion of this section focuses on Paul's hope. The NIV captures the force of the text well in making "I eagerly expect and hope" introduce the content of Paul's hope.[90] The anticipation of his deliverance accorded perfectly with his lifelong hope that Christ would be glorified in him.

Paul stated his hope in two ways.[91] First, he hoped that he would not be ashamed; second, that Christ would be exalted in his body. What did he mean that he would not be ashamed? This certainly does not express the feeling of guilt which the English word often conveys. There is an objective aspect to it. Here Paul was using the objective aspect of "hope" or "trust" as it was used in Isa 28:16. He quoted this verse both in offering the gospel and as one of its foundations (Rom 9:33; 10:11). The verses from Romans help interpret Paul's understanding of the passage. In Rom 9:33, he contrasted a stumbling over a stone (Christ) with those who do not stumble (i.e., are not put to shame). In Rom 10:10-11, Paul stated that the one who confesses Christ "with his mouth" after believing "in his heart" will not stumble (i.e., be put to shame). Confession seals the commitments, and those commitments do not lead to embarrassment. This suits the context of Isa 28:16, where the Lord spoke through the prophet that Israel should remain true to the Lord. If it did, it would not be "put to flight." These texts have little to do with being ashamed to confess Christ. They do not speak to the point of timidity. Rather, they speak to the security of

---

[89] In Greek, the former is a subjective genitive and the latter is a descriptive or even appositional genitive.

[90] Hawthorne, *Philippians*, 39, makes a good case for taking the two ὅτι clauses as parallel, as providing two reasons for Paul's joy. His interpretation depends on taking "salvation" as deliverance from Rome, and with the second ὅτι Paul looked to his spiritual triumph. The suggestion fits well with the Greek of the text, although the parallels are a little contrived. However, the flow of thought seems to fit better with understanding this portion as a modifier of the previous. That is, Paul's expected spiritual deliverance is completely in accord with his anticipated success in standing true to the Lord. We have taken these verses to have one primary statement with the second ὅτι clause as a modifier of it.

[91] This interpretation understands the second ὅτι clause to be a restatement of hope. It is appositional rather than parallel, as the previous footnote explains. It is unusual for Paul to have a clause express the nature of the hope since he normally did it with a genitive. The natural way to read this, however, suggests an exception.

believers and the certainty that they are on solid foundation when they believe on the "cornerstone."

Paul expected, therefore, not to be put to shame. He confidently had confessed Jesus as Lord. It was not a thoughtless or quick confession; it was the direction of his life. He had Old Testament Scripture to support his contention that the Lord aids those who confess him. Perhaps his thoughts turned to the day of judgment. That was the greatest test, and Paul hoped to be bold (not to "be ashamed") on that day. The context, however, points to the present life, as the contrasting clause to this one makes clear. He expected God would give him the grace so that he would not be put to shame in his confession here and now. The Roman trial was another opportunity for him to triumph in Christ. In no way would he fail. Christ would give him the strength.

The positive side of Paul's hope was that Christ would be exalted in his body. This clearly identifies the hope with an earthly situation rather than the final judgment. The first clause of the section presents the hope that Paul would stand strong through the various situations of life. This clause makes that hope concrete. They both refer to the same aspects of existence. The use of the term "body," which Paul used for the physical body, and the discussion of life or death as the means of accomplishing this hope demonstrate Paul's present expectation. Two matters help interpret Paul's statements here: "sufficient courage" and "in my body."

The phrase "have sufficient courage" translates a strong Greek expression (lit., "have all presence"). Usually, Paul employed it referring to the proclamation of the gospel (2 Cor 3:12; Eph 6:19) so that it described boldness in witness. However, it describes a courage of life. He hoped that he would have the courage to live or die as a true Christian should. Paul's ministry encompassed both living and speaking, and he needed courage for both. He had enjoyed success before, but now he faced greater tests. He expected to end as he began, courageous in his witness.[92]

The location of this final witness was "in my body." Paul consistently used the term for the physical body, and there is no need to suggest some metaphorical use of the term here.[93] In Rom 6:6 Paul spoke of the crucifixion with Christ to "paralyze the body [physical] of sin" (author's translation). Later, in 6:12-14, he made it clear that the body was the mortal body, and sin had to be overcome there. Further, in a positive command, in Rom 12:1-2 Paul employed the metaphor of sacrifice to exhort the believers to consecration. He still used the terms of the physical body. It is not surprising, therefore, that he thought here

---

[92] Some object to another interpretation besides a speaking ministry because of a pattern of Pauline usage of the phrase. It is not impossible for him to have used the phrase in other contexts, however (2 Cor 7:4), and this was an unusual situation to address. To confine Paul's use of the term in such a way unnecessarily encumbers his expression.

[93] See R. H. Gundry, *SOMA in Biblical Theology: With Emphasis on Pauline Anthropology*, SNTSMS 29 (Cambridge: University Press, 1976), 37.

in terms of the body's responsibility in Christian commitment.

Paul knew that Christian commitment cannot happen apart from the body. In fact, Christian growth requires a focus on the body as the vehicle of expression of the true person, and as the instrument for receiving the communications of others. The person is intimately connected to the body, and Paul easily localized Christian commitment in the physical parts of his body. Since, therefore, he had committed his body to God and served him through the body, he had to continue to glorify him there as well. The immediate context confirms this conclusion where, in 1:24, he again referred to life in the body.

No matter what it took or what it cost, Christ would be honored by everything about this apostle. Paul's commitment to Christ, his confession of him, and his understanding of the power of God to sustain the believer demanded no less.

Paul's Commitment to the Philippians (1:21-24). In vv. 21-24, Paul revealed a deep inner struggle. The contrasts between life and death indicate that Paul seriously contemplated the possibilities of both. Of course, he did not have the power over his destiny; it was in the hands of God (perhaps as he might work through Rome). However, he faced the alternative situations with forethought. In his own mind, he resolved the tension by the same principle that guided his life to that point. He would serve to the end.

1:21 The themes of life and death explain how Paul would glorify God in his body—even death would not keep him from it. These themes also prompted him to evaluate the purpose of living. With this introduction to 1:21-24, it seems that the section explains the commitment of the previous verses (vv. 18b-20). As far as Paul was concerned,[94] "to live is Christ and to die is gain." This differs from what others thought and what might have been expected. Normally, one would say to live is gain and to die is Christ, but Paul reversed these. At death a Christian gains a more intimate relationship with the Lord. The statement "to live is Christ" is magnified by the statement "to die is gain."[95]

Often Paul spoke of Christ as his life. In Gal 2:20 he said, "I live by faith in the Son of God." In Col 3:4 he stated that Christ "is your life." These two passages differ in context and concern. The emphasis in Gal 2:20 is soteriological; in Col 3:4, Paul speaks to the mysterious union between Christ and the believer. Paul did not mean precisely either here, however. In this context he spoke of glorifying Christ through whatever means he had, and that provides the interpretive environment. The statement is completed by envisioning death as a better state than life. Thus, "to live is Christ" must mean that Paul so totally wanted to glorify Christ that as long as he lived everything about him was to

---

[94] This is a dative of reference.

[95] Some commentators want to break the equation and make it say something like "to live or die is Christ." That is unnecessary and confuses the passage.

point people to Christ. This was accomplished in part by the chains which were "manifested in Christ" (1:13); but even if he were called to die, it would be an occasion for Christ to become prominent. Death was a gain because he would see the Lord, enjoy him, and no longer endure the difficulties he was called to bear on earth.

1:22-24   These verses describe both Paul's dilemma and his resolution of it. The literary pattern emphasizes his conviction that he would remain, that the result of his trial would be life not death. In 1:22 he expressed the conviction that fruit would result from his continued physical life. The way the discussion takes place reveals the interpretation of "fruitful labor for me" (1:22). This statement is matched by the conviction that he would remain for the sake of the Philippians (1:24). While it may appear that the "fruit" was some spiritual development in Paul's life, the context clearly relates "fruit" to the service Paul performed. In between these two statements, he posed the troublesome question of his choice. "What shall I choose? . . . I am torn between the two."[96] It was helpful to them for Paul to remain; the fruit was what resulted from his work for others. The longer Paul lived, the more people would be touched by his life.[97] Many understand Paul to say that he would reap the harvest of his past work. Therefore it would benefit him to remain in the flesh.[98] These interpretations, however, seem to neglect the fact that Paul's rewards, and therefore his "benefits," awaited him at death. That is why dying was gain. Further, this passage reveals Paul's concern for others, not himself (1:24, 26). He must have been thinking of the future and the harvests that would come from his life should God allow him to continue on this earth.

Beyond the discussion of rewards, however, Paul clearly expressed the desire to be with Christ (1:23). It was better. The discussion of rewards clouds the basic issue. Paul's longing for death was, in reality, a longing for a more intimate, open, and total relationship with Christ himself. Such a relationship could only occur after death. The practical dilemma, therefore, consisted of whether Paul would choose his own preference or remain to benefit others. His

---

[96]This chiastic arrangement emphasizes the expectation that he would continue to serve them. The question is there, but it remains a question. The answer is clear: They needed him.

[97]This verse has had many diverse interpretations. The syntax is ambiguous. Paul introduced the statement with a first-class condition format, εἰ ("if"), but where the apodosis begins is not clear. Is it with "this will mean fruitful labor" or with "what shall I ask?" The NIV takes the former and makes the rest of the one sentence in Greek introduce a new idea. There are three ways of rendering it: If my living on in the body means that I could reap the fruit of my past toil, then I do not know which to prefer. If I am to live on in the body, that will mean that I can reap the fruit of my toil. Yet I do not know which to prefer. What if my living on in the body means that I could reap the fruit of my toil! I do not know which to prefer. The second appears to be the best even though it means introducing an apodosis with καί ("and"), and the τοῦτο ("this") seems unnecessary. There are fewer problems with it.

[98]It may be that every Christian wants to see the work he has done and to enjoy it. Paul, however, wanted to see Christ more than all.

conviction was that he would remain. While the statement obviously takes an optimistic perspective on the trial Paul faced, it spoke more to his conviction regarding his life service. His work remained unfinished. He thought, therefore, that God would have him remain and accomplish it.

One final concern emerges from these verses. Some commentators introduce the problem of the doctrine of soul sleep here.[99] Generally those who do must address the fact that these verses do not teach the doctrine. They must harmonize the passage with what they have deduced from others. Paul directly stated that in death he would be "with Christ," and the language speaks of being immediately in Christ's presence. Further, Paul would hardly have been comforted by being away from Christ after death. He was already with him and looked forward to a more open relationship with him at death. Why would Paul want to sleep (away from the conscious presence of Christ which he enjoyed on earth) when his tension resulted from the desire to enjoy Christ more fully? Finally, making this passage conform to an already assumed position such as soul sleep is difficult.[100] The natural way to read the passage speaks against it, as do the other Pauline discussions of life after death. The fact is, Paul did not discuss the doctrine in this text at all. He simply expressed his conviction that if he died he would gain because death was a departure whereby he would be in the presence of the Lord (*syn Christō*, 1:23).

PAUL'S CONFIDENCE OF FUTURE MINISTRY (1:25-26). **1:25**   The second section of this passage begins here. It not only looks back to the discussion of 1:18-20 but also expresses Paul's hope in new ways. Specifically, Paul shared his confidence that he would remain with the Philippians to advance the gospel and to further their progress and joy in the faith as they saw him again.

Looking back, Paul based his statement on the confidence expressed in 1:18-20. The glory of Christ would be achieved best by Paul's remaining on earth to continue his ministry. Paul did not tell the readers why he felt this conviction. Perhaps he knew that Rome had no reason to punish him, and his optimism lay in the confidence that Rome would do justly. At a deeper level, his confidence grew out of his understanding of the ministry God had given him. Paul lived for others. He knew their needs well, and he knew that they would grow spiritually through his presence with them. This statement applied the

---

[99]Caird says that Paul taught consistently that "Christians who die remain in a state of sleep until the Advent of Christ, who will then raise them to eternal life" (113-14). This conclusion is not so clear, however, even from the passages he draws upon for support (1 Thess 4:13-5:11; 1 Cor 15:35-55; 2 Cor 5:1-10; Rom 8:18-25). For example, there is a two-part experience in 1 Thess 4:13-18, as Paul said those who are asleep (a euphemism for death) in Jesus will be raised with him. They are alive and conscious; they come to be reunited with their bodies. It is the resurrection that awaits the Advent, not the presence with Christ.

[100]Caird, an advocate of soul sleep, states, "This verse seems to present the contrary view that those who 'die in the Lord' go directly into his presence" (113). He then attempts to explain why the obvious cannot be so to his mind.

hope that Christ would be glorified (1:20) to the realities of daily life. He might have chosen to go on to heaven and enjoy fully the Lord whom he loved, but the task was unfinished, and he must remain.[101]

Paul would remain because of their needs, which he first stated in an overview and then in specific terms. The overview is "for your progress and joy in the faith." The word "progress" (*prokopēn*) was used earlier of the advancement of the gospel message (1:12). There Paul's circumstances pushed the message forward into new territory. In a similar way, his return to the church would push its faith forward. As the events became opportunities for preaching the gospel, his presence with the church could only help it. This advancement of its faith was also called a joy. Both "progress" and "joy" are modified by "in the faith."[102] As the Philippians matured in their understanding of Christ, their joy in the faith would deepen and would be encouraged. This thought is repeated in v. 26.

1:26 The specific statement is that Paul's presence would bring great joy.[103] It was a joy in Christ through Paul's release. A similar statement occurs in 4:10, where Paul said, "I rejoice greatly in the Lord that at last you have renewed your concern for me." Their financial support caused Paul to worship and praise the Lord, who sent it through them. Naturally, the gift brought joy, but the greater joy was what it meant in the work of the Lord. Applying that understanding here, Paul realized that his presence provided an occasion for worship and praise. In spite of the similarity of 1:26 and 4:10, two different words describe "joy." In 4:10, Paul used *chairō*, "to rejoice" or "be glad."[104] Here, the word is *kauchēma*, "to boast or be proud."[105] *Kauchēma* often suggests an occasion or object of the joy and has the sense of "taking pride in" something specific.[106]

Three complementary phrases explain the ground of their glorying. First, it would "overflow" in Christ Jesus. For Paul, Jesus was always the basis of joy. Second, it would be through Paul as representing Christ. Paul, as apostle, brought Christ to them, and they longed to see him again. He was their best example of Jesus. Third, they would boast because of Paul's presence with

---

[101] His confidence of remaining receives emphasis two ways. First, twice he stated that he expects to remain (μένω and παραμένω). Second, the word παραμένω is a perfective form, stressing his expectation to remain "beside" them.

[102] The Granville Sharp rule applies here: Two nouns joined by καί and introduced by one article refer to the same person or thing. Progress and joy are two sides of the same idea. The construction "in the faith" is an objective genitive, that is, "Progress and joy directed toward their faith."

[103] In Greek, this verse is a purpose clause that shows the goal of his statement. Dividing the commentary into "overview" and "specific" seems to satisfy the demands of that construction. The overview is expressed with "εἰς" which also speaks to a goal of living; the specific is expressed with ἵνα showing purpose.

[104] *BAGD*, 873.

[105] *BAGD*, 426.

[106] Vincent said it "is the *matter* or *ground* of glorying, not the *act* of glorying" (30).

them again. Additionally, there may be an overtone of joy that the trial would be over and that the work of the Lord could go forth.

Paul's words express his optimism. Without a doubt, he expected to continue his ministry after the trial. Even so, he contemplated the realities of what could happen and how he would respond to the worst of situations. He would triumph. If he went to be with his Lord, that was triumph. If he stayed with them, they would be helped. But as he understood the work of the Lord, he would remain to further their faith.

This passage suggests that Paul anticipated a visit to Philippi upon his release. The same expectation occurred in Colossians and Philemon. Paul's plans to go to Spain had been postponed. Perhaps he sought the strength of fellowship that his converts provided. Perhaps he knew they needed him. At any rate, they would prosper if God allowed him to remain on earth.

3. Exhortation to Christlike Character (1:27-2:18)

This verse begins a new section of the epistle. A change of tone signals a change of direction. Paul moved from information to exhortation, and three primary exhortations occur: 1:27-30; 2:1-4; 2:12-18. Both before (1:12-26) and after (2:19-30) the exhortations, Paul shared information about himself.[107] The word "only" ("whatever happens," NIV) also marks a change, such as seen in Gal 2:7-9.[108] Paul's concerns about Christian relationships surface during this discussion.

(1) A Unified Stand (1:27-30)

[27]Whatever happens, conduct yourselves in a manner worthy of the gospel of Christ. Then, whether I come and see you or only hear about you in my absence, I will know that you stand firm in one spirit, contending as one man for the faith of the gospel [28]without being frightened in any way by those who oppose you. This is a sign to them that they will be destroyed, but that you will be saved—and that by God. [29]For it has been granted to you on behalf of Christ not only to believe on him, but also to suffer for him, [30]since you are going through the same struggle you saw I had, and now hear that I still have.

In this first section of commands, Paul urged the church to be true to the faith. Paul's actual words were, "to walk worthily of the gospel of Christ." The command may be taken broadly, but Paul's specific concern was a unified stand for the gospel. Both of these elements were important. The church at Rome stood for the gospel, but there was no unity. That hurt its witness. The

---

[107]The change of tone is noted most dramatically by a change from indicative verbs to imperatives in these sections. There is a parallel:

Indicative verbs:	1:12-26	2:19-30	4:10-15
Imperative verbs:	1:27-2:18	3:1-4:9 (basically)	

[108]See Silva, 89-90, for a good discussion of this.

Philippians had the opportunity to witness to the world by their unified stand for the gospel. This would be particularly impressive if they stood strong through the sufferings they were called to endure. Two matters need to be discussed: the nature of their stand (1:27-28) and Christian suffering (1:29-30).

THE NATURE OF THE PHILIPPIANS' STAND (1:27-28). **1:27** The main verb "conduct yourselves" (*politeuesthe*) called the church to appropriate conduct. It is an unusual term, and the verb form occurs only here and in Acts 23:1. Normally Paul used the verb "walk" (*peripateō*) to describe a Christian's conduct. Here he used the verb "conduct yourselves as citizens" (*politeuō*). Scholars differ as to the exact force of the word in this text. It was a word built upon the Greek *polis* (city) and had overtones of citizenship responsibilities. Paul made conscious use of the term. The noun form occurs in 3:20 in calling the Philippians to appropriate ethical conduct. There he stated that "our citizenship is in heaven." No doubt the readers would have associated the word with the Roman citizenship which they prized so much. This was Paul's way of reminding them of the obligations of people who participate in a society. In this case, the society was of Christians whose strongest ties were in heaven.

Paul expressed his concern for the church earlier (1:24-26). He so longed for its maturity that he was convinced that God would leave him on earth to help it grow in faith. In reality it could grow with or without him, and now he spoke of the possibility that he would not come. If he were absent, perhaps because of the unfavorable verdict in his trial or unexpected delays, he still longed to hear of its good spiritual condition. Paul had no inflated ideas about his importance.The church was capable of standing for the gospel.

The Christian's stand is "in one spirit." This is the first of the several words for unity that bind together 1:27-2:4. The word "spirit" is used in parallel with the word "soul" (1:27b; "as one man," NIV), and thus refers to the attitude that should characterize the church. It naturally cannot refer to the Holy Spirit, nor does a combination of the Holy Spirit working to strengthen the human spirit satisfy the parallel constructions. Paul drew on the imagery of persons to describe the function of the body of Christ. It is unnecessary to distinguish between "spirit" and "soul" here. They both explain the immaterial part of persons, and the point Paul made was that the church was to unite inside and out. Both "one spirit" and "one soul" mean that there was no divisiveness. The differences between the words are minimal.

The stand is explained in two complementary ways.[109] The positive statement is "contending" for the faith of the gospel. The imagery changes again. Before, Paul used the idea of a Greek *polis* to explain the Philippians' relationship to the Lord. Then he used the metaphor "stand," which was taken from the military. Paul's mind moved to the athletic games where he had seen team

---

[109]Two participles modify the verb "stand." They are "striving together" and "not being frightened."

sports in action. The metaphor is rare, occurring only twice in the New Testament (cf. Phil 4:3). If the Roman military element appreciated the military associations with the word "stand," the Greek population would identify with the necessity of "contending as one man" as was demanded in athletic games. It does little good for individuals on a team to contend individually rather than as part of the team. Similarly, the church was to contend "as one man." Complete harmony of purpose and coordination of various elements was necessary to achieve God's purposes.

The struggle was described in positive terms. The Philippians were to contend "for the faith of the gospel." The expression "faith of the gospel" has many possible interpretations, and there is little clear precedent in the New Testament that favors any one of them.[110] The context assumes that people opposed the church and its message. That means that this construction probably relates to its taking the gospel to the world. Paul must have meant "contending for the advance of the gospel." The NIV translators have captured that meaning by the statement "for the gospel."[111] The team effort supplied by the church would present the gospel to the world. Together the members also would explore the implications of the gospel in each other's lives.

1:28 The second explanation of standing firm is negatively stated: "without being frightened." The term occurs only here in the New Testament and suggests a reflex action resulting from being startled.[112] The church was to have an unflinchable steadfastness, even in the midst of persecution. Whoever the opponents were at this point, they were not to intimidate the Philippians.[113]

The fact that the church stood fast became a sign.[114] The question is, To whom was it a sign? Scholars have taken two positions regarding the rest of this verse. First, some see the steadfastness as a confrontation to unbelievers and a confirmation to believers. Therefore, the same situation produced a twofold result. Unbelievers would see the stand of the church and know that destruction

---

[110]The genitive construction "of the gospel" could be descriptive ("a gospel-faith"), objective ("a faith directed toward the gospel"), subjective ("faith produced by the gospel"), or appositional ("a faith which is the gospel"). Of these, the second is the least likely. The word "faith" ($\pi i \sigma \tau \iota \varsigma$) is also capable of a semantically active ("faith") or passive ("faithfulness") translation, and can even be a synonym for "message."

[111]This takes the construction $\tau \hat{\eta}$ $\pi i \sigma \tau \epsilon \iota$ with a true dative force.

[112]It was used of horses which "spook" because of something that scares them.

[113]The opponents in mind may have been Gentiles from outside the church, or they may have been Judaizers whom Paul addressed in 3:2ff. Apparently, these opponents were used to having their way with Christians, for Paul urged the believers not to give in to intimidation.

[114]The Greek text again is ambiguous. The pronoun "which" is feminine, and scholars question its antecedent. It could be "sign" ($\check{\epsilon} \nu \delta \epsilon \iota \xi \iota \varsigma$ within the clause it introduces, by attraction), "faith" (1:27), or the entire situation. Paul normally used the neuter pronoun to refer to a previous clause or list of commands (see Eph 2:8-9; 1 Thess 5:17-18). Here the flow of thought suggests that the entire clause, with the verb "stand" and the two participles ("contending . . . not frightened"), form the antecedent. The gender probably results from an attraction to "sign" within the clause.

was coming. They would be warned to accept the truth. On the other hand, the church would be encouraged by its own stand, knowing that God strengthened it and that salvation was sure. This interpretation contrasts the words "to them" (*autois*) and "of you" (*hymōn*) in 1:28.[115]

Others interpret the construction with reference to the non-Christian world entirely. They point out that the words "to them" precede the rest of the sentence and must mean that both aspects of the church's steadfastness were a sign to unbelievers. Thus, they would know of their destruction and the believers' salvation. This makes better sense of the passage. The fact, then, that the Philippians could stand firm in the face of adversity proved their relationship to the Lord. Others could see a hidden strength. Paul did not enumerate the ways he knew the church would be confronted by such a proof. Apparently it was the inner strength to live and die for what the Philippians believed. Such strength had to come from God himself, not from mere human resources.

CHRISTIAN SUFFERING (1:29-30). The reason unbelievers would arrive at that conclusion is that God granted suffering to Christians. The text makes a direct connection between "the sign" and suffering, using a Greek word which must be taken as providing a reason.[116] These verses speak to the nature of Christian suffering (1:29) and the Pauline model of suffering (1:30).

The Nature of Christian Suffering (1:29). **1:29** Paul spoke straightforwardly about Christian suffering. In this text he clearly said it was a privilege, that God had in fact graced them with suffering.[117] That raises serious questions, and it is necessary to understand Paul's thought carefully. The suffering was "on behalf of Christ," as stated twice in 1:29. The words "on behalf of" appear to be vicarious, i.e., in his place. The words recall Col 1:24, where Paul stated that he suffered eschatologically, "for the sake of his body." The phrase does point out that Paul had in mind the specific suffering that comes to Christians as they serve Christ.

The fact that suffering was connected with believing reinforces Paul's claim that it is a grace gift. Paul lived with persecution, and he realized its redemptive value, but here he did not address that. The key to this phrase "on behalf of Christ" is Phil 3:10 where Paul revealed his deepest desire of knowing Christ. That knowledge involved knowing resurrection power and the fellowship of suffering. Suffering confirms Christians' faith, brings them into closer contact with the Lord, and provides a vehicle for making commitment real and tangible. It is one thing to accept suffering and resign oneself to it. It is another to realize the privileges that come through it.

---

[115]Hawthorne, *Philippians,* 59-60, makes a good case for this interpretation. His syntactical reconstruction is entirely possible, but one must question whether it is the best. Silva states, "The sense thus achieved is attractive but the syntax is barely defensible" (95).

[116]The word is ὅτι, but one might expect γάρ.

[117]The word translated "granted" is "granted as an act of grace."

The Pauline Model of Suffering (1:30). **1:30** Paul's life provided the model of the suffering he identified here. In 1:30 he used athletic imagery again ("struggle," *agōna*) to remind the believers that they would go through what he did. In a parallel, 1 Thess 2:14-16, Paul explained that his suffering related to calling the Gentiles to Christ so that they could be saved. The universal nature of the gospel presented a problem to Gentiles, who had their own religions, and to Jews, who wanted the Gentiles to accept Judaism. The result was that Paul suffered at the hands of both groups, and the church at Philippi would do so as well.[118] Paul had to develop a theology of suffering. He did so without becoming calloused to human need and without accepting suffering as good. The danger for Christians at Philippi and elsewhere was that as they endured suffering they would have one of those reactions. Suffering is evil because it comes from sin in the world. Paul stopped far short of mixing good and evil, which would make evil (suffering) a good thing. He did, however, realize the benefits and privileges of being involved in a battle for the truth and that battle scars were inevitable. The supreme model of that was Christ. Similarly, Christians should remember that general suffering sometimes comes because they live in a world which suffers as a result of sin, that Christians are called to a unique Christian suffering because of their identification with righteousness in an evil world, that it is a divinely given privilege to be involved in this battle, and that the struggle becomes redemptive in attesting the grace gift in their own experience. The Philippians were, therefore, to take heart if they were called to suffer. Their steadfastness would demonstrate the reality of their relationship to God.

(2) A Unified Mind (2:1-4)

[1]If you have any encouragement from being united with Christ, if any comfort from his love, if any fellowship with the Spirit, if any tenderness and compassion, [2]then make my joy complete by being like-minded, having the same love, being one in spirit and purpose. [3]Do nothing out of selfish ambition or vain conceit, but in humility consider others better than yourselves. [4]Each of you should look not only to your own interests, but also to the interests of others.

Paul's thoughts turned from the need to withstand pressure from the outside to the attitudes that were to characterize Christians. In 1:27 he exhorted them to unity, and here he continued that thought. The passage unfolds in three parts: the basis of Paul's appeal to unity (2:1); the essence of unity (2:2a); and the expression of unity (2:3-4). In actuality, these three are part of another long sentence in the Greek text, and there is one basic command: "Make my joy complete."

---

[118]There is no evidence as to who caused the suffering of which Paul spoke. There was no organized persecution at Philippi. The text was a general orientation for them as Paul reflected on his experience in many places in the empire.

THE BASIS OF PAUL'S APPEAL TO UNITY (2:1). **2:1**   Four statements form
the basis of Paul's appeal to the Philippians. The statements are introduced by
"if" in both Greek and English. Although the word "if" brings doubt to mind,
these clauses express little hesitancy. They should be translated "assuming . . .
then make my joy complete."[119] All four statements introduce the command of
2:2, and they identify Paul's avenue of approaching the church. Paul gently
reminded the believers of what he and they had in common.

The four statements recall the blessings of being in a Christian community.
The first statement is, "If you have any encouragement from being united with
Christ." Commentators differ on the precise meaning of the word translated
"encouragement" (*paraklēsis*). The Greek word is capable of meaning *encouragement* or *exhortation*. The tone of this section is warm and gentle, as Paul
appealed to their common experience of Christ. The best understanding of the
word seems to be "encouragement" that comes from Christian commitment.[120] Second is the blessing of "comfort from his love." The NIV correctly
translates this as affirming Christ's love for his people. The "fellowship with
the Spirit" is the third statement of blessing. All agree that this refers to the
Holy Spirit. The question is whether this is fellowship brought by the Spirit or
fellowship in the Spirit.[121] Finally, there is "tenderness and compassion."
Again these terms refer to the mercies shown them by the Lord. These statements make a strong emotional appeal. Their rhetorical value clearly surfaces,
and though Paul approached the Philippians gently here, the combined effect
of the statements was powerful. The church had a common experience of
grace, and Paul built upon that in his exhortation. Since the other three of these
qualities seem to be spiritual in nature, it is best to take this as a fellowship the
Holy Spirit provides.

THE ESSENCE OF UNITY (2:2a). **2:2a**   Paul wrote to produce like-
mindedness. His approach shifted from the blessings they shared in Christ to
the Philippians' responsibility to Paul, their spiritual father. Paul's joy would
be complete when they stood together in unity. His references to joy here
suggested the anticipation of presenting a mature group of Christians to the
Lord. His joy was that his life work would amount to something in God's
economy and in the lives of other people (1 Thess 2:19-20). This personal
appeal, therefore, was a way of encouraging them onward for the glory of God.

The content of his exhortation is that they be "like-minded." The verb used

---

[119]The clauses are the fourfold protasis of a first-class conditional sentence. The apodosis is
the imperative in 2:2. First-class conditions are translated "since" by many, but it is clear that that
translation cannot be sustained (see Matt 12:27). This class of condition sets up a logical
relationship where an assumption occurs in the protasis and a conclusion based upon it occurs in
the apodosis.

[120]Many take the word to mean "exhortation." See Lightfoot, 107. Caird, 116, takes "in Christ"
as going with all the four statements, but its position and the symmetry of the four argue against it.

[121]2 Cor 13:13 speaks in favor of "fellowship produced by the Spirit."

here occurs ten times in Philippians (of twenty-three times in the Pauline corpus). It speaks to the intellect (i.e., a way of thinking), but it goes beyond that. It incorporates the will and emotions into a comprehensive outlook which affects the attitude. With this word and the contexts in which it occurs, Paul spoke of the values and ambitions which surface through the mind. This is unity. It is not found in an identical life-style or personality. It occurs when Christian people have the same values and loves. Paul sought that in this church.

THE EXPRESSION OF UNITY (2:2b-4). **2:2b**   Three characteristics express the unity of the church. They are goals for which to strive, and they provide the measurement of success. The three are stated in different ways, and either grammatical or logical units express them. The first is the same outlook. Three ideas combine to emphasize its different aspects: having the same love as Christ did; having a harmonious affection;[122] and valuing the same thing. The NIV translates "having the same love, being one in spirit and purpose" (2:2b). Together these speak to the unity found among those who are going the same direction. There is nothing superficial about it. This unity comes from the core of one's being.

2:3   The second measurement is humility. Paul expressed this both negatively and positively. Negatively, the Philippians were to avoid "selfish ambition" and "vain conceit." Selfish ambition motivated the preachers Paul described in 1:17. Perhaps that was fresh in his mind. It led him to think about conceit, a seeking of glory which is, in reality, empty because it focuses on the individual rather than on the Lord. The positive side corrects improper attitudes. They were to act in humility.[123] Before the New Testament era, the word "humility" had a negative connotation. The adjective related to it "was frequently employed, and especially so, to describe the mentality of a slave. It conveyed the ideas of being base, unfit, shabby, mean, of no account. Hence 'humility' could not have been regarded by the pagan as a virtue to be sought after."[124]

Nonetheless, "humility" introduces a key theme of the passage. Paul further described it in 2:3 and 2:5-11. He urged the Philippians literally to "count others as excelling over themselves." This also relates to the mind and values. The word "excelling" ("better," NIV) occurs in 3:8, where the pursuit of Christ excels anything Paul had before he engaged in it. The word "consider" occurs in the hymn to Christ (2:6), as does the word for "humbled" (2:8). Since the

---

[122] The Greek is literally "like-souled," a term that occurs only here in the New Testament. It recalls "one soul" of 1:27 and suggests the sharing of a life principle.

[123] A significant grammatical distinction is to be made between the negative and positive attributes. The negative is expressed by κατά and the accusative; the positive, by the locative or dative. It could be that this is a locative of sphere (operate within the sphere of humility) or a dative of reference (with reference to humility, consider others as excelling).

[124] Hawthorne, *Philippians*, 70. See also W. Grundmann, *TDNT*, 8:1-27.

model of Christ loomed in Paul's mind, Christ's actions provided the necessary motivation. Christ's humility is the standard for evaluating the worth of others and actions toward them. This does not mean that personal concerns should be overlooked. Elsewhere Paul clearly stated that Christians must take care of their own affairs as an act of love for the congregation (1 Thess 4:9-12). The next verse implies the same truth. Humility begins with a realistic appraisal of oneself and others as being in the image of God.[125] This relates intimately to the next characteristic, where the topic is continued.[126]

2:4 The third measurement is consideration. The Philippians were to "look out" for others' interests as well as their own. Some Greek texts insert the word "also" in this sentence so that it reads "also the things of others." This may reflect an early interpretation, and it surely is a correct inference. Some then interpret this exhortation to mean that the church is to focus on the good qualities of others in the church.[127] A way to unity, then, is watching to see how God works in others the qualities he desires in everyone. The focus shifts to others rather than personal spiritual qualities. The interpretation is attractive. It answers the problem of self-centeredness and false glory. It also does not relieve Christians of an obligation to care for their own things. It expresses the dynamics of church relationships and fits the example of Christ. In reading the text, however, it seems that Paul had more in mind. A natural reading suggests a broader reference point than merely spiritual qualities. Any concerns of others were to become the concerns of all! The Philippians were to imitate Christ, and it seems unlikely that Christ focused on the good spiritual qualities of the people for whom he left heaven. He died in spite of the fact that they were not spiritually attractive.

(3) The Example of Christ (2:5-11)

[5]Your attitude should be the same as that of Christ Jesus:
[6]Who, being in very nature God,
did not consider equality with God something to be grasped,
[7]but made himself nothing, taking the very nature of a servant,
being made in human likeness.
[8]And being found in appearance as a man,

---

[125] Martin says, "The practice of humility consists in giving to other people a dignity and respect which Christians expect of themselves, especially as both parties are seen in God's sight (cf. Rom 12:3,10)" (89).

[126] Christian humility has four basic elements that Christians must realize. They must acknowledge that God has gifted them to serve in his economy in some way, and they must find that/those gift(s); that God enabled them to do what they do; that they do not have every gift, but that they need what others have as well; and that they must answer to God for how they use their gifts for his kingdom.

[127] The interpretation is aided by the meaning and use of the word "look" (σκοπέω). It generally means *to make something an aim or object of concern*. That would mean that each person was to make the good qualities in others his aim, asking that God work them in him as well.

> he humbled himself
> and became obedient to death—
> even death on a cross!
> [9]Therefore God exalted him to the highest place
> and gave him the name that is above every name,
> [10]that at the name of Jesus every knee should bow,
> in heaven and on earth and under the earth,
> [11]and every tongue confess that Jesus Christ is Lord,
> to the glory of God the Father.

Paul exhorted the Philippians to proper attitudes in 2:1-4. In 2:5 he repeated that exhortation. The repetition emphasizes its importance. Even more, however, it introduces the model of humility and servanthood: the Lord himself. Philippians 2:6-11 recalls the attitude and actions of Christ as he left the glories of his preexistent, eternal state to assume humanity and die vicariously. The Philippians were to imitate him because, in so doing, the problems of disunity would be solved.

The thrust of the passage is clear, but scholars have debated almost every aspect of these verses. They have debated the form of the text. Is it a pre-Pauline hymn known and appreciated by the early church? If it is a hymn, what is its arrangement and order? In addition to the form of the text, they have debated the function of the text in the context of the epistle. Is it theological, presenting Christology and soteriology as a foundation for the Philippians' action? Is it ecclesiological, exhorting them to unity in the church? Is it psychological, explaining how persons are to view themselves and their positions in life? Once questions of form and function are answered, there are questions about the details of exegesis. Almost every word of the text has been debated. The following analysis cannot indicate the breadth of the debate. Rather, significant conclusions are presented, along with suggestions as to how the hymn functions in its context.

THE FORM OF THE TEXT. The basic question regarding form is whether these verses are an early Christian hymn.[128] Most contemporary scholars interpret these verses as a hymn because of the rhythmical quality, rare words and phrases, and motifs. The second portion of the passage, 2:9-11, goes beyond the demands of the immediate context. It seems to be the second stanza of the hymn about Christ. Although the exaltation theme presented there contributes to the context, here Paul advocated humility, not exaltation. If the verses do

---

[128]The literature on this subject is extensive and bewildering. Perhaps the best presentation is in Martin's works on the passage: *Carmen Christi, Philippians 2:5-11 in Recent Interpretation and in the Setting of Early Christian Worship* (Cambridge: University Press, 1967) and *An Early Christian Confession: Philippians 2:5-11 in Recent Interpretation* (London: Tyndale, 1960). V. Taylor also has a helpful study of the issues involved in this passage: *The Person of Christ in New Testament Teaching* (London: MacMillan, 1966), 62-79. An extensive bibliography is provided in Hawthorne, *Philippians*, 71-75.

constitute a hymn, which seems reasonable, they reveal something of the worship of the early church. At least two characteristics predominate: They express a depth of theology which reveals in particular a highly developed Christology; they reveal that the early church had formulated its Christology in cryptic but powerful language. Further, the fact that Paul could appeal to the (apparently) well-known hymn indicates the widespread interest the early church had in Jesus.[129]

Scholars agree on little about the precise form of the hymn. Commentators accept from two to six verses with various arrangements. They normally appeal to theological themes for structure, rather than grammatical indicators.[130] Some believe Paul added his own comments so that the structure is irregular. Theological or other reasons compelled him to amplify what the Philippians already knew. It seems clear that the verses move in two directions, which must be considered the focuses of the text. Philippians 2:6-8 speaks of Jesus' servanthood; 2:9-11 speaks of his exaltation. A change of subjects from Jesus as actor (vv. 6-8) to God as initiator (vv. 9-11) confirms these divisions.

The structure of the two portions is as follows. The first three verses have within them a contrast which makes a negative and a positive statement. The main verbs reveal the pattern:

> He *did not consider*
> but He *emptied* himself
> He *humbled* himself

There are, with each, participles which further explain these actions. The second three verses present God's response. They may be pictured

God *exalted* him		every knee *should bow*
	in order that	
and *gave* him		every tongue *confess*

Unlike the first section, these clauses do not have participles modifying them. Their form is straightforward, using simple statements to present the results of Jesus' actions.

THE FUNCTION OF THE TEXT.   The discussion of how the hymn contributes to the epistle occupies the thoughts of scholars. In general, three positions attempt to answer the question. First, some consider the function of the hymn

---

[129] Further discussion of hymns may be found in the commentary on Col 1:15-20. Some object to the term "hymn" to describe these verses. The title does not suggest these "hymns" were sung. The themes of this passage may be found in the broader context of Philippians. This passage, however, is commonly identified as a hymn.

[130] Hawthorne, *Philippians*, 6-77, presents a good representation of these various positions.

to be primarily theological. Especially among older commentators, attention was devoted to discussions of the meaning of the hymn. For some, context mattered little. In other words, the hymn was approached for its own interests, without taking into account the impact of the problem at Philippi. Second, some were concerned with the ecclesiological aspects of the hymn. Since the problem which prompted including the hymn concerned the fellowship of the church, its application to the church naturally predominated. Another aspect of the ecclesiological interpretations was that some became preoccupied with what the hymn revealed about the setting of the early church. Employing form and source techniques, the hymn was viewed as a window to view early church order and worship. Naturally many interesting and fruitful suggestions arose when it was viewed this way. The problem which frustrated much of this study, however, is the fact that the only context that has survived is the Epistle to the Philippians. No one can be sure that the material even had another context. Third, some scholars focused on the psychological aspects. They assumed that Paul wanted the individuals of the church to implement the model of self-sacrifice seen in Christ. This view often overlooked the theological significance of the hymn.

Each of these approaches to the text is valid. Two major questions arise from the options. Is it necessary to isolate one of these approaches at the expense of the other two? Most today want to do just that. They assume that if a psychological motif predominates, for example, then the theological (or other) has no importance. There is no reason multiple reasons could not have guided Paul in his application of this text to the church. Typically in the epistles, Paul expressed theological truths, then described their application to a specific context.[131] It would be natural to use a theologically loaded text to make a psychological point. In fact, that procedure strengthens the argument by providing it with a solid foundation.

The second question pertains to the theology of the hymn. Is it proper to exegete the hymn theologically if its ethical function is primary? Rather than explore the meaning of the hymn, some bypass the difficult questions it poses in favor of making an application. They assume that since Paul's concern was moral (the nature of self-sacrifice), the illustration is the point. Generally, these interpreters do not seek the explanation of important words and ideas. Rather, the impact of the hymn in its totality, as opposed to its content, becomes the total message.

Such a procedure fails at two important points. First, it does not take account of the point of illustration. Paul picked this hymn *because* it conveyed what he wanted. That means that he accepted the content of the hymn and saw in it the greatest example of proper attitudes. Second, the illustration loses its impact if

---

[131]This occurs in small portions of the text (e.g., Col 2:8-3:4), as well as the larger progress of the epistles where most of them begin with theology and move to ethics.

the details have no significance. The dramatic distance Jesus traveled from the "form of God" to "the death of the cross" dramatically reveals the servant mind that each believer was to have. Hermeneutically, this material first calls for a serious exegesis of the content of the hymn as a free-standing theological expression. Further, the hermeneutical task involves applying that to the church. No one in the church could repeat what Christ did. They did not start where he started, they could not suffer the way he suffered, and they could not be exalted to the position he occupied. That is not the point. The mind of Christ is the point of application, and that loses its impact without its theological foundation. The older interpreters who asked questions about the Christology of the passage, the meaning of the emptying, and the nature of the exaltation asked the proper questions. That dimension was essential. At the same time, however, the application of the text to individuals and the church at large completes the text as it stands in its canonical form.

One final concern must be expressed. Many interpreters question the Pauline authorship of these verses. Specifically, they point out that this hymn has a decidedly Semitic background which seems to translate an Aramaic original;[132] typical Pauline themes are missing;[133] and there is, according to some, an un-Pauline emphasis on the "servant of the Lord" from the Old Testament.[134] The situation, however, could account for many differences in wording; linguistic data are not conclusive; Paul did write in poetic style (1 Cor 13; Rom 8:31ff.); and many Pauline elements are present in the hymn. In actuality, no one can know whether Paul wrote these words originally or only incorporated them. Further, it matters little in the interpretation of this text, although it contributes to an understanding of Pauline Christology. What does matter is that Paul chose to use this material to make his point; it is consistent with his views about Jesus, and he put his approval on it by building his argument around it. In fact, some scholars believe the entire epistle serves as a commentary on these verses, though that is unlikely. The hymn serves to illustrate and explain the exhortations of its content.[135]

ANALYSIS OF THE TEXT.   These verses contain two parts: an introduction

---

[132] These are participles functioning as main verbs, non-Greek constructions like "having been found . . . as", repetition of "threes" (three stresses to a line, three lines to a strophe, three-fold division of the cosmos, three-fold theme of preexistence, humiliation, exaltation).

[133] Such as redemption (no ἡπέρ, περὶ ἡμῶν, or any substitutionary idea is explicit), resurrection (the hymn moves directly to exaltation), the church.

[134] These come from E. Lohmeyer, *Die Briefe an die Philipper, und die Kolosser und an Philemon* (Göttingen: Vandenhoeck, 1953).

[135] E.g., W. S. Kurz, "Kenotic Imitation of Paul and of Christ in Philippians 2 and 3" *Discipleship in the New Testament* (Philadelphia: Fortress, 1985), 103-126, argues that the epistle basically urges the church to imitation of Christ (primarily) and of Paul (secondarily). In this, these verses are central to the exhortation. The point is well made but may be overdone. He argues persuasively that the book is a unity because of the literary parallels.

in the form of a command (v. 5) and the hymn to Christ (vv. 6-11). The hymn has two movements: the humility of Christ (vv. 6-8) and the exaltation of Christ (vv. 9-11). The following commentary will focus on conclusions and major questions. Space forbids the type of analysis that deals adequately with each contested portion.

The Introduction to the Hymn (2:5). **2:5** Paul introduced the hymn to Christ by looking both backward and forward. Looking back, he picked up the theme of the proper attitude which he commended in 2:2 (with the word "like-minded") and 2:3 (with the word "considered," also found in 2:6). Looking ahead, Paul anticipated the epitome of the proper mind, Jesus.

Two primary questions arise in 2:5. What is the meaning of "your attitude should be the same as," and what is the sense of "Christ Jesus"? The NIV handles these problems by presenting a highly dynamic, almost paraphrased translation. The KJV says, "Let this mind be in you, which was also in Christ Jesus." The differences come from the Greek text chosen as well as the translator's preference. The first question relates to whether the verb translated "your attitude should be" (*phroneite*) is active or passive. The KJV takes the passive, "let this mind be." Most Greek texts have the active form, and that is the better reading.[136] It should be translated, "You think this in you." The second question concerns "in Christ Jesus," which occurs at the end of the verse. As the text stands, another verb is needed to make a complete statement, and some translators add "was." The sense then is "have this mind in you which *was* in Christ Jesus." Others have repeated the main verb of the first part of the sentence for a translation like: "You think this in you which you think in Christ Jesus."[137] That means that the Philippians were exhorted to think properly as Christians, as those "in Christ Jesus." The translation has much to commend it.[138] Immediately, however, Paul appealed to the attitude of Christ, and the most natural reading is to understand Paul to say, "Think this in you which Christ thought in him."

The Hymn to Christ (2:6-11). Paul commended Jesus' disposition by appealing to his attitude (v. 6) and his actions (vv. 7-8). The order is both logical and chronological. One led to the other. Paul employed the same order in vv. 1-4, where he addressed the attitude (v. 2) first, then actions toward each other (vv. 3-4). Perhaps Paul's exhortation was based on the hymn which he

---

[136]Hawthorne, *Philippians,* 80, takes the passive form as best. Almost no one agrees with him.

[137]This comes from A. Deissmann, *Die neutestamentliche Formal "in Christo Jesu"* (Marburg: N. G. Elwert'sche Verlagsbuchhandlung, 1892), 113-17; E. Käsemann, "A Critical Analysis of Philippians 2:5-11," in *God and Christ: Existence and Providence* in *Journal for Theology and Church* (New York: Harper & Row, 1968), 45-88, and a good case is made by Silva, 107-111, who also quotes these sources.

[138]Most notably, it makes good, straightforward sense of the Greek text which is difficult at best, and it takes the usual sense of Paul's phrase "in Christ"—the soteriological environment of the church.

anticipated. In this text Jesus' attitude (presented negatively to make a positive point) led to his redemptive actions.

2:6   The main verbs are the key to the structure, and Jesus' attitude is presented in the first. Jesus "did not consider equality with God something to be grasped." Precise knowledge of why that was so remarkable comes from the phrases which modify and explain the significance of his attitude.

Two parallel statements show the exemplary nature of Jesus' thoughts. The first is "being in very nature God," which is compared to the second, "equality with God." The former is normally translated by the English word "form," which is true to the literal meaning of the Greek *morphē*. Commentators have debated hotly the meaning of the word "form."[139] Basically, the word means "form, outward appearance, shape";[140] but since it occurs only in 2:6 and 2:7 in the New Testament, the context must determine its precise meaning. Clearly, the "form of God" and the "form of a servant" must mean the same thing. Some take that to mean that the visible appearance of God is not a factor because he is invisible, and therefore the text calls for a nuance of the word. This meaning should not be dismissed too quickly, however. The hymn called the readers to consider the preexistent state of Jesus, when he was in the form of God. Physical eyes cannot see spiritual realities, only spiritual eyes can. Given the context, it would not be uncommon to use the term to state that he actually "appeared as God" to those who could see him. Nothing in the context requires that human eyes see the form. Similarly, the "very nature of a servant" does not require that human eyes be able to see that form, although with spiritually enlightened eyes one sees it. The question is whether he had that form. Surely the actions described of him here are appropriate to the servant role, and they appear in his death on the cross. The word "form" means an outward appearance consistent with what is true. The form perfectly expresses the inner reality.[141]

The description "very nature of God" parallels "equality with God." "Equality with God" is, therefore, another explanation of Jesus' nature. The form of the expression stresses the manner of his existence since the word "equal" is actually an adverb showing how he existed.[142] In the Greek text,

---

[139] Hawthorne, *Philippians*, 81-84, provides perhaps the most complete survey of possibilities. He includes: "form" is equal to "glory" ($\mu o \rho \phi \acute{\eta}$ = $\delta \acute{o} \xi \alpha$), based upon parallel passages; "form" is equal to "image" ($\mu o \rho \phi \acute{\eta}$ = $\epsilon \grave{\iota} \kappa \acute{\omega} \nu$), based on Gen 1:26-27 and 3:1-5; "form" is "mode of being," based on the Gnostic parallels; and "form" is "condition" or "status." Each of these has extensive support and implications for Paul's (the hymn's) motif. Hawthorne does not accept any of them.

[140] *BAGD*, 528.

[141] Lightfoot, 127-33, drew a correct distinction between $\mu o \rho \phi \acute{\eta}$ and $\sigma \chi \tilde{\eta} \mu \alpha$ by saying "that which is intrinsic and essential with that which is accidental and outward." The distinctions will not always hold, but they seem generally true. He preferred to equate the form with "attributes" and spoke of a transfer from "objects of sense to the conceptions of the mind."

[142] J. Müller, *The Epistles of Paul to the Philippians and to Philemon*, in *The New International Commentary on the New Testament* (Grand Rapids: Eerdmans, 1955), 80, says, "Christ could have

the phrase is introduced with an article so that it should read "the equality with God," referring back to something already identified as equality.[143] Thus "form of God" and "equality with God" refer to the same state of existence,[144] and the NIV correctly translates "in the form of God" as "in very nature God."

Two other matters relate to Jesus' preexistent state. The first is the meaning and force of the participle "being." The word basically meant "to exist originally"[145] but later was used as an intensive form which meant "really exist." The result is that Jesus "really existed" in that form. The force of the participle ("being") is debated as well. Most interpreters take it with a concessive force ("although being"), and that stresses the dramatic nature of Christ's humility.[146]

The second matter is the meaning of "something to be grasped." Some understand the words to mean "something to hold on to," while others take them to mean "something to rob."[147] Often Jesus is contrasted with Adam, who selfishly attempted to rob God of what he had no right to possess. He wanted to be "like God." This contrast may have been in Paul's mind, but any suggestion that requires the sense of aspiration to "equality with God," as though it were not Jesus', cannot fit the passage.[148] With this understanding, Christ would have refused to do what Adam did. He refused to grab what was not his.

---

existed and have appeared only as God, only in a manner equal to God: it was a right which was due to him; he need not have gone into another manner of existence." This captures the thought well.

[143] The Greek text uses an infinitive to express this phrase. Infinitives may occur with or without the article and have generally the same force. Here the article appears to call to mind the previous reference since the same sense could be achieved without the article.

[144] Some scholars point out that literally the text states "in the form of God" and not that he *was* the form of God. The locative sense they affirm means "in the sphere of God"; apparently the sense would be that Jesus existed "within God's sphere," rather than "as God." The point of that distinction would be difficult to understand. All beings exist "within God's sphere" (presence) as Paul reasoned in Acts 17:28. Paul's point must have been that Jesus was uniquely "in the form of God." If anything, he meant that Jesus "emerged within God's form." Given this difficulty, and Paul's general Christology, this phrase must mean that he was in nature God.

[145] The etymology of the term means "under the beginning," stressing the original state of affairs. In actuality, it is somewhat synonymous with "to be," but stresses the reality of existence (*BAGD*, 838).

[146] Hawthorne, *Philippians*, 85, takes the participle causally. "Precisely *because* he was in the form of God." The idea is attractive, but the text speaks of giving up what one has, and the concessive emphasizes that more.

[147] The question is whether ἁρπαγμόν is active ("to rob") or passive ("to be held"). It is difficult to see how "equality with God" should be robbed since he already possessed it. If a grasping were to take place, it would have to be a grasping of something other than equality with God, but that is precisely what the text identifies.

[148] Many interpreters have pointed out that the Adam/Christ contrast lay behind Paul's thinking when he spoke of the human Jesus. The contrast helpfully explains the "in Adam"/"in Christ" motif. The objection here is to any idea that Adam and Christ were equal in what they wanted, to grasp equality with God. Jesus had it; Adam sought it.

Two factors speak against that understanding. First, the text more naturally reads "not to be clutched." Since he already possessed "equality with God," Jesus had nothing to grasp. He was able to release the appearance of deity. Second, when the word "grasped/clutched" is studied with words like "consider" (*hēgeomai*, 2:3,6) the "idiomatic expression refers to something already present and at one's disposal."[149] The passage may mean, therefore, that Christ did not think of his equality as "something to use for his own advantage."[150]

2:7 The hymn moves from attitude to actions. Two verbs describe successive actions as Jesus gave himself for humanity: "He made himself nothing" and "he humbled himself." Each has a phrase modifying it. The first of Jesus' choices was to empty himself. The NIV translation "made himself nothing" captures the spirit of the passage but overlooks many theological discussions of the past. Historically, interpreters have wondered of what did Jesus empty himself? The question shows that a theological interest predominates in the passage. Most modern interpreters, however, point out that the hymn does not speak to that point. The contrasts between "Lord" (v. 11) and "servant," (v. 7) and "very nature of God" (v. 6) and "human likeness" (v. 7) express the emptying. Thus the emptying is that God became human, Lord became servant, and obedience took him to death. The verb "emptied" (NASB) does not require a knowledge of what was emptied (Rom 4:14; 1 Cor 1:17; 9:15). Often it is translated simply "to render void, of no effect."[151] This passage affirms simply that Christ left his position, rank, and privilege. They were "of no effect."[152]

Two ideas modify the verb "made himself nothing." They are: taking the very nature of a servant and being made in human likeness. These statements explain both how this took place and what it means. Paradoxically, being "made nothing" means adding humanity to deity rather than subtracting deity from his person. The language has a vagueness to it; that vagueness allows for theology which cannot be expressed easily, a theology of the relationships between the divine and human in Christ.

The relationship between these ideas reveals further the movement to death. Some interpreters take the two ideas to be simultaneous, so that being a servant

---

[149]R. W. Hoover, "The Harpagmos Enigma: A Philological Solution," *HTR* 64 (1971):95-119. See also N. T. Wright, "Harpagmos and the Meaning of Philippians 2:5-11," *JTS* 37 (1986): 321-52.

[150]Hoover, 118.

[151]*BAGD*, 428.

[152]The theological question is important and should not be totally cast aside. This passage does not tell us enough to make judgments about it. The most that can be said is that Jesus left the appearance of deity to accept another form of existence. Some argue for a low Christology on the basis that he really became human. Nothing in the text suggests that being human required him to be less than God. Most of the theological discussion regarding the kenosis of Christ involves reading in other assumptions, either high or low regarding Christ. It is best to leave unanswered questions the text does not raise and, therefore, does not answer. A good discussion of problems associated with a kenotic theory that limits the divine nature of Christ is found in Müller, 83-85.

and becoming human explain each other and refer to the same action. Others see a progression: first servanthood, then humanity. Certainly the first, the "very nature of a servant," speaks to an attitude which produced the action of assuming humanity. It logically precedes.

Because of the close relationship between these modifying ideas, their content should be seen in parallel, rather than with fine distinctions of meaning. The "very nature of a servant" means that Jesus' outer actions (appearances) conformed to the inner reality. Jesus' servanthood issued in humanity and, later, obedience to death. Some assume that his servanthood was his humanity. That brings questions of how humanity is servant and to what is its slavery.[153] These questions, however, go beyond the text, and they cannot be answered from the passage. This text says simply that he was genuinely a servant. It does not explain what that means, other than the giving of his life in death.[154]

The description "human likeness" really stresses Jesus' humanity. While on the surface it may seem to say that Jesus was not really man, that conclusion finds almost no support. In fact, likeness "does not suggest any degree of unreality in Christ's humanity; the word is almost a synonym for 'form' (*morphē*) and 'image' (*eikōn*); but it leaves room for the thought that the human likeness is not the whole story."[155] It must be seen in light of the next statement, that he was found "in appearance as a man" (v. 8). The change from the plural ("human likeness") to the singular ("appearance as a man") may reinforce that conclusion. Finally, the verb "being made" (v. 7) contrasts with "being" (2:6). He existed originally in the form of God; but at a specific point, he became human.

With these words, the text praises the attitude of Jesus. The hymn was to be used in worship, and as such, it was doxological. The total impact was to move the church to appreciate and imitate Jesus' actions. Each word contributes to the meaning. Certainly interpreters need not read more into the text than was intended, but overtones of Christology exist which cannot be dismissed. First, it affirms Jesus' preexistence. Before he came to earth, he existed fully as God, in essence and appearance. Second, he became human. Like the movement from riches to poverty in 2 Cor 8:9, this text follows the movement from the exercise of lordship to the obedience of the servant. The hymn teaches that Jesus added servanthood to lordship as he added humanity to deity. In so

---

[153] F. Craddock, *Philippians, Interpretation: A Bible Commentary for Teaching and Preaching* (Atlanta: John Knox, 1985), 41, represents many commentators who suggest that Jesus became subject to the "elements" like all persons are. They point to Gal 4:3-5 and 1 Cor 2:8 as proof passages. The suggestion is interesting but leaves many questions unanswered. Further, as pointed out in the text, it is doubtful that the nature of the slavery is important to the hymn.

[154] It also has become common to link the "form of a servant" with the "Servant of the Lord" texts of Isaiah. See Martin, *Philippians*, 97. They are noteworthy because of their suffering motif, but the legitimate objection may be made that the Servant of the Lord was an honored position, and that is far from the meaning of this hymn.

[155] Beare, 83. This well states the point.

doing, he elevated humanity beyond what it had known before, as Heb 2:6-8 affirms (quoting a fulfillment of Ps 8:5-6, LXX). Paul easily affirmed both the deity and humanity of Jesus by using (and not correcting) this hymn. The words convey significant theological meaning that adds reality to the impact of the worship experience. Recalling this servanthood also exhorted the believers to unity.

2:8 Having entered the world of humanity, Jesus "humbled himself" (2:8). This describes a second stage in Jesus humility. Like the first statement, two ideas modify this one, explaining the extent of Jesus' actions. First, when he was found in fashion like a man, he chose humility. This statement reinforces the previous section of the hymn, but it also introduces a new phase of Jesus' action. At this point, people can identify with him. Second, he became obedient to death. The text does not suggest to whom Jesus was obedient, though most obviously God willed such an action. As a true servant, Jesus chose to obey even when it cost his life, and that further in a most ignoble way. The impact of crucifixion on the Philippians would be great. No Roman could be subjected to such a death, and the Jews took it as a sign that the victim was cursed (Gal 3:13). Perhaps it made a point to Paul's opponents as well, whom he described as "enemies of the cross of Christ" (Phil 3:18). The cross, so dear to Paul and other devout Christians, was an embarrassment to many. That, in itself, demonstrates the extent to which Jesus went.[156]

2:9 Again the passage changes both tone and structure. The hymnic character continues, but God becomes the subject, rather than Christ, and the purpose of God's actions becomes evident. God exalted Jesus. Two statements reveal the nature of God's actions. First, he "exalted him to the highest place"; second, he "gave him the name that is above every name." The two relate to each other so that together they express God's action.

Jesus' exaltation is stated graphically. The word translated "exalted to the highest place" actually means *superexalted*.[157] Some scholars have taken the word in a comparative sense, that God exalted him more than before. Thus they seek a new position for Jesus after the ascension.[158] Others, however, point out that this is a superlative degree. He was exalted "to the highest," a contrast which compares the lowliness of the "death of the cross" (v. 8) with the exaltation of restored glory.[159] Finally, many interpret this in the context of the

---

[156]Silva, 121-22, points out that the one other time "obedience" occurs of Jesus in the Pauline corpus is Rom 5:19, where Paul contrasted Adam's disobedience with Jesus' obedience. The parallel has fruitful possibilities.

[157]*BAGD*, 842, says "to raise someone to the loftiest height." Literally it means to *exalt above*.

[158]H. A. Kent, "Philippians," *EBC* (Grand Rapids: Zondervan, 1978), says, "Implicit in this exaltation is the coming consummation mentioned in the next verses, when his triumph over sin and his lordship will be acknowledged by every being" (11:124-25). The new status, therefore, is the acknowledgment of his rule.

[159]Beare, 85.

human Jesus. The hymn describes the exaltation of humanity in Christ.[160]

In determining a solution, several matters must be kept in mind. First, the action of "superexaltation" occurred as a consequence of Jesus' voluntary humility.[161] It clearly came because of his servantlike attitude and actions. Second, these actions began in eternity past. The sequence of thought is that his attitude was such that he was able to add humanity. A position that rewards Jesus as man, therefore, seems to enter the drama in the second act. Surely God's blessings took into account the attitude which prevailed in Jesus' preexistent state. That is the primary point of the passage. Third, "superexaltation" should be taken seriously. It was not something that happened to the earthly Jesus only; it began in eternity past. Fourth, it has overtones of a change of position, even though exaltation lies at the heart of its usage.[162] Fifth, the exaltation involved granting to Jesus the title "Lord" (v. 11). This places the focus on function as well as being. The "superexaltation," therefore, is as much a functional matter as an ontological one. These scholars argue for an interpretation that elevates Jesus *in position* more than before, while recognizing that he could be no more than God before or after.

The second portion of the exaltation is that God "gave him the name that is above every name." Though the introduction to this portion of the hymn suggests that God's blessings were the outcome of Jesus' humility, this verb implies a gratuitous giving of honor. Jesus was not "paid" for his servanthood; nevertheless, as a consequence, God chose freely to grant him a high name. Most agree the "name that is above every name" is the title "Lord." Further, most agree that the title refers to Jesus' character, as well as to his function.[163] This corresponds to Peter's preaching at Pentecost (Acts 2:36) and to the view of the early church generally. The new factor is that, by virtue of Jesus' humility, he became the object of adoration in the Godhead, as well as the administrator of God's affairs. The worship accorded him in 2:10-11 supports this fact. Other passages speak to his function of Lord as well (1 Cor 15:24-28; Eph 1:20-23). Now, since the ascension, all that God is comes to us through Jesus, and all who come to God do so through Jesus.

---

[160]Caird says, "It is the man Jesus of whom it is said that *God has highly exalted him.* The heavenly Christ returns to the high dignity he possessed before, but with this difference that he returns as man, and as a man who by his self-humbling has made common cause with his fellow men and become their representative" (123). Silva opts for a similar interpretation.

[161]The introductory conjunctions to 2:9 make that clear. They are διὸ καί ("wherefore also"). They naturally suggest that God chose to reward Jesus for his actions.

[162]Martin, *Philippians*, 101, points out that Paul's terms introduced with ὑπέρ are "generally elative in force."

[163]Caird expresses the view of those who take "Jesus" as the name given: "There is an obvious difficulty, however, in identifying a name given at Christ's exaltation with that by which he was known to his contemporaries during his earthly life. For this reason, the majority opinion is that the new name is 'Lord'" (123).

2:10-11 The hymn explains the goal or purpose of God's exalting Jesus. Quoting the LXX of Isa 45:23, with its own additions, two parallel ideas express Jesus as the object of worship. They are: every knee should bow and every tongue should confess. Employing typical imagery of the part for the whole, the knee and the tongue stand for worship and confession that Jesus is Lord.

Ultimately, every creature in the universe will acknowledge who Jesus is. Two concerns must be discussed: the meaning of "at the name of Jesus" and the description of which persons acknowledge him. The phrase "at the name of Jesus" may mean that he is the object of worship,[164] that he is the medium of worship,[165] or that he provides the occasion and focus of worship.[166] The context clearly reveals that Jesus is to be the object of worship, as the name "Lord" and his exalted position indicate. That rules out Jesus as a medium of worship, but more may be required by this expression. In fact, more is intended. Wherever Jesus' name (and character) has authority, he will be worshiped. Since he is authoritative everywhere, as the next phrase indicates, he will be worshiped everywhere. The emphasis of this text, however, is not directly on the worship of Jesus. The language is that of triumph. The bending of the knee was a posture of submission, as was confessing "Jesus Christ is Lord." The hymn, therefore, speaks to Jesus as the conqueror of all and should be seen as parallel to such texts as 1 Cor 15:24-28. Thus the hymn points out that everyone will acknowledge the position of Jesus in the universe.

The second concern of this first purpose clause is the persons who submit to Jesus' lordship. The text states, "in heaven and on earth and under the earth." The meaning of the text is that it is *the knees* of beings located in these places.[167] Paul could and did use personification to speak of the relation of inanimate objects to Christ (Rom 8:19-22), but this context is confined to persons.[168] Jesus' lordship encompasses spiritual beings (those of "heaven"— good or evil),[169] living human beings (those of "earth"), and dead persons as

---

[164]In which case the phrase ἐν τῷ ὀνόματι is basically equivalent to πρός showing the object. Those who argue for this unique use of the preposition ἐν point out the necessity of it because of context.

[165]This takes the preposition ἐν in an instrumental sense and makes it equivalent to διά with a genitive. Some commentators who take this position remind the readers that this is the language of prayer, and that in prayer the worshiper comes to God "through Jesus' name."

[166]This may take ἐν as a normal locative of sphere. It is in the sphere of his name that people worship. This is accepted here.

[167]The adjectives are masculine, not neuter, since they imply persons whose knees are the point of reference.

[168]Lightfoot, Martin, Silva, and a host of others broaden the reference to include "things." Paul's theology does include creation itself giving glory to God (Col 1:20), but that seems foreign to his thought here. There is no reason to extend it beyond persons.

[169]The heavens are often considered the place of all spiritual beings, both good and bad. See notes on Col 1:15-20 and Ephesians, especially 6:12. The term seems to be broad here, including all living spiritual beings.

well ("under the earth").[170] Thus the hymn includes every conceivable habitation of personal beings.

The second purpose statement is that "every tongue will confess that Jesus Christ is Lord." In a parallelism typical of poetry, both the universal nature of Jesus' lordship and the acknowledgment of it are reemphasized. "Every tongue" includes the same beings as "every knee" which bows. The confession "Jesus Christ is Lord" encapsulates this aspect of the Christian faith and may well have been the earliest Christian confession.[171]

Honoring Jesus in this way fulfills God's plan. He elevated Jesus to the position of lordship (v. 9), and the confession is "to the glory of God the Father." There is perfect unity in the Godhead. The actions of Jesus in his exaltation bring glory to the Father. Thus the Father honors the Son, and the Son honors the Father. In this dynamic, both display selflessness, and both receive honor.

This is an eschatological picture. The hymn brings the future into view by describing the culmination of history, when all persons will acknowledge Jesus' lordship. No evidence states that such acknowledgment will bring salvation, however. That must be cared for in the present, before Jesus conquers his enemies. The church bears witness to Jesus' lordship by confessing to the world "Jesus Christ is Lord" and offering salvation to those who accept that confession and make it the central part of their lives (Rom 10:9-10). Paul recognized, therefore, that some people will voluntarily accept the reality that Jesus is Lord and participate in his reign of glory. Others will deny that lordship and, in the end, be conquered by the Lord himself. For them, it will be too late to participate in the glory, and they will be destined to the punishment appropriate for those who resist the Lord.

In using this hymn, Paul reminded the Philippians of the greatest example of servanthood. The first section, on selflessness, applied directly to them. They were to be like Christ, the chief servant. Christ's attitude was to become theirs. They were to focus on giving rather than receiving. If God chose to exalt them, they would be truly exalted, but there were no guarantees of what that meant. True servanthood can never be perceived as simply an alternate route to the top, to exaltation.

Christ acted selflessly to accomplish the will of God. He even died to provide salvation as a part of the divine plan. God chose to honor him, determining

---

[170]This phrase seems to be the equivalent of Hades or Sheol, the place of the dead. In the hymn the writer simply included every dimension of personal beings.

[171]The title "Lord" had relevance to Gentiles, who identified it with sovereignty, and to Jews, who associated it with the Jehovah of the Old Testament. Sometimes a fuller confession included "Lord Jesus Christ," which included the messianic significance of this sovereign one. An older but still helpful work in this regard is V. Neufeld, *The Earliest Christian Confessions*, NTTS (Leiden: Brill, 1963).

that Christ would be the focus of the Godhead in its interactions with creation. Because of Jesus' actions, the way to honor God is to honor Christ. Even so, the glory Christ receives is a glory given to the Father. Again, a shared servant-hood works to the mutual benefit of all involved. The church had to learn this lesson. It would learn this lesson by focusing on Christ himself. Appropriately Paul employed a hymn to teach the lesson. Hymns were used in worship, and it was through worship that these attitudes would make their way from the mind to the heart and from attitudes to appropriate actions.

(4) The Command to Obedience (2:12-18)

¹²**Therefore, my dear friends, as you have always obeyed—not only in my presence, but now much more in my absence—continue to work out your salvation with fear and trembling, ¹³for it is God who works in you to will and to act according to his good purpose.**
¹⁴**Do everything without complaining or arguing, ¹⁵so that you may become blameless and pure, children of God without fault in a crooked and depraved generation, in which you shine like stars in the universe ¹⁶as you hold out the word of life—in order that I may boast on the day of Christ that I did not run or labor for nothing. ¹⁷But even if I am being poured out like a drink offering on the sacrifice and service coming from your faith, I am glad and rejoice with all of you. ¹⁸So you too should be glad and rejoice with me.**

Following the extended hymn to Christ, Paul returned to his primary concern. The passage resumes the thought of 1:27 with the concern of whether Paul might be present or absent. More importantly, however, Paul identified and applied what he considered the central thrust of Jesus' attitude, obedience (2:8). For Paul, obedience was also a primary responsibility of the church and expressed an essential ingredient in Christian living. These verses have three movements to them, all of which extend the central idea of obedience. First, the Philippians were to devote themselves to practical Christianity (2:12-13) by working out their salvation. Then, they were to be characterized by positive steadfastness (2:14-16), never succumbing to complaining or grumbling. Finally, they were to participate in Paul's personal joy in ministry (2:17-18), not only rejoicing with him but also sharing his outlook.

PRACTICAL CHRISTIANITY (2:12-13). Paul immediately applied the example of Christ to the problems in the Philippian church. In so doing, he urged the believers to work out their salvation (v. 12) and provided a reason for doing so (v. 13).

The Command to Work Out Their Salvation (2:12). **2:12** One central theme ties these verses together. The Philippians were to make salvation work in their lives. It will be helpful to determine the nature of the word "salvation" and whether this refers to the church at large or the individuals within it.

Salvation was central to Paul's theology. Normally the word has its full soteriological sense of spiritual deliverance from sin and the world.[172] Paul described salvation as a past event (Eph 2:8-9) and as a future consummation (Rom 13:11). Here he spoke of working out salvation. Many recent commentators have opted for the meaning "well being," as a better translation for *sōtēria* ("salvation," NIV) although this is highly unlikely.[173] Personal salvation brings with it responsibilities which Paul related to Christians' obedience. The responsibility was to live in accord with their salvation, letting the implications of their relationship with Christ transform their social relationships. Paul really meant, in the first place, that they were to act like Christians.

To live like Christians, the Philippians were to have an attitude of obedience. The obedience was not to Paul, although apparently his presence encouraged it in their lives.[174] The obedience was to God. The church members were to solve their problems as an act of obedience to God. Such obedience confirmed the fact that they were truly saved. Perseverance, whether in individual purity or harmonious group relations, was expected of Christians.

In addition to obedience, the Philippians were to be sober. The precise words are "fear and trembling." These words reminded them of their relationship to God and that they were to conduct their lives with a seriousness and reverence due him. After all, he worked in them.

Did Paul's exhortation refer to individuals or to the church at large? Many contemporary interpreters understand the words to address the church collectively. Basically, this position recognizes that Paul was concerned with a group problem. In order to promote harmony and unity, he told the group to work out their salvation. That position has some difficulties, however, as well as some strengths. Those who take that position correctly interpret the text in light of the context of Philippians. Paul did, indeed, want to correct the group, but often he provided more instructions for dealing with a group problem. He did that in 4:2ff., where he invoked the help of a third party. Further, the group would have had difficulty changing without the individuals devoting themselves to the task of personal change as well. Finally, this approach must make salvation refer to the wholeness of the group, and that would be very strange for Paul. Instead,

---

[172] Paul used the word "salvation" nineteen times in his writings . By far the majority carry the full soteriological sense. Phil 1:19 is the most likely time when it may refer to a generic "deliverance." *BAGD*, 801, gives "deliverance" as a meaning of the term but indicate no Pauline references in their listing. It states that 1:19 means "to appropriate it for oneself."

[173] Representing this view, Martin, *Philippians*, says it is "the health of the church which was sorely distressed by rivalries and petty squabbles" (102). He provides five reasons for taking it that way: "salvation" can mean wholeness; after 2:5-11 it is inappropriate to stress individual salvation; "your own" cannot mean each church member concentrating on his own soul's salvation; the state of the Philippian church needed just this call; and "fear and trembling" are manward attitudes involving a healthy respect for each other. Silva, 135ff., consistently refers to this as "the new view," pointing out that it is not the view of the older commentaries.

[174] He wrote with some apprehension that they would act differently if he were not there. This may well mean that he entertained the idea that he would die before seeing them again.

Paul must have meant the individuals of the group were to live consistently with their salvation. If they did so, the group problems would be solved.

The Reason for Working Out Their Salvation (2:13). **2:13** Paul often provided reasons for ethical commands. The reason the Philippians were to work out their salvation was the soberness of realizing that God worked in them. The text emphasizes God.[175] Using a play on words, Paul said they were to "work out" because God "works in." God's work in them provided both the motivation and the ability to do his good pleasure. Two factors indicate that Paul meant God initiated their interest in him. First, the context was one of salvation. Although the implications of salvation concerned Paul, they could not be separated from the total experience of salvation. Second, the work of God culminated in "his good purpose." The term generally relates to the ultimate will of God (see Eph 1:5,9), his own glory. The application to the Philippians should have been clear. First, without God's taking the initiative, they would not have had the opportunity to work *out* salvation because they would neither want to nor be able to do so. Second, the fact that God started the work in them gave them a stewardship responsibility. They were to be true to his purposes, handling the gift of salvation with utmost care. After all, they were God's showcase (Eph 3:10), and the way they handled their salvation reflected on the God who gave it. This passage closely resembles 1:6, where Paul expressed his confidence in them because God began a work in them and would complete it.

The emphatic use of words for "work" built on the same root in Greek presents an unusual contrast. Paul presented both the work of God ("works in") and the work of the individual Christian ("work out"). Paul recognized the place of each. Divine initiative called for a human response. While he believed that, ultimately, all of salvation, considered in its broadest scope, depended on God's initiative and power, he never tolerated passive Christianity. Human energy could never accomplish the work of God, yet God did not accomplish his purposes without it. The two functioned in perfect harmony, and people cooperated with and contributed to what God did in them and in the world. It is both comforting and sobering to realize that God initiated the relationship. It is equally sobering to realize that nothing short of full cooperation with God's working confirms personal salvation. Thus both the divine initiative and human response accomplish his purposes. Here, the Philippians were to apply their salvation to the problems of selfish ambition, strife, and egocentric actions which divided the church (2:3-4). Their salvation demanded it; their responsibility to God called for it.

POSITIVE STEADFASTNESS (2:14-16). The second sentence of the paragraph changes directions slightly. Appealing perhaps to an Old Testament

---

[175]The actual subject of the sentence is "the one working in you"; "God" occurs in the normal predicate position, first in the sentence. Even though a normal construction and "God" is not the subject, the predicate position is typically emphatic in these constructions.

precedent, Paul warned of the dangers of murmurings and arguing. Paul knew that selfishness and vainglory led to complaints. He may, therefore, have been heading off even more problems in the community.

Another possible rationale for this entire section may rest in Paul's quoting Deut 32:5 (LXX) in 2:15. In Deuteronomy Moses made his farewell address. He complained that Israel was a "crooked and perverse generation," and that no doubt brought to mind the people's "grumblings" against Moses in the wilderness.[176] Paul may have used the text because he thought in terms of his own farewell (his absence, 2:12). The combination of the two seemingly different ideas of "work out your salvation" and "do everything without complaining" could have come from his realization of Moses' disappointment with Israel, who failed at both these points. Perhaps Paul wanted to be sure his fruit lasted. All three of the major portions of this section fit that motif, including the idea of sacrifice with which Paul ended the section. The fact is, the Philippians had the possibility of being blameless among a crooked generation. Israel was blameworthy, and Moses called them the crooked generation.[177] In this section Paul issued a command (v. 14) and gave an extended purpose for the command (vv. 15-16).

The Command to Stop Complaining (2:14). **2:14**   The command has positive force although it is framed negatively. The use of the words no doubt comes from the Old Testament text, but their appropriateness to Philippians is a question. What would the positive command be? Would it be to trust God in everything since complaining is at the root a failure to accept God's plans and provisions? That seems unlikely because the problems within the group still govern the context. Perhaps it was to be accepting of the ways and efforts of others in the church since Paul warned about self-seeking (2:3-4). Whatever the problem, it was a concern which affected the moral life of the church and its witness to the world. Paul implied that if dissension stopped the church would be on its way to purity of life and action.[178]

The Purpose of the Command (2:15-16). **2:15-16**   Employing terminology like his prayer in 1:9-11, Paul looked for the completion of the Philippians' character. They were to become pure and blameless. The terms speak to the

---

[176]Significantly, Paul used the word "grumbling" (γογγυσμός) only here in the New Testament. He did use a cognate form (γογγύζω, "to grumble") in 1 Cor 10:10, describing the wilderness experience of Israel. Conceivably the wilderness experience governed his thoughts at this point.

[177]The clear reference to Deut 32:5 makes this suggestion a real possibility and provides a good rationale for what is otherwise a disconnected thought. Beare, 89ff., boldly associates these ideas. It also subtly but perhaps powerfully countered the Judaizers who prided themselves as the people of God, the heirs of Israel.

[178]The plural words and the fact that "arguing" may be a strong word may suggest a deep problem of continual arguments within the congregation. Martin, *Philippians,* 104, suggests that they were actually going to court before unbelievers as at Corinth. He probably goes beyond the evidence since Paul did not handle it the same way as he did there.

moral nature of their lives. They were to have complete Christian character, and they were to have no offense in relation to others.[179] This hope was further expressed by Paul's statement, "children of God without fault in a crooked and depraved generation." This statement explains the first so that "without fault" incorporates "blameless and pure." They were children of God already; Paul hoped they would become blameless.

This consistent character is particularly striking when viewed against the backdrop of the world. Two metaphors describe the contrast between Christians and non-Christians. First, using the words of Deut 32:5, Paul described the world as distorted and depraved. The use of such language stressed the moral distinctiveness of Christians. Purity and blamelessness were the standard by which the distortions of the world were measured. Thus Paul meant that the world was morally crooked, distorted by its failure to understand the word of God. The ministry of the church, then, was to provide a straight model for distorted lives.

The second metaphor comes from astronomy. The Philippians, with their unblemished moral character, shone like stars in the universe. Even with their imperfections, they were the light of the world to those in darkness.[180] This mission was accomplished by their holding out the word of life.[181] All assume that the "word of life" is the gospel, of which Paul had so much to say in this epistle. The word "hold out," however, may mean "holding fast"[182] or "proffering."[183] The immediate context supports "holding fast" because Paul's discussion concerned moral conduct. By their lives, the Philippians were actually holding fast to the gospel. By so doing, their lives also became the measuring rod and illumination of the world around them.

Paul ended this section with a personal appeal. His converts were his life. Equally, his life was Christ. Like other seeming paradoxes, this one blended perfectly in Paul's mind. He urged them to progress in their lives so that his efforts would be profitable. Looking to the day of Christ, the day of judgment, he wanted to have fruit from his labor. Using athletic imagery, he stated he

---

[179]The words "blameless," "pure," and "faultless" are likely synonyms which should not be pressed into strong differences of interpretation. Two emphasize personal relationships ("blameless," and "without fault"), and one emphasizes personal character ("pure").

[180]Some interpret the word "shine" as a command and translate it "you must shine" (the Greek form is the same for indicative and imperative). It is highly unlikely that an imperative would be found in a subordinate clause (relative) which is itself subordinate to a purpose clause. The indicative reading is the better. Paul described their function. There is also significant discussion regarding the voice of the verb: passive ("you appear") or active ("you shine"). The active sense is attested in Matt 24:27 and should be accepted here.

[181]The NIV takes this as temporal and ministry oriented ("as you are holding out"), but the commentary makes this manner and related to steadfastness ("by holding fast").

[182]*BAGD*, 285.

[183]Caird, 126, believes this translation accords better with the star metaphor and with the theme of living for others.

wanted not "to have run . . . for nothing." At other places, he expressed that desire in terms of his personal understanding of Christ (3:12-14).

Here he related it to his ministry. Was he selfishly motivated in this? Two factors require a negative answer to the question. First, Paul's life was Christ (1:20-21). Paul knew that everything he did, Christ actually did, and all of his glory was for Jesus' glory. Paul's energies, therefore, contributed to the glory of Christ whom he so much loved. Second, it hardly seems consistent in a context devoted to selflessness and warning about personal ambition that Paul would so blatantly express his own selfish wish. That the Philippians were to live a certain way for his benefit would be the height of egoism. In baring his concerns, Paul openly spoke in terms of his ministry. He had previously just as openly revealed his deepest motivation to please Christ. There was no conflict!

PERSONAL JOY IN MINISTRY (2:17-18).   Paul's concern for the Philippians' steadfastness did not replace his joy for them and their service to the Lord. In this last portion of 2:12-18, Paul employed sacrificial terms to explain that he was not dissatisfied. The introductory words are "but even if." They suggest a sharp contrast. The question is the nature of the contrast. Paul did not merely accept his lot as an apostle; he rejoiced in the faith of the church no matter what the cost to him. The words introduce a deliberate affirmation of Paul's trust in the Lord. Whatever happened—whether he was released from prison or died a martyr's death—he was confident the Lord had called him into apostolic ministry on behalf of the Philippians, and not even the prospect of death could diminish his joy.

2:17   The sacrificial terminology of these verses supplies another metaphor to explain. Three words recall the sacrificial system: "poured out" (*spendomai*), "sacrifice" (*thysia*), and "service" (*leitourgia*). "Poured out" refers to a drink offering that accompanied the sacrifices. "Sacrifice" was the actual offering, and "service" accompanied the offering. These last two appear to combine to speak of a sacrifice; the first, "poured out," definitely referred to a procedure of pouring a drink offering either before or after the offering itself.

Paul said he was being poured out. The present tense verb suggests something already happening, although it may have been happening in kind and would culminate in the future. Some interpret this to mean his impending martyrdom, of which Paul was certain. Others think of it in terms of his apostolic ministry, which often included suffering. While Paul may have entertained the idea of martyrdom, he was not unduly pessimistic at this point. His language is reflective. It seems to be a verbalization of thoughts about his life and its meaning. The conditional sentence in which this occurs ("even if") suggests an element of doubt about the matter.

Regardless of its interpretation, Paul's "being poured out" accompanied their sacrifice. While many think of Paul's life as the offering, that blurs the metaphor. Further, there is no reason he would not use more direct terminology to express sacrifice, as he did in Rom 12:1. The sacrifice was that of the Philippians. Most likely, he meant that their support of him, including the gift mentioned in 4:10, was a sacrifice and service to God. He used that terminology in 2:30 and 4:18 when speaking of the gift.[184] Understood this way, the "sacrifice and service coming from your faith" would be that which their faith produced. Thus their response to God in faith produced the sacrifice of the gift to Paul.[185]

The use of this terminology reveals Paul's humility about his own importance. In the ritual, the sacrifice was primary; the drink offering was secondary. If Paul placed himself in the position of the drink offering, he saw their gift as the primary matter and his own circumstances as secondary. Their support, in fact, enabled him to be a drink offering. Without it there would have been no need. This balances the statement of 2:16 that Paul "boasted" in their continuing to the end as a source of pride. If that seemed arrogant, though in actuality it was not, this countered it. They were the important ones; his part was complementary.

2:18 Rather than being discouraged about his circumstances, Paul had great joy. In 2:18 four times joy is prominent. Twice the words "joy and joy with" ("glad and rejoice with," NIV) occur. One time Paul used them to explain his feelings about being a part of their offering. The other, he urged them to feel the same way.

In this section, the mind of Christ occurs in the thoughts of Paul. He urged the Philippians toward the goal of blamelessness. As for him, he was happy with his service to them and with them. If Christ's act were one of sacrifice, Paul's life was too. It was "poured out like a drink offering" along with those whom he loved so much.[186]

This ends the first section of exhortations. From 1:27-2:18 Paul's commands provide the tone and organization of the text. He urged the Philippians to stand true, to have the mind of Christ, and to work out their salvation in obedience. Above all, they were called to be like Christ.

4. Paul's Future Plans (2:19-30)

[19]I hope in the Lord Jesus to send Timothy to you soon, that I also may be cheered when I receive news about you. [20]I have no one else like him, who takes a genuine interest in your welfare. [21]For everyone looks out for his own interests, not

---

[184]Not all agree with that. Some take it as their blameless character being the sacrifice to God (Caird, 127). Many have equated the "pouring out" with the sacrifice itself so that they believe Paul was speaking of his own death as the sacrifice which was directed toward them. That does not seem to fit the context or the grammar.

[185]This takes the construction to be a subjective genitive.

[186]Often commentators point out the use of sacrificial terminology in Paul. In Rom 15:16 he spoke of his priestly function of offering up the Gentiles. In Rom 15:27 Gentile "service" is commended. In 2 Tim 4:6 Paul used the term "poured out" of his martyrdom. In Rom 12:1-2 cultic language is compounded. Finally, in 2 Cor 9:12 sacrificial language describes the gift that meets the needs of the saints. The closest reference to Phil 2:18 is 2 Tim 4:6, and the idea of martyrdom in 2 Timothy may well have been in Paul's mind in Philippians.

those of Jesus Christ. [22]But you know that Timothy has proved himself, because as a son with his father he has served with me in the work of the gospel. [23]I hope, therefore, to send him as soon as I see how things go with me. [24]And I am confident in the Lord that I myself will come soon.

[25]But I think it is necessary to send back to you Epaphroditus, my brother, fellow worker and fellow soldier, who is also your messenger, whom you sent to take care of my needs. [26]For he longs for all of you and is distressed because you heard he was ill. [27]Indeed he was ill, and almost died. But God had mercy on him, and not on him only but also on me, to spare me sorrow upon sorrow. [28]Therefore I am all the more eager to send him, so that when you see him again you may be glad and I may have less anxiety. [29]Welcome him in the Lord with great joy, and honor men like him, [30]because he almost died for the work of Christ, risking his life to make up for the help you could not give me.

These verses form a break in the letter. Paul exhorted through commands from 1:27-2:18, and he returned to that in 3:1-4:8. Here he provided information about his situation and his intent to visit the Philippian church when he could. In these verses, Paul promised to send Timothy and Epaphroditus and praised them for their good character and service to him and to the Lord. These two stand as further examples of the mind of Christ. They both served unselfishly, considering others better than themselves. They were of value to the church at Philippi, as is clear, but they were of equal importance to Paul at this time in his life.

The character of Timothy and Epaphroditus does not explain why Paul wrote about them. This section has often been called a travelogue because it reveals Paul's travel plans,[187] and Timothy and Epaphroditus fit into those plans. That raises the question of why Paul would reveal his plans to the Philippians. Perhaps they were concerned about when he would see them and anxiously awaited some news regarding his situation. They had both a financial and a fraternal interest in the apostle. No doubt that was a primary concern of the apostle in disclosing this information. Even so, it is necessary to explain why these verses occur in this part of the text. The answer must be that while Paul thought of the mind of Christ he was reminded of two who represented that character and had especially been selfless in their service to him. Since they each had a special relationship to the church at Philippi, Paul took the opportunity to discuss their character, their value to the ministry, and their proposed journey to Philippi. If Paul were not enough of a model of Christlikeness, these two beloved friends were.

---

[187]Generally such travelogues come at the end of an epistle, though not always. The fact that it occurs here fuels the fire of those who see multiple letters incorporated into this canonical one. The matter is not definitive enough to be a substantive argument in favor of fragments since 1 Cor 4:17-19 has almost identical content, including Timothy as an envoy for Paul. Travelogues may be studied from R. W. Funk, "The Apostolic *Parousia*: Form and Significance," *Christian History and Interpretation: Studies Presented to John Knox*, ed. W. R. Farmer, C. F. D. Moule, and R. R. Niebuhr (Cambridge: University Press, 1967), 249-68.

(1) Concerning Timothy (2:19-24).   Timothy is mentioned first. He was the companion of Paul whom Paul called a servant with him (1:1). Often Paul sent Timothy on missions for him, and he intended to do that again.[188] Perhaps the church would be surprised to see Timothy and Epaphroditus, rather than Paul, and some explanation was needed. Paul, therefore, first explained his plans to send Timothy (v. 19), commended Timothy for his character (vv. 20-23), and explained that Timothy was only a temporary substitute for Paul (v. 24).

THE SENDING OF TIMOTHY (2:19)   **2:19** Knowing he could not visit Philippi, Paul hoped to send Timothy. As always, his plans were subject to the will of God; therefore he stated, "I hope in the Lord Jesus." The expression was not simply tacked on to Paul's statement, nor was it an escape clause in case the plans did not materialize. Rather, Paul naturally thought in terms of commitment to God's will, and the expression disclosed the principle by which he lived his life. Perhaps part of that hope was that Timothy would be sent soon. Paul could not release him yet (v. 24), but he hoped that would change and Timothy could be on his way quickly.[189]

Paul hoped to receive news concerning the church. Good news would lift his spirits, which may have been somewhat depressed by the difficulty in the church. Paul used an unusual term for the expected lift of his spirits, "cheered" (*eupsycheō*), which showed how important this was to him. Of course, other means of gathering information were available to Paul. If there were no better courier of news (v. 20), there was certainly the possibility of mail. These did not suffice. Paul wanted accurate, reliable information. Timothy knew them well. He could read between the lines of their comments. Further, Paul appreciated this church, and in his absence, his right-hand man should go. Thus, he planned to send Timothy on another important mission.

THE COMMENDATION OF TIMOTHY (2:20-22).   **2:20** These verses contain one of the highest commendations possible. Both the commendation itself and the reason it was given deserve comment. The commendation includes a statement and three reasons to support it. They evidence the reality of Paul's words. Simply stated, Paul sent Timothy because he was "like-souled" ("I have no one else like him," NIV). Some have questioned whether Paul meant Timothy was like Paul, but all the evidence suggests that Timothy was a partner in ministry, sharing Paul's commitments and burdens. Significantly, Paul did not commend Timothy for like desires, his word "like-souled" suggest that the basic life prin-

---

[188]Timothy's character is noted in how Paul used him on these trips as well. Paul sent him to troubled spots where he could be "oil on the waters" (1 Cor 4:17). Most notably Timothy had a significant ministry in Macedonia. Paul sent him to three churches in that province, Berea (Acts 17:14), Thessalonica (1 Thess 3:1-2), and Philippi.

[189]Some have suggested that Paul was disposed to send him before he was really ready to do so since he obviously needed Timothy for some reason. Perhaps even some problem at Philippi caused Paul to change his plans. These ideas are purely speculative, and the text does not suggest them.

ciples coincided. Apparently, for Timothy to live was Christ as well, and he conducted his affairs in that way.

Paul gave three evidences that what he said was true. First, Timothy had a "genuine interest" in the affairs of the church at Philippi. The NIV translation weakens a strong statement in the Greek text. The word root has the idea of "legitimate" ("born in wedlock," *gnēsiōs*),[190] and the adjective form is used of Timothy in 1 Tim 1:2. That has led some to suggest that Timothy was Paul's son and as a son he "naturally" inherited the interests of his father.[191] That, however, goes beyond the normal sense.[192] Paul's commendation was that Timothy had acquired a concern for others that had become second nature in its genuineness.

2:21-22 Timothy's concern for others manifested itself in other ways. The second reason for commendation was that Timothy sought the things of Jesus Christ rather than his own interests. The wording recalls v. 4, and with it Paul provided a model of what he meant there. Finally, Timothy's worth was found in his commitment to Paul. Paul had no sons. Timothy took care of Paul as though Timothy were a natural son. The dangers he endured in that service, such as at Philippi (Acts 16:19-40), proved his genuineness even in life-threatening situations.[193] Paul added to his commendation by pointing out that though Timothy served as a son his primary commitment was to the gospel, not to Paul.

Why did Paul go to such lengths to commend one the Philippians already knew well? It is not likely that they would be disappointed with seeing Timothy because they apparently had a positive relationship with him. It is not likely that they hoped instead for Paul to come. They knew Paul's circumstances, so much so that they anticipated his needs in Rome and sent Epaphroditus ahead of Paul. Surely they knew Paul could not come even if he wanted to. He still awaited trial. Any word from Paul would have been welcomed. Further, some have suggested that Epaphroditus failed in the mission given him by the Philippian church, and perhaps they would be disappointed in seeing him since he was supposed to stay with Paul as their helper. Yet they knew of his serious sickness, and they had responded to it in a way that increased Epaphroditus's desire to see them. If they were angry with him, he hardly would have sought

---

[190] *BAGD*, 163.

[191] Martin, *Philippians*, 117.

[192] Every use of the word in the New Testament is metaphorical. It is used of Timothy and Titus as "a true child in the faith" (1 Tim 1:2; Titus 1:4), but that probably does not mean that they were brought to Christ by Paul. The events surrounding their salvation are unknown, but Paul gave credit to Timothy's mother and grandmother for their impact on his life (2 Tim 1:5). Further, in 2 Cor 8:8 it refers to "genuine love." Perhaps most telling is the one other use of the adjective in Phil 4:3, where the expression "loyal yokefellow" occurs. Surely there the "yokefellow" was not born to it. The adverb is used only here (Phil 2:20).

[193] The Greek word is "tried by the fire and refined" (δοκιμήν), therefore "tested."

to return home. Further, even if Timothy were sent to "soften" the impact of Epaphroditus's return, that was no reason to commend Timothy as Paul did.

Apparently, Paul commended Timothy because he remembered Timothy's value to the ministry. Paul quickly praised his fellow-workers, and after thinking about Christ's servanthood, he remembered that he lived with a servant, Timothy, who had the same disposition. Further, in sending such a valued helper, the church would realize his esteem for them as well. They could not be disappointed with Paul's actions.

THE IMPORTANCE OF TIMOTHY (2:23-24).   **2:23-24** Obviously Timothy had a significant role in the work of Paul. Although he represented Paul in delicate situations, Paul reluctantly allowed him to do so. Two statements in the text reveal Timothy's importance to Paul and the work of the gospel. First, Paul needed Timothy a while longer (v. 23). When he knew "how things [would] go," Timothy would be free to come. No one knows why Paul felt that way. What is certain is that Timothy uniquely sustained Paul during the uncertainty of his trials, and Paul felt he could hardly get along without him.[194] Later, as Paul knew of his impending death, he called for Timothy to stand with him (2 Tim 4:9-11). Second, Timothy replaced Paul, who desired to come when he could. In sending Timothy, Paul sent the best he had—an extension of himself—and a costly gift to them. After all, they had sacrificed for him as well.

(2) Concerning Epaphroditus (2:25-30)

With a similar style of commendation, Paul explained why he sent Epaphroditus to the Philippians. This section has a commendation of Epaphroditus (v. 25), a reason Paul sent him (vv. 26-28), and a command to honor him (vv. 29-30).

THE COMMENDATION OF EPAPHRODITUS (2:25). **2:25** Paul wanted to send Timothy, but he also found it necessary to send Epaphroditus. That raises many questions. Why would Paul have felt that way? Would Epaphroditus not be of service to Paul as the church originally intended? Did something happen to sour him or Paul? Was he physically impaired in a way that limited his usefulness? Further, it would seem that Epaphroditus could make the trip without Timothy, so perhaps Timothy accompanied him for his sake, as well as to find out about the church. The text provides no answer to these questions. For that reason, even though imaginative suggestions abound, it is best to state what the text does and leave the rest to conjecture.

Paul commended Epaphroditus as he identified him. First to be mentioned was Epaphroditus's relationship to Paul. Obviously Paul expressed a fondness and deep appreciation for him. Paul reminded them of Epaphroditus's

---

[194]The physical difficulties combined with a natural anxiety regarding the long awaited trial. Paul was sixty to seventy years old and had known physical problems. Additionally, the church at Rome was divided regarding his worth as an apostle and preacher (1:12-18), and few were there to comfort him.

relationship to him on their behalf. As for Paul, Epaphroditus was a brother, a fellow-worker, and a fellow-soldier. These descriptions emphasize partnership by employing familial, vocational, and military terms. Each of them provides insight as to how Paul saw the work of the gospel. Epaphroditus was an equal; there was no hint of inferiority or failure.

Epaphroditus's service had been a gift from the church to Paul. The NIV translation describes Epaphroditus as "your messenger [*apostolon*], whom you sent to take care [*leitourgon*] of my needs." The words "messenger" (*apostolon*) and "servant" (*leitourgon*, a word suggesting religious service which the NIV fails to translate clearly) state his mission. He came with news of the church's love and a gift from them. He also determined to stay and care for Paul. This action demonstrated the love of the church in sending and supporting Paul, and it showed the self-giving character of Epaphroditus, who left home to serve in difficult circumstances.

THE REASON PAUL SENT EPAPHRODITUS (2:26-28). **2:26-28** Before discussing the reason he sent Epaphroditus, Paul described his situation. Perhaps he had some concern that they would not understand. After all, Epaphroditus was well enough to travel, and they would not know of his difficulties. The verses tell of his sickness. Apparently on the way to Rome, Epaphroditus fell sick. He traveled on to Rome, perhaps after some delay for healing, and met Paul. When he arrived, however, the situation was not like it was when he started. The church made known its concern about Epaphroditus's well-being, and Paul wanted to assure the believers their messenger was well. Even the discussion of his sickness has the flavor of selflessness about it. Epaphroditus was concerned only for the impact his sickness would have on them (v. 26), and Paul agreed that Epaphroditus's return to Philippi would have more profit than the service he would render to the apostle (v. 28).

The sickness was severe. Three times Paul informed them of that fact (vv. 26,27,30). It almost cost Epaphroditus his life, and Paul understood that kind of service. The church, though it had heard Epaphroditus had been sick, had no way of knowing what he went through, so Paul reinforced Epaphroditus by this disclosure.

The scene is filled with emotion as well. Epaphroditus was filled with deep emotion over the Philippians' reaction to his circumstances.[195] Some have suggested he was homesick. That is not as likely as the fact that he felt his sense of responsibility toward them and wondered how they would respond to his inability to carry out their wishes. This feeling grew from a sense of responsibility on his part. Perhaps he was anxious about how they would treat him, but the text seems to indicate that he participated fully in the decision to return, and that would not be likely if he had dreaded seeing them.

---

[195]The words "ἐπιποθῶν ἦν" (periphrastic construction) and "ἀδημονῶν" are strong terms individually, and together they make a powerful statement.

Paul also expressed his own emotion. He took Epaphroditus's sickness to heart, realizing no doubt that he was sick because of his love for Paul. A special relationship develops when some willingly risk their lives for others. Paul expressed his feelings by the word "sorrow" (*lypē*), which occurs three times in the Greek text of vv. 27-28 (the third usage in v. 28 is a form of *lypē* and is translated "less anxiety" in the NIV).[196] It was better for Epaphroditus to return home than to die in service to Paul. Further, Paul expected that the church would be eager to see him.

THE COMMAND TO HONOR EPAPHRODITUS (2:29-30).   **2:29** Was there any doubt that the church would honor Epaphroditus? Paul wanted to make sure that it would. Therefore, he urged the members to welcome Epaphroditus appropriately,[197] with the honor due to men like him. If they had doubts about whether Epaphroditus had failed, Paul relieved those concerns. Men like him deserved honor, and the Philippians were to provide it. He had risked his life for Paul, but he also had done it in demonstration of his love for them. He endured sickness near to death for their sakes.

2:30   Paul ended this section by reminding the Philippians that Epaphroditus really served them. He had no chance to serve Paul. They were to realize that this man attempted to do what others, no doubt, could not or would not do. He had acted on their behalf. Paul's words "to make up for the help you could not give me" translate literally "to fill up your lacks of service toward me." The terminology suggests that something was missing. In fact it was. Although the word "lacks" (*hysterēma*) does not necessarily mean that they had failed or that Paul judged them because of it,[198] here "lacks" seems to have its normal meaning. The church intended to do more than it could do without Epaphroditus or someone like him. The gift had to be carried to Paul, and it came with a promise that someone would be with Paul to care for him. It was a special way the church chose to honor the beloved apostle. Thus, their gift, as they intended it, had three stages. First, they collected the gift. Second, they selected a courier to go to Paul. Third, that courier was to remain with Paul for an extended time, presumably at the church's expense. They intended all three, but the church at large could only do one. The rest was the responsibility of Epaphroditus. What they could not do, the "lacks" in their ministry, he attempted to do. Thus "lacks" may mean the remainder of what was intended but which, to this point, had not been done. In confirmation of this interpretation, the word for "service" seems to be the equivalent of "gift."[199]

---

[196]Twice the noun occurs in 2:27 (λύπην ἐπὶ λύπην), and once the negative adjective occurs in 2:28 (ἀλυπότερος). The word may be used of intense sorrow, even that caused by childbirth. *BAGD*, 482.

[197]Greek is προσδέχομαι.

[198]Silva, 163, points to Col 1:24 and 1 Cor 16:17-18 as parallel statements to this one.

[199]See notes on 2:17.

Paul ended this section of the epistle by commending the service of these two Christlike men. Both thought of others before their own concerns, and both served the Lord and the church. They would journey to the church in Paul's stead, in the hopes that he would soon follow.

──────────────── *SECTION OUTLINE* ────────────────

III. EXHORTATIONS TO CHRISTIAN LIVING (3:1-4:9)
   1. Exhortation to Avoid False Teachers (3:1-21)
     (1) Paul's Experience Explained (3:1-16)
        Apostolic Safeguard (3:1)
        True Circumcision (3:2-6)
          Decrying the False (3:2)
          Describing the True (3:3-6)
        True Values (3:7-11)
          Evaluation of Paul's Former Life (3:7-8)
          Aspiration of the New Life (3:9-11)
        True Zeal (3:12-16)
          Paul's Desire to Fulfill His Call (3:12-14)
          Paul's Encouragement to Other Believers (3:15-16)
     (2) The False Teachers' Character Exposed (3:17-21)
        Encouragement to Imitate Paul (3:17)
        Characteristics of Paul's Opponents (3:18-19)
        Characteristics of True Believers (3:20-21)
   2. Miscellaneous Exhortations (4:1-9)
     (1) Exhortation to Steadfastness (4:1)
        The Address to the Readers
        Exhortation
     (2) Exhortation to Unity (4:2-3)
     (3) Exhortation to Joy and Peace (4:4-9)

────── III. EXHORTATIONS TO CHRISTIAN LIVING (3:1-4:9) ──────

At this point in the epistle, Paul turned his thoughts more directly to the false teachers and to Christian living. The epistle contains an interchange of instruction and exhortation, and here commands predominate again. They continue until 4:10, where Paul thanked the Philippians for their gifts to him. Two concerns occupied Paul's mind. First, certain persons attempted to undermine his ministry, and Paul had to counter them. Second, the problem of disunity demanded one final appeal, and Paul provided it with more direct and confrontational language. These two concerns form the logical divisions of the text.

1. Exhortation to Avoid False Teachers (3:1-21)

Before addressing the concerns of the text, a brief discussion of the identity of Paul's opponents will be helpful. Two questions must be answered regarding the opponents, and scholars have been significantly divided regarding both questions. First, were these the same persons who were addressed in chpt. 1?

Second, were the same persons addressed throughout chpt. 3? Some discussions of these matters assume that there are multiple epistles contained in this one, and therefore, the suggestions have no contextual boundaries. For advocates of these positions, the only evidence for the opponents' identity comes from the pieces of information contained in these fragments. Thus, for example, 3:1-16 may be totally unrelated to 3:17-21. The fragment hypothesis, however, leaves many unanswered questions.[1] It is best to discuss the opponents within the context of Philippians itself.

Were the persons identified in 3:2ff. the same as those of chpt. 1? Major differences surface in ecclesiology and Christology. Primarily, in chpt. 1 Paul accepted the opponents' message even though he objected to their motivations. They preached Christ. Here, he warned about the message, basically approaching it as non-Christian. In chpt. 1 the opponents were within the church, but those of chpt. 3 were outside. Further, Paul's criticisms were different. In chpt. 1 he said nothing negative about their theology. In chpt. 3 his criticisms focused on theology. The opponents of these two chapters could not have been the same people.

Did Paul address the same persons throughout chpt. 3? That question is not as easily answered. Scholars debate whether Paul addressed one, two, or three different groups. Advocates of the one-group interpretation assume either Jewish or Jewish-Gnostic opposition. The Jewish nature of the attackers appears in their boast of circumcision (3:2); their methods of operation which reminded Paul of "dogs" (3:2); their claim to "perfection" (3:12-14);[2] their "belly-service" ("Their god is their stomach," 3:19), which may refer to rituals and Jewish food laws; and their boast in their shame (3:19), which refers to circumcision. Some contend, however, that Paul did not denounce Jews by claiming they opposed the church.[3] Others see a Jewish-Gnostic opponent. They point out that Paul's argument included the typical Gnostic themes of knowledge, perfection, and resurrection from the dead (presumably avoiding suffering); and that the nature of 3:17ff. fits a Gnostic audience better. However, Paul's argument against them assumed that they were preoccupied with the flesh and fleshly attainments (3:2).

Often interpreters contend that there were two or three groups. Evidence for two groups occurs in the differences between 3:1-16 and 3:17-21.[4] Advocates

---

[1] See the introduction to this commentary for some of these questions.

[2] These verses do not represent their claims, but Paul revealed his attitudes, they say, because of their claim to perfection. Paul countered it by his confession of not having arrived.

[3] This seems difficult to see in light of 1 Thess 2:13-16, where he described the Jews as those who "oppose all men."

[4] These include J. B. Lightfoot, *St. Paul's Epistle to the Philippians*, reprint ed. (Grand Rapids: Zondervan, 1953); M. R. Vincent, *Critical and Exegetical Commentary on the Epistles to the Philippians and to Philemon, ICC* (Edinburgh: T & T Clark, 1897); and F. W. Beare, *The Epistle to the Philippians, HNTC* (San Francisco: Harper & Row, 1959).

point out that the tone changes between these two sections and that there are, in reality, two kinds of arguments. The greatest obstacle for them is the lack of transition between the two passages, which would seem appropriate if Paul changed his focus. Recently some have advocated three groups. Generally, the three are Jewish legalists who advocated strict adherence to the law (vv. 1-6), libertines who had the opposite view of law (vv. 17-21), and perfectionists who believed they had attained already (vv. 12-14). However, these verses are not necessarily mutually exclusive in the characteristics they describe. It is entirely possible that one or two groups held a theology that united these seemingly diverse positions.

The resolution of these approaches may await more evidence. Those who point to the Jewish nature of the opposition may well explain everything in the chapter. Strict legalism could easily produce a sense of perfectionism, and Paul certainly could have described them as preoccupied with their bellies and genitals and totally oriented to this life. That is easy enough to see, but the question remains, Does that answer a natural reading of the text? Strong evidence exists for either one or two groups of opponents. Since the chapter may be naturally read with these being Jewish, non-Christian opponents, that approach will be assumed. This makes the problem of Philippians similar to that of Galatians and Colossians. The Jewish reaction to the gospel made inroads into the church and threatened a syncretism between them.[5] Thus, while Paul addressed Jews outside the church initially, he purposed to warn Christians within the church who might have been influenced by them. That caused a mixed argumentation and exhortation.

(1) Paul's Experience Explained (3:1-16)

[1]**Finally, my brothers, rejoice in the Lord! It is no trouble for me to write the same things to you again, and it is a safeguard for you.**
[2]**Watch out for those dogs, those men who do evil, those mutilators of the flesh.** [3]**For it is we who are the circumcision, we who worship by the Spirit of God, who glory in Christ Jesus, and who put no confidence in the flesh—** [4]**though I myself have reasons for such confidence.**

If anyone else thinks he has reasons to put confidence in the flesh, I have more: [5]**circumcised on the eighth day, of the people of Israel, of the tribe of Benjamin, a Hebrew of Hebrews; in regard to the law, a Pharisee;** [6]**as for zeal, persecuting the church; as for legalistic righteousness, faultless.**

[7]**But whatever was to my profit I now consider loss for the sake of Christ.** [8]**What is more, I consider everything a loss compared to the surpassing greatness of knowing Christ Jesus my Lord, for whose sake I have lost all things. I consider them rubbish, that I may gain Christ** [9]**and be found in him, not having a righteous-**

---

[5]This may also have affected Ephesians since it contains a major discussion of the relationships between Jews and Gentiles in Christ. If so, that means that some form of the problem prevailed in all of Asia. The introduction to Colossians discusses some of the supporting evidence.

ness of my own that comes from the law, but that which is through faith in Christ—the righteousness that comes from God and is by faith. [10]I want to know Christ and the power of his resurrection and the fellowship of sharing in his sufferings, becoming like him in his death, [11]and so, somehow, to attain to the resurrection from the dead.

[12]Not that I have already obtained all this, or have already been made perfect, but I press on to take hold of that for which Christ Jesus took hold of me. [13]Brothers, I do not consider myself yet to have taken hold of it. But one thing I do: Forgetting what is behind and straining toward what is ahead, [14]I press on toward the goal to win the prize for which God has called me heavenward in Christ Jesus.

[15]All of us who are mature should take such a view of things. And if on some point you think differently, that too God will make clear to you. [16]Only let us live up to what we have already attained.

Paul had traveled the road the false teachers traveled. In this passage, Paul drew on his theological pilgrimage. He knew the weaknesses of a legalistic approach to salvation, and he knew the joys of coming to God through Christ. In his career he had experienced both, and he knew that one excluded the other. A subtle danger, however, was the threat that some would become legalistic Christians. In their enthusiasm they would hold together two polar theologies, their untrained theological minds allowing them to practice what threatened the existence of the church they loved. The best means of countering both was for Paul to explain his experience.

APOSTOLIC SAFEGUARD (3:1). **3:1** Paul began this section with a verse of transition. Two matters in it call for brief discussion: the use of the word "finally" and the statement that he was repeating his warning. First, the use of "finally" has been misunderstood by many. It literally means *to (toward) the rest*, and that meaning fits here.[6] The word occurs again in 4:8. Second, Paul claimed to repeat what he had stated earlier. Some relate that repetition only to the command to rejoice, which precedes it,[7] but that construction seems awkward, as do the defenses for it. Others understand the expression to refer to the warnings about the Jewish opponents. Previously, when present, Paul had spoken against them; now he wrote. The Greek text does not say that Paul wrote before; that idea comes from the statement "to write the same things to you." When did he express these concerns? Some say it was in a previous letter. Others say it occurred in some oral communication, possibly through Timothy and Epaphroditus, who carried the letter. Any of these explanations would suffice and do not violate the meaning of the text. In any case, from this warning came

---

[6]C. F. D. Moule, *Idiom Book of New Testament Greek* (Cambridge: University Press, 1953), 16ff., says that it may imply the end in a final sense ("finally"), or it may point to the rest ("and so" or "it follows then, that"). Some theories of multiple letters have supported their cases by the use of "finally," but there is common enough usage of it in the second sense in Paul so that no case can be made based on this adverb alone (1 Thess 4:1,2; 2 Thess 3:1).

[7]G. Hawthorne, *Philippians, WBC* (Waco, Tex.: Word, 1983), 124.

two observations: Paul believed this matter was significant enough to address repeatedly, and the problem most likely persisted long enough for continued communication about it. The Philippians needed to realize that Paul lived for the spiritual well-being of his converts and that his instruction was intended to prepare them for the attacks against their faith. He found it no problem to write; they would find the instruction helpful.

TRUE CIRCUMCISION (3:2-6). Immediately Paul addressed the problem. Although he focused on the message of the false teachers—circumcision— Paul also discussed their methods. In this there can be no doubt as to his conviction regarding them and their religious activities. Paul's writing revealed his concern that the church realize the nature of its opponents. His style became graphic and picturesque, a sign of his interest in the subject.[8] Both the terms which describe the opponents and the definition of true Christians would appeal to a Jewish audience.

Decrying the False (3:2). **3:2** With three rapid, terse statements Paul warned the church about the false teachers. The warnings also described the false teachers. Three times the verb "watch out for" (*blepete*) occurs.[9] The objects of the verb also characterize the false teachers for what they really were. First, they were "dogs." Eastern people generally hated dogs.[10] The Jews often described Gentiles that way, but here Paul applied the term to Jews. Perhaps he envisioned the packs of ravenous dogs which roamed the countryside eating whatever they could. They were scavengers. With this definition, Paul may have implied that they were simply following him, anxious to pick up those who were not theologically grounded after his missionary activity. Obviously Paul spoke in irony, turning the tables on these false teachers.

The two other descriptions were direct plays on words with Jewish ideas. The second was "those who do evil." These Jews, oriented to salvation by the good works of the law, had pride in their exemplary lives. Probably, like the Paul of the past, they considered themselves blameless. In reality, however, what they supposed to be good works were not. They hindered the gospel, providing a stumbling block to genuine faith. Describing their character, not their activity, Paul warned against their zealous activities.[11] Third, they were

---

[8]This is known in the quick, pithy sentences which open the passage and in the frequency of figures of speech here. Hawthorne, 123, lists six figures of speech found here: anaphora (repetition of the same word), paronomasia (sound-alike words), polysyndeton (repetition of καί in close succession), alliteration, short disjointed sentences, and chiasm.

[9]Three factors reveal the urgency of his address: the imperative mood verbs; the repetition of the same verb, "watch out for" (βλέπετε), even when it is unnecessary; and the fact that the clauses are in asyndeton (no connective conjunctions). Some do not believe the verb deserves such attention and have concluded that there were no opponents outside the church. See D. Garland, "The Composition and Literary Unity of Philippians," *NovT* 27 (1985): 165-66.

[10]Michel, *TDNT*, 3:1101-4.

[11]Significantly, Paul did not say, "They do evil works." That would focus on their activities. He said they *were evil workers*, placing the emphasis on their character and motivation.

"mutilators." In a figure of speech employing sound-alike words, Paul turned his thoughts to their circumcision.[12] Circumcision represented the first requirement of the law and symbolized their approach to God. They took great pride in it, as 3:19 reveals. Paul recognized that their circumcision was simply a cutting. It had no value apart from genuine faith in Christ.

Describing the True (3:3-6). Paul described a genuine response to God in two ways. In 3:3-4a he characterized Christians generally, consciously contrasting them to his Jewish opponents. In 3:4b-6, he appealed to his own religious background as proof of the validity of his theology.

3:3-4a Genuine believers in Christ were the truly circumcised. Paul referred here to a spiritual circumcision rather than physical. In God's economy, spiritual circumcision was always more important. The Old Testament said as much (Jer 31:31-34; Ezek 36:26ff.), and Paul confirmed it elsewhere (Rom 2:25-29). Physical circumcision served to identify someone with the Jewish nation and had value for purposes of ministry, but it had no value in commending someone to God.[13] Spiritual circumcision was a matter of the heart (Col 2:11).

The spiritually circumcised were described three ways. Each part of the description is linked together by the fact that in the Greek text the three are preceded by one article that goes with them all. The three together, therefore, characterize genuine Christians. Paul identified himself with that group, even though he also had physical circumcision. By so doing, he anticipated the discussion of the choices which became apparent when he chose Christ (3:7ff.). By stating that "we" were the true circumcision, Paul associated himself with Gentiles and Jews who relied on Christ rather than religious ritual.

The three characteristics involve worship, glory, and confidence. First, true believers worshiped by the Spirit of God. Using a term that often referred to temple service (*latreuō*), Paul identified inward, spiritual worship in contrast to the legalism of outward conformity to the law. The Spirit energizes and focuses Christian worship. Second, true believers glory in Christ Jesus. The term "glory" means to boast (*kauchaomai*), and Paul consciously contrasted the boasting of good works with boasting that is in the work of Christ. Third, true believers have no confidence in the flesh. Again he referred to a righteousness that trusts in human initiative and energy to gain spiritual blessing. Paul came to the place where he realized his own efforts were useless, and that attitude paved the way for his trust in Christ.

---

[12]The sound-alike is with the ending of the words "circumcision" (περιτομή) and "mutilation" (κατατομή). The KJV attempts to capture this pattern by translating the contrasts as "circumcision . . . concision." The NIV misses Paul's rhetorical device entirely.

[13]This is clear in Paul's handling of Timothy and Titus. Timothy was circumcised *before* his journeys with Paul (Acts 16:3) in order not to be offensive to his Jewish countrymen. Paul forbade Titus to be circumcised, however, because he was Greek, and circumcision would only hinder his ministry to his countrymen (Gal 2:3).

Following this general description of Christians, Paul appealed to his background as proof of his point. The immediate concern was "confidence in the flesh." Since that attitude is basic to all human life—all naturally trust in their own abilities—Paul picked up that point. Further, it seemed to be the pride of the Jewish opponents and, therefore, their downfall. They trusted in their flesh to gain salvation.

Paul's background naturally divides into two logical categories: heredity and achievement. Paul listed seven components which spoke of his background. The last three are introduced by the preposition "according to" (*kata*). They belong together since *kata* provides a standard of measurement and refers to achievements. The other four form the first group, and each identifies some part of Paul's heredity. Clearly, though he had the best of advantages by birth and made the most of his religious opportunities, they fostered a spirit of pride which kept him away from his goal of gaining salvation.

3:4b-5a The natural attributes are identified in a list that includes four components, but their exact relationship to each other is difficult to understand. The pattern of these relationships is one of inclusion.[14] Two statements occur. Paul was "an eighth-day person" ("circumcised on the eighth day," NIV), and he was a "Hebrew of Hebrews." Each of these has a modifier, and the effect is to divide them into two distinct points. First, Paul was a true Israelite. Starting at the point of their interest, he disclosed that, with reference to circumcision, he was an "eighth-day one."[15] If his opponents were circumcised, he was too, and his was completely in accord with the law. Further, he was of the people of Israel. This set him apart from Gentiles. Second, Paul was a Hebrew. The chiastic arrangement (an inverted relationship between the elements of parallel phrases) places the tribe of Benjamin first. He had an enviable ancestry and remained true to that heritage. He was a Hebrew of Hebrews. On one hand, this may have meant he was not a Hellenist or Hellenist sympathizer. Since he was born in Tarsus, his opponents could have assumed that he was. On the other hand, it may have referred to Paul's ability to read the Scriptures in Hebrew. In any case, the stress on the correct pedigree removed a potential question about Paul's credentials when he confronted the Jewish teachers.[16]

---

[14]The inclusion is a grammatical pattern that helps explain the semantic relationships between the components. The first and last components are in the nominative case, and the second and third are in the ablative case. This suggests that the second and third are secondary. Two possibilities exist: The ablatives modify the first nominative; the ablatives modify one nominative each so that a chiasm results. This latter explanation is more likely. This enabled Paul to build his argument to a climax with a "Hebrew of the Hebrews," the high point of his pedigree.

[15]"Circumcision" is a dative of reference which serves to introduce a statement.

[16]Lightfoot, 146-47, provided a good description of the importance of these statements. He also pointed out that the four are in an ascending order, reaching a climax with the fourth statement.

3:5b-6a   Paul moved from heredity to achievement. He had made the correct choices as a Jewish boy and adult. Three items provide the standard to measure these achievements: the law, zeal for the nation, and righteousness.[17] First, Paul had chosen to be a Pharisee. Each devout Jewish male would sympathize with some organized approach to the law since it was the heart of Jewish life. The Pharisees were noted for their love for the law, strict interpretation of it, and ethical consistency. Paul obviously had excelled in all three (see Acts 22:3ff.; 26:5). Second, Paul had persecuted the church. This had been a matter of zeal. In the first century, Jewish men often measured their commitment to God and the nation by how they opposed foreign religion and rule. Since Paul had persecuted the church, he had put into action his love for the nation and the law. He had taken his beliefs to an extreme that even his opponents did not, using physical force to eradicate Christianity (see Acts 9:1-2).[18]

3:6b   Third, Paul had attained the righteousness of the law. Obviously Paul did not mean that he had lived perfectly in accordance with the law. In this context, he boasted of externally verifiable qualities that demonstrated the religious standing he had before he became a Christian. If the other two points regarding achievement could be verified, which was the case, this one must have the same capability. Paul's point was that he had an outwardly perfect record! He had never been accused of breaking any law[19] and, therefore, "showed himself blameless."[20] This does not cancel out the testimony of Rom 7:7-12. At one time, he had perceived himself as "alive, apart from the law" (Rom 7:9) but that time had passed quickly. He knew his inner spiritual condition, but publicly he was above reproach.[21] These seven characteristics of heredity and achievement reveal that Paul's accepting Christ did not occur because he was marginally Jewish. He had not failed in his own religion. He had seen a better way and had chosen to follow it.

TRUE VALUES (3:7-11).   The second section of this warning explains Paul's real values. The false teachers were evil workers (see 3:2). While Paul's evaluation was penetrating, he realized that their outlook was the same as his had been. In fact, the burden of this entire section is carried by a theme of Paul's life before and after Christ. The real value Paul found was in knowing Christ

---

[17] Each of these is introduced by κατά.

[18] Lightfoot stated graphically the sense of Paul's statement: "I persecuted, imprisoned, slew these infatuated Christians; this was my great claim to God's favour" (148).

[19] So M. Silva, *Philippians, WEC* (Chicago: Moody, 1988), 175. His discussion of this verse is quite to the point. It is difficult to determine whether or not the NIV translation "legalistic righteousness" means this or not. It is a good attempt to translate in light of the contextual considerations.

[20] Lightfoot, 148.

[21] K. Stendahl, "The Apostle Paul and the Introspective Conscience of the West," *HTR* 56 (1963): 199-215, takes a different view which has had significant impact on interpretation. He argues that Paul simply chose a better way, and that he had no sense of guilt about his sin. The context, however, seems to support the view taken in this commentary.

personally. That brought a true zeal for perfect character not found through the law.

This section is intensely theological, yet practical. After describing dissatisfaction with his natural attainments, Paul described succinctly and successively what has come to be known in the topical arrangements of classical systematic theology as "justification" (v. 9), "sanctification" (v. 10), and "glorification" (v. 11). Since they occur together under one subject in Paul's testimony, clearly he considered them to be linked together, each growing out of the other. Further, the passage calls to mind 2:5-11, which combined theology and ethics. There are even verbal parallels between the two: "consider" (2:6; 3:7,8), "form" (2:7 "taking the very nature"; 3:10 "becoming like him"), "found" (2:8; 3:9), and "Lord" (2:11; 3:8).[22] Paul probably linked these in his own mind, though they address two very different situations. This passage makes clear, however, that theology and life go together and that the antidote to poor living is proper theology. If the Philippians understood the richness of Paul's life, they would not follow the false teachers.

Evaluation of Paul's Former Life (3:7-8). These two verses are characterized by two consistently employed literary patterns. The first is comparison. Paul compared his pre-Christian life with his life with Christ. The second is progression. Paul described the former and the present life progressively, sometimes with the same words or cognates. This is a powerful passage. It combines personal experience with deep theology. Some have suggested that this is Paul's theology in brief statement.[23]

3:7-8 The first side of the comparison is Paul's terminology for his former life. Three times he described it, and each is progressively more vivid. First, he considered his gains as loss. The perfect tense form of "considered" (*hēgemai*) suggests a completed evaluation with present effects.[24] He came to realize that they were loss. Second, he continued to affirm that decision. In 3:8 the present tense of "consider" joins with the object "loss." Paul meant that this was a proper appraisal and a good decision. The point receives further emphasis by the repetition of the word "loss" in a verbal form: "I have lost all things." Third, in 3:8 Paul expressed his conviction more firmly with the verb "consider" and the object "rubbish" (*skybala*).[25] There is increasing intensity, as though the mere thought of that decision brought a renewed appraisal that his former life was useless compared to what really mattered.

---

[22] These two ideas come from Silva, 178. His analysis of this section is particularly insightful.

[23] Ibid., 177-78. Silva calls this section "The Essence of Pauline Theology." He correctly captures the significance of these verses. They are theology expressed through personal testimony.

[24] This is not a matter of tense only because the perfect can stress the completion of the action or the abiding results. The idea comes from the tense in contrast with the present tense in 3:8 and from the impact of the context.

[25] Some scholars are prone to translate this as "garbage." It is used for "dung," however, and the strongest possible contrast makes best sense of this passage.

Paul reflected on the Damascus road experience (Acts 9:1ff.). At that time he saw the foolishness of his past life and embraced a new way. His negative appraisal, therefore, expressed an important component of salvation. No one can choose Christ who does not reach a similarly negative conclusion about his own efforts.

The other side of the contrast explains why Paul considered his heredity and achievements so useless. They did not bring him to Christ. Three times Paul expressed that the goal was Christ. First, he said it was "for the sake of Christ" (3:7). This is the idea of exchange in seed form. Second, he said it was for the sake of "the surpassing greatness of knowing Christ Jesus my Lord" (3:8). The advance in this statement is that a knowledge of Jesus excelled what Paul had before. The word "surpassing" suggests something of more excellence than that to which it is compared.[26] Therefore, knowing Christ was better than the combined value of his former life. Some interpret this knowledge in a Gnostic context and claim that Paul spoke of a general religious knowledge. This is a Jewish context, however, and the knowledge of which he spoke is probably to be understood in light of the Old Testament "knowledge of God," now applied to Christ. Seen this way, "knowledge" means "a personal response of faith and obedience to God's self-revelation."[27] Third, Paul said he counted all things as loss "that I might gain Christ" (3:8). Here Paul clearly developed the idea of exchange. It was impossible to hold on to the former values and still have Christ. It was one or the other, and Christ exceeded anything and everything else. The three statements express repentance regarding Paul's former attitudes about salvation. He turned away from the past to gain Christ.[28]

Aspiration of the New Life (3:9-11). Paul explained what was better. The structure of the text is somewhat confusing. First, two verbs are parallel, but one explains the other. The parallels are: "that I may gain Christ" (v. 8) and "be found in him" (v. 9). Second, a parenthesis explains what that means—it is having a Christian righteousness, not a legal one. Third, the idea is restated: "that I may know him" (v. 10, KJV). The NIV makes this a new sentence, "I want to know Christ." Finally, the ultimate concern is expressed in v. 11, "to attain to the resurrection from the dead." The section, therefore, has three movements, one for each verse division.

---

[26] The word, ὑπερέχον, occurs only five times in the New Testament, three of which are in Philippians. In 2:3, Christians are to consider others "better." In 4:7, the peace of God is "better" than knowledge. Here, knowledge of Christ is "better" than the former ways.

[27] G. B. Caird, *Paul's Letters from Prison* (Oxford: University Press, 1976), 137. He states further, "Here he takes up the Old Testament phrase and fills it with a specifically Christian content and with a peculiarly personal intensity." Since the Jewish teachers would be particularly offended by Gnostic concepts, it seems best to understand this in terms of its Jewish origins. To this point, at least, there is no hint of Gnostic influence in the epistle.

[28] Repentance is primarily a change of attitude about God, salvation, and sin. The attitude toward sin does not predominate here. However, there is a definite change of attitude about the way of salvation, and thus the passage stresses one aspect of repentance.

3:9 The first statement expresses Paul's existence in relation to Christ. Being in Christ was at the heart of Paul's theology. He saw all persons as either in Adam or in Christ (Rom 5:12-21). His desire to be in Christ meant to be in union with the Lord and thus to have the covering of Christ's righteousness surrounding him and the resources of Christ available to him. Paul equated the words "gain Christ" (v. 8) and "found in him" (v. 9). Together they present two different points of view. From one perspective, Paul gained Christ. From another, he was found in him. The passive verb, "found in him," often has the meaning of "prove to be" or "be present."[29] It takes the perspective of a divine investigation of one's relationships. At the great day of judgment, Paul wanted to be found in Christ.

Significantly, Paul defined being in Christ in terms of righteousness. Being found in Christ means being clothed with God's righteousness rather than one's own. This is the heart of the matter. Fellowship with God is always based on righteousness. The Old Testament makes that clear, for example in the case of Abraham (Gen 15:6; see also Ps 143:12), and Paul continually affirmed it (Rom 4:1ff.). The basic question for all persons is the question of righteousness.

In Scripture, righteousness is often a legal term, not a moral one. It means that a judge would pronounce someone righteous. Naturally, the ideal was that the person would actually be righteous, but the focus is on what the judge said. The verdict did not necessarily depend on the moral realities. In accord with that, the primary question of both Judaism and Christianity was "what must a man do if God is to declare that he is in the right and so give judgment in his favour? The Jewish answer was that he must obey the Law of Moses."[30] For Paul, a righteousness attained by the law was only a relative self-righteousness. The best that could be hoped for was the blamelessness of which he spoke in 3:6b, but which he nonetheless had found inadequate for gaining salvation. Thus, the law provides one approach to righteousness, but it is a flawed approach. The problem is not the law. Paul taught that the law is good (Rom 7). The problem is the sin which indwells each person (Rom 7:13-25). Clearly, no one has the kind of righteousness that will secure a verdict of innocent when God examines the life.

The alternative was God's righteousness. Twice in the context of God's righteousness "righteousness" and "faith" occur (one time "righteousness" is assumed as the subject of the clause). Although they parallel each other, one explains the other by adding to the concept to complete it. First, Paul simply stated that righteousness is through the "faith of Christ" ("faith in Christ," NIV). Further, he clarified that it is a righteousness *from God* and based upon faith.

---

[29] Caird, 137.
[30] Ibid., 138.

The construction "faith of Christ" is ambiguous in Greek. Two questions emerge regarding it, one semantic and the other syntactical. The first is the meaning of the word "faith." The second is the precise meaning of the genitive Greek construction "of Christ."[31] Regarding the meaning of the word "faith," the tension is between the semantically objective meaning (*trust*) and the semantically subjective meaning (*faithfulness*). Both are attested in Scripture (objective, Rom 4:9; subjective, Rom 3:3). Normally Paul meant "faithfulness" when the word was a quality of "God" or "Christ," as it is here.[32] The syntactical question is the nature of the statement "of Christ." It could mean belonging to Christ, produced by Christ, directed to Christ, or simply of Christ.[33] Most likely, it is the faithfulness which is in Christ and should be read "of Christ." This first statement, therefore, appears to mean that righteousness is made available to people through the faithfulness of Christ.

Paul explicitly stated that this righteousness comes to people *from God* and *based on that faithfulness.*[34] Paul rejected his own faithfulness to the law, realizing it was insufficient. His hope was the faithfulness of Christ. This verse, then, brings a knowledge of how God makes his righteousness available: It is through Jesus' faithfulness and a person's total reliance on him.

The passage further contrasts Christ and the law. Paul never spoke against the law. Rather, he spoke about the individual's inability to keep it. In this text he contrasted two means of coming to God: by works and by grace. If one chooses works, the law sets the standards and determines the success of that endeavor. Paul had tried that and found it unacceptable. If one chooses grace, Christ's life and death become the hope. Paul found grace and faith to be the

---

[31]The literature is growing on this subject. The most comprehensive recent monograph on the subject is R. Hays, *The Faith of Jesus Christ: An Investigation of the Narrative Substructure of Galatians 3:1-4:11,* SBLDS 56 (Chico, Calif.: Scholars, 1983), esp. 158ff. An earlier historical, syntactical, and theological survey may be found by this author in "A Study in the Concept of Belief: A Comparison of the Gospel of John and the Epistle to the Romans" (Unpublished doctoral dissertation, Southwestern Baptist Theological Seminary, 1976, 173-89). Other significant contributions include J. Barr, *The Semantics of Biblical Language* (London: Oxford University Press, 1961), 161-205; and criticisms of Hays by M. Silva in *Conflict and Context: Hermeneutics in the Americas,* ed. M. L. Branson and C. R. Padilla (Grand Rapids: Eerdmans, 1986), 274-80.

[32]The adjective πιστός occurs frequently with "God" and "Christ" as a quality meaning "faithful," so the idea is not foreign to New Testament thought (of God: 1 Cor 1:9; 1 Cor 10:13; 2 Cor 1:18; 1 Thess 5:24; 2 Tim 2:13; Heb 10:23; 1 Pet 4:19; 1 John 1:9; of Christ: 2 Thess 3:3; Heb 2:17; 3:2; Rev 1:5; 3:14). When πίστις is followed by a genitive of person, faith is a quality of that person, i.e., God (Rom 3:3), Abraham (Rom 4:12), and Christ (Rom 3:22). When it occurs with God or Christ, however, the objective meaning of "trust" does not apply since "trust" is not a quality of God. A rule develops: when applied to deity, it means faithfulness; when applied to man, it may mean either.

[33]These would be possessive, subjective, objective, or descriptive genitives respectively.

[34]The same argument occurs in Rom 3:21ff. and Gal 2:20. A related idea occurs in Gal 3:26 which states "faith in Jesus Christ," and one wonders why the difference in the construction (ἐν rather than the simple genitive).

only way to have fellowship with God. Grace means that persons cast themselves on the mercy of God, trusting that what Jesus did will be applied to them. Grace freed Paul from self-effort *to gain* salvation and enabled him to devote himself to the things that *follow* salvation. The problem with the false teachers Paul countered was that they had not learned what Paul had learned.

There is also a contrast between two "righteousnesses." Keeping the law produced an *achieved* righteousness; trusting Christ brought an *imputed* righteousness. Paul's hope was the righteousness that God gave.

3:10 Paul turned his thoughts to knowing Christ. Some understand the words "know Christ" (which are an infinitive in Greek) to express the purpose of gaining Christ and being found in him. In this sense, the purpose of being found in him would be to come to know him. That seems somewhat awkward for Paul but is a possibility. A better approach is to understand the infinitive as consecutive, further defining "to be found in him" (v. 9). This, then, gives the content of Paul's deep desire, i.e., to come to know Christ in a life-shaping way.

In this verse two ideas complement each other: the power of Christ's resurrection and the fellowship of sharing in his sufferings. They provide a theological foundation for Paul's thought, as well as a model for Christian growth. Christians must be like their Lord.[35] Here another chiasm occurs. The first elements are the power of his resurrection (v. 10) and attaining the resurrection from the dead (v. 11). The second elements are fellowship of sharing in sufferings (v. 10) and becoming like him in his death (v. 10). The literary arrangement indicates that Paul's deepest ambition was resurrection power. While the chiasm expresses these four statements in two, the logical order preserved Paul's theology.

3:11 The definition of resurrection power depends on Christ's experience since the only available model is Christ. The power displayed through Christ's resurrection is also available through Christ. It is divine power and all of God's attributes appear in Christ. Resurrection power has two phases. First, at conversion believers experience the power of a spiritual resurrection. They are given new life.[36] A new spiritual energy characterizes the new life in Christ. Yet this powerful life only begins at conversion. Successively and progressively the moral life must be changed, the physical body ultimately transformed, and believers brought to the eternal resting place of resurrection, heaven itself. The transformation does not happen at once. It culminates in the attaining of the resurrection from the dead. The resurrection occurs at the time of the Lord's return to earth. (1 Thess 4:13-18). That will finalize the application of resurrection power to the Christian.

Paul longed for the complete resurrection in his own life. Any contemplation of existence without the completed process made him uncomfortable

---

[35] The frequent references to Christ in this passage unmistakably speak to this point.

[36] See the commentary on Col 2:8-3:4.

because no one can conceive of himself without a body.[37] Resurrection power achieves the entire process. Paul's longing to know Christ, therefore, was a longing to be like Christ in his glorified state.

Knowing Christ also meant identifying with his death. This involved participating in suffering and being conformed to his death. Paul spoke of sharing in Christ's sufferings in various ways,[38] but here he paralleled Rom 6:1-11. In Romans the suffering was the death of Christ into which Paul had been baptized. He thus participated in what Christ did for him when he died.[39] Paul did not expect to contribute to Christ's sufferings, i.e., by taking on himself some redemptive suffering as Jesus did, neither did he mean that he would suffer and die as Jesus did. The theological substructure of this passage is the Christian's identification with Christ.[40]

Paul also spoke of his identification with Christ's death. Being united with Christ in his death was a spiritual reality, but being conformed to his death was the daily process of living. Again Rom 6:11 provides the theological parallel. The task of the Christian is, in part, to realize that the nature of salvation is a death. By constantly choosing that death to sin and self, a conformity to Jesus' death occurs. Jesus completely died to self and became a sacrifice for others. It was the greatest demonstration of commitment to the will of God, and it was that death which brought his resurrection life. Paul realized that conformity to Jesus' death made him a candidate for resurrection power. This helps explain the spiritual discipline mentioned in 3:12-16.

In longing to know Christ, therefore, Paul sought a complete relationship with him. Situations may differ, but each Christian has the hope that resurrection power results from death and that conformity to Jesus' death brings life. In fact, the more obedient one is to Christ, thus conformed to his death, the more resurrection power becomes available. Further, Paul longed for the completion of his Christian hope. Someday he would enjoy complete transformation of character, newness of body, and a perfect environment. He would live in heaven with his Lord.

---

[37]This is the burden of 2 Cor 5:1-10. He longed there to be clothed with the new body, at which time the work of salvation will be complete. In that text, he also implied that he expected a time when he would be in heaven without his body, i.e., a "naked state." Since the body is both the vehicle through which we communicate and receive communication and the "housing" which shapes our self-identity, we cannot conceive of existence without it. The dead in Christ will have an intermediate state of existence, but Paul looked forward to the completion of salvation.

[38]See, for example, Rom 8:17; 2 Cor 1:5; Col 1:24; Acts 9:16. See also the commentary on Col 1:24.

[39]This preserves the basic meaning of "participation" which the Greek κοινωνία implies. It has little to do with "completing tribulations," as Col 1:24 states. Rather, it is expressive of "benefitting from" by participation.

[40]W. Grundmann, *TDNT,* 7:786-87, provides a full range of compound words used to express the theology of identification with Christ.

TRUE ZEAL (3:12-16).   Paul's attention turned to true zeal in living the Christian life. He continued his argument against his Jewish opponents through his personal experience. What should occupy the thoughts and focus the energy of genuine Christians?

The passage falls into two distinct parts. First, in 3:12-14, Paul expressed his desire to achieve what God had in store for him. Then, in 3:15-16 he issued a call to follow his pattern of living. The Greek of this section is particularly difficult, but the thrust is abundantly clear. Paul was in the process of achieving. In case he was misunderstood in 3:4-11, he clarified that he had not yet arrived. One of the key words of the passage is "pursue" ("press on," NIV; *diōkō*, 3:12,14). It stresses an active commitment to the call of Christ.

Some commentators suggest that in this section Paul addressed his opponents. They say that he consciously countered a perfectionistic group, sometimes called "divine men," who claimed their own completeness. Others suggest that Paul produced this section because the Jewish opponents of 3:2 taught that perfection could be achieved by keeping the law. Still others see Paul continuing the logic of 3:4-11, issuing a warning because of a tendency to misunderstand his teaching. His introduction of 3:15 with the words "all of us who are mature," (lit., "perfect"), however, suggests that there may have been some irony in his tone. The context does not require an opponent, and it is unlikely that he envisioned one. A group within the church may have misunderstood his teaching on justification and taken it to their own "logical" conclusions, which were theologically unacceptable.

Paul's Desire to Fulfill His Call (3:12-14). **3:12-13a** Twice, in similar terms, Paul expressed his imperfection. The first expression presents this in three ways (v. 12), and the second expression summarizes the three ways into one (v. 13). The three are: "Not that I have already obtained," "have already been made perfect," and "I press on." The basic question is, What did Paul lack and, therefore, seek? Three times the word root for "received" occurs (3:12; *lambanō*; *katalambanō*, twice). The word is ambiguous, and no object occurs with it.

The precise definition may refer to mental or experiential attainment. Used of the mind, it means *to understand* (or *understand fully* with *katalambanō*).[41] This would mean that Paul did not yet understand the significance of Christ or that he did not know him completely. If the use were experiential, "to grasp something," Paul stated that he did not yet have in hand what he desired. The understood object of the verbs would determine which definition applies.

What did Paul hope to attain? In these verses two phrases suggest an answer: "have already been made perfect" and "Christ Jesus took hold of me." "Have

---

[41] See, e.g., John 1:5; Acts 4:13; Eph 3:18. *BAGD*, 464-65, lists several meanings for the term. It states that Phil 3:12 means "to make one's own, apprehend or comprehend mentally or spiritually."

already been made perfect" (*teteleiōmai*) occurs only here in the Pauline corpus. It contrasts with the verb "obtained." Through his past experiences ("obtained," aorist tense), Paul had not yet achieved completion (*katalambanō*, perfect tense).[42] The question is whether Paul referred to a perfect knowledge or experience. Was his call to a complete knowledge of Christ or to a complete identification with him in character?

The context has a bearing on the problem (3:9-11).[43] Those who understand Paul's desire in the mental sense, to know Christ completely, point out that the primary verb in these verses is "that I may know him" (see 3:10). That knowledge, then, involved knowing Christ's power and suffering. Because that knowledge was related closely to experience, clearly he wanted to know in his experience the full implications of his union with Christ. However, the text seems to argue against that understanding.[44]

Those who understand Paul's desire in the experiential sense point out that the object of the verb "obtained" is "the resurrection from the dead" of 3:11. It seems best, therefore, to understand Paul as saying he had not completed the experiential process begun in his salvation. He looked forward to the resurrection from the dead and, secondarily, to the process of conformity to death which would bring it forth.

"The resurrection" fits this context and answers the problems raised in the text. First, it easily explains why Paul had not attained. He looked to the end of time when the resurrection would occur. Second, it is helpful to remember that a first-century heresy stated that the resurrection was already past. Paul countered it in 2 Tim 2:18 (cf. 1 Cor 15:12ff.; 2 Thess 2:2). Something similar may have concerned Paul here when he pointedly affirmed the necessity of continued growth.[45] Third, this fits well with Paul's prayer in 1:9-11. He hoped to be pure and blameless at the day of Christ. Fourth, the idea of "the power of the resurrection" (v. 10) must be taken with the death that precedes it. Thus the thought of conformity to the will of God ("becoming like him in his death," v. 10) continued to be a goal because resurrection power is available in death. The best explanation of this desire is that Paul looked ahead to the completion of his salvation.

---

[42] See A. T. Robertson, *A Grammar of the Greek New Testament in the Light of Historical Research* (Nashville: Broadman, 1934), 901.

[43] This is known by the flow of thought and the fact that the objects of these verbs are omitted. The rule of thumb is that no object needs to be supplied if the existing subject naturally supplies it. That rule applies here. Thus the Greek text looks back to these verses to find its object.

[44] This objection is that, in typical Jewish fashion, Paul thought of knowledge as applied to action; it was experiential. Therefore, even if the stress of these verses is on knowledge, it is on knowing by experience, a concept quite in keeping with the meaning of the verb chosen, γινώσκω. For a complete defense of the "knowledge" position, see Hawthorne, 151ff.

[45] The theological misunderstanding involved the denial of a physical resurrection, which Paul countered by implication here as well.

3:13b-14   The content of Paul's goal is given. Repeating the word "press on" of v. 12, Paul employed athletic imagery to make his point.[46] Since the Greek athletic games captured the imagination of all of the peninsula, Macedonia included, it spoke vividly to the readers.[47] The manner of attainment is explained by two participles. First, "forgetting what is behind" comprehensively expresses Paul's future orientation. What was done was done! Both the nostalgia of the former life and the "good ole days" of his Christian life would paralyze him in terms of what God wanted in the future. Every day was a new adventure. Second, he was "straining toward what is ahead." This word continues the athletic metaphor. It is particularly graphic, bringing to mind the straining muscles, clear focus, and complete dedication of the runner in his race to the prize. Both mental and physical discipline were necessary.

The goal is the heavenward call of Jesus Christ. The text is ambiguous here. The "goal" ("mark," KJV; *skopos*) is the "goal marker" in English.[48] It was the focus of the eye when a runner ran the race. For Paul, it was probably the model provided in Christ who demonstrated both obedience unto death and the resurrection. The prize is explained as the heavenward call (*anō*). The NIV translates it, "for which God has called me heavenward," correctly seeing that the word *anō* refers to heaven as opposed to earth.[49] The translation seems to make the call at the beginning of the race, however, rather than the end. That corresponds to Paul's life if the call is understood as at the time of conversion, but there is no hint of that here. It seems best to take it as the call associated with the resurrection. At that day there will be a call to heaven. Further, in 3:21, Paul mentioned the resurrection and the transformation that will occur then. He lived for the day when the heavenward call would come, like a victory in a race. Rather than slack off, as some were prone to do, the thought of it motivated him to further purity and service. He would get to know every dimension of Christ (reign and suffering), through every means. The joy of the process kept him going, but he realized that the ultimate joy was the completion of God's work in his life.[50]

Paul's Encouragement to Other Believers (3:15-16).   Paul came to his point at the end of this section. His experience correctly set a pattern for all believers. If they would understand it and join with him, they would avoid the

---

[46]The word "press on," διώκω, means "to run swiftly in order to catch some person or thing." (ThayLex, 153). It was used in both hunting and athletics. As to the former, it described the pursuit of game, stalking it with relentlessness. In athletics it meant to run so as to gain the victory.

[47]The imagery is well developed by Hawthorne, 154.

[48]Ibid.

[49]See the notes on Col 3:1-4.

[50]The syntax of the interpretation is as follows: "toward the goal" (κατὰ σκοπόν) provides a standard of measurement, strictly, and is not the goal in sight (therefore Christ is the model and standard); "unto the prize" expresses the direction of the striving; "of the heavenly call" (τῆς ἄνω κλήσεως) is appositional, expressing what the call is. It is a call to "come up" to heaven, just as victors ascended the victory platforms.

influence of the false teachers. Three movements occur in this command to the church: a call to unity, a warning of misconduct, and an exhortation to continue.

3:15a   First, Paul called the Philippians to unity. The words "take such a view of things" use the verb "be minded" which characterized 2:1-11. It occurs again later in this verse. The word includes both thoughts and values. The church was to value these truths as Paul did. Several problems occur in this verse. First, who did Paul mean by the word "mature"? He called the believers "mature" ("perfect," *teleios*), but in light of the relative infrequency of the word as a description of persons, questions arise.[51] Two primary possibilities exist regarding it. Conceivably, Paul addressed a group of people who shared his outlook and were perfect in their understanding of their imperfection or in their desires to be perfected. This meaning requires different uses of two words built on the same root, which is awkward.[52] On the other hand, Paul could have been speaking in irony, addressing a group of people who assumed they were perfect. If so, he was calling them to admit their imperfect knowledge about such matters and accept his evaluation.[53] The choice between the meanings is difficult, but the latter is likely the correct reading.

3:15b   Second, Paul warned about misconduct. The interpretation depends in part on knowing who Paul addressed. It could have been a correction to the false teachers or instructions to mature Christians. Some scholars take the position that Paul meant that those who differed with him had a right to their own positions because ultimately the way they thought did not matter. That hardly seems consistent with Paul's attitude.[54] Others argue that Paul really meant it would do little good to try to convince the false teachers of their error. God would reveal it to them.[55] Another possibility is that Paul turned his thoughts to the general problem of disunity in the congregation, which he addressed in 4:2ff.[56] Paul did address the mature and realized that God would work in them. Further, his words were corrective, i.e., that God would correct their wrong attitudes in the course of time. Their misunderstanding involved their perfectionistic ideas, which had reached a deep level of personal commitment, evidenced by Paul's use of the term "think differently" (*phroneō*).[57]

---

[51] Paul employed the term eight times, but only descriptively of persons who had "attained perfection" twice (1 Cor 2:6; Phil 3:15). He did speak of it as a goal of maturity several times (1 Cor 14:20; Eph 4:13; Col 1:28; 4:12).

[52] The verb τελειόω (3:12) expressed his imperfection; the adjective τέλειος (3:15) would be awkward in a different meaning.

[53] This was suggested by Lightfoot, 153, and developed more fully by Hawthorne, 156.

[54] Caird, 144-45, provides eight convincing reasons why that approach cannot be correct.

[55] Hawthorne, 156.

[56] Silva, *Philippians*, 206. This seems quite unlikely since it makes an abrupt shift in the text.

[57] The Greek adverb "differently" occurs only here in the New Testament. Outside the New Testament, it has the idea of having "the wrong frame of mind." Silva, *Philippians*, 207.

3:16 Third, Paul gave an exhortation. The believers were to remain steadfast. What they achieved to this point was to guide them into the future as the standard by which they would walk collectively. Here Paul used another relatively rare term, which the NIV translates "let us live up to" (*stoicheō*). Generally it means an *orderly walk* or *a disciplined walk*. It has overtones of a collective discipline, of all walking in the same row or by the same measure.[58] Two emphases appear in this sentence. First, they were to remain true to what they had. Second, they were to remain true with a collective discipline that was to characterize the entire church. This meant that they would not follow the infatuating teachings of Paul's opponents, and it also meant that they would seek to implement in their own lives what they already knew to do.[59] That included knowing Christ and looking forward to the resurrection.

The last sentence summarizes this section by presenting a challenge to continue in the faith. Obviously some believers had tendencies toward deviating from what they had learned from Paul. In rebuking the false teachers, Paul presented his own testimony and urged the group at large to have the same attitude. While the exhortation related primarily to 3:12-16, it ended Paul's first line of apology against his opponents. It also placed faith in the church members' attitudes and ability to continue in the things they had learned.

(2) The False Teachers' Character Exposed (3:17-21)

[17]Join with others in following my example, brothers, and take note of those who live according to the pattern we gave you. [18]For, as I have often told you before and now say again even with tears, many live as enemies of the cross of Christ. [19]Their destiny is destruction, their god is their stomach, and their glory is in their shame. Their mind is on earthly things. [20]But our citizenship is in heaven. And we eagerly await a Savior from there, the Lord Jesus Christ, [21]who, by the power that enables him to bring everything under his control, will transform our lowly bodies so that they will be like his glorious body.

Paul continued to warn the church about the false teachers. The format remains the same as vv. 1-16: the literary pattern is comparison and contrast. Now, however, the text moves to plural rather than singular subjects so that the entire church is included (vv. 20-21). Some interpreters see a change of opponents to the libertines; others see a consistent reference to enthusiastic Jewish teachers, as at vv. 1-16. They were probably the same opponents. If they were a new group, Paul handled them in a veiled manner, with no introduction and no conclusion to their teaching. Paul also implicitly described them as non-

---

[58]*BAGD*, 769, says "be in line with, stand beside, hold to, agree with, follow." It occurs in the New Testament in Acts 21:24; Rom 4:12; Gal 5:25; 6:16.

[59]W. Schenk, *Die Philipperbrief des Paulus Kommentar* (Stuttgart: W. Kohlhammer, 1984). Cited in Silva, 207. Schenk states that ἐφθάσαμεν is equivalent to κατελήμφθην, so that "what we have already attained" equals "what we received." That would tie the passage together and form a fitting end to the section.

Christian. They were enemies of the cross (v. 18), their citizenship was on earth rather than heaven (v. 20), and they did not have the same destiny as Paul and the church (v. 21).[60] Structurally, after an introductory statement setting the direction for these verses (v. 17), Paul described the opponents (vv. 18-19) and then contrasted them with true believers (vv. 20-21).

ENCOURAGMENT TO IMITATE PAUL (3:17).   **3:17** Earlier Paul urged the church to imitate Christ (2:5-11); here he urged the Philippians to imitate him. The theme occurs in other places in Paul's writing (1 Cor 4:16; 11:1; 2 Thess 3:7-9), but it seems awkward to the present-day Christian. There is no egotism here, as two factors in the text make apparent. First, he realized that they would follow other Christian models as well. The words "join with others in following my example" [61] naturally meant that they would follow Paul, but later in the verse he urged them to follow others with the same goal. Second, vv. 1-16 reveal that imitation is the literary style Paul used. He recalled his own experience to persuade them to follow him. To state that they should follow him was no more prideful than the pattern he employed in this chapter. It rather grew out of it.[62]

In addition, Paul urged them to imitate others who were like-minded. The word for "take note of" (*skopeō*) occurs elsewhere in this passage. It meant the Philippians were to have the lives of others in their sights or to make living like these their aim. In Paul's absence they were to find other models who were true to his commitments. The principles Paul taught worked in the lives of their friends, who could be followed in Paul's absence.

CHARACTERISTICS OF PAUL'S OPPONENTS (3:18-19). **3:18**   Paul delivered his final blow against the false teachers. Emotion characterizes the text, and Paul confessed his tears as he wrote. It is the only recorded instance that the apostle Paul cried. Why was there such emotional involvement with these deceptive teachers? Paul described them and then explained their characteristics. He was sad, first of all, because he had to make repeated warnings about them. They apparently followed him about, seeking to entice people away from the truth. Doubtless, repeated efforts to counter that brought on fatigue. Second, he called them enemies of the cross. The statement must mean more than that they refused to accept the cross as God's way of reconciliation. It means that they actively opposed the message of the cross and hindered those who would take advantage of its work. Paul cherished the cross. For him, the fact

---

[60]This is an implication from the way the contrast proceeds.

[61]The word has the common Greek prefix "with" (σύν), which typically describes the theme of being "in Christ." The reference does not explicitly mean that others were following Paul—it could be that he meant others along with him were following Christ. The former would not be too harsh, however, because Paul did in fact set the pace for many people.

[62]A. T. Robertson, *Paul's Joy in Christ: Studies in Philippians* (Nashville: Broadman, n.d.) insightfully says: "Keep your eye on the goal if you can see it. If not, keep your eye on one who knows the way to the goal and who is going there" (118).

that the false teachers did not revealed who they were. The strong emotion parallels the emotion of Rom 9:1-3, where Paul prayed that he could be anathema for his kinsmen. Apparently these teachers were his own people who should have accepted the Messiah, but they chose instead to hinder the truth wherever they could.[63] This was organized, active opposition to the gospel.

3:19 Paul exposed these teachers by revealing their character. Four statements explain their theology and practice, although little is known about them. The first characteristic looks to their eternal condition: Their end was destruction. Destruction does not necessarily mean *loss of existence* since its opposite is salvation (1:28).[64] The direction they were going was enough to warn the church. The second and third characteristics point to the way they had lived before that time. These two belong together because they are linked in the Greek text by one relative pronoun.[65] Those who identify the opponents as libertines point out that Paul decried excessive food and sexual pleasures. Since this is a Jewish context, the statement must refer to dietary laws and circumcision of which they were so proud. They had become so preoccupied with kosher foods that they spent more time contemplating them than thinking about God.[66] Similarly, they were preoccupied with their circumcision, boasting of it wherever they went. Although Paul generally did not speak of circumcision as a shame, here the term applied because of the focus on the genitals, which should have been a private matter. When made public, it was distasteful. Clearly, these matters engendered pride in the teachers, and Paul criticized them severely. Finally, they minded earthly things. Since they were earthly in orientation,[67] their religious shortsightedness came because they could not see beyond time into eternity.

CHARACTERISTICS OF TRUE BELIEVERS (3:20-21). **3:20-21** Paul ended this comparison by presenting a Christian perspective. He specifically contrasted the earthly with the heavenly. Paul stated that "our citizenship is in heaven." The metaphor had rich meaning to the Philippians.[68] Immediately their thoughts would have turned to an analogy with their earthly citizenship. They were proud of their Roman citizenship, but the analogy would have con-

---

[63] In a similar vein, Paul explained the Jewish opposition as a "hindrance to all men" in 1 Thess 2:13-16. The similarities between the passages and Rom 9:1-3 suggest he had the same persons in mind.

[64] It is also used of the lost who are physically alive in Luke 19:10.

[65] Two relative pronouns introduce the first three characteristics. The first, ὧν, literally reads "whose end is destruction." The second relative ὧν joins the two into one clause and reads literally "whose God is their stomach and their glory is in their shame." The next characteristic does not have the relative pronoun introducing it.

[66] Food was a major concern to the religions of the first century. It came into the Christian churches as well (e.g., Rom 14-15; 1 Cor 8-10; Col 2:8-10). The issues were complex, but this one seems to be rooted in the Old Testament regulations.

[67] The discussion on Col 2:20-3:4 helps explain this from Paul's perspective.

[68] See the introduction for the significance of the city as a colony with Roman citizenship.

veyed more. Philippi was an outpost colony, and, interestingly, Paul was at the home base in Rome. Regularly they awaited news from the capital to know how to conduct their business. When Paul said that they belonged to a citizenship, he spoke directly to them. Though they belonged to a city, the political entity spanned several geographical areas. Similarly, the church was an outpost of an entity which had its own capital, heaven. Although "citizenship" may call to mind a place, Paul used it of a people. They awaited the Savior from that citizenship. He would come with power sufficient to subdue everything and with ability to transform their bodies to be like his. They would naturally associate subduing power with a Roman emperor, but transforming power was unique to Christ. Once again, Paul spoke of the resurrection as the climax of his Christian experience. By implication, the false teachers would not share in the resurrection of the just because their expectations were earthly rather than heavenly.

One final point occurs in v. 21. Paul focused on the physical body which would be transformed so that it became like Christ's body. Two factors are significant. First, the body is destined for eternity. It should be treated accordingly, and people should not make earthly existence *in the body* their ultimate concern. The tragedy of the false teachers was, in part, that they did just that. They focused on some aspect of the body that would not last beyond this life.[69] Second, Paul's hope involved a physical transformation. His theology included the fact that redemption culminated in a change of the body itself. The spirit was already in a resurrection with Christ; the body awaited that change.[70] This statement reiterates the hope expressed in v. 10. The power of the resurrection would be complete when Jesus exerted his power toward the bodies of believers. Paul characterized the body now as one of humiliation (*tapeinōseōs*). In so doing, he addressed the limitations Christians have on earth. The body is not suited to heaven unless a transformation takes place. In that sense, it symbolizes a Christian's state of humiliation. Someday, however, it will be a body of glory, fully suited to the needs of heaven and displaying the glory of Christ himself. This was a significant hope, fully pastoral in motivation. It should have caused the believers to press on until that great day.

2. Miscellaneous Exhortations (4:1-9)

Paul's mind turned to various matters in the church. Throughout the epistle there are hints of disunity among the congregation, and Paul countered that disunity with strong doctrinal (2:1-11) and practical (2:12-18) instruction. This chapter presents the only tangible evidence as to what the problem might have been, and the evidence is scarce. Several exhortations occur in these verses: to steadfastness (4:1), to unity (4:2-3), to joy and peace (4:4-7), and to the proper outlook (4:8-9).

---

[69] Again, Col 2:20-3:4 should be read in this light.

[70] E.g., Rom 8:19-25; 1 Cor 15:42-44, 50-54.

Some interpreters question where this section begins. Since 4:1 is obviously transitional, a case may be made for including it in the previous section. Grammatically it is natural for a "so then" (*hōste*) clause to look forward.[71] There is a parallel in 2:12, which, looking forward in the text, applies the truths of Jesus' self-emptying to the church. Here, Paul applied the truths of chpt. 3 to the practical church life. For that reason, 4:1 is included in the exhortations of the final chapter.

(1) Exhortation to Steadfastness (4:1)

[1]Therefore, my brothers, you whom I love and long for, my joy and crown, that is how you should stand firm in the Lord, dear friends!

4:1 Immediately Paul changed his tone in this verse. The previous passage contains the emotion of argumentation; now he spoke with the warmth of a dear friend. Two sections occur in this verse: the address to the readers and the exhortation.

THE ADDRESS TO THE READERS. In the address Paul made three statements about the church. First, the members were "brothers." The term occurs frequently in Philippians[72] and helps express the oneness they had with each other and with Paul. Second, he said, "whom I love and long for." The first term, built on a form of *agapē*, stresses the strong tie that bound them together in love. The second word, "long for," occurs only here in the New Testament. It speaks of Paul's desire to fellowship together.[73] Just because they were Christian brothers did not guarantee that Paul would feel this way about them. Their relationship grew out of the fellowship in the gospel. Third, Paul called them his "joy and crown." These terms turned the readers' thoughts to the end of time. Joy is a common theme in the epistle. This use is unique, however, because the church *was* Paul's joy. He did not mean that they replaced the joy of the Lord, but rather that life was better because he knew them. They brought him joy even while he was awaiting trial. Further, their response to the gospel would bring him joy on judgment day. The imagery of the crown speaks of the reward God gives. The Philippian believers were Paul's crown. The fact that they believed guaranteed Paul's rewards. Clearly, a strong tie existed between Paul and the church.[74]

EXHORTATION. Out of this friendship grew exhortation. Paul urged them to steadfastness. Perhaps the language came from the military and, therefore, had significant meaning for the city populated by military families. The Roman

---

[71]Moule, 144, says it is an inferential particle, meaning "and so, accordingly." These suggest the possibility of a forward-looking idea as well.

[72]1:12; 3:1,13,17; 4:1; 4:8,21.

[73]*BAGD* translates ἐπιπόθητοι "longed for, desired," 298. Hawthorne, 178, says it is the emotion of "homesick tenderness."

[74]The passage parallels 1 Thess 2:19-20 and Phil 2:16.

armies were known for standing unmoved against the enemy. The church was to stand in the same way. A more significant question is, How was it to stand? The words "that is how" translate the Greek *houtōs*, a word that shows manner. The church was not to be weakened by disunity, turmoil, or wrong values. It was to stand together to accomplish God's will. The exhortation recalls 1:27, and it was an important aspect of church life.

(2) Exhortation to Unity (4:2-3)

[2]I plead with Euodia and I plead with Syntyche to agree with each other in the Lord. [3]Yes, and I ask you, loyal yokefellow, help these women who have contended at my side in the cause of the gospel, along with Clement and the rest of my fellow workers, whose names are in the book of life.

4:2-3 At this point Paul addressed the problem of unity. It is the first specific problem known about the church, but Paul may have been concerned with it from the beginning of the epistle. The location of this discussion in the epistle suggests two different characteristics of the problem. On one hand, its occurrence in a prominent place in this section of the epistle suggests that the problem had some significance. It was more than a passing disagreement. It had the potential of splitting the church into two groups. On the other hand, it occurs near the end of the epistle and is handled in a relatively soft manner. Apparently it was not enough of a problem to cause Paul undue alarm. Paul had faith in the women themselves and the church's ability to correct the problem.

Nothing is known about these women or the dispute between them. Many scholars have attempted to identify them, but the conclusions are all conjecture, and the best course of action is to stay within the bounds of Scripture.[75] Some suggestions may be drawn from the knowledge of Acts and Philippi. Women occupied a prominent place in the church. They were among the first converts. The controversy occurred between two notable women who played a major part in church life. Whatever the cause, several factors emerge about the problem: It was significant enough that the women could not solve it themselves; it probably was not a doctrinal problem since Paul spoke to such matters when they arose; it was divisive enough to cause the church to write to Paul about it; the entire church was asked to intercede on behalf of these women;[76] and the fellowship and ministry of the church faced a major crisis because of it.

In writing how to solve the problem, Paul identified a process and a reason for it. The process began with the women themselves. In addressing them,

---

[75]Lightfoot, 158, provided the evidence for the names in the inscriptions. Hawthorne, 179, surveys the kinds of suggestions that have been made regarding their identity.

[76]Certainly that was the point of making the problem public in an epistolary form. Some go further and suggest that the "yokefellow" is the church at large, an unlikely conclusion. (Hawthorne, 180, reaches this conclusion perhaps because Clement was also named in the text.)

Paul used the term "I plead with" twice, once before each woman's name. The repetition stressed the personal interest Paul felt, and it also called them to reconciliation. Naturally, the best solution was for them to solve their own problem. The word translated "agree" (*phroneō*) is encountered frequently in this epistle. These women were to have the same attitudes and values that Christ had (2:5-11).

If the women could not resolve the problem themselves, they were to secure a mediator. Apparently the dispute was not moral, and neither woman was guilty of theological heresy. If so, Paul would have urged the erring one to submit to the Lord and the church.[77] This was a true disagreement, and a third party could help resolve it. Paul simply identified the third party as "loyal yokefellow." Throughout history, many scholars have attempted to identify this person, but too little evidence exists.[78] Some conclude that this is a name, Suzuge, and therefore Paul appealed to a prominent person in the church.

Next, Paul presented reasons for helping the women. First, they were Christian sisters. The last statement reveals Paul's confidence that their names were in the book of life.[79] Paul seldom stated such confidence about people.[80] Second, they fought with Paul for the gospel. Employing an athletic term again, he spoke of their value in the spread of the gospel. They not only helped Paul in his work[81] but also fought alongside Clement and other unnamed fellow workers. Strangely, nothing is known about Clement. Apparently, knowing about Euodia, Syntyche, the yokefellow, and Clement was unimportant. "God *knows* them, and that too as righteous, as his own."[82]

Church government is another interest sparked by this passage. Some suggest that the women had leadership roles in the congregation. However, Paul said nothing about the offices of these women. Nor did he say they preached as they labored for the Lord. Nevertheless, two indications of church order emerge here. First, Paul's appeal to an individual to mediate the problem may indicate that this individual was in a place of authority. Everyone knew both his

---

[77] This is clear in 1 Cor 5:1-5 in morality and in Gal 2:11-14 and 2 Tim 4:10 in theology (assuming Demas's departure was theological). Paul did not hesitate to address persons when he felt they were in error.

[78] Hawthorne, 179-80, provides an excellent list of these attempts. Some are totally speculative, including Paul's wife (possibly Lydia). The best course is silence.

[79] The statement regarding the book of life may refer to the fellow workers of Clement and Paul or to the women. The Greek is unclear. Commentators have taken it both ways. Beare concludes that Paul's certainty regarding it seems to convey the idea "of comrades who have died in the faith" (145). The text more naturally includes these living women in the word "whose." The gender is ambiguous (ὧν), and the phrase "Clement and the rest of my fellow workers" seems parenthetical.

[80] For the book of life, see Exod 32:32-33; Pss 69:28; 139:16; Dan 12:1; Qumran (1QM 12:3); Luke 10:20; Rev 3:5; 20:15; 21:27.

[81] Paul frequently acknowledged women for their contribution to the gospel. Rom 16 contains a list of ten women who significantly helped in his ministry.

[82] K. Barth, *The Epistle to the Philippians* (Richmond: John Knox, 1962), 120.

identity and his right to intervene. Perhaps he was the pastor of the church.[83] Second, the matter became public, and the church was to handle such matters in a way that few do today. The congregation was a partnership. As the body of Christ, the members were to address such matters objectively, frankly, lovingly, and spiritually.[84]

(3) Exhortation to Joy and Peace (4:4-9)

[4]**Rejoice in the Lord always. I will say it again: Rejoice!** [5]**Let your gentleness be evident to all. The Lord is near.** [6]**Do not be anxious about anything, but in everything, by prayer and petition, with thanksgiving, present your requests to God.** [7]**And the peace of God, which transcends all understanding, will guard your hearts and your minds in Christ Jesus.**

[8]**Finally, brothers, whatever is true, whatever is noble, whatever is right, whatever is pure, whatever is lovely, whatever is admirable—if anything is excellent or praiseworthy—think about such things.** [9]**Whatever you have learned or received or heard from me, or seen in me—put it into practice. And the God of peace will be with you.**

These verses naturally divide into two major sections (vv. 4-7; vv. 8-9), but they unite around the theme of peace. In 4:7 Paul wrote of the peace of God that sustains Christians during times of hardship. In 4:9, he wrote of the result of proper thought life (4:8)—the God of peace will be present.

The passages differ from each other in significant ways. Philippians 4:4-7 speaks primarily to those occasions in life when peace is lacking. They are the times when troublesome circumstances interrupt the normal flow of events. Paul gave three commands to help the readers solve these problems. In 4:8-9, Paul organized his thoughts to address the need for a peaceful environment. The cultivation of the proper environment brings with it the God who is peace. Some commentators see these commands as applying to the church collectively rather than to individual Christians. Because of the distributive nature of the Greek plurals, it is impossible to determine this. Often commands made collectively must be implemented individually. The commands also occur in passages describing the application of truth. In these Paul moved from the problems of the church to individual concerns. He probably had both individual Christians and the church in mind.

---

[83] Some apply the passage as though Paul were the pastor of this church. They derive pastoral principles from the text. While some of the principles may apply, Paul was not the pastor of the congregation, nor was he a former pastor intruding into the affairs of a previous pastorate. Care must be exercised in these analogies.

[84] F. Craddock, *Philippians, Interpretation: A Bible Commentary for Teaching and Preaching* (Atlanta: John Knox, 1985), speaks well at this point: "Notice that Paul does not, as some pastors do, regard matters such as this as private, to be settled outside the church lest anyone be disturbed. No, in Paul's view, this is precisely the nature and function of the congregation as a partnership" (70).

Philippians 4:4-7 falls into two sections. Three imperatives are followed by a promise (indicative) for those who followed Paul's words. The first two commands are emphatic.

4:4-5   First, Paul commanded the Philippians to rejoice. He repeated the command immediately, thereby emphasizing its importance. Their joy was to be in the Lord, and it was to be unchanging. The circumstances of Paul's life reminded him of the joy available in the Lord, and he wished that joy for them as well. Paul knew that no situation is beyond the Lord's help. Christians can always rejoice in that, if nothing else.

Second, Paul exhorted them to gentleness. No single word translates *epieikes* well, and commentators consistently insist that the word contains an element of selflessness. The gentle person does not insist on his rights. "It is that considerate courtesy and respect for the integrity of others which prompts a man not to be for ever standing on his rights; and it is preeminently the character of Jesus (2 Cor 10:1)."[85] The word occurs in Paul's writing as a characteristic of Christian leaders (1 Tim 3:3, of bishops; Titus 3:2). Fairness and magnanimity were to be developed so that they were visible to all. They were to characterize the church. Paul made this emphatic by reminding them that the Lord was at hand. The statement sobers Christians for two reasons: He will come as judge, expecting to see this quality in his people; having personified the quality himself, he knows what it is like.

4:6   The third command is negative, but it has a positive thrust: "Do not be anxious about anything." Jesus spoke about anxiety in the Sermon on the Mount (Matt 6:25-34), where he stated the most common causes of anxiety. They are: physical attributes (v. 27); clothing (v. 28); food and drink (v. 31); and the future (v. 34). Even in contemporary life with its complexities, the same simple concerns cause anxiety. Prayer cures anxiety. Here three words describe prayer. Each contributes to a proper understanding of the comprehensive nature of the prayer life.[86] The point, however, is that prayer relieves the problem of anxiety. The center of the verse is the significant part: Prayer is to be offered "with thanksgiving." The attitude of gratitude accompanies all true approaches to the Father.

4:7   The answer to anxiety is the peace of God. Paul made three statements about this peace. First, it is divine peace. He did not envision a situation where circumstances changed or external needs were met. This peace was a characteristic of God which invaded the Christian. Second, it "transcends all understanding." "Transcends" translates the word *hyperechousa* ("excellent"),

---

[85] This excellent definition comes from Caird, 150.

[86] In this context, the three have the following meanings: "'Prayer' (προσευχῇ) denotes the petitioner's attitude of mind as worshipful. 'Petition' (δεήσει) denotes prayers as expressions of need. . . . 'Requests' (αἰτήματα) refers to the things asked for." H. A. Kent, "Philippians," *EBC* (Grand Rapids: Zondervan, 1978), 11:152. These distinctions are based on the context and should not be pressed here or in other texts.

which is found in 2:3; 3:8, and here in a compound form. Paul contrasted knowledge and peace at one point: Peace excels over knowledge. No doubt he had in mind situations where knowledge is insufficient. Sometimes it cannot explain, and sometimes explanations do not help. Peace, however, is always appropriate and meets the need of the heart. Finally, this peace will "guard your hearts and your minds in Christ Jesus." "Guard" is a military term, implying that peace stands on duty to keep out anything that brings care and anxiety. For these reasons, prayerful people are peaceful people.

4:8-9   Paul turned his thoughts to providing an environment of peace by unified thought. The church was to make these matters its collective goal, and God would rule in them. Individual Christians were to also conduct their lives in this way. This speaks to the need of rearranging life and thought through discipline so that the God of peace can freely work.[87]

These verses have a definite structure. They contain two lists, each introduced by its own verb. The first list completes a clause with the main verb "think about such things" (*logizesthe*, v. 8). The word means far more than simple thought. The church was to count on these things and to chart its course according to them. The second list completes the verb "put into practice" (*prassete*, v. 9). By using these two verbs, Paul combined the mental and ethical concerns of his Jewish background with Christian thought. For him, knowledge always led to responsible Christian living. Some scholars point out that many secular moral philosophers could have produced the lists since there is little that is distinctive to Christianity. Because Paul seldom used many of these terms, these scholars say he probably borrowed them.[88] Paul may have discovered a list of virtues which was acceptable to him, but the motivations and resources to develop these qualities in a Christian manner come only from the Holy Spirit who produces such fruit within.

Paul addressed the thought life first. He identified seven qualities which should characterize Christians. "True," in the ethical sense as used here, means "truthfulness, dependability."[89] "Noble" translates a rare word which has a broad meaning. Used primarily by Paul in the Pastoral Epistles, it has the idea of "worthy of respect, honor, noble."[90] It is primarily used of church leaders,

---

[87] In actuality, the former seems to speak to occasions of outbreaks of anxiety. This speaks to ordering a personal environment to prohibit such outbreaks.

[88] Beare states the case strongly and representatively: "It is almost as if he had taken a current list from a textbook of ethical instruction, and made it his own; these are nothing else than the virtues of the copybook maxims. It follows that Paul had come to recognize that there was a genuine capacity for moral discernment in the pagan society around him, and that the things which were counted honourable by good men everywhere were in fact worthy of honour, worthy to be cultivated by a Christian believer" (148). Many accept this type of conclusion, but there are two parts. If Paul did borrow a philosophical list and approve it, that does not mean that Christians should cultivate the qualities of the pagan society around them. Surely Paul Christianized the list.

[89] *BAGD*, 36.

[90] *BAGD*, 746-47.

where various persons are urged to be respectable. "Right" is a translation of the Greek *dikaiosynē*, normally translated "just" (KJV). It implies giving to God and people a justness that is worthy of them. This definition differs from Paul's normal use, but it well describes the ideal Christian virtue. "Pure" translates a word meaning "pure" or "holy" in relation to God. "Lovely" is found only here in the New Testament and has a fundamental meaning of "that which calls forth love" (*prosphilē*).[91] It covers a host of qualities but basically means that the person should be attractive, lovable. "Admirable" occurs only here in the New Testament, and it means whatever is "praiseworthy, attractive,"[92] therefore likely not to offend. "Excellent" (*aretē*) means *morally excellent*. The word was seldom used by Paul, but in 1 Pet 2:9 and 2 Pet 1:3,5 the word describes Christian virtue. Finally, "praiseworthy" means *worthy of praising God*. These characteristics would unite the church and present a good testimony to the world.

After presenting the standard for the thought life, Paul turned to Christian practice. The church was to cultivate the things it saw in Paul. Again the theme of imitation predominates. Recalling 3:1-16, Paul urged it to use him as a model of effective Christian living. This kind of living would result in the God of peace being with them. Often Paul greeted his friends with a prayer for peace, such as in the salutation of this epistle (1:2). In this passage the means to the answer of that prayer appear. God's peace especially resides in those who have ordered their lives in accordance with God's will. This includes proper and disciplined thoughts and good Christian living. Thus the two sets of instructions on peace complement each other. When anxiety appears, the cure is prayer. When the life is disorderly, the cure is mental and practical discipline.

---

[91] Hawthorne, 188.
[92] *BAGD*, 327.

SECTION OUTLINE

IV. EXPRESSION OF THANKS FOR THE PHILIPPIANS'
    SUPPORT (4:10-20)
    1. Paul's Situation (4:10-14)
       (1) Appreciation (4:10)
       (2) Contentment (4:11)
       (3) Adaptability (4:12)
       (4) Dependency (4:13)
       (5) Blessing (4:14)
    2. Paul's Attitude Toward Those Who Gave (4:15-20)
       (1) Commendations (4:15-17)
       (2) Blessings (4:18-19)
       (3) Doxology (4:20)

IV. EXPRESSION OF THANKS FOR THE PHILIPPIANS' SUPPORT (4:10-20)

The final section of the epistle addresses finances. Paul thanked the Philippians for remembering him and his needs, as they had before. Because of their pattern of giving, they were a double blessing. Typical of Paul, however, he used this occasion to teach the church spiritual truths. An introductory statement of thanks led to an explanation of Paul's outlook on things. This was followed by identifying some of the benefits for those who gave.

1. Paul's Situation (4:10-14)

[10]**I rejoice greatly in the Lord that at last you have renewed your concern for me. Indeed, you have been concerned, but you had no opportunity to show it. [11]I am not saying this because I am in need, for I have learned to be content whatever the circumstances. [12]I know what it is to be in need, and I know what it is to have plenty. I have learned the secret of being content in any and every situation, whether well fed or hungry, whether living in plenty or in want. [13]I can do everything through him who gives me strength.**

[14]**Yet it was good of you to share in my troubles.**

(1) Appreciation (4:10)

4:10   Apparently some time elapsed between gifts from the Philippian church. It may have been years between the gifts mentioned in 2 Cor 8 and the one delivered by Epaphroditus. Perhaps Paul had despaired of their love for him since so much time elapsed and since they were the ones who remembered him financially and a financial gift uniquely expressed love. Their gift was a cause of joy in the Lord. Perhaps they expected Paul to be joyful because of the gift but, as the context clearly reveals, his joy was in the Lord. Spiritual relationships brought the most satisfaction: their love for him because of Christ's love and his love for the Lord. Thus it was natural for a material gift to become an occasion for Christian joy. The Christian nature of this relationship is supported by the word Paul used for "concern." It is the key verb of the epistle, *phroneō*. Paul used it consistently to point out proper Christian attitudes in following the mind of Christ. He must have consciously alluded to that in his choice of the word.

Although some time elapsed between the gifts, Paul remained in the Philippians' thoughts. He explained that they were mindful of him all along (the same verb occurs, *phroneō*), but they lacked opportunity. The lack was probably that Paul did not have need, but some interpret it as the church's inability to provide what they desired. Since when they were motivated to give, they created the opportunity by sending Epaphroditus as their minister, Paul's situation best explains the reference.

Paul may have moved between mild rebuke and sympathetic understanding in this section. On one hand, lest some misunderstand him as being too critical, he explained that they had no occasion to give.[1] On the other hand, the phrase translated "indeed you have been concerned" is introduced by a causal construction (*eph ho kai*).[2] That makes the meaning "you have renewed your concern for me *because* you have been concerned." Rather than a rebuke, this makes Paul's situation the reason they could not respond and implies that they wanted to respond all along. It makes good sense of the passage.

Paul's statement did not reflect his own need. He had learned to be at home with whatever God supplied to him. He stated three reasons he fared well even without their gift.

(2) Contentment (4:11)

4:11 The first reason Paul did not need the gift was his own contentment. Twice in these verses he stated that he had learned contentment. One word, *emathon*, was natural to use. It speaks to having arrived at a fact of understanding. The other word, *memyēmai*, often appears in the mystery religions. It means to *learn the secret* and conveys the idea of a secret knowledge to which adherents of the mystery religions aspired.[3] The word conveyed what Paul

---

[1] G. B. Caird, *Paul's Letters from Prison* (Oxford: University Press, 1976), expresses the idea of many by interpreting this as, "You lacked the means" (153). M. Silva, *Philippians*, WEC (Chicago: Moody, 1988), 231-32, suggests that the awkwardness of the passage is partly cultural, in that we do not understand their ways, and partly circumstantial. The awkwardness also comes in the natural difficulty of expressing thanks without asking for more.

[2] The construction occurs four times in Paul's writing and each time it appears to make a correction of thought (Rom 5:12; 2 Cor 5:4; Phil 3:12; 4:10). See BDF, 235.2, 123.

[3] Paul may have deliberately chosen the word to explain in irony that Christians have their secrets too.

desired. Contentment is learned through experience. Paul used another rare word for "to be content." The etymology means "self-reliant,"[4] and the context supports that meaning. It is a self-sufficiency because of Christ, however, as Paul clearly stated in 4:13. He meant that he came to grips with his circumstances and fared well in and through them because of his own relationship to Christ. He did not need help.[5]

(3) Adaptability (4:12)

4:12 Circumstances were the arena of spiritual growth, and through them Paul developed adaptability. In this verse Paul presented three contrasts that provided the occasion for learning and explained the nature of contentment. The first and last speak to physical needs in general, while the middle refers to food. In these varied experiences, Paul displayed spiritual equilibrium. He was equally unaffected by poverty and riches. This knowledge is learned by walking with Christ, who is the sufficient one, and by developing a solid theology of material things. Things ultimately do not matter. Relationships matter. Paul's attitude contrasted with the false teachers'. They were preoccupied with food and other earthly matters; Paul could rise above any set of circumstances.

(4) Dependency (4:13)

4:13 Paul depended on Christ for strength. The expression "through him who gives me strength" clearly refers to the indwelling Christ, and Paul could accomplish all that God wanted through the strength he provided. Some people abuse this verse by taking it out of context. They assume Paul was making a comprehensive statement about the spiritual abilities of a Christian. Some even act as if there were nothing they could not do. Paul did not mean that. Two factors in the text reveal why. First, the passage discussed material and physical needs. In the day to day economic fluctuations, Paul knew a stability that enabled him to rise above them. The rule of context means that this must be applied to economic matters.[6] Second, Paul expressed his dependence on the power of the Lord. In this, he knew that where the Lord led him, he had power. The will of God limited the application of the strength he knew. Many who misapply this verse step out of God's will for their lives. They hope to cover their actions by a blanket promise of power, but power comes in the will of God. Thus, Paul expressed a crucial paradox. He was strong when he was weak! He was independent (self-sufficient) only when he was dependent! Although Paul

---

[4] *BAGD*, 122. It only occurs here in the New Testament.

[5] J. B. Lightfoot, *St. Paul's Epistle to the Philippians*, reprint ed. (Grand Rapids: Zondervan, 1953), stated well that the meaning of the word αὐτάρκης is "independence of external circumstances" (163).

[6] This does not directly refer to his ministry, even though it was in the course of ministry that he encountered these circumstances. It certainly does not apply to spiritual powers, although in some ways the principle remains. The apostle meant he could get along well in this life because of Christ.

realized the necessity of living in a Christian community, he also knew what it meant to face life's problems alone and still triumph through them.

It may be more difficult to triumph in the good times than in the bad. A Christian's victory comes from a conscious dependence on the Lord and his power, and that is easier understood when times get hard! One mark of maturity in Christ is that the mature know how to depend on the Lord in every situation of life, not only in those for which they assume they need help. Paul modeled this lesson for them and thus even in his thankfulness taught the truths of Christian living.

(5) Blessing (4:14)

4:14 As a summary of this section, Paul reminded the readers that their share in his work was good. The NIV translates this accurately but perhaps too casually: "You share in my troubles." Two important terms indicate the significance of their contribution to Paul. First, they participated with him. The Greek *sygkoinoneō* emphasizes that participation. The basic translation, "fellowship," means *a deep partnership of two going the same direction*. This is heightened by the preposition "with" (*syn*), which has a perfective force here.[7] Second, Paul identified their partnership specifically as with his "troubles" (*thlipsis*). The term naturally implies hardships of any kind,[8] but it had a deeper significance for Paul. In Col 1:24 he spoke of suffering the "tribulations of the Christ" (the same Greek word) so that his difficulties in spreading the gospel actually related to the Messiah.[9] In reflecting on his tribulations, Paul realized the eschatological significance of his ministry and that those who supported him participated in that themselves. Their gifts evidenced their willingness to identify with the new era inaugurated by Jesus.

This expression contains the first hint of the significance of Christian giving. It also explains something of Paul's hesitancy in expressing his own needs to them. The Philippians recognized Paul's strategic place in the spread of the gospel, the mystery revealed to him (Eph 3:1-13). Others, particularly the Jewish Christians, had difficulty accepting Paul's ministry. The gifts from Philippi meant that the church eagerly participated in the work of God and that their gifts were, in reality, contributions to the spread of the gospel to other Gentiles. Paul knew he would suffer because of his distinctive apostolic calling. He accepted this suffering joyfully and learned the secret of triumph over any circumstance. Paul's ministry simply provided an occasion for sharing in the gospel. He knew that he handled sacred resources when they came from the people of God (see 4:18). Their gift was good because it demonstrated that

---

[7] Such compounds may be directive, pointing to an object, or perfective, stressing the meaning of the verb. Here the perfective force comes through. It stresses a complete, deep partnership with Paul.

[8] *BAGD*, 362, says primarily "of the distress that is brought about by outward circumstances."

[9] See the exegesis of that passage in the Colossians commentary.

they understood God's working in the world and that they willingly supported it through God's servants.

2. Paul's Attitude toward Those Who Gave (4:15-20)

Paul's thankfulness turned to commendation and promise of reward. Both the nature of their giving and its motivation pleased the Lord.

(1) Commendation (4:15-17)

[15]Moreover, as you Philippians know, in the early days of your acquaintance with the gospel, when I set out from Macedonia, not one church shared with me in the matter of giving and receiving, except you only; [16]for even when I was in Thessalonica, you sent me aid again and again when I was in need. [17]Not that I am looking for a gift, but I am looking for what may be credited to your account.

4:15 Paul commended the church for the way it supported him. Its support was unique. It was the only Macedonian church to support him. Paul disclosed one of the reasons he remembered the Philippians fondly "from the first day until now" (1:5). When they first heard the gospel, they saw its implications for others and shared in its propagation. Since Paul committed his life to the progress of the gospel (1:12) and measured his success by the proclamation of the gospel (1:18), their giving promoted a natural friendship. The early days in Macedonia had been difficult. Paul suffered physically in Philippi. In Thessalonica his work caused an uproar (1 Thess 2:9), which resulted in his departing the city (Acts 17:5-9). These difficulties were only external. Perhaps the greatest difficulty was that the other churches failed to help him. In this, Philippi was different! From the very first it supported his work, evidencing the genuineness of salvation and love for Paul.

The other churches failed in their obligations to the gospel. Paul called the Philippian support a matter "of giving and receiving" (4:15). When he stated that other churches did not support him, he used the common word for "fellowship" (*koinōneō*) which so characterizes this book. Subtly and without complaining, Paul pointed out that others had received but not given. They had a one-way relationship in the gospel. Paul expected rejection and loneliness in his work; it came as no surprise. He was, however, troubled for two reasons. First, when they received they had a responsibility to share. Second, they missed the spiritual blessings that came from giving. The Philippians understood both principles and acted on them. That brought joy to Paul's heart.

4:16 Paul also commended them because their support was immediate and consistent. He remembered that they supported him in Thessalonica, the city he had entered after being asked to leave Philippi. Beyond that, they continued to support him. His statement in 4:10, however, reveals that at some time their support ceased. Perhaps the deeper meaning of their giving enhanced Paul's joy when they gave again.

4:17 Paul commended them because their gifts were an investment. Financial terms dominate this passage.[10] The gifts were an investment in the work of God and in their future. Some believers may have mistakenly assumed that Paul sought gifts, but he clearly stated he sought the blessings it would bring to the givers.[11] Paul saw beyond the physical act to the spiritual transactions taking place. Even in acknowledging their support, his servant attitude surfaced. He thought of their growth and blessings.

(2) Blessings (4:18-19)

[18]I have received full payment and even more; I am amply supplied, now that I have received from Epaphroditus the gifts you sent. They are a fragrant offering, an acceptable sacrifice, pleasing to God. [19]And my God will meet all your needs according to his glorious riches in Christ Jesus.

Paul's commendation led him to speak of how the Philippians benefited from supporting him. He understood well that genuine giving seeks no personal benefits. He lived that way, and so did they.[12] Nevertheless, giving brings blessings to both giver and receiver. First, Paul stated what he received from their gifts. Further, using financial language, Paul stated that his need was met. He had sufficient resources to carry on God's work. Any obligation they had to him had been paid in full. Their responsibility was satisfied. The gift brought by Epaphroditus exceeded what Paul might have expected, and they were to feel no obligation to give more.

4:18 Paul also listed two benefits to the giver. First, God was pleased. In terms reminiscent of Rom 12:1-2, Paul pointed out that their gift was an acceptable Christian sacrifice. Like Rom 12, this passage teaches that physical activity can become spiritual in motivation and importance. Romans states that dedicating the body to God is a spiritual act. Here, Paul revealed that giving was a spiritual exercise. Since Paul used the language of the Old Testament sacrificial system, perhaps even his terms subtly countered the Jewish false teachers.

Paul had developed a comprehensive theology of stewardship. Its most thorough statement occurs in 2 Cor 8-9, where he solicited support for a famine relief offering.[13] He stated that the Macedonians led the way in giving, and

---

[10]This was pointed out long ago by H. A. A. Kennedy, "The Financial Colouring of Phil. 4:15-18," *ExpTim* 12 (1900-1901): 43ff. Some of these are: "fruit," "increase," "account," and "full payment."

[11]The Greek is graphic. "Gifts" is really τὸ δόμα, "the gift." It stressed the giving/receiving aspect. It is contrasted with another articular expression τὸν καρπόν, "the fruit."

[12]In our day, it helps to be reminded of this truth. Giving should not be perceived as an alternate way of receiving. That is a contradiction of terms. In God's economy, however, giving is blessed, and the blessings outweigh the sacrifice.

[13]The theological aspects of giving as presented in 2 Cor 8-9 are developed in R. Melick, "Collection for the Saints: 2 Corinthians 8-9," *CTR* 4 (Fall, 1989): 97-117. There are soteriological

most likely the primary church to give was Philippi (2 Cor 8:1-5). Their giving was exemplary because they gave out of "rock-bottom poverty."[14] Their contribution was a "fragrant offering" to God because of its sacrifice, its Christian motivation, and its significance to the spread of the gospel.

4:19 The second benefit to the believers was that they would experience God's provision. Just as God had met Paul's needs in the work of the gospel, so God would meet their needs. The context of this promise deserves careful attention. Paul spoke to those who actively supported the work of the Lord. His statement of 4:15 indicates what he meant: God meets the needs of those who give to him. In the context of ministering being ministered to occurs.[15]

God's supply is "according to his glorious riches in Christ Jesus." Often commentators point out that the statement says "according to" and not "out of."[16] "According to" means that the supply is suited to the resource and like it in kind and extent. God, therefore, bountifully blesses those who give with glorious provision in accord with his glory and for his purposes.[17] Since the glory is associated with Christ—it is "in Christ"—Paul probably spoke of one of the benefits brought to those who are in Christ. "Glorious riches" are available to those who give as the Philippians did.

(3) Doxology (4:20)

[20]To our God and Father be glory for ever and ever. Amen.

4:20 The section closes with a doxology to God the Father. The thought of the glorious nature of what the Lord supplies no doubt prompted Paul to think of the ultimate purpose of life: to bring glory to God forever.[18] The doxology expresses a prayer concerning all the affairs discussed in the epistle. Through whatever means, in every age, and through all creatures, may God be glorified. Once again, Paul's thoughts moved beyond the present to the future, or, as in other places in the epistle, he consciously remembered the ultimate purpose of life. It is to bring glory to God now and forever. In so doing, the believer will join a great host of creation glorifying God for eternity.

---

aspects: It is a Christian grace demonstrating the completion of grace in the heart; it is true to the example of Jesus Christ; it expresses the concept of Christian community. In that text there are also eschatological aspects which overlap with Philippians.

[14]The Greek of 2 Cor 8:2 describes their poverty as "according to the depth" or bottom. The expression "rock-bottom" comes from P. Hughes, *Commentary on the Second Epistle to the Corinthians* (Grand Rapids: Eerdmans, 1962), 228.

[15]This is much the same as the Lord's prayer: "forgive us . . . as we forgive" (Matt 6:12).

[16]The Greek is κατά rather than ἐκ.

[17]The construction "in glory" (ἐν δόξῃ) has been taken as: in a glorious manner he will provide; in the kingdom of glory after this life; and equal to his glorious riches. This latter seems best suited to the context.

[18]The idiom translated "for ever and ever" really captures the idea of the ages to come. It is based on the Hebrew idea of heaven as a future age.

──────────── **V. CONCLUSION (4:21-23)** ────────────

[21]Greet all the saints in Christ Jesus. The brothers who are with me send greetings. [22]All the saints send you greetings, especially those who belong to Caesar's household.
[23]The grace of the Lord Jesus Christ be with your spirit. Amen.

4:21-22 The conclusion of Philippians is typical of other epistles, including exhortations to greet the brothers and greetings from Christians in the place of writing. These concluding remarks are abbreviated, but significant. Paul sent greetings from three groups of persons with him. First, greetings were sent from the brethren who surrounded him, his team of men who supported him and served with him. No doubt they knew the church well. Second, greetings were sent from other saints with whom Paul had contact. The term "all the saints" must mean those in the church at Rome, who were not specifically a part of Paul's band of men. Such greetings were commonly exchanged as a mark of Christian friendship and brotherhood. Finally, greetings came from Christians in Caesar's household. The unusual manner of identifying them as a "household" suggests that they were not family members. Most assume that they were in Caesar's civil service. Perhaps because of Philippi's importance as a colony and financial center, some of them had regular business contacts with the Christians at Philippi.[1] The interchange of greetings was an important way of maintaining contacts with the Christians around the empire.

4:23 Paul's final words implored the grace of God. He ended like he began—with a prayer for grace. Possibly he had a collective church spirit in mind,[2] but most likely he referred to the spirits of individuals. The spirit stands for the entire person, spiritually sensitive through this aspect of human beings. God communicated with their spirits, and through them he brought the riches of his grace wherever it was needed. In an epistle which presents clearly the polarities between law and grace, works and faith, and self-righteousness and divinely imputed righteousness, it is significant that the final line should be grace. Fittingly he reminded them that everything good they had came because of God's grace.

---

[1] F. W. Beare, *The Epistle to the Philippians, HNTC* (San Francisco: Harper & Row, 1959), 158, points out that one Poppaea, a proselyte to Judaism, was Nero's mistress. It is not likely that she became a Christian, but it shows that the household included people of other faiths than the religions of Rome.
[2] Ibid.

Colossians

──────────── **INTRODUCTION** ────────────

Christianity faced one of its most severe challenges in the complex and confusing intellectual climate of ancient Colosse. Perhaps due to the nature of the times, the location, and the ideological climate, what had begun well faced a major threat to Christianity's very existence. False teachers were urging the people to move away from their Christian roots and to accept other religious ideas. Although Paul did not found the church at Colosse, it manifested Pauline traits, and Paul felt the responsibility to address its problems. This little epistle contains distinctive teachings about the person and work of Christ, about Christian living and relationships, and about Paul's conception of his ministry.

Studying the epistle is an adventure in Christian theology. It reveals Pauline thought and authentic Christian living. The pages of the text are alive with relevance and challenge the reader to a more reflective and informed faith.

Paul constructed his arguments to counter false teaching and to teach orthodox theology. One theme predominates: the centrality of Christ. No other epistle is as Christocentric as this one. Whether the reader spends countless hours with Colossians or reads it only casually, every encounter with the text brings one face to face with the Lord whom the text introduces so well. Every occasion to read it leaves its mark indelibly on the mind. This commentary provides another exposure to the powerful little letter.[1]

1. The City and Its People

No one knows when Colosse was founded. As early as the time of Xerxes of Persia (485-465 B.C.), it was a thriving community. Herodotus, a Greek historian, said it was a "great city of Phrygia" in 480 B.C.[2] No doubt its early greatness came in part from its location. Colosse sat on the main East-West road from Ephesus to the East, at the entrance to a pass in the Cadmus range of mountains. In this location, westbound travelers came to it first when they entered the Lycus valley. Travelers, such as Paul and his company, traversed this same road from Antioch (Syria) to Tarsus, through the Cilician Gates on to Derbe, Lystra, Iconium, and Colosse. They could continue westward to Laodicea and 100 miles to Ephesus and possibly 1000-1200 land miles to Rome.[3]

The location of Colosse provided the resources to make the city great. The Lycus River ran through the valley. The river was a branch of the Maeander River and became known as the Little Maeander. The area suffered frequent earthquakes, one of which did severe damage to Laodicea and Hierapolis,

---

[1] Many commentaries provide a wealth of information. As a starter, the serious student should consult the following: P. O'Brien, *Colossians, Philemon, WBC*; E. Lohse, *Colossians and Philemon, Her*; J. B. Lightfoot, *St. Paul's Epistle to the Colossians and to Philemon*; R. P. Martin, *Colossians and Philemon, NCB*, also *Colossians: The Church's Lord and the Christian's Liberty*; F. F. Bruce, *Ephesians and Colossians, NIC*; C. F. D. Moule, *The Epistles of Paul the Apostle to the Colossians and to Philemon, CGTC*; W. Hendriksen, *Colossians and Philemon, NTC*; C. Vaughan, *Colossians: A Study Guide Commentary*, and "Colossians," *EBC*; Dibelius and Greeven, *An die Kolosser, Epheser, an Philemon, HNT 12*; G. B. Caird, *Paul's Letters from Prison (Ephesians, Philippians, Colossians, Philemon)*, and John Callow, *A Semantic Structure Analysis of Colossians*; R. E. O. White, "Colossians," *BBC*. Many more could be mentioned along with even more helpful articles, dictionaries, introductions, etc.

[2] This information comes from J. B. Lightfoot, *St. Paul's Epistles to the Colossians and to Philemon*, reprint ed. (Grand Rapids: Zondervan, 1959), 15. Even one hundred years after the first publication of this work in 1879, it remains one of the significant commentaries. Lightfoot's introductory work on the epistle is especially useful, and his analysis of the false teaching has guided scholars since its writing. He provided extensive bibliography that bears on the backgrounds.

[3] Excellent graphs and maps of these relationships are presented in W. Hendriksen, *Colossians and Philemon, NTC* (Grand Rapids: Baker, 1964), 6-9.

neighboring cities, in the year A.D. 60.[4] No doubt Colosse suffered as well. The beautiful valley had lush pastures for grazing sheep. The abundance of wool supported a flourishing garment industry. One of the branches of the Lycus River left chalk deposits that were useful for dyeing cloth.[5] The valley prospered from both ranching and industry.

By the time of the apostle Paul, Colosse's importance had waned. Strabo, about twenty years before Paul, called the city a "small town."[6] The two neighboring cities eclipsed Colosse. Laodicea, mentioned in Col 4:15-16, was most prominent. The Romans made Asia a province in 190 B.C. and selected Laodicea as a *conventus*, the capital of a district of twenty-five towns.[7] The Romans also changed the road system, and Laodicea became an important junction of the East-West highway and four other roads. This meant it was ideally suited for commerce, banking, and general prosperity (Rev 3:14-22).

Hierapolis almost equally eclipsed Colosse. Located about six miles from Laodicea, it formed the third member of the triangle. Paul mentioned that a joint venture of churches in these three cities supported Epaphras in his ministry to Paul; that was entirely feasible, given the geographical and cultural intercourse among them (Col 4:13). Hierapolis was noted for its mineral baths. One of the hot wells, the Plutonium, issued a deadly vapor. Superstitions about it abounded, and many temples of various sorts surrounded this city.[8] By the time of Paul, therefore, for commercial interests one went to Laodicea; for luxury and pleasure, to Hierapolis.

The cities had a mixed population. The natives were Phrygian. Because of the military and commercial heritage of the valley, however, Greeks may have settled in the area during the Greek period of dominance. To this were added Jews of the Diaspora,[9] Romans involved in politics, and various ethnic groups drawn by commercial interests. The exact population mixture of Colosse during this time is unknown. From the epistle, both Jews and Gentiles lived there and became part of the church.

2. The Founding of the Church

The origins of the church at Colosse are obscure. Clearly, Paul did not found it since he said as much in 2:1; however, Paul addressed the church as though it were his responsibility. He considered it in some sense a Pauline community, taking liberty to address problems within it as though he had the authority to do so. Some suggest that Paul's authority came because he was the "apostle to

---

[4]Lightfoot, 3, 38. In note 1, p. 38, he listed the known earthquakes in the area.

[5]Hendriksen, 10. Pliny noted that there was a river in the city which turned brick into stone (Lightfoot, 15).

[6]Cited in Lightfoot, 16.

[7]Ibid., 7.

[8]Ibid., 12-13. Even the name Hierapolis possibly means "Holy City."

[9]See the evidence later in the "The Problem at Colosse."

the Gentiles" and had a proprietary interest in all Gentile congregations. They support this conclusion from the Letter to the Romans, the other church to whom Paul wrote but whom he had never met. In writing to the Romans, Paul spoke to vital issues of misunderstanding in the fellowship. This suggests that it, too, was Pauline. In Romans, however, Paul introduced himself to gain support for a mission to Spain (Rom 15:24). His advice regarding the problems comes from a "softer voice" than Colossians. The church at Colosse had no resources to offer Paul, as the Roman church did, and Paul's writing to them appears to reveal a special interest in their well-being, though, of course, he shared a similar concern for all the churches. The Colossian church was Pauline in a way that the Roman church was not.

The most common suggestion regarding the founding of the church is that Epaphras founded it. Probably that is correct. Paul identified his fellow-prisoner Epaphras as a Colossian (4:12), a servant of Christ (4:12), and an envoy from the other churches in the valley (4:13). Further, Paul stated that the Colossians heard the word from Epaphras (1:7). The church most likely began during Paul's third missionary journey, while he taught in the school of Tyrannus in Ephesus. Luke recorded that all of Asia heard the word during that time (Acts 19:9-10). Epaphras met Paul in Ephesus, became a student and able minister, and took the word to his own people. This reckoning dates the founding of the church at about A.D. 53-55, some seven to ten years before Paul wrote the epistle.

3. The Occasion

Determining the occasion of a letter involves two parts. First, the basic question is, Why did Paul write the letter at all? This deserves serious attention, and most scholars concentrate on that question. The second matter is, Why did Paul write the letter when he did? This is a question of expediency. The two issues do not necessarily intertwine. Conceivably, a reason for writing could be delayed or accelerated depending on the availability of couriers, time of year, circumstances of the author, and many other matters. This fact alone provides insight into the relationships of the four epistles commonly called Prison Epistles, as well as the context of the letter.

Why did Paul write? False teachers threatened to undermine what Epaphras had taught. More disconcertingly, the implications of their teaching threatened to remove the church from its strong Christian foundation. Since Paul saw himself as the apostle responsible for the well-being of the church, he thought it imperative to respond to the teaching personally. The nature of the teaching is discussed later under the heading "The Problem at Colosse," and that section should be consulted regarding this matter.

Why did Paul write when he did? Three of the Prison Epistles belong together: Colossians, Ephesians, and Philemon. Paul wrote Philemon, urging him to forgive and restore his runaway slave, Onesimus. Significantly,

Onesimus and Tychicus traveled together to Colosse with news of Paul's situation, and they carried the letter Paul wrote. Piecing this information together, the following scenario best explains the immediate occasion.

Sometime during Paul's imprisonment, he met the runaway slave Onesimus. Suggestions that Onesimus sought out Paul do not fit the data. It seems highly unlikely that Onesimus had run away as a Christian, and Paul stated in Phlm 10 that he became a son in prison.[10] Because of this new commitment to Christ, Paul encouraged Onesimus to return to Philemon. Generally, such a decision came with great anxiety and an urgent need to settle the matter, and Onesimus no doubt felt that way. Therefore, at the earliest convenience, Paul sent Onesimus to Philemon with the letter. Philemon probably belonged to the church at Colosse, and Paul took advantage of the situation to address his other concern: the problem which Epaphras had discussed with him. Epaphras had earlier journeyed to Paul to help him in whatever way he could, representing the three churches of the Lycus valley.[11] Further, since Onesimus and Tychicus had to travel through Ephesus to get to Colosse, Paul took advantage of the occasion to write to his good friends at Ephesus. This suggests that the problem at Colosse did not require an emergency response from Paul. At least equally pressing was Paul's desire for Christian restitution between Onesimus and Philemon.[12]

4. The Authorship

Recently many scholars have doubted the Pauline authorship of Colossians. Others continue to affirm it. D. Guthrie pointed out, "There is no shred of evidence that the Pauline authorship of the whole or any part of this epistle was ever disputed until the nineteenth century."[13] At that time, however, some questioned Pauline authorship because the content did not resemble Paul or because they set the letter in the context of second-century Gnosticism.[14] Since that time, the authorship question has been discussed on basically three fronts: the context of the "philosophy," the style of writing, and the theology. The first of these, contextual considerations, depended largely on determining that Paul

---

[10]Paul likely would not have appealed to Philemon if he were a harsh master; and, if Onesimus had a history of fickle Christian commitment, Paul likely would not have put his reputation on the line for him. The tone of the situation suggests that Paul and Onesimus met in prison.

[11]The text contains no hint that Epaphras did not know how to respond to the heresy or that he came to Paul seeking help and counsel in the matter. Col 4:13 suggests that he was sent by the churches as an act of good will from them to Paul.

[12]It is entirely possible, of course, that the two events coincided so that both situations could be addressed with urgency. However, Paul spoke of Epaphras as though he had been with him long enough to accomplish good work, and that suggests the greater urgency came from Onesimus.

[13]D. Guthrie, *New Testament Introduction*, rev. ed. (Downers Grove, Ill.: InterVarsity, 1990), 576.

[14]For the first, E. T. Mayerhoff; for the second, the Tübingen School of F. C. Baur. (See Guthrie, 489-95).

combatted some form of Gnosticism. Although, a full orbed Gnosticism did not develop before the second century, a type of incipient Gnosticism, perhaps co-mingled with Jewish thought, existed in the mid-first century. Nevertheless, the last two concerns, style and theology, are primary.

The two basic arguments against Pauline authorship are the style of writing and theology. The question of style deals with vocabulary and use of language. The epistle contains an unusually high number of words which are only used one time in the New Testament (*hapax legomena*), but we should remember that the subject matter of Colossians differs from the other Pauline writings. When Colossians is compared to the other Pauline writings, many expressions and forms of writing differ. Again, these unusual terms may be explained by the different situation or the fact that most of these occur in pre-Pauline mate-rial (see discussion at 1:15-20) or in the discussion of the heresy. Those parts naturally have a higher incidence of unfamiliar expressions. In a thorough investigation of vocabulary and style, E. Lohse concludes that "on the basis of the observations made about the language and style of the letter, no final deci-sion can yet be reached on the question of Pauline or non-Pauline authorship of the letter."[15] Particularly when Ephesians is considered, the parallels are strik-ing. Ephesians has become a battleground as well, but the Letter to Colossians reads smoothly with or without Ephesians,[16] and the conceptual parallels between the two make a strong case for the same author in both.

The concern over Pauline authorship also focuses on theology. In particular, the issues are Christology, ecclesiology, and eschatology. Lohse states that each of these doctrines underwent tremendous change so that "Paul cannot be considered to be the direct or indirect author of Col."[17] He suggests that a Pauline school arose around Ephesus and that the epistle was the product of that environment and various elements of Hellenistic Christianity.

Others disagree with this assessment. P. O'Brien points out that the cosmic application of Christ's rule simply makes plain an earlier Pauline theme.[18] The Christology fits well with the teaching of Phil 2:6-11; 1 Cor 8:6; 2 Cor 4:4; 8:9. Pauline ecclesiology is reflected in the concept of the "body of Christ." That metaphor was used by Paul in writings much earlier than Colossians.[19] It was, however, extended to include new dimensions, but that may be the result of a situation which called for a slightly different application. Further, the applica-

---

[15]E. Lohse, *Colossians and Philemon, Her* (Philadelphia: Fortress, 1971), 91. See his excellent presentation of the data of parallels in the Pauline literature in 84-91. For a good evaluation of the data in support of Pauline authorship, see P. O'Brien, *Colossians, Philemon, WBC* (Waco, Tex.: Word, 1982), xlii-xlix; and Hendriksen, 29-38.

[16]See the comment by Julicher quoted by Lohse, that the question of interpolations "would never have arisen but for the presence of the epistle to the Ephesians beside it" (90).

[17]Lohse, 181. See his discussion of theological changes in 177-83.

[18]O'Brien, xiv.

[19]See N. T. Wright, *Colossians and Philemon, TNTC* (Grand Rapids: Eerdmans, 1986), 33.

tions of Jesus' universal lordship differ in Colossians and Ephesians, one referring to cosmic rule, the other to his rule over the church. Similarly, eschatological elements in Colossians resemble those of the other epistles, and other Pauline parallels are frequent. Paul did not major on eschatology, however, because the church was preoccupied with Christology and soteriology.

While the questions of authorship are quite complex, some general observations about method may be helpful.[20] Many of the recent theories of critical scholarship arise from a procedure of methodological doubt. That is, skepticism becomes the tool of learning. The result is that, rather than approaching the text with sympathy for its statements and the history of its study, some approach the text to see why it cannot be what others decide it is. Doubt has a place in the reasoning process, but it should not overrule good arguments to the contrary. Often good explanations are rejected simply because they are traditional. Along with this is a second methodological principle, that of determining proper standards for comparison. Since the objective data are limited, scholars can easily drift into subjective standards of comparison that are psychological and sociological, as well as theological. For example, determining what Paul should have said or would have said in a given situation is almost impossible once one departs from what Paul did say. A third concern is about a kind of focused-theology approach. Many assume that Paul's theology was only one-tracked. This means, first, that he could not speak to any subject other than the one addressed by him in his undisputed writings. Second, if he did speak to another issue, he had to speak from the perspective of his one foundational principle. While there can be no doubt about the general contours of Pauline thought, Paul could have written on subjects that required basing an argument on another theological foundation.

As these assumptions work into practice, some specific areas may be addressed. First is the assumption that a developed theology determines the date or author. This assumption moves in two contrary directions. Sometimes a writing is given a late date because it shows mature thought on the part of the writer. At the same time, some assume the writing is from another writer because of the belief that a writer cannot mature in his presentations. The second assumption relates to the questions of vocabulary. The specific words chosen to address an issue arise from the issue itself. When the situation to be addressed changes, the vocabulary with which it is addressed also changes. For example, some assume that Paul could not have written Colossians because it does not contain his distinctive vocabulary (i.e., 2:6-3:4). Yet when discussing the problem in those texts, some of the same people suggest that Paul employed the terminology of the opponents. Naturally their terminology would not be his, and both arguments should not be used together in the authorship question.

---

[20]This is more in keeping with the nature of this commentary series which attempts to focus on theological thought more than matters of introduction.

Finally, some have pointed to theological and ideological differences in a literalistic and pedantic fashion. They say that if the same terms and constructions are not used the author is not the same. Yet they may be quick to point out that Paul used different metaphors to make a point. Thus the arguments *may become* circular. Care should be taken here.[21]

Interesting and challenging questions are to be answered regarding Pauline authorship. Most of the objective concerns, however, have been sufficiently answered, as Lohse and others affirm. The questions of theology are the primary obstacles. That broadens the discussion to its most subjective level. Too many factors affect the particular formulations of theology. No compelling reason has been given for rejecting the traditional authorship. Paul addressed a unique situation. Perhaps that solves more problems than it raises.

5. The Date and Origin

From earliest times, most scholars dated the Epistle to the Colossians from Rome during Paul's first Roman imprisonment. The letter affirms that Paul wrote from prison (Col 4:10) and that Aristarchus (Col 4:10) accompanied Paul to Rome (Acts 27:2). Recently, however, scholars have debated the site of the imprisonment. Now three different suggestions vie for attention: Rome, Ephesus, and Caesarea. The details of argumentation are available from many sources. Only an overview may be done here, but it will provide an orientation to the suggestions that have been made.[22]

The position that Paul was in Rome at the time of writing has various lines of support in addition to the traditions. Luke's description of the situation in Rome certainly allows for the type of ministry Paul described in his imprisonment letters. Paul was under house arrest with a great deal of freedom (Acts 28:30). Further, many of the names of persons associated with Paul in the Prison Epistles are also found in Philemon. Particularly, the runaway slave Onesimus is mentioned. He may have gone to the imperial capital to avoid recapture. When the data are compared to the Book of Acts, no other imprisonment fits the required details as well.

Many question this conclusion. The most significant concern is the distance between Colosse and Rome, which is variously estimated as 1000-1200 land miles. Would a runaway slave have had the resources to make such a long trip and the courage to be on the open road subject to recognition? Others also traveled to and from Colosse to Paul. Does the distance prohibit that? A second

---

[21] This discussion does not suggest that the methods identified have been useless to scholarship. Much has been learned which would not have been learned had not someone questioned. This discussion was simply to warn of inconsistent applications of principles brought on by a tendency to disprove.

[22] For good surveys of these issues in succinct form, see the following: R. Martin, *Colossians and Philemon, NCB* (Grand Rapids: Eerdmans, 1973), 22-32; P. O'Brien, xlix-liv; N. T. Wright, 34-39; and Guthrie, 472-78.

concern is Paul's apparent change of plans if Rome is the place of origin. Earlier he wrote of his plans to go to Spain when he could (Rom 15:23-24). In Philemon, however, he indicated he would go to Asia and urged Philemon to prepare a room for him (Phlm 22). Would this be likely from Rome?

Some, therefore, have suggested a Caesarean imprisonment. According to Acts, Paul was imprisoned in Caesarea for two years, awaiting transport to Rome. Advocates suggest that Onesimus more likely would have fled there, and Paul more easily could have envisioned a trip to Colosse by land on his way to Rome. Even after his appeal to Caesar, that was a possibility. This suggestion also has its problems. Since Caesarea had a small population, Paul probably would not have needed the extensive missionary staff he had during his imprisonment. Further, Onesimus would have had no reason to flee to that particular city since several other larger ones on the way would have provided more anonymity. Most scholars reject this view.[23]

A third suggestion is that Paul wrote from prison in Ephesus. Although Acts does not record an Ephesian imprisonment, it does speak of serious difficulties there and an imprisonment is quite likely (2 Cor 11:23; 1 Cor 15:32). In 2 Cor 1:8 Paul also wrote about serious trouble in Asia. G. S. Duncan, the first to suggest this hypothesis, thought that the imprisonment came after the Demetrius riot (Acts 19:23-41).[24] If this scenario is correct, several events seem to fit in place better. First, this allows for the fairly extensive travel reflected in the epistle. Second, Paul's request that a room be prepared for him soon makes good sense because he was only one hundred miles away. Third, many suggest that the church at Colosse appears to have been young, and the Ephesian location supports that conclusion.[25] It reduces the time between the founding of the church and Paul's letter. Finally, some objective evidence supports this view. A few traditions of limited value suggest that Paul was there. In the Marcionite prologue to Colossians, for example, it states: "The apostle already a captive writes to them from Ephesus."[26]

---

[23] The advocates are, most recently, W. G. Kümmel, *Introduction to the New Testament* (Nashville: Abingdon, 1973), 245; B. Reicke, "Caesarea, Rome, and the Captivity Epistles," *Apostolic History and the Gospel: Essays Presented to F. F. Bruce*, ed. W. W. Gasque and R. P. Martin (Grand Rapids: Eerdmans, 1970), 277-82. G. Hawthorne, *Philippians*, WBC (Waco, Tex.: Word, 1983), xxxvi-xliv, makes a strong case for Caesarea as the origin of Philippians.

[24] See G. S. Duncan, *St. Paul's Ephesian Ministry: A Reconstruction with Special Reference to the Ephesian Origin of the Imprisonment Epistles* (London: Hodder & Stoughton, 1929). See especially pp. 111-15, where he claims this occurred on the feast to Artemis in the year A.D. 57.

[25] Wright reflects others when he states: "Colossians has, however, increasingly given me the impression of a letter to a church which, very young in the faith, needs to be strengthened, informed about what has actually happened to its members in their becoming Christians, taught how to pursue Christian maturity, and warned against a threat most dangerous for those only recently converted from paganism" (35). The argument has plausibility, but the telling statement is "increasingly given me the impression."

[26] Quoted in Martin, 27. An impressive list of scholars accept that conclusion, including recent writers Martin, 30, and Wright, 39.

Of these suggestions, more scholars accept Ephesus than Caesarea. The Ephesian hypothesis has much to offer and would satisfy most of the data. One major problem, however, is, Why would Paul write a letter to the Ephesians when he was in prison in Ephesus? Admittedly, the earliest manuscripts of Ephesians do not contain any destination, so it is impossible to tell who received the letter first. On the other hand, no manuscript exists with any other stated destination. Apparently at least one copy of the letter was sent to the church at Ephesus.[27] The similarity of Colossians and Ephesians suggests that they were written by the same author at approximately the same time.

The Roman imprisonment seems to account for the data best. Both a stronger tradition and the parallels to Ephesians support it. In light of these factors and the fact that the Ephesian imprisonment is a hypothesis without solid factual data, it seems best to accept the Roman origin. If it were from Ephesus or Caesarea, however, nothing would be gained or lost from the message of the epistle. The historical context would be slightly altered.

6. The Relationship to the Other Prison Epistles

Traditionally, four epistles are grouped together as the Prison Epistles. They are so called because Paul stated in each that he was in prison (Col 4:10; Eph 3:1; 4:1; Phil 1:12-14; Phlm 13,23). The Book of Acts only records two imprisonments of significant length, Caesarea and Rome, and scholars have assumed traditionally that the four were written from the same location. Further, the situation had to allow for the free interchange of persons and ideas, as well as the opportunity to write. The Roman imprisonment fits that best.

The relationships among the four epistles, however, have not always been clear. Three of them go together by virtue of the circumstances they share. The same person served as courier for Colossians and Ephesians (Tychicus, Eph 6:21-22; Col 4:7,8). Tychicus traveled with a runaway slave, Onesimus, who returned to his master, Philemon (Col 4:7; Phlm 12). Further, Archippus occurs in both Col 4:17 and Phlm 2. The most likely conclusion, therefore, is that these three epistles belong together. Philippians must be considered separately.

Paul had a specific reason for writing these letters when he did. Obviously the church at Colosse faced a serious theological threat. Philemon reflects a personal situation, and Ephesians does not hint of any problem unless it is racial tension in the church. It seems possible that the Letter to Philemon prompted all three. Onesimus's desire to restore his relationship with his master probably provided the incentive for writing. It seems natural that Paul wrote Philemon first. Since Philemon probably belonged to the church at Colosse, Paul took opportunity to write Colossians second. It has an extended message to slaves and masters which makes it unique among Paul's writings.

---

[27]Many have suggested that Ephesians was a circular letter and that the one copy which survived was the one sent to Ephesus. It would seem strange that the church needed even a copy.

In this letter, he wrote what had been on his mind for some time, ever since Epaphras informed him of the situation. The close parallels with Ephesians suggest that the two go together, but the question is whether Ephesians is an embellishment from Colossians or whether Paul shortened Colossians from Ephesians. Ephesians seems to have more explicit ethical details, though the Christological sections are equal. Colossians was most likely written second, and, since the road to Colosse passed through Ephesus, Paul wrote to the church there too.

Philippians is somewhat different from the other three. It has a different style of writing and a different tone. Its theology resembles Galatians, Romans, and the Corinthian Letters,[28] but in it Paul stated he was in prison. Further, in the other three, Paul gave no evidence of concern about his trial. In Philippians, however, although Paul was optimistic, he expressed a natural concern about the future. Finally, a different messenger carried the letters. Epaphroditus, who was a representative from the church at Philippi (Phil 2:25) carried Philippians, and Tychicus carried Colossians. The order is that Philippians was written at a later date than the other three and was carried by a different courier.

Colossians has significant parallels to other Pauline writings. The most extensive parallels occur with Ephesians. Paul followed the same general outline, communicated basically the same ideas, and wrote with a common theme. The theme of Colossians is the cosmic Lord Christ; the theme of Ephesians is Christ the Lord of the church.[29]

The parallels offer some helpful insights about the text. First, the problem at Colosse was localized. It did not spread the one hundred miles west to Ephesus. Even so, the basic Christological answers to the false teachers apply equally to Ephesus, as do the ethical imperatives. Second, the two epistles must be studied together. They help to interpret each other. The specifics may vary as they were applied to a given situation, but the outline of thought and the concepts are parallel. In this commentary, therefore, references to Ephesians are made where appropriate. Both Ephesians and Colossians contain similarities to the Epistle to the Romans. For that reason, comparisons are made with Romans to explain Paul's thought in Colossians.

7. The Problem at Colosse

The Christians at Colosse faced a major threat to their orthodoxy. Like many letters, this one countered a specific movement threatening to remove the church from Christ. Paul affirmed the centrality of Christ in both doctrine and practice. While most commentators agree that a problem threatened the church, there is no consensus as to its exact nature. A brief survey of the primary

---

[28] Some, therefore, think it was written in the mid-50s like those other epistles.

[29] The most extensive list of parallels in English between Ephesians and Colossians is in W. Hendriksen, *Exposition of Ephesians*, NTC (Grand Rapids: Baker, 1967).

historical contributions follows, along with an overview of the data. Details of the situation await the commentary section.

(1) The Data

The criteria for discovering the context suggest fertile ground for speculation. Paul dealt with a specific heresy; but because he basically answered problems rather than describing them, the situation of the church remains obscure. Specific data come from two complementary approaches: the general content of the epistle and the specific texts that discuss the problem.

The general content encompasses many sections. They include the prayer for knowledge to do the will of God (1:9-11), the hymn to Christ (1:15-20), the sufferings of the apostle explained in mystical terminology (1:27-2:5), the confrontation of the false teachers (2:8-3:4), and the ethical portions employing the vice and virtue lists (3:5-17).[30] Each has had interpreters who claimed either heretical contexts or tendencies for these portions. For the most part, however, defining the heresy consists of analyzing 1:9-20 and 2:8-3:4. The significant features of 1:9-20 are the cosmic presentation of Christ, his role in creation and redemption, and his authority because of his death on the cross. Colossians 2:8-3:4 contains more detailed elements to consider.

Others refer to the number of unusual words in the epistle. In the Greek text there are 34 *hapax legomena* and 63 words which occur less than 5 times in the New Testament. Significantly, of the *hapax legomena*, 83 percent occur in 1:9-3:17, the passage considered most reflective of the heresy. Of this 83 percent, 38 percent occur in 2:8-3:4. The same general phenomena occur in words used less than 5 times in the New Testament. Fully 80 percent occur in 1:9-3:17, with 32 percent occurring in 2:8-3:4. The technical use of other terms, such as *plērōma* (fullness), *philosophia* (philosophy), *embateuō* (go into great detail), and *gnōsis* (knowledge), are discussed much. A major question remains whether these words are really technical terms. Are they catchwords from other religions? Are they doctrinal statements from the heretical groups? Could Paul simply have been employing unusual terminology because of the heresy he opposed? In this century, earlier interpreters often saw technical definitions. M. Dibelius, for example, built a case for the context on the technical use of one term alone (*embateuō*).[31] On the other hand, M. Hooker claimed that the

---

[30] The passages which contain polemical elements have been identified by C. A. Evans, "The Colossian Mystics," *Bib* 63:2 (1982) 192-94. The sections are identified along with the nature of the polemic. He identifies the following polemical portions: 1:1-2; 1:3-8; 1:9-14; 1:15-20; 1:21-23; 1:24-29; 2:1-7; 2:8-15; 2:16-19; 2:20-23; 3:1-4; 3:5-11,12-17; 3:18-4:1; and 4:2-6,7-18. Every portion of the epistle is included. The value of his list is the grouping together of the verses along with the polemic he brings.

[31] M. Dibelius, "The Isis Initiation in Apuleius and Related Initiatory Rites," *Conflict At Colossae*, ed. F. O. Francis and W. A. Meeks, 2nd ed. SBLSBS 4. (Missoula, Mont.: Scholars, 1975), 61-121.

terms suit the situation and do not reflect the heresy itself.[32] Although her suggestions do not receive universal acceptance, her concerns show the relative subjectivity involved in making such judgments. At any rate, building conclusions on the data requires tedious and disciplined exegesis of the individual words and the several passages involved.

The major text for determining the context is 2:8-3:4. There several matters call for attention. They include: "fullness" (*plērōma*) (2:9); "delights in false humility and the worship of angels" (2:18); "what he has seen" (2:18); "Do not handle! Do not taste! Do not touch!" (2:21); and "self-imposed worship, their false humility and their harsh treatment of the body" (2:23). Recently many have considered these as phrases from the heretical teachers themselves. If they are not actual quotes, they must be terms particularly suited to the teachings advocated by the heretics. They became a vehicle for countering the philosophers in their own terms. The concentration of these rare terms in 2:8-3:4 confirms the obvious: This text provides the *locus* for determining the problem which Paul countered.

(2) Historical Context

The context addressed by the apostle shapes the concrete meaning Colossians has today. Indeed, the task of discovering the context has led to various suggestions which have rightly colored the presentations of both entire commentaries on Colossians and even Pauline theology as a whole. The quest for context began in earnest in the nineteenth century and developed into a science in the twentieth.

NINETEENTH-CENTURY CONTRIBUTIONS. Two significant works dominated the nineteenth century. The direction-setting work of F. C. Baur questioned the integrity of the epistle and dated it after the lifetime of Paul. This opened the door to many second-century contextual suppositions. He worked also for an evolutionary explanation of the phenomena of Christianity and its writings and invited comparisons between Christianity and non-Christian parallels. In many ways, all subsequent study reacts to Baur. Some support him, some modify him, and others counter him.

By far the most lasting contribution of the nineteenth century was the work of J. B. Lightfoot in his *St. Paul's Epistles to the Colossians and to Philemon*.[33] Lightfoot's conclusions remain viable one hundred years after his commentary, and many arguments simply repeat or expand his views. He saw the problem as an incipient Jewish Gnosticism which characterized the Essenes. The religious and philosophical parallels pointed to an early date of the epistle written

---

[32]M. D. Hooker, "Were there False Teachers in Colossae?" *Christ and Spirit in the New Testament: Studies in Honor of Charles Francis Digby Moule*, ed. B. Lindars and S. S. Smalley (Cambridge: University Press, 1973) 315-31.

[33]J. B. Lightfoot, *St. Paul's Epistles to the Colossians and to Philemon*, 3rd ed. (London: Mac-Millan, 1879).

by the apostle Paul. He left a twofold legacy: the idea of incipient Gnosticism and the Jewish nature of the heresy.

TWENTIETH-CENTURY CONTRIBUTIONS. Twentieth-century interpreters develop and shape one or more of the ideas of the nineteenth century. Some, such as Dibelius[34] and Lohse,[35] reaffirm the Gnostic or "pre-Gnostic" context. Others, such as S. Lyonnett,[36] F. Francis,[37] F. F. Bruce,[38] W. Hendriksen,[39] A. Bandstra,[40] and O'Brien,[41] hold to a more Jewish context.

The first major essay of the twentieth century was written by Dibelius.[42] He studied the Isis initiation in Apuleius and, impressed particularly by a technical use of the term *embateuō*, determined that Colossians addressed a similar initiatory rite. For him, Colossians provides proof that Christianity joined with a mystery cult of the "elements" by about A.D. 56.[43] This occurred before the time of Paul. Paul's task, therefore, was to demonstrate the distinction between the cult and Christianity. Many objections arise. Dibelius does not explain the distinctive element of Christianity that made it survive. He states its survival depended on its exclusivity, but the exclusive nature is unexplained. Further, Christianity dominated the Isis cult by offering a better solution to life. Lyonnet's evaluation is representative of the reservations among contemporary scholars. He states regarding Dibelius's analysis of the temple rites: "But the sense of the passage is one of the most controversial, the text itself is scarcely certain, and it would be imprudent at least to erect a whole theory on this single term."[44]

Later scholars modify Dibelius's position. G. Bornkamm argues that the problem was a Gnosticized Judaism that added pagan elements.[45] These

---

[34]Dibelius, *An die Kolosser, Epheser, und Philemon, HNT*, 3rd ed. rev. by H. Greeven (Tübingen: Mohr, 1953).

[35]Lohse's comments, being more recent, reflect this tradition better. He says: "Consequently the adherents of the 'philosophy' cannot be considered Essenes, members of the Qumran community or proponents of heretical Jewish propaganda. . . . because of the emphasis placed on knowledge as well as its world-negating character, [but they] can be termed Gnostic or, if a more cautious designation is desired, pre-Gnostic" (129).

[36]S. Lyonnet, "L'etude du milieu litteraire et l'exegese du Nouveau Testament: Les adversaires de Paul a Colosses," *Bib* 37 (1956): 27-38, which is translated as "Paul's Adversaries in Colossae," *Conflict at Colossae*, 1147-61.

[37]F. O. Francis, "Humility and Angelic Worship in Col 2:18," *Conflict at Colossae*, 163-95.

[38]F. F. Bruce, *Ephesians and Colossians, NIC* (Grand Rapids: Eerdmans, 1957), 165-69.

[39]Hendriksen, *Colossians and Philemon*, 17-21.

[40]A. J. Bandstra, "Did the Colossian Errorists Need a Mediator?" *New Dimensions in New Testament Study*, ed. R. N. Longenecker and M. C. Tenney (Grand Rapids: Zondervan, 1974), 329-43.

[41]O'Brien, xxxviii.

[42]Dibelius, "The Isis Initiation."

[43]Ibid., 91.

[44]Lyonnet, 150.

[45]G. Bornkamm, "Die Haresie des Kolosserbriefes," *Theologische Literaturzeitung* 73 (1948): 11-20. This is reprinted in *Conflict at Colossae*, 123-45.

included Iranian-Persian elements and Chaldean astrology. Thus syncretism resulted. Although the Gnostic position has faded in popularity, some still advocate it.

The contemporary climate understands Paul's letter in a Jewish context. Three significant writers contribute to this understanding, though they, in their own way, built on the work of Lightfoot. Lyonnet leads the way in several penetrating articles.[46] He states that the terms used to support the ties between Christianity and Gnostic cults occurred outside Gnostic circles but persisted in other philosophies as well. Particularly, they often occurred in Jewish (Christian) contexts. He concludes that the opponents were Christians attracted to Judaism.

Francis also sees a Jewish Christian context, but it was a context of mystical asceticism.[47] The terms employed could well be Jewish rather than Greek, including "humility to the flesh," "entering [*embateuō*] into visions," and "worship of angels." These concepts and similar terminology appear at Qumran and, for Francis, may well represent a like religious group. Bandstra confirms Francis's arguments and notes that the Gnostic influence at Colosse was not clearly established.

The prevailing view, therefore, is that the Colossian heresy was some form of Judaism. Most likely it was typical of reactionary Judaism, such as practiced at Qumran, since many of the terms occur in that literature. Little has been done, however, to trace the connection between Qumran and Colosse.

(3) The Jewish Context

Historical inquiry reveals a sizeable Jewish community in the Lycus valley at the first century. Josephus recorded that Antiochus the Great (223-187 B.C.) imported two thousand Jewish families from Mesopotamia and Babylon to Lydia and Phrygia.[48] Lightfoot calculated the Jewish population at A.D. 62 to be more than eleven thousand adult freemen, plus women, children, and possibly slaves.[49] The entire Jewish population, however, "would probably be much larger than this partial estimate implies."[50] The attractions of the areas were of some concern to the Jewish scholars. Reflecting a concern for the northwestern migration to the area, one rabbi wrote, "The wines and the baths of Phrygia have separated the ten tribes from Israel."[51]

---

[46]In addition to "Adversaries," mentioned above, he wrote "Col 2,18 et les Mysteres d'Apollon Clarien," *Bib* 43 (1962): 417-35; and "Saint Paul et le gnosticisme: la lettre aux Colossiens," *Le Origini delo Gnosticismo*, ed. U. Bianchi (Leiden: Brill, 1967), 538-61.

[47]Francis, 163-95.

[48]See Josephus, *Antiquities* XII.iii.4.

[49]Lightfoot, 20. He came to this conclusion by noting that a contraband temple offering was taken by Flaccus, the propraetor of Asia. The contraband offering was twenty pounds of gold from the single district. He estimated the amount per family.

[50]Ibid., 21. He pointed out that there were larger seizures from neighboring areas.

[51]*B. Sabb.* 147.b.

The New Testament also bears witness to a sizeable community of Jews in the area. Acts 2:9-10 states that Jews from Asia and Phrygia were at Pentecost. Many of the books of the New Testament reflect Jewish Christian interests there. Paul's writings are instructive in this regard. For example, Galatians counters the energetic activities of Judaizers; Ephesians obviously deals with two religious communities which had to realize their unity (2:1-11); and 1 Timothy may reflect theological problems prompted by study of the Old Testament and the law (1:8-11). The writings of John reflect the cultural mixture as well. The Gospel of John contains many elements intended to persuade a Jewish audience of the messiahship of Jesus, and the Revelation is similar in genre to the Jewish apocalypses of conservative Judaism. Significantly, all of these New Testament books address situations in Asia Minor and deal with problems which are, at least in part, Jewish. Many have also compared them with Gnostic elements assumed in their teachings. Clearly, a study of their contexts reveals there was a large and vocal Jewish element in the area. It also reveals that many Jews converted to Christianity.

Finally, the ministry of John the Baptist spread quickly and significantly into this area. Although John lived a short time, his ministry enjoyed a worldwide impact. Acts 18:24-26 records the ministry of Apollos, who apparently advanced the teachings of John the Baptist at Ephesus. Apollos's influence may have been significant by the time he met Priscilla and Aquila. Much later, about A.D. 85-95, John the apostle wrote his gospel from around Ephesus. A distinctive of this writing is the large space devoted to John the Baptist and his witness to Jesus. It would seem that forty years after Apollos the impact of John the Baptist would be diminished, yet the apostle John thought it significant enough to build upon it for his Gentile readers.

The tie between the Essene Jews and the Colossian church may be the misunderstood influence of John the Baptist. Years ago Dibelius commented, "The Christian congregation probably borrowed baptism, as an eschatological sacrament, from the circle of John the Baptist. But the Christians of the hellenistic world felt the need to understand it as a hellenistic mystery."[52] There is an obvious connection between John the Baptist and the Palestinian Christian communities. Possibly, the relationship extended into Asia Minor, where disciples of John the Baptist turned to Christ. When they did, they brought their ascetic and strict ethical concerns with them into the church.

Conceptual and theological factors support the strongly Jewish nature of the Epistle to the Colossians. Obvious ties existed between reactionary Judaism and Christianity in the Lycus valley. Naturally a conflict between them arose.

(4) The Focal Text: Colossians 2:8-3:4

In discussing Paul's argument in Col 2:8-3:4, three matters emerge. First, an introductory statement provides a cryptic analysis of the problem. Second, the

---

[52] Dibelius, "Isis Initiation," 95.

primary concerns are detailed. Finally, the problem is carefully defined and exegetical solutions are suggested. This important section serves as a window to the theology of Colossians.

INTRODUCTORY STATEMENT. Paul introduced the problem in 2:8. Set in a context of watchfulness lest the Christians be captured, the verse discusses both the medium and the measurement of the heresy. The medium is "hollow and deceptive philosophy." Two matters emerge here. First, the teaching characterized itself as a philosophy (no doubt Paul referred here to the position of the adversaries). This articular noun, occurring only here in the New Testament, points to a specific and organized formulation of thought. A similar articular construction occurs in v. 14 (*tois dogmasin*), which confirms this observation. Paul did not decry philosophy itself, but this particular formulation. Second, the teaching led nowhere. It was empty and deceiving. The problem, then, was not simply random or periodic speculations about life in the hope that something good would come. This system of thought appears organized and aggressive.

Paul measured the teaching by three instructive criteria. Together they profile the teaching in a way that reveals its destructive nature. First, it was *traditional*. Although the phrase "human tradition" points to the source of the teaching, it may not point to antiquity. Paul's point was not that the teaching was old; rather, it was human.

Second, the teaching "depends on . . . the basic principles of this world" (*kata ta stoicheia tou kosmou*). This much-discussed phrase may be technical or nontechnical since both may occur in the New Testament.[53] Technically, it refers to a tenet of the heretical teachers and/or the supernatural beings believed to exert their power and influence over the physical and human world. If the technical use occurs here, it is the only such use of the phrase in the New Testament. Nontechnically, it refers to imperfect teachings or conditions. The elements of the world contrast with the higher truths of Christianity. Favoring this view, the passages outside of Colossians refer to the physical elements (2 Pet 3:10,12) or elementary matters generally (Gal 4:3-9) or the basics of the Christian faith specifically (Heb 5:12). Either position reconciles easily with a Jewish context for the teaching, though the so-called pre-Gnostic elements call more naturally for the technical application. Whatever position is taken, clearly Paul regarded the *stoicheia* as inferior and, in that sense, elementary.[54]

Finally, the heretical doctrine was non-Christian (*ou kata Christon*). This by itself does not suggest it was outside the church. It does mean that it belonged

---

[53]For a nontechnical use of στοιχεῖα, see Heb 5:12 and 1 Pet 3:10,12. The technical use, if it is employed, is best represented here.

[54]The use referring to supernatural beings is preferred by Martin, J. Moffatt, F. C. Baur, Dibelius, A. Deissmann, and Lohse, among others. Preferring the nontechnical are Hendriksen, H. Meyer, E. Burton, Moule, Lightfoot, and Bandstra.

outside the church. The real problem here is involvement in Christian matters with a non-Christian orientation.

Together these three characteristics provide understanding about the false teaching. It was a nonrevelational, spiritually juvenile, sub-Christian system of thought.

PAUL'S CONCERNS. Paul identified several concerns. They may be understood broadly in theological categories, moving to specific matters within each category. After a presentation of the thematic arrangement of the passage, a brief interpretation is offered.

Thematic Arrangement. The passage deals with both theology proper and practice. Thematically, the first of the theological sections addresses soteriology in a chiastic literary pattern. The chiasm (from the Greek letter *chi* [*X*]), which is an inverted relationship between the syntactic elements of parallel phrases, includes both supernatural beings and the regulations, what may be classified loosely as angel worship and asceticism. The chiasm of 2:9-15 is as follows:

A   For in Christ all the fullness of the Deity lives in bodily form, and you have been given fullness in Christ, who is the head over every *power* and *authority.*

B   *In him you were also circumcised,* in the putting off of the sinful nature, *not with a circumcision done by the hands of men* but with the circumcision done by Christ, having been buried with him in baptism and raised with him through your faith in the power of God, who raised him from the dead.

B´   When you were dead in your sins and in the uncircumcision of your sinful nature, God made you alive with Christ. He forgave us all our sins, *having canceled the written code, with its regulations, that was against us* and that stood opposed to us; he took it away, nailing it to the cross.

A´   And having disarmed the *powers* and *authorities*, he made a public spectacle of them, triumphing over them by the cross.

A	B´
who is the head over every *power* and *authority*	having cancelled the written code, with its regulations, that was against us

B	A´
In him you were also circumcised . . . not with a circumcision done by the hands of men	And having disarmed the *powers* and *authorities*, he made a public spectacle of them

The uniting theme is soteriological. The work of Christ, specifically his death, holds the two sections together.

The second of the theological sections describes the practical aspects of Christ's death in terms of Christian attitudes toward the law. Two imperatives provide the literary key, dividing the passage into two applications. The first relates to asceticism (vv. 16-17): "Do not let anyone judge you by what you eat or drink." The second refers to angel worship (vv. 18-19): "Do not let anyone . . . disqualify you." Since they discuss the practical applications of soteriology, they speak to a theology of sanctification.

The two concerns of asceticism and angel worship unite the passage. A matrix of thought and the outline take note of both. Angel worship is dealt with in vv. 9-10,15. The concept of asceticism is addressed in vv. 11-14.

Finally, Paul spoke of the application of these theological truths *in practice*. Colossians 2:20-3:4 present positive principles, as well as strong warnings, to be observed in the Christian life. These also grow out of theological foundations, as was typical for Paul. Thematically, two interrelated patterns reveal the connection of these sections. First, 2:20-3:4 speaks of the implications of union with Christ. In characteristic Pauline terminology, Paul linked Christian living to the death and resurrection of Jesus. Second, these two themes extend the teaching of 2:8-19. The semantic parallels reveal this motif.

This thematic overview suggests an outline with parallel focal points. It is as follows:

> Introduction (2:8)
> Theological Implications of the Heresy (2:9-19)
> > Soteriological Implications (2:9-15)
> > > (Death with Christ)
> > Sanctification Implications (2:16-19)
> > > (Life with Christ)
> Practical Implications of the Heresy (2:20-3:4)
> > Soteriological Implications (2:20-23)
> > > (Death with Christ)
> > Sanctification Implications (3:1-4)
> > > (Life with Christ)

The passage seems cluttered from an organizational perspective because of the interchange between theological principles and their extensions into life. The particulars of Christian living presented here, however, occur in the theological section. This reveals Paul's integration of thought and practice. The specifics, such as diet, days, do's and don't's, concretely illustrate the point. When Paul moved to sanctification, he left behind the particulars. After all, as Paul reminded the Romans in a similar context, the "kingdom of God is not a matter of eating and drinking, but of righteousness, and peace and joy in the Holy Spirit" (Rom 14:17). A preoccupation with the things of earth *in any fashion* distracts one from the kingdom of God.

Interpretation. The thematic and literary analysis aids interpretation. A survey of contents demonstrates that each section of the text reveals Paul's polemic.

The previous survey reveals that the theological passage divides into two areas: soteriology (2:9-15) and sanctification (2:16-19). The soteriological section contains two matters: "angel worship" (2:9-10,15) and "asceticism" (2:11-14). The two receive almost equal emphasis. Syntactically, the outside members of a chiasm receive primary emphasis. On one hand, Paul concerned himself more with the cosmic Christ, a seeming fascination of the Colossians. On the other hand, the ascetic problem occupied more space in the text.

In dealing with this issue, Paul confronted two typically Jewish problems which plagued the church. Fascination with supernatural beings characterized many groups of Jews from the time of Daniel through the Intertestamental Period.[55] This specific infatuation was needless. In his work, Jesus dominated them. He created them (he is their head, 2:9-10; see also the hymn to Christ of 1:15-20). When many rebelled, for Paul focused here on the evil supernatural beings, Jesus conquered them, embarrassing and exposing them publicly (2:15). They deserved *no* following.

The other Jewish problem stems from the heart of Jewish life. In vv. 11-14 Paul addressed circumcision and the law. Perhaps these represent the entire system since in Rom 2:17-29 these two focal points characterize Judaism (the law in vv. 17-24; circumcision in vv. 25-29). Circumcision was no longer necessary. Spiritual circumcision, the more important matter (cf. Rom 2:29), occurred at baptism when one identified with the death, burial, and resurrection of Christ (see Col 2:11-12 where syntactically being buried and being raised explain baptism). Physical circumcision introduced one to the spiritual blessings of Israel and to the requirements of the law. Here Paul argued that *neither* circumcision *nor* the requirements of the law continue in effect.

Similarly, at the time of conversion, forgiveness occurred. Paul related this to the law with specific terminology suggesting a legal framework and system.[56] Surely Paul meant that Christians no longer fear the condemnatory aspects of the Commandments. They have no obligation to them. Neither of these perspectives, however, characterized the heretics of Colosse.

Thus the soteriological heresy failed to appreciate the central place of Jesus. Rather, its advocates accepted a supernatural hierarchy other than the Trinity and gave themselves to scrupulous and legalistic requirements which they assumed commended them to God. This indeed was the heart of the problem and even today is still one of the roots of secularism.

---

[55] Of course, these references may refer to the Hellenistic speculation about the supernatural. The point is that there is no reason why this cannot be considered natural to Judaism.

[56] The phrase is "handwriting of ordinances." There are, of course, many problems interpreting the phrase.

The issue of sanctification, viewed from a theological perspective, extends these errors of thought into errors of life. Colossians 2:16-17 explains that the legal requirements of the law prepared the way for the Messiah. They lacked the substance that Christ would bring. They were external and did not deal with the heart of the matter (Paul explained the latter in 2:23).

Similarly, readers were not to become preoccupied with the "worship of angels," as some were prone to do. Until recently the phrase "worship of angels" was a thorn in the flesh for interpreters. Most understood the genitive construction as objective, the worship *directed* to angels. The interpretation fit the incipient Gnostic viewpoint well, but it was difficult to reconcile with the strongly Jewish flavor of the passage. Francis devoted himself to the phrase and found that it bore striking similarity to the Essene community of Judea. As a part of their worship, the Essenes sought to worship *with the angels*. They aspired to higher forms and expressions than normal, hoping to worship with the angels.

A study of the phrase "voluntary humility" confirmed Francis's viewpoint. He noted evidences of self-imposed hardships of fasting which allowed the believer to enter new vistas of religious experience. They probably believed self-induced trances evidenced their super-spiritual position.[57] The religious experience came from fasting and strenuous, voluntary self-deprivation. The writer used the term "humility" (*tapeinophrosynē*) to describe these rigorous religious activities.

When the two concerns of "worship of angels" and "voluntary humility" are understood in this fashion, one complements the other. Gnostic and pre-Gnostic speculations become unnecessary, though the possibility of the pre-Gnostic influence remains. The point is that two seemingly dissimilar religious activities join in one religious outlook. Whatever interpretation holds, clearly Paul addressed a religious community endangered by mere human tradition.

The problem was not likely entirely Jewish in origin. Paul's detailed argument about Jesus as the Creator and Redeemer, particularly with reference to supernatural beings, suggests a more Hellenistic orientation. The fact that he continually called them "principalities, rulers, thrones, and dominions" suggests a greater categorization of angelic beings than is normally found in Scripture. For this reason, a probable explanation is that the heresy was primarily Jewish, particularly in its origins, but had some secular elements included, which later became part of a Gnostic system of thought.

Practicality. When Paul turned to *praxis*, his reference points remained salvation (conversion) in 2:20-23 and sanctification (Christian living) in 3:1-4. Regarding conversion, Paul asked, "Why are you willingly subjecting yourself to regulations?" After liberation from a legal system, obeying such a system

---

[57]This evidence occurred in Hermes, particularly.

again was a step backward. Three reasons are given for not submitting to regulations. First, the believers had died with Christ. This mystical but experiential union means that ties to this world have been severed. Second, submitting to these commands assumed a this-world orientation. Third, these things have no lasting value—they perish when used and have no real effect on the lusts of the flesh. The principle espoused is that any spiritual slavery—voluntary or otherwise—other than a slavery to Christ robs one of spiritual freedoms. A preoccupation with matters confined to this age saps spiritual energy.

The principle Paul elucidated relates only to external, amoral matters. In 3:5-17 he clearly commanded the readers to be known by qualities of character which accompanied their new life. Sloppy or careless living has no place among Christians. Unfortunately, too many times Christians give scrupulous attention to such regulations as found here while overlooking the weightier matters of a moral nature. The development of Christian character brings eternal rewards.

Finally, Paul turned to the practical aspects of sanctification or Christian growth (3:1-4). These are to desire and delight in things above rather than things below. Christians must focus on Christ. Three reasons provide incentive.

First, Christians are raised with Christ. As death with Christ satisfies the past life, their resurrection with Christ opens new dimensions of living.

Second, Christ is life. This does not mean he provides life, which, of course, he does. Here Paul stated that Christ is the life principle. Believers are sustained for time and eternity by the spiritual power given to them by Christ. Unbelievers, of course, have a different life principle. Natural eyes cannot see what makes Christians live as they do. Their motivations, values, and actions seem strange. The life principle remains hidden.

Third, Christians will triumph with Christ. Someday he will manifest himself, when he comes to this earth again. The unseen spiritual realities will break through this age, and the now-secret source of life will be manifest. At that time, all Christians will share in the glory of the revealed Christ. There is an eschatological verification of the truthfulness of Christianity, and Christians anxiously await that great day. These more important concerns were to attract the interests of the Colossian Christians.

Paul's accusations were devastating. The system of thought threatening the Colossian church was of human tradition, it was elementary, and it was non-Christian. Theologically, it divorced Christ from his place in the Godhead and separated itself from Christ. It invalidated Christ's death. By adding its requirements of human effort, it made the death of Christ insignificant, if not unnecessary. Practically, the heretics alienated themselves from Christ, the source of real life. No doubt this, too, resulted from their natural perspective. Human ideas do not embrace the thoughts of the Spirit, and human eyes do not see them.

(5) *Conclusions*

Having surveyed matters of the context of the Epistle to the Colossians and the primary focal passage, Col 2:9-3:4, the situation may be related to the subject at hand. This problem appeared within a religious community. Even if incipient Gnostic elements surfaced, they were certainly secondary. The deeper problem may have been the age-old clash of the human mind versus the Spirit or human tradition versus the revelation in Christ. Similar issues may exist in the relationships between Christianity and philosophy, psychology, natural science, and the behavioral sciences. At many points, merely human ideas attempt to reformulate Christian truth, to remake it in their image. While not blatantly secular, such situations reveal the priority of reason over revelation.

On the other hand, the problem also arises when Christianity becomes only tradition. The specific practices addressed in Colosse may well have had revelational roots. They were extensions of Old Testament law. Orthodoxy without orthopraxy leads to *de facto* secularism. Creeds without conviction and structure without substance lead the unsuspecting away from God. If the previous concern were reason over revelation, this one was the priority of assent over action.

The answer lies in a positive and comprehensive commitment to Christ. Human reason and tradition do not necessarily contradict revelation. Indeed, the *imago dei* consists in part of a structured, organized capacity to think and act. Theological reflection provides the answers. The origin of secularism is separation from the source of spiritual life. To counter the subtle philosophy that threatened Colosse centuries ago, Christians today will find it imperative to know Christ personally and intimately, theologically and practically. They must never allow any philosophical system, whether good or bad, to replace that relationship.

8. The Theological Structure of the Epistle

Colossians divides naturally into two sections. Like many Pauline epistles, the first part consists of theological instruction (1:1-3:4); the second part, ethical (3:5-4:18), though elements of both theology and ethics are present in each part. These components undergirded Paul's message and prepared the believers for the onslaughts of the false teachers. The two primary sections each have traditional material supporting them. The first section, which is theological, builds around the hymn to Christ of 1:15-20. Although it illustrates the nature of the gospel, it forms a high point in the first part of the epistle. In the beginning of Colossians, Paul praised the readers because he knew they were a part of the kingdom of Christ (1:3-8). Immediately he followed his thanksgiving with a petition that they would continue to grow into all the wisdom which God provides for his people (1:9-14). They had every reason to be thankful for what God did since he rescued them from their spiritual enemies and qualified them for an inheritance.

The hymn to Christ follows. It explains lyrically the centrality of Christ in creation and redemption (1:15-20). This is followed by application to the Colossians and Paul. Their reconciliation is described in 1:21-23, and Paul's place in God's plan of redemption is explained in 1:24-2:7.

The practical section of the epistle also builds on traditional materials. The domestic code (*Haustafeln*) occurs in some form in several letters, including Ephesians and 1 Peter. No doubt the early church developed a commonly accepted list of expectations for these relationships. When Paul wrote to Ephesus and Colosse, he embellished an understanding known in the church and perhaps received from the Lord himself. This list has some distinctives (see the commentary), but the basic teaching also occurs elsewhere. At any rate, two sections of the epistle are clearly defined by the centrality of the hymn and the family behavior code.

The transition section contains many difficulties in analyzing the structure.[58] Beginning with 2:8, two independent commands appear which normally form major dividing points. In 2:8 Paul warned, "See to it that no one takes you captive." Colossians 2:16-19 begins with "therefore" which is, apparently, subordinated to 2:8. This means that 2:8-19 forms one unit with two parts. The parts are theological in nature. The first discusses the theology of salvation (2:8-15); the second presents the theology of sanctification (2:16-19). The Greek word "therefore" (*oun*) holds these two sections together.

The second command occurs in 2:20, "Why . . . do you submit to [the world's] rules?" The paragraph occurs independently but is followed by three paragraphs introduced again by "therefore." The question is, Where does a break occur, if one occurs?

The relationships of the "therefores" must be determined. Significantly, "therefore" occurs only four times between 2:8 and 3:17. The two imperatives mentioned seem to break the sequence into two sections. Is there another break?

A thematic analysis helps to resolve the difficulty. Colossians 2:20 begins a common theological theme, that of the death and burial of Christ. The section on "The Problem at Colosse" pictures the relationships well. The death of Christ naturally called for a section on the resurrection of Jesus. From a thematic perspective, 2:20-3:4 stand together because of the "in Christ" motif. Further, the discussion in these verses develops the idea introduced in 2:12. It seems that the first major section begins at 1:3 and ends at 3:4.

---

[58]Commentators do not agree on where the dividing points should be. C. Vaughan, "Colossians," *EBC*, ed. F. E. Gaebelein (Grand Rapids: Zondervan, 1978), 11:170; Wright, 45; Guthrie, 560, e.g., break the text at 3:1. Others see the major break at 3:4: R. Martin, *The Church's Lord and the Christian's Liberty* (Grand Rapids: Eerdmans, 1972), vii; Lightfoot, 127; and Moule, 113. Moule seems correct in stating of 3:5-17: "This paragraph marks the transition from what is primarily theology to the application of this doctrinal matter to life and conduct."

Colossians 3:5 begins a new direction. The theme of Christian purity continues, but the discussion has moved to a more practical level than 2:16-3:4. It deals with the actual outworkings of theology in life. For these reasons, this commentary takes 3:5-4:18 as a second unit of thought, developing the theology of the believer's death and resurrection with Christ.

It may seem awkward to the reader of English translations to break the text in this manner. Nevertheless, this appears to be the turning point in a carefully woven argument. The epistle, then, contains three distinct movements: the salvation experience and growth of the Colossian church (1:9-23), illustrated by the hymn to Christ; the commands to thought and life which apply the truths of the hymn and their salvation (2:8-3:17); and a practical section in which Paul drew in part from a common understanding in the early church (3:18-4:18). The significant place of transition is 3:5, indicated by the use of "therefore" (*oun*) and the shift to the imperative mood (*nekrōsate*, "put to death"). The three movements, therefore, call for a twofold division. The outline of the epistle follows.

─────────────── **OUTLINE OF THE BOOK** ───────────────

I. Salutation, (1:1-2)
    1. The Writers (1:1)
    2. The Readers (1:2a)
    3. The Greeting (1:2b)
II. The Preeminence of Christ in Christian Theology (1:3-3:4)
    1. Paul's Thanksgiving and Prayer for the Colossians (1:3-23)
        (1) Paul's Thanksgiving for the Colossians (1:3-8)
        (2) Paul's Prayer for the Colossians (1:9-14)
        (3) The Hymn to Christ (1:15-20)
        (4) The Salvation of the Colossians (1:21-23)
    2. Paul's Place in Christ's Kingdom (1:24-2:7)
        (1) Paul's Ministry to the Churches (1:24-29)
        (2) Paul's Ministry to the Colossians (2:1-7)
    3. Paul's Defense of the Faith (2:8-3:4)
        (1) Against the Theological Threat (2:8-19)
        (2) Against the Practical Threat (2:20-3:4)
III. The Preeminence of Christ in Christian Living (3:5-4:6)
    1. Order in the Christian Life and the Church (3:5-4:1)
        (1) The New Person (3:5-17)
        (2) Family Relationships (3:18-4:1)
    2. Prayerful Cooperation in Ministry (4:2-6)
        (1) Prayer (4:2-4)
        (2) Wisdom (4:5)
        (3) Careful Communication (4:6)

IV. Final Matters (4:7-18)
   1. Those Who Journeyed to the Church (4:7-9)
   2. Those Who Sent Greetings (4:10-14)
   3. Those to Whom Greetings are Sent (4:15-17)
   4. Final Greeting from Paul (4:18)

SECTION OUTLINE

I. SALUTATION (1:1-2)
1. The Writers (1:1)
2. The Readers (1:2a)
3. The Greeting (1:2b)

I. SALUTATION (1:1-2)

Paul addressed this epistle to a congregation previously unknown to him (1:4; 2:1). That in itself appears strange since he knew well the churches in the area. The road from Galatia to Ephesus probably passed through Colosse, so Paul's travels no doubt took him into the region from the time of the second missionary journey onward. Nevertheless, the Apocalypse of John identifies several churches in the area that are not mentioned in Pauline literature. These include Smyrna, Pergamum, Thyatira, Sardis, and Philadelphia (Rev 2-3). Though they may have been founded later than Paul's travels, they appear to have been old enough by the time of the writing of Revelation to have developed their spiritual condition. The point is that, while Paul knew many of the churches "by face," he did not know them all. It is inconceivable, however, that they did not know of him.

This lack of personal knowledge does not alter significantly the introduction. In the Epistle to the Romans, another church Paul did not know personally, the salutation is quite lengthy and informative. Paul wanted to enlist the Romans' help for a mission to Spain (15:24). Such a cooperative venture was best served by providing information about himself. Here, however, the salutation follows a normal pattern for the first-century world in general and the Pauline epistles in particular. This may reveal a significant mutual secondhand knowledge between apostle and church. The introduction contains the three elements normally included in first-century correspondence: the writer(s), the readers, and a greeting.

1. The Writers (1:1)

[1]Paul, an apostle of Christ Jesus by the will of God, and Timothy our brother

1:1 This letter had two writers, Paul and Timothy, although later the epistle clarifies the fact that Paul was the primary writer.[1] Here he identified himself as an apostle. The title appears in most of the Pauline Epistles (but not Phil

---

[1] Apart from the obvious Pauline flavor to the letter, in contrast to other writers of the New Testament, the plural verbs are used through 1:9, then singular verbs replace them. Perhaps at the point of the substance of the letter Paul reverted to his own primary authorship.

or 1, 2 Thess), and it provides a reference point for understanding Paul. He seems to have used the term here to call attention to his authority. This situation demanded confrontation. The fact that Paul did not identify himself with the usual term "servant of Jesus Christ" emphasizes the authoritative element in this introduction. Paul's apostleship, however, was "by the will of God." The phrase was to remind the readers of the divine call on his life. His was an apostleship by God's initiative, not by his own efforts. Thus two ideas converge in this designation. First, Paul's apostleship contained all the elements associated with that office. Second, God called him to the office. The first description, therefore, combines both authority and humility.

The office of apostle included several elements.[2] Primarily, an apostle had to know Christ personally and have witnessed the resurrection (Acts 1:21-22). Paul claimed that he had seen the risen Lord (1 Cor 9:1) and, therefore, had witnessed the resurrection (1 Cor 15:7). Further, Paul's message came from divine revelation with no human intermediary (Gal 1:15-17). At times he argued forcefully that his apostleship was equal to the other apostles and was, therefore, to be received by the churches.[3] His address to the church at Colosse came because of his apostleship and the supervisory responsibilities it entailed.

Paul included Timothy because of Timothy's share in the ministry.[4] Timothy had a close relationship with Paul, but his relationship to the Colossian church is unknown. Perhaps Paul included Timothy because he was from the general area of the church and because he was the "heir apparent" of Paul's ministry. Timothy came from Lystra and Derbe, to the east of the Lycus valley. He also traveled with Paul on the second journey and, as much as any of Paul's companions, knew of the church's situation. Timothy later assumed the major oversight of the churches in that area, judging from his prominence at Ephesus and the directions given him in the Pastoral Epistles which bear his name. Since Timothy would carry on Paul's work, including him served to introduce him to the Colossians as a knowledgeable leader. He had demonstrated an interest and

---

[2]Much discussion involves the technical and nontechnical use of the term. While it does seem that the term may be used in a general sense of "anyone sent," clearly it has the technical use as well. That is, it may designate one of those who were called to a specific office. Obviously the technical sense is found here, and that is the reason for such discussions as are found in 2 Corinthians and Galatians, where Paul's apostleship was questioned. No one would question the generic sense of "sent." The discussion makes sense only in light of Paul's claim to a special official function.

[3]Some scholars have asked whether the church made a mistake in selecting Matthias to replace Judas, rather than Paul. But there is no indication that Paul or the others thought it was a mistake, even though Paul did not have the specific qualifications demanded by the eleven. There appear to have been more than twelve apostles anyway. The question must be decided in favor of the church's decision.

[4]Timothy's part must have been significant. He is frequently mentioned in the Pauline Epistles, and Paul included him in many salutations as he does here (2 Cor 1:1; Phil 1:1; Col 1:1; 1 Thess 1:1; 2 Thess 1:1).

ability in church relations, at times undertaking important missions for Paul involving tense interpersonal relationships (e.g., Thessalonica).

Timothy was called simply "the brother."[5] Since Timothy did not hold the office of apostle, this appropriate term described him. His unique relationship to Paul revealed that he was a true partner, a brother in the fullest sense. Of course, all who read the letter would know that Timothy was a brother to them all in the work of the gospel.

2. The Readers (1:2a)

2To the holy and faithful brothers in Christ at Colosse:

1:2a The readers were Colossian Christians who were described by a two-fold location. First, in the original text, they were in Colosse. The geographical name located them in terms of this earth, a specific context, and a clear concern. Second, they were known as "holy and faithful brothers in Christ." Their spiritual location, "in Christ," demonstrated a tie to a higher society, the Christian community. This latter designation provided an orientation for the remainder of the epistle. The Colossians were located in Christ. Their spiritual environment provided common ground for the appeal of Paul, a fact which he stated clearly in Phil 2:1-4. Both geographical and spiritual locations brought distinctive responsibilities: one to the people of this earth, the other to the concerns of the Lord. The Colossian church should have been beyond the heresy that threatened them since they were "in Christ."

In designating the church members as Christian, Paul referred to them as "holy and faithful brothers."[6] The word "holy" (*hagiois*) can be translated "holy ones" (NIV) or "saints" (NASB). Early in Paul's ministry, he addressed congregations as "churches" (1, 2 Thess; 1, 2 Cor; Gal). Later he consistently used the term "saints"or "holy ones" (Rom; Phil; Col; Eph;).[7] While there is a consistency in the pattern, too much could be read into the progression. The term "saints" conveyed the ideas of separation and holiness expected in the Old Testament (Num 23:9) and included the righteousness already imputed to these believers because of the work of Christ on their behalf. The parallel term, "faithful," stressed their consistency in spite of the heresy that threatened. The term may suggest that the heresy was impending rather than actually present in the church. At any rate, these Christians were designated as holy and faithful in spite of their obvious shortcomings in the areas addressed in the epistle itself.[8]

---

[5]He is also called the "brother" in 2 Cor 1:1 and Phlm 1.

[6]It is noteworthy that Paul used the term "brothers" for them. He obviously made a conscious association with Timothy and, thus, Paul as well.

[7]This is noted by J. B. Lightfoot, *St. Paul's Epistle to the Philippians*, reprint ed. (Grand Rapids: Zondervan, 1953), 32.

[8]Grammatically, the Granville Sharp rule joins these two adjectives so that both refer to the same persons. The adjectives are used to modify the term "brethren."

3. The Greeting (1:2b)

Grace and peace to you from God our Father.

1:2b   This greeting was typical for Christian and non-Christian epistles. It is impossible, however, to think of Paul addressing a Christian congregation with nothing more than the typical secular greeting (thus the use of *charis* rather than *charein*). Obviously the terms are filled with Christian significance. "Grace" pointed the readers to the basis of their new life in Christ, as well as the state of grace in which they were to conduct their lives. "Peace" was a prayer for the general well-being of the readers. The two are sequential, grace preceding peace, and both come as gifts from God, designated more personally here as "our Father."[9]

---

[9] No doubt the term "peace" reflects the general and comprehensive meaning of the Hebrew שָׁלוֹם, which Paul would have heard so frequently as a Jewish boy. The epistolary pattern of Greek letters was well suited to expressing it. The Greek term "peace" almost carries the same significance when used this way. See comments on Phil 1:2.

II. THE PREEMINENCE OF CHRIST IN CHRISTIAN
    THEOLOGY (1:3-3:4)
    1. Paul's Thanksgiving and Prayer for the Colossians (1:3-23)
        (1) Paul's Thanksgiving for the Colossians (1:3-8)
             Expressed to God in Prayer (1:3)
             Encouraged by the Colossians' Christian Growth (1:4-8)
                The Nature of the Colossians' Growth (1:4)
                The Basis for the Colossians' Growth (1:5-8)
        (2) Paul's Prayer for the Colossians (1:9-14)
             The Character of Paul's Prayer (1:9a)
             The Content of Paul's Prayer (1:9b)
             The Purpose of Paul's Prayer (1:10-14)
        (3) The Hymn to Christ (1:15-20)
             Introduction to the Hymn to Christ
             The Structure of the Hymn
                Two-Stanza Arrangement
                Three-Stanza Arrangement
             The Authorship of the Hymn
             The Contents of the Hymn
                Jesus: Lord of Creation (1:15-17)
                Jesus: Lord of the New Creation (1:18-20)
        (4) The Salvation of the Colossians (1:21-23)
             The Colossians' Former Condition (1:21)
             The Colossians' Present Condition (1:22-23)
    2. Paul's Place in Christ's Kingdom (1:24-2:7)
        (1) Paul's Ministry to the Churches (1:24-29)
             To Complete the Afflictions of Christ (1:24)
                Suffering for the Colossians
                Suffering for the Christ
             To Complete the Word of God (1:25-27)
                The Role of Paul
                The Revelation to Paul
             Paul's Message, Method, and Purpose (1:28-29)
        (2) Paul's Ministry to the Colossians (2:1-7)
             The Object of Paul's Concern (2:1)
             The Purpose of Paul's Concern (2:2-3)
             The Reason for Paul's Concern (2:4-5)
             The Application to the Colossians (2:6-7)

3. Paul's Defense of the Faith (2:8-3:4)
    (1) Against the Theological Threat (2:8-19)
        To the Doctrine of Salvation (2:8-15)
            The Nature of the Threat (2:8)
            The Answer to the Threat (2:9-15)
        To the Doctrine of Sanctification (2:16-19)
            Concerning Asceticism (2:16-17)
            Concerning Angel Worship (2:18-19)
    (2) Against the Practical Threat (2:20-3:4)
        To the Doctrine of Salvation (2:20-23)
            The Nature of the Attacks (2:20-21)
            Reasons Not to Submit (2:22-23)
        To the Doctrine of Sanctification (3:1-4)
            The Nature of the Christian's Higher Calling (3:1-2)
            Reasons to Seek the Higher Calling (3:3-4)

———— II. THE PREEMINENCE OF CHRIST IN ————
CHRISTIAN THEOLOGY (1:3-3:4)

1. Paul's Thanksgiving and Prayer for the Colossians (1:3-23)

(1) Paul's Thanksgiving for the Colossians (1:3-8)

[3]We always thank God, the Father of our Lord Jesus Christ, when we pray for you, [4]because we have heard of your faith in Christ Jesus and of the love you have for all the saints—[5]the faith and love that spring from the hope that is stored up for you in heaven and that you have already heard about in the word of truth, the gospel [6]that has come to you. All over the world this gospel is bearing fruit and growing, just as it has been doing among you since the day you heard it and understood God's grace in all its truth. [7]You learned it from Epaphras, our dear fellow servant, who is a faithful minister of Christ on our behalf, [8]and who also told us of your love in the Spirit.

Typically, Paul opened his epistles with an expression of thanksgiving for the church.[1] He approached his readers this way even if he had never seen them (here and Rom), if substandard Christianity characterized them (Cor), or if heresy threatened (Col). Remarkably, Paul's faith in the working of God brought to mind genuine thankfulness for the Christian experience of believers everywhere.

Structurally, the section is one long sentence with modifiers. This, too, is typical for Paul in these expressions. The main verb is "we are giving thanks" (*eucharistoumen*). Two subordinate clauses modify Paul's thanksgiving, v. 3

---

[1]This is true with the exception of Galatians, where the breaking of the pattern becomes an exegetically significant matter in itself. It is due to the importance of the heresy threatening Galatia which was different in kind from this one.

("when we pray for you") and vv. 4-8 ("because we have heard of your faith in Christ Jesus"). Thus there is one main idea with two rather complicated sub-thoughts.

Paul framed the prayer in the plural form "we." As already noted, the plural is used consistently until 1:9, then the verbs become singular. Some, such as C. F. D. Moule, note this is an epistolary plural in which Paul really meant himself but naturally wrote in the plural.[2] Others note that this is a genuine plural describing the prayers of the group with Paul.[3] Most likely Moule is correct. Paul divulged his own prayer life, using the common plural designation.

In the ancient world, epistles often opened in this fashion. Commonly after salutations, thanksgivings were expressed to the gods, followed by reasons for such thanksgiving.[4] This observation confirms the fact that Paul followed generally accepted forms of writing for his own culture. However, he clearly deviated from the normal patterns as the situation dictated, freely filling the letters with his own content.

Pauline literature contains two basic types of thanksgivings. The first is the sevenfold structure, beginning with a verb of thanksgiving and ending with a "that" (*hina*) clause of content. The second begins similarly, but includes a different "that" (*hoti*) clause which notes the reason for the thanksgiving.[5] In Colossians Paul employed the sevenfold introduction which included vv. 3-10. However, the pattern is not clear-cut, particularly since the final element, the "that" (*hina*) clause, occurs in this one.[6] Interruptions to the flow of thought allowed the apostle to interject his own free-flowing ideas suited to this particular situation.[7]

The expression "we thank God" occurs frequently in the Pauline Epistles. The term implies both a statement of thanksgiving for what is received from

---

[2]C. F. D. Moule, *The Epistles of Paul the Apostle to the Colossians and to Philemon*, CGTC (Cambridge: University Press, 1962), 48.

[3]J. B. Lightfoot, *St. Paul's Epistle to the Colossians and to Philemon*, reprint ed. (Grand Rapids: Zondervan, 1959), 231, on Col 4:3.

[4]P. O'Brien, *Colossians, Philemon*, WBC (Waco, Tex.: Word, 1982), 8, points out a simple pattern: thanks offered to the gods, assurance that the gods were petitioned regularly, and the reasons for the thanksgiving are given. The pattern occurs in Hellenistic writings as well as those of Hellenistic Judaism from the time of the third century B.C.

[5]P. Schubert, *Form and Function of the Pauline Thanksgivings*, BZNW 20. (Berlin: Topelmann, 1939), 10-39, 54-55, gives a complete analysis of these introductions, including a comparative chart. See also P. O'Brien, *Introductory Thanksgivings in the Letters of Paul*, NovTSupp 49 (Leiden: Brill, 1977), 62-104.

[6]The elements are: expression of thanksgiving, object of thanksgiving, a temporal word (adverb) noting frequency of thanksgiving, a pronominal phrase, a temporal participle, a causal participle, and a content clause introduced by ἵνα. O'Brien, *Colossians, Philemon*, 8.

[7]The verses are complicated grammatically. In addition to the main verb and the two primary participles, two relative clauses and three comparative clauses follow in sequence, each adding ideas to what was previously stated. This run-on type of sentence characterizes Paul's introductions and doxologies.

God and an element of praise for God's character which originated it. While it is helpful at times to distinguish between praise and thanksgiving, the former being related to God's character and the latter his actions, generally the two blend together. This is the case here. A pattern also emerges in Paul's prayers of thanksgiving. When he concentrated on what God had done for others, he normally employed the verb "give thanks," as he did here. When he was personally involved in the benefits in mind, he preferred the phrase "God be blessed" (or its equivalent). If that pattern holds true here, Paul focused on the goodness of God in the lives of the Colossians. Since he had no personal acquaintance with them, he did not participate directly with them in these blessings. Paul rejoiced whenever God bestowed his blessings on his people.

EXPRESSED TO GOD IN PRAYER (1:3).   **1:3**   The first factor to note about Paul's thanksgiving is that it occurred in prayer. While this may seem obvious, subtle emphases are to be noted here. First, the passage contains various synonyms for prayer. Together they demonstrate the importance of prayer for Paul. He could pray in times of difficulty, and he could pray in times of joy. The synonyms, particularly "pray" (*proseuchomenoi*) and "give thanks" (*eucharistoumen*), emphasize two aspects of prayer. The more general term "praying" speaks to the activity itself, while "giving thanks" is a specific form of prayer. In like manner, the word "asking" (*aitoumenoi*, 1:9), another synonym for prayer, emphasizes the specific request made. Thus the words collectively stress prayer in its various aspects.

Since Paul often emphasized the activity of prayer, he wanted to share the fact that he actually remembered them in prayer. The joys and concerns of the Colossian congregation meant enough to Paul that he prayed about them. When this is compared with the other epistles, a sizable impression emerges regarding the extent of Paul's prayer life. He prayed for all the churches.

Several factors appear regarding Paul's prayers. First, they were continual. The church was regularly in Paul's mind and thoughts. Second, the prayer was directed to God. Finally, the prayers were intercessory, "when we pray for you." This phrase indicates the prayers involved people more than events. While Paul feared the negative church-wide impact of the threatening heresy, he was more concerned with the effect on the individuals who would be swept away by it.

In praying to God, Paul added that God is "the Father of our Lord Jesus Christ." In a sense the focus of the entire epistle rests in this phrase since it contains precise details about the relationship between these two members of the Godhead. There is a major textual variant here regarding whether the phrase should be read "the God and Father of our Lord Jesus Christ" or "the God *who* is Father of our Lord Jesus Christ." This latter construction emphasizes the unique relationship between God and Christ and also demonstrates which concept of God Paul holds. As it stands, the construction is both ambiguous and rare. However, it seems best to understand the statement "the God *who* is

Father of our Lord Jesus Christ" as the better reading.[8] Thus, Paul believed strongly in one God, the one known in connection with Christ. He also drew attention to the fact that the avenue to and from God is Christ since the Son is the way to the Father.

In summary, this short clause reveals that Paul was a man of prayer. He had a significant prayer list of persons for whom he often prayed. He included Christians he had never met, such as the Colossians. Paul's concern for others included both thanksgiving and praise for God's working in people. There was obviously a close relationship between Paul's practice and his prayer. Finally, the ultimate source of blessing and the church's well-being was God who was revealed through Christ.

ENCOURAGED BY THE COLOSSIANS' CHRISTIAN GROWTH (1:4-8). The second factor which led to Paul's thanksgiving was the growth of the Colossian Christians. The structure of this Greek sentence, which began in v. 1, is somewhat complicated because Paul's mind moved quickly from one theme to another and one idea grew out of another. The participial modifier is "because we have heard" (1:4) and all that follows depends logically and grammatically on it. Thematically, however, the direction of the passage shifts with the introduction of "this gospel" in v. 6. Colossians 1:7-8 modify the term "gospel" and logically depend on it. The passage that remains, therefore, may be considered from the twofold standpoints of the nature of their growth (1:4) and the basis of their growth (1:5-8).

The Nature of the Colossians' Growth (1:4). **1:4** The presence of faith and love evidenced the Christian character of the Colossian church. Although Paul had never visited the church, he knew well its Christian experience and accepted it as genuine.[9] The first of these, faith, marks the church as Christian. Without doubt, Paul was pleased to find Christians at Colosse, but the presence of faith was just the beginning. The construction used here stresses more. It suggests the practice of faith more than its presence. The phrase "faith in Christ Jesus" is not the same as "faith directed toward Christ Jesus." The latter statement would be written literally "faith into (unto) Christ Jesus." This construction, "faith in Christ Jesus," points to the sphere of faith rather than its object.[10] Naturally, Paul assumed that the object of faith was Christ, for that is

---

[8]This is the more difficult reading, which is to be preferred if all other matters do not militate against it. A similar construction occurs in 3:17. For a fuller defense of this position, see Moule, 48-49.

[9]The Greek construction of "because we have heard of your faith" is actually the verb ἀκούω followed by the accusative case, suggesting a hearing with comprehension. It seems strange in this type of context since the qualitative hearing (genitive case) would seem appropriate.

[10]See, e.g., Moule, 49. Other Pauline texts employ the same construction or a slight modification of it (Eph 1:15; 1 Tim 3:13; 2 Tim 3:15; possibly Rom 3:25). While the object is implied in the locative of sphere, the environment is more pronounced.

the only appropriate direction for faith. Thus Paul had heard that the church was Christian. He further had heard that it was living its faith in the risen Lord. Its members were practicing, faithful Christians. In this commendation, Paul resumed what he introduced in 1:2 with the term "faithful brothers in Christ."

Paul used various means to express different aspects of faith. This may be seen generally in the various prepositions used with the noun "faith." He spoke of faith as a conduit through which a relationship with God is achieved ("through faith"). He also spoke of faith directed toward God and based on Christ ("on faith") and faith as a sphere in which a Christian lives ("in faith").[11] This variety of expression represents Paul's more abstract view of faith. Generally, Paul contrasted faith with works. For him, like John and the other New Testament authors, only by faith can one approach God. Yet John spoke of faith as an activity which characterizes a Christian. He preferred the verb "believe" rather than the noun for faith and showed a decisive tendency toward using participles to describe believers. In the Greek text, these participles show the active, dynamic nature of faith. Both Paul and John correctly identified different aspects of the relationship to God.

The second evidence of the Colossian Christians' growth was the presence of love. Typically, Paul employed the term *agapē* for Christian love, as he did here. Of significance, however, is the fact that he used the article with the noun, pointing to a specific expression of love. It is "the love you have for all the saints." The employment of the articular noun ("the love") and the qualifying phrase ("you have for all the saints") reveals two truths about the nature of the church's concern. First, it was sacrificial. The term *agapē* reminded them of the sacrificial love of Christ for them. Second, within the Christian community it was indiscriminate. The love was directed to all the saints. Appropriately, Paul used the preposition "unto" (*eis*) for love's dynamic. Love has little value if it is held only among the saints. It must be expressed to others. Both the nature of love as a relational quality and the necessity of "giving it" call for this construction in contrast to the one used for faith.[12]

Perhaps Paul praised them for this basic characteristic of love, which is in line with the words of Jesus in this regard. Jesus indicated that love is the moral basis for unity in the Christian community (John 17:20-26). Such love fulfills two divine objectives: It represents Jesus to the world, especially in his physical absence, and it perfects the body of Christ. By commending the church for its love, therefore, Paul acknowledged a genuine and mature Christianity.

The Basis for the Colossians' Growth (1:5-8). After expressing thanksgiving for the Colossian Christians' maturity in Christ, Paul presented the

---

[11] The prepositions are, respectively, διά, ἐπί, and ἐν.

[12] The construction here is εἰς πάντας. The preposition εἰς shows direction. It contrasts with the construction ἐν Χριστῷ used with faith. Faith is in the sphere of Christ; love works out toward all.

reason for their growth. It was their hope.[13] Hope provided the basis for Christian growth since the most basic elements of faith toward God and love toward others grow out of hope. In reality, without hope there is no reason for faith or love, and everything is directed to ourselves and our world. Paul modified the concept of hope in two ways.

1:5a-b The first statement about Christian hope was that it is a present reality. It was preserved for them in heaven. In Scripture the term "hope" may be used subjectively, as an attitude of heart, or objectively, as the reality for which hope is expressed. Paul used the subjective meaning in Rom 5:1-11; 8:24, where he stressed the attitude of trust necessary to provide Christian security in the world. Subjectively hope is an attitude or feeling of anticipation that things will work out as desired. On the other hand, Paul used "hope" often in an objective sense. In that case, it meant that reality to which subjective hope aspires. Without doubt Paul used the objective sense here. This is evident because of the modifying participle indicating the location of the hope ("in heaven"), the modifying clause "that you have already heard about in the word of truth, the gospel," and the parallels in other New Testament writings (Gal 5:5; 1 Pet 1:3). Paul believed that the hope offered in Christ inspires assurance and, as a result, produces spiritual fruit. The basis of believing Christ (faith) and serving others (love) is that this world is not the end. There is an afterlife where the deeds done here will be evaluated and rewarded. Christians have an understanding of the rewards and blessings of heaven.

1:5c The second statement about hope is that it comes from the proclamation of the gospel. The actual expression of the gospel is "the word of the truth of the gospel," which the NIV translates "the word of the truth, the gospel."[14] Although some translate the phrase "the word of the true gospel," which is possible in Greek, there is no evidence that Paul would call a non-Christian message a "false gospel."[15] It is not a gospel at all, real or counterfeit. His statement stresses the truth and should be read "the truth, which is the gospel which came

---

[13]The construction is διά in the accusative case. Conceivably, the modifying phrase could go in several directions: it could modify "we give thanks," "love," or both "faith and love." It cannot easily modify "we give thanks" because it is too far removed in context, and the triad of faith, hope, and love generally occur together as modifiers. Again it does not naturally go with love alone because the modifying relative clause ἣν ἔχετε κ.τ.λ. seems to conclude the modifying of ἀγάπη, and the balanced structure of πίστις plus modifier and ἀγάπη plus modifier call for a third idea rather than a second modifier. It seems best to understand that hope goes with both faith and love.

[14]This follows A. T. Robertson's explanation, among others, that the genitive construction should be read "the truth which is the Gospel." It understands the second genitive construction "of the gospel" as appositional. Many agree with this analysis. A. T. Robertson, *A Grammar of the Greek New Testament in the Light of Historical Research* (Nashville: Broadman, 1934), 498. Moule seems to have preferred the word "of the true gospel" (115).

[15]In Galatians Paul argued regarding the true gospel, but according to Gal 1:7, he did not consider the heretical message a gospel. Rather it is "not another" (οὐκ ἔστιν ἄλλο). He seemingly refused to call another message by the term "gospel."

to you." Paul, therefore, emphasized the fact that the gospel message they heard was, in fact, sufficient as a word of truth. They should have had no need to seek some new teaching. The preachers of the gospel had given them the word of truth.

This latter fact deserves amplification. The gospel is dynamic. Even though the message comes through the instrumentality of human messengers, Paul saw the gospel as "in motion," moving from place to place and incorporating gospel preachers into it. It was not the property of those who preached it. The gospel belonged to God and was his way of saving the world.[16]

1:6 Three statements trace the movement of the gospel from God to the Colossians through Epaphras.[17] First, the general nature of the gospel's advance is given in v. 6. This simple statement expresses a major concept about the nature of the spread of the message. "In all the world, the gospel continues to bear fruit and increase."[18] The actual terms used, when pressed to their original ideas, suggest reproductive capability ("bearing fruit") and maturing capability ("increasing"). Together the terms teach that the gospel is productive; it accomplishes the work God intends. Significantly, the same terms occur in v. 10 in Paul's prayer for the Colossian Christians and their growth in the knowledge of God's will.

In using the word "gospel" in this fashion, Paul focused on the person and work of Christ. Although he had a major concern about spreading the message of the good news of the cross, the life communicated through the message captured his imagination here. The advance of the gospel is in reality the advance of the work of God in changing the lives of those who hear and believe the proclamation.[19]

Second, the meaning of the term "gospel" receives further explanation from the second modifying clause: The gospel came to Colosse (v. 6). When it did, they knew the grace of God in truth. From Paul's perspective, grace was the introduction to the gospel as well as its most basic element. The gospel of God's grace relieved people of their sins and brought them into a right relationship with God.[20]

1:7-8 Third, Paul devoted significant space to a discussion of Epaphras who had taken the gospel to the Colossians (1:7-8). Epaphras worked closely

---

[16]The word "came" is παρόντος, itself somewhat unusual in this regard. It "came alongside them" as part of its movement.

[17]These are noted in the text by the recurrence of καθώς modifying the concept three times (twice in v. 6 and once for vv. 7-8).

[18]The Greek construction is graphic. The verbs are presented in periphrastic form which "marks more clearly the durative force," H. E. Dana and J. R. Mantey, *A Manual Grammar of the Greek New Testament* (New York: Macmillan,1927), 231. Moule commented that there is probably no significance to the middle voice as over against the passive. Moule, 50-51.

[19]See the discussion of this in Phil 1.

[20]The reference to truth reminds of the "truth which is the gospel" of v. 5.

with Paul and was most likely the founder of the Colossian church. At this time, he informed Paul of the members' deep love prompted and promoted by the Spirit (1:8). Thus, the gospel message advances through the world calling persons to Christ, communicating the message of grace, and being entrusted to the servants of Christ like Epaphras who proclaim it.

The church at Colosse was healthy in many respects. It had a living faith, an indiscriminate love for all Christians, and a solid hope of life eternal through the gospel. These virtues are solid ground for genuine thanksgiving.

(2) Paul's Prayer for the Colossians (1:9-14)

⁹For this reason, since the day we heard about you, we have not stopped praying for you and asking God to fill you with the knowledge of his will through all spiritual wisdom and understanding. ¹⁰And we pray this in order that you may live a life worthy of the Lord and may please him in every way: bearing fruit in every good work, growing in the knowledge of God, ¹¹being strengthened with all power according to his glorious might so that you may have great endurance and patience, and joyfully ¹²giving thanks to the Father, who has qualified you to share in the inheritance of the saints in the kingdom of light. ¹³For he has rescued us from the dominion of darkness and brought us into the kingdom of the Son he loves, ¹⁴in whom we have redemption, the forgiveness of sins.

After expressing thanksgiving to God for the condition of the Colossian church, Paul offered a prayer on its behalf. The prayer reflects the specific threat to the church and, in its own way, combats the heretics. The section is quite complex, including an extended sentence containing 218 words in the Greek text. The subject matter moves rapidly from one idea to another. Inserted into the text is a lengthy passage on the person and work of Jesus. Many have pointed to a chiastic arrangement of this long section, beginning with a prayer for the Colossians and concluding with a statement applying the redemptive work of Christ to these believers (in 1:21-23).[21] Two themes predominate. The first (1:9-14), in the form of a prayer, focuses on the spiritual well-being of the Colossian Christians and petitions God for their continued growth. The ideas quickly move to praise for what God had done in calling them to Christ. The second theme (1:15-20), in the form of a hymn, praises God for the work of the Son, Jesus. Thinking about the blessings of God in the lives of the Colossian Christians caused Paul to pray on their behalf. The text includes the character of Paul's prayer (1:9a), the content of Paul's prayer (1:9b), and the purpose of Paul's prayer (1:10-14). Structurally these form a unit. The character of Paul's prayer contains the main verb of the clause, "pray," which is followed by a clause in Greek providing the content of the prayer.[22] These are concluded by an infinitive ("to be filled") and its modifiers which supply the purpose.

---

[21] Those who see a chiasm here point out that the chiasm actually extends beyond sentence to include the application in vv. 21-23.

[22] This is done by means of a ἵνα clause in the Greek text.

THE CHARACTER OF PAUL'S PRAYER (1:9a).   **1:9a**   Three statements describe the character of Paul's prayer. They are the occasion prompting it, the specific nature of the prayer, and its consistency.

The occasion must be noted from two complementary ideas: the condition of the church and the danger to the church. The introduction, "for this reason," points to the previous section, 1:3-8, and identifies the spiritual condition of the church.[23] Paul expressed great joy when he heard of the Colossians' salvation. The joy continued from that day, and that, too, became an occasion for prayer. Additionally, Paul saw the dangers in the theological heresy and what it would do to the congregation. The words of the prayer clearly reveal Paul's concern about the future of the church. Thus, while the grammar looks backward to the heritage of the church, the content looks ahead to the danger faced by the congregation. Both the joy of its Christian experience and concerns about the threatening philosophy prompted Paul to engage in prayer.

The specific nature of the prayer occurs in two complementary verbs found here, "praying" (*proseuchomenoi*) and "asking" (*aitoumenoi*).[24] Although the terms are basically synonymous, when used together they stress slightly different aspects of prayer. The first, "praying," is a general term, the most common for prayer in the Pauline Epistles. It covers the entirety of the prayer life. The second, "asking," is more specific. It expresses a particular request that God intervene in the lives of the people for whom Paul prayed.[25] Thus Paul's general prayer took a specific form. He prayed that they would know the will of God in their lives.

The prayer also is consistent. Paul employed the negative words "not stopped praying for you"[26] with an obvious positive meaning, i.e., that Paul prayed regularly and consistently for them. Often Paul expressed this characteristic of his prayers.[27]

THE CONTENT OF PAUL'S PRAYER (1:9b).   **1:9b**   Paul prayed specifically for a knowledge of the will of God, for "God to fill you with the knowledge of his will through all spiritual wisdom and understanding." The prayer carefully notes the situation at Colosse, and Paul included the definition of the knowledge of God's will and the sphere of achieving that knowledge.

---

[23]The construction διά τοῦτο may, of course, look forward. Generally, however, the construction points back to what has been addressed, which forms a foundation for what is to come.

[24]Both verbs are complementary participles of manner, explaining the means which effect the prayer.

[25]Since this is the only time in the Pauline Epistles that the terms occur in juxtaposition, this conclusion is a matter of contextual judgment. Often words for prayer occur, but these are unique in tandem here.

[26]οὐ παύομαι, a common term in Pauline introductions. Robertson points out that the Greek παύομαι is only followed by a participle (Robertson, 1102). The participles, therefore, should be considered as complementary to the verb.

[27]E.g., Rom 1:9; 1 Cor 1:4; Eph 1:16; Phil 1:4; 1 Thess 1:2; 2 Thess 1:3; 2 Tim 1:3; Phlm 1:4.

The Greek word used for "knowledge" (*epignōsis*) had many applications, both religious and non-religious. It is a compound form including the word "knowledge" (*gnōsis*) and a preposition (*epi*) which at times slightly alters its meaning. A secular use of the term "knowledge" occurs in the New Testament in 1 Pet 3:7, where Peter urged husbands to live with their wives according to knowledge (*gnōsis*). He meant that they should have a personal understanding of their wives' specific needs. Generally in the New Testament, however, the word has a religious use. It was also a favorite word of the Gnostic philosophers/religionists. It was, for them, the way of enlightenment that bridged the gap between the visible, material, evil world, and the invisible, spiritual, and (often) good world of reality. The battle between good and evil took place in the spiritual world; for the Gnostics, the visible world was influenced, even controlled, by spirit beings which they called "aeons." Human beings, being material and evil, could only hope for salvation by a flash of insight (of knowledge, *gnōsis*) which would lift them above worldly matters. Although Gnosticism took many specific forms and must be considered a movement rather than a specific religious expression, all Gnostics had these common beliefs.

Many feel that Colossians reflects this type of Gnostic character and environment. For them, Paul wrote with a Gnostic or incipient Gnostic pattern of thought. That is, of course, possible, but the work of many other scholars places Gnosticism in the second century, and Paul wrote Colossians in the first. The two, therefore, simply do not share a common environment.[28] The most that can be said is that Colosse and early forms of Gnosticism shared an early ideological environment which later blossomed into Gnosticism. Some call that incipient Gnosticism, but many question whether Colossians reflects any Gnostic tendencies at all.

Paul used the term "knowledge" in both general and theological ways. For example, in Rom 3:20 Paul stated that through the law one could gain a knowledge (*epignōsis*) of sin. There it expressed an understanding of sin in relation to law, but the term had little special significance. Normally, however, the term in the Pauline Epistles referred to a knowledge of God. It stressed a true knowledge of God and his will. It was also, generally, the appropriate term for personal rather than intellectual knowledge. Since Christians have a personal relationship with God, who is also a personal being, the term is correctly chosen.[29]

---

[28] See discussion of historical context in "Introduction" to Colossians.

[29] Grammarians question whether the term for "knowledge" with or without the preposition makes much difference. The Greek preposition ἐπί is often prefixed to the word. Some say that the form with the preposition intensifies, drawing attention to an accurate knowledge contrasted with a simple, perhaps undefined knowledge (see T. Abbott, *The Epistles to the Ephesians and to the Colossians, ICC* [Edinburgh: T. & T. Clark, 1897]; H. Cremer, *Biblico-Theological Lexicon of New Testament Greek*, 4th ed. [Edinburgh: T & T Clark, 1895], 159-60; R. Trench, *Synonyms of the New Testament* [New York: Scribners, 1864], 124). Others take the compound term as directive,

In his prayer, Paul clarified the environment in which Christian knowledge is gained. Obviously, such knowledge must come from God since he alone clearly reveals his own mind.[30] In this context, Paul stated that God takes the initiative to reveal himself (and his will). The human response is to trust him to do it. A rather awkward Greek construction expresses that fact. The verb "to fill" is in the passive voice, "to be filled," yet here it occurs with a direct object (accusative in Greek). The construction is as odd in Greek as it is in English. The point is that God discloses a knowledge of himself. It was unthinkable that someone could simply learn to know God. Most truths may be learned; divine truth must be revealed!

Knowledge of God's mind comes from spiritual resources. Getting to know God is qualitatively different from other quests. The human responsibility is to place oneself in an environment conducive to spiritual growth where God can reveal his mind. Specifically, this environment is identified as "through all spiritual wisdom and understanding." Some, as O'Brien, see this as the essence of the will of God, i.e., that "the perception of God's will consists in wisdom and understanding of every sort, on the spiritual level."[31] The NIV is better suited to both the Greek text and to the logic of the passage. While the two words convey different nuances of meaning, together they make a clear point. Spiritual understanding includes wisdom: the acquisition of knowledge and the application of that knowledge to a specific concern. It, therefore, consists in the ability to "act and think spiritually." Spiritual wisdom goes beyond natural wisdom. Thus, wisdom becomes not only a goal but also a means to an end. Christians must place themselves in that spiritual environment with the hope and expectation that God will reveal his will regarding specific matters. Paul's point was not the difficulty of knowing God; it was the attitude required by the seeker of knowledge. In Christ God always makes himself known.

THE PURPOSE OF PAUL'S PRAYER (1:10-14).   Paul prayed with a goal in mind. The purpose of the prayer is "that you may live a life worthy of the Lord." It is wisdom applied to living, not simply wisdom related to knowledge.

---

i.e., pointing to a specific object of knowledge. Often great difficulty occurs in forcing such distinctions. Here, if a shade of meaning is to be pressed, the directive is to be preferred. Paul, therefore, prayed for a specific knowledge of God's will. The term ἐπίγνωσις and cognates differ from οἶδα and its cognates at least slightly. The former generally stresses either an accurate knowledge or a personal knowledge (a knowledge of relationships). The latter generally relates either a complete knowledge or a factual knowledge (a knowledge of intellect). Although there is significant overlap in some contexts, these distinctions generally prevail in the New Testament.

[30]This is presented rather interestingly by the passive voice verb πληρόω followed by an accusative object. It is unusual in general, but common enough for grammarians to discuss it (cf. BDF, 87). The only exact parallel with the verb πληρόω is Phil 1:11 (see the discussion there). In both "the fruit of righteousness" and "the will of God" the divine element is pronounced and the thought overrules the grammatical form. Paul's grammar is always subject to his thought.

[31]O'Brien, *Colossians, Philemon*, 21. The quote is actually from Moule, 53, with which he is in agreement.

The prayer was directed to transformation of character and witness. In this Paul differed radically from the Greek thought that surrounded him. His thought grew out of his Jewish heritage. In the Old Testament and Qumran literature, the proper response to God is the "walk."[32] The rabbis devoted much time and thought to the "walk" that God required.[33] One of the first commands from God was given to Abraham who was told to "walk before me and be blameless" (Gen 17:1). From that time, the term "walk" became synonymous with obedience to the grace of God.[34] Paul's purpose was clearly ethical rather than intellectual; it related to character more than to abstract thought. That the Christian's walk concerned Paul is confirmed by the characteristics he identified here. These accompany a true knowledge of God's will. They are presented in vv. 10-14 by four clauses (participles in Greek) which may be divided into three ideas.[35] These are continued growth, strength, and thanksgiving to the Father.[36]

1:10 The first characteristic of those in God's will is continued growth in the spiritual life. The two phrases which come together form a twofold division: effective service and growth in knowledge. The two words imply metaphors which are complementary. First, "bearing fruit in every good work" refers to the reproductive aspect of the Christian's calling. This need not be confined to evangelism, though that cannot be excluded. It refers also to the fruit of the Spirit in a Christian's life which, at times, is called fruit-bearing. The suggestion is that those who know the will of God will be successful in their Christian activities. Second, there will be an increase in the knowledge of God. This teaches that the "server" will benefit from service by an increased understanding of God both mentally and experientially. The term "growing" suggests qualitative or quantitative growth. Since it was used in connection with the spread of the gospel (1:6), some see it as synonymous with the phrase

---

[32] H. Seesemann, *TDNT*, 5, 944, points out this is not found in classical Greek and therefore one must look to Hebrew parallels. Some of these are found in Qumran (see O'Brien, *Colossians*, 22); others, in contemporary Judaism.

[33] Their term is הֲלָךְ, a word which gave rise to the division of the study of law into *hagaddah* (law) and *halaka* (ethics).

[34] The Hebrew term here is הָלַךְ which is related to another term for "walk," יָלַךְ. Together they comprise the majority of uses of the English translation "walk," often in an ethical context as here.

[35] Some commentators see four distinct elements, although they may subdivide them into smaller categories. They suggest that the four are: fruit bearing, increased knowledge, strength, and thanksgiving. O'Brien took this position (*Colossians, Philemon*, 23). In actuality, the better approach is to understand that there are three sets of ideas, the first of which has two segments. Those who take vv. 12-23 as a new section of thought, if not grammar, see three expressions here as well. They, however, understand the last of the participles, εὐχαριστοῦντες, as part of the next section, and the first three are included in this segment.

[36] The evidence for this is only the first two participles are joined by the Greek καί, the prepositional phrases form a balance with a prepositional phrase for each participle, and there is a chiastic arrangement of the first two participles.

"bearing fruit."[37] If that is the case, however, the modifier "in the knowledge of God" should be consistent with the phrase "in every good work" of that previous verse. That parallel is unlikely. Both terms express the environment in which the growth takes place. Therefore, this last phrase is better understood as "increasing in the realm of the knowledge of God." Bruce was no doubt correct when he stated that obedience to the work of God brings further knowledge of God himself.[38]

This first characteristic has two focal points. First, it clearly demonstrates that God's will is related to growth in Christian experience. Again Paul stressed that real knowledge issues in life. Second, two complementary aspects of growth are identified. Christian service is a natural response to the will of God, but so is gaining spiritual understanding. A close relationship exists between these two. In the arena of service, one learns more about personal faith, the Lord, and God's will.

1:11 The second characteristic of those who know the will of God is power to persevere. The Greek text stresses the idea of power by employing two different terms in a complementary sense. The first is *dynamis* which may be defined as "the potentiality to exert force in performing some function." The second is *kratos* which indicates "the power to rule or control."[39]

Actually two forms of that root word are used here so that the text reads "being strengthened with all power." Thus Paul stressed the nature and application of the power available to the Christian. The context generally has a specific application for the power expressed, and that is found here. They needed power for enduring the circumstances of life and relating positively to other people. Again two terms explain the empowering for the believer in the will of God. They are "endurance" (*hypomonē*) and "patience" (*makrothymē*). "Endurance" is "the capacity to continue to bear up under difficult circumstances."[40] Generally in Scripture, this word refers to the events of life which must be endured. On the other hand, "patience" is "a state of emotional calm in the face of provocation or misfortune and without complaining or irritation."[41] This provocation usually comes from other persons. The two ideas complement each other. Neither circumstances nor people are to upset the person who walks in the will of God. Divine power is available to those who know Christ.

---

[37]This was the position of Chrysostom's translation which he said was "increasing the number of converts."

[38]F. F. Bruce, *Commentary on the Epistles to the Ephesians and the Colossians*, NIC (Grand Rapids: Eerdmans, 1957), 186.

[39]J. P. Louw and E. A. Nida, *Greek-English Lexicon of the New Testament based on Semantic Domains* (New York: United Bible Societies, 1988), 680, 681.

[40]Ibid., 308.

[41]Ibid., 307. They continued to state with reference to translators, "In a number of languages 'patience' is expressed idiomatically, for example, 'to remain seated in one's heart' or 'to keep one's heart from jumping' or 'to have a waiting heart.'" These idiomatic equivalents agree with the biblical picture of calmness in difficulty.

1:12 The third characteristic of those who walk in the will of God is joyful thanksgiving. The text describes this as heartfelt, genuine thankfulness that grows out of the experience of salvation. Christians should never forget what God has done for them, and they should allow that life-changing experience to bring them daily joy. Here the thanksgiving is directed to God himself, rather than Jesus Christ. Paul wanted believers to realize that the plan of salvation was initiated by God the Father. It was accomplished by God the Son. Often Christians direct their thanks to Christ. It is a proper form of praise. In this context, however, Paul pointed first to the Father's role. The role of the Son is described later (1:15-20). God is to be thanked because he qualified believers for an inheritance (1:12); he rescued believers from darkness (1:13a); and he brought believers into the Son's kingdom (1:13b). Thus, those who walk in the will of God are conscious of their salvation. They continually thank God for it.[42]

First, God the Father qualified believers for an inheritance. Colossians 1:12 states, "who has qualified you to share in the inheritance of the saints in the kingdom of light." Each portion of the statement is significant. Basically, the statement expresses the fact that God takes the initiative in bringing Christians into the realm of his righteous presence. The Greek term translated "qualified" occurs only here and 2 Cor 3:6.[43] There Paul used the term for God's work in making him, as well as others, able ministers. Here it refers to bringing one into salvation. The employment of this rare term suggests that both salvation and ministry require specific character qualities and that no one possesses them by himself. God qualifies people for both by a supernatural working. Here the term has a soteriological use. The context clarifies that God gives to people what they need to be a part of his kingdom. The basic need is righteousness. Since Paul used Old Testament language throughout this context, perhaps he thought in terms of Lev 11:44, "Be holy, because I am holy" (see also 1 Pet 1:15). No one can claim that standard of holiness, apart from God's declaration. When God qualifies people for his kingdom, he supplies righteousness, a necessary prerequisite for salvation (see Rom 4:1ff.). Since he declares believers to be righteous by his grace, he alone qualifies a person for entrance into the kingdom.

The descriptions of the inheritance of the kingdom come from the Old Testament. The words "share" and "inheritance" are the same words used for ancient Israel's portion of the promised land.[44] As to the former, Paul consciously compared God's working in Israel then with his working in Christians.

---

[42] In thanking God the Father, this section parallels Eph 1:3-22. There God is to be blessed because of his plan of salvation.

[43] The term is ἱκανόω, which is translated as "make sufficient, qualify," *BAGD*, 374.

[44] The first word μερίδα (*share*) occurs in Gen 31:14; Num 18:20; Josh 13:16; 14:2; 16:1. In all but the first occurrence, the term refers to the promised land. The first speaks of the inheritance to be received by Rachel and Leah. The second word κλῆρον (*inheritance*) had the same connotation to Israel.

It specifically referred to the dividing of the land so that each tribe would get its allotment of the inheritance. Here, Paul applied that situation in Israel to the allotment of the believers. God gives believers a spiritual inheritance, the redemption that is in Christ.

The Christian's inheritance is described as "of the saints in the kingdom of light." The word "saints" was used by Paul only for Christians, never for supernatural beings. It points to the fact that what God has done in Christ he did primarily for people. The location of the inheritance is the kingdom of light. Drawing on typically Jewish terminology, especially that of the Qumran covenanters, the expression contrasts the realms of light and darkness. The Jewish idiom "sons of light" indicates people who love truth and morality. Appropriately those who walk in the knowledge of the will of God are reminded of their position in God's kingdom. Some understand the inheritance to consist of the saints in Christ. This means that the believer receives a relationship with other believers as a part of his inheritance. The interpretation finds support in the Epistle to the Ephesians, which emphasizes the mutual relationships among fellow believers. The concept is foreign to Paul's thought here, however, and has little to commend it to the heresy at Colosse. A better understanding is to take the inheritance as that which is appropriate to and promised to the saints. It refers to the blessings reserved for Christians. This particular statement, therefore, speaks of God the Father's activity of calling his people to their promised inheritance. The same idea is found in Paul's statement of 1:5, that there is a hope reserved for them in heaven. God's initiative guarantees that his people will be able to inherit what is promised them.

1:13-14   The second statement about the Father's work is that God rescues believers (1:13). It refers to God's redemptive activity, and the terminology comes from warfare. The terms "rescued," "dominion," and "kingdom" emphasize this truth. Paul contrasted "the dominion of darkness" with "the kingdom of the Son he loves." In this context, they parallel the ideas of darkness and light of the previous verse. Perhaps this is distinctively Pauline because he included the contrast along with other ideas found here in his earlier testimony before King Agrippa (Acts 26:15-18). Although the words occur in different forms, there are parallels between this context and Acts 26:18: the idea of entering light ("to open their eyes"), to move from darkness to light, the dominion of darkness (called the dominion of "Satan" in Acts), the forgiveness of sins, the inheritance, and God's people described as saints. Thus Paul may have recalled his commission from the Lord at the time of salvation. The commission impressed him significantly since some twenty-five years later Paul wrote with vivid, verbal memory of that call.[45]

---

[45]This should be noted in the argument for Pauline authorship since both the concepts and many of the words are identical.

The significant difference between Acts and Colossians, however, is the identification of the spiritual situation of the unbeliever. Both accounts express that situation by the Greek term *exousia*, which refers to *authority, right, a holder of authority (an authority)*, or *a sphere of authority*. It points to a legitimate right to rule, rather than the power necessary for that activity. In both books, it stresses the sphere of authority, describing it as a sphere of darkness. In Acts 26:18 the unbeliever's environment is equated to "the power of Satan." The change from Satan, in Acts, to darkness, in Colossians, may be because of the Jewish nature of this book.[46] The terminology parallels the Jewish concepts of the world as the rule of Satan, which is often described as darkness in contrast to light. Paul also consistently used the word for the supernatural powers in Ephesians and Colossians.[47] It occurs eight times in these two books, and it is the exclusive meaning in them. Obviously the "kingdom" is not a geographical place since these believers did not change location when they changed kingdoms. In Christ, God invaded Satan's territory and delivered people.

In parallel with the statement that God rescued believers, Paul stated that "he . . . brought us into the kingdom of the Son he loves." Pauline literature contains few references to the kingdom of Christ. Sometimes Paul used the phrase "kingdom of Christ," while at other times he used the phrase "kingdom of God." He did seem to distinguish between them. The kingdom of Christ is an intermediate kingdom which will someday be handed over to the Father. This is taught directly in 1 Cor 15:24. The ultimate state of existence for the believer is the kingdom of God, but God planned for Christ and his kingdom to be the focus in the interval between the cross and the return of Christ. Most of the time when Paul referred to a kingdom, he referred to the kingdom of God. Many times the kingdom concept provided the ethical incentive for purity, i.e., that the unrighteous will not inherit the kingdom of God.[48] Other times Paul's ethical commands were based on the fact that the kingdom of God is a spiritual dimension rather than physical (Rom 14:17; 1 Cor 4:20; 15:50). Two clear references, however, speak of the kingdom of Christ (1 Cor 15:24; Col 1:13). Paul consistently spoke of the need of being in God's kingdom, and the way to do that is to be placed in the kingdom of Christ. Christ will bring the believer to God and his kingdom.[49]

---

[46] The light/darkness theme was prominent in Gnosticism as well and is found in the New Testament materials which reflect that background (e.g., the proposition of 1 John 1:5).

[47] The only exception to this exclusive usage is 1 Cor 15:24 where ἐξουσία refers to a power. Otherwise, the term in this sense is reserved for Ephesians and Colossians (Eph 1:21; 2:2; 3:10; 6:12; Col 1:13,16; 2:10; 2:15). Interestingly there are four occurrences in each book.

[48] These references are the most numerous in the Pauline literature: 1 Cor 6:9,10; 15:50; Gal 5:21; Eph 5:5.

[49] This basic idea is found in the Pauline conception of faith as well. Paul conceived of faith in Christ as the way to a relationship with God.

The third statement about the work of the Father is that "he . . . brought us into the kingdom of the Son he loves, in whom we have redemption, the forgiveness of sins" (1:13-14). This passage anticipates 2:8-3:4, which further develops the work of Christ. Two statements describe the entrance into the kingdom. They anticipate the hymn to Christ and Christ's kingdom. Paul stated that in Christ God provided redemption and forgiveness. Together they emphasize a payment securing freedom and the forgiveness for sins. In this text, both occur together so that one helps explain the other.[50] Paul easily conceived of a price paid and forgiveness granted.[51]

The two terms complement each other. The word "redemption" belongs to the slave market. It involves the payment of a price to secure freedom, and Paul clearly identified that price as the death of Christ. In Rom 3:24ff., Paul spoke graphically to this point by stating that God presented Jesus as a "sacrifice of atonement" for sins. Paul stressed the facts that God initiated redemption and that Jesus' death was the necessary price of salvation. In Romans he linked propitiation and redemption. The terms describe two different aspects of salvation. Sin produces an objective problem: God's justice demands satisfaction because his entire constitution moves against sin. The objective problem must be resolved in salvation. Paul described that by the term "propitiation" (NASB) or "sacrifice of atonement" (NIV). The term "redemption" speaks of emancipation from slavery. Paul used it to refer to the slavery of sin. The death of Christ was also the payment for release from slavery. Thus, complementary terms describe the different aspects of salvation. Although redemption includes the payment of a price, Scripture contains no thought about the one who receives the price. The idea cannot be pressed beyond the explicit statements of Scripture and the insights that come from the contexts in which it occurs.[52]

The second term, "forgiveness," stresses the loving nature of God. In these two expressions, therefore, the justice and the mercy of God combine. The term is uncommon in Paul, occurring only two times,[53] and it is fairly infrequent in the New Testament (seventeen times).

---

[50] Probably the best explanation is that "forgiveness" is in apposition to "redemption." The two are not identical, but they are complementary. Whatever relationship is sustained, "forgiveness" helps to shape the meaning of "redemption." They are two distinct terms (some say metaphors) which refer to the same transaction. That both occur together here indicates that neither is sufficient in itself, and that both influence and express the concept.

[51] This goes against those who argue that different metaphors for the work of Christ as appropriate to different situations must be accepted. Usually they think of forgiveness as a more adequate concept than redemption, which, some say, smacks of a pagan deity who must be "bought." But Paul put both of these together without any thought of contradiction, and he knew the meanings he intended better than we. They are truly complementary. We should not, therefore, opt for one as opposed to another.

[52] In older days much discussion ensued regarding who received the price of payment. Origen is reputed to have said the price was to the devil! Paul never pressed the metaphor far enough to develop that aspect of it. It is best to take the part Paul used and leave the rest alone.

[53] Interestingly enough, they are in Eph 1:7 and Col 1:14.

A tension arises from the combination of the two terms. Forgiveness implies a free act of grace, but redemption implies the payment of an appropriate price to secure freedom. Is God demanding of satisfaction, or is he willing to forget and suffer the wrong himself? Perhaps Bruce's reason for the occurrence of the two terms explains this unusual combination. He suggested that perhaps a second-century heresy was surfacing as early as this. In the early second century, some heretics distinguished between "remission of sins" as a first state received at baptism and "redemption" as a later and perfect state.[54] This two-fold presentation of salvation only characterized one segment of (heretical) Christianity, however, and its appearance is later than the Epistle to the Colossians. Perhaps, Bruce suggested, an anticipation of the heresy explains the occurrence of the two terms together here. Although this explanation may be correct, little evidence supports the idea that the combination of the terms occurred because of a specific heresy Paul combatted.

Whether that explains the words' appearance in combination, the theological problem remains. How can both terms be true of God? The answer lies in understanding that God chose to appease himself. Since he was the only one qualified to satisfy his nature, if justice were to be done, he had to do it. He was under no obligation to act as he did. God's sacrifice was an act of mercy. The cross represents the interrelationship of two aspects of God's nature. His forgiveness and justice go hand in hand.[55]

Paul related each of these reasons for thanksgiving to God the Father. This relationship is consistent with Paul's presentation of the work of the Trinity. The passage parallels Eph 1:3-14, where the entire scope of salvation, incorporating the work of the Father, Son, and Spirit, is attributed to the grace of God the Father.[56]

In summary, a personal knowledge of God's will is accompanied by three characteristics. First, continued growth in the knowledge of God comes in the arena of service. Second, power is given to endure both difficult circumstances and people who seem to counter the work of God. Finally, joyful thanksgiving is offered to God the Father for what he has done in planning and effecting salvation. The discussion of the work of Christ and the entrance into his kingdom prompted Paul to pen the words of a hymn to Christ. The hymn occupies the next section of this epistle.

---

[54]Bruce, 191-192, n. 55. He refers to Irenaeus, *Heresies* i. 21.2.

[55]The literature on these concepts is extensive. Helpful discussions occur in L. Morris, *The Apostolic Preaching of the Cross* (London: Tyndale, 1955), 11-64; and D. Hill, *Greek Words and Hebrew Meanings, Studies in the Semantics of Soteriological Terms* (Cambridge: University Press, 1967), 49-81.

[56]This is seen in the grammar of the passage, in which all of the statements modify "blessed be God" (Eph 1:3). It is confirmed by the threefold repetition of the statement that these things were done to the praise of his glory and/or grace (1:6,13,14).

(3) The Hymn to Christ (1:15-20)

[15]He is the image of the invisible God, the firstborn over all creation. [16]For by him all things were created: things in heaven and on earth, visible and invisible, whether thrones or powers or rulers or authorities; all things were created by him and for him. [17]He is before all things, and in him all things hold together. [18]And he is the head of the body, the church; he is the beginning and the firstborn from among the dead, so that in everything he might have the supremacy. [19]For God was pleased to have all his fullness dwell in him, [20]and through him to reconcile to himself all things, whether things on earth or things in heaven, by making peace through his blood, shed on the cross.

INTRODUCTION TO THE HYMN TO CHRIST. This section continues the thought of Paul's prayer. Several indicators reveal this. First, the long sentence begun in 1:9 continues with no grammatical break. Second, the theme of giving thanks to the Father advances into this section, amplifying the statement "giving thanks" (1:12). Third, Paul had been describing the kingdom of Jesus, the Son. He now moved to a poetical description of the nature of that kingdom.

The passage moves in a slightly new direction as it focuses on the Son. In transition, Paul discussed Jesus as Redeemer, but the work of Jesus described here goes beyond human redemption. It describes Jesus as Lord. The hymn is complete in itself, but it contributes to the flow of thought in the epistle. For this reason, it first must be studied as an entity rich in theological content. Then it must be placed in its immediate context to determine the contribution it makes to the argument of the epistle.

This passage has received as much discussion in recent times as any section of the epistle.[57] In this century, scholars have concluded that vv. 15-20 contain a hymn to Christ.[58] As such, it reflects the worship of the early church. The themes are far from abstract, removed, theological affirmations about Jesus. They are living, vibrant, essential elements that found a significant place in regular worship. The criteria for determining the presence of hymns includes lyrical style and linguistic abnormalities. The stylistic factors are mainly reflected in the "certain rhythmical lilt"of the passage.[59] The linguistic features include

---

[57]The literature is extensive. Perhaps the best English summaries of approaches to this section are R. Martin, *Colossians: Church's Lord and the Christian's Liberty* (Exeter: Paternoster, 1972), 40-55; O'Brien, *Colossians, Philemon*, 32-42; and E. Lohse, *Colossians and Philemon, Her* (Philadelphia: Fortress, 1971), 41-46. Many other monographs and periodicals discuss the various aspects of this passage as well.

[58]The terminology "hymn" does not demand that this was sung in the congregational worship. It could mean that it was a poetic, lyrical presentation of theology. The form it takes was didactical, intended to teach in an easily rememberable fashion.

[59]R. Martin, *Carmen Christi, Philippians ii. 5-11 in Recent Interpretation and in the Setting of Early Christian Worship* SNTSMS 4 (Cambridge: University Press, 1967), 12. This rhythmical lilt is known when the passage is read aloud, thus giving evidence that the feel of the passage was carefully planned.

unusual words, distinctive theological expressions, and any features which cause a break between the passage and its context.[60] By these criteria, this passage must be considered an early hymn.

Although scholars agree that this is a hymn, they do not agree on the exact structure of the hymn. The first major recent analysis, done by E. Norden, notes that the hymn consists of two stanzas of unequal length.[61] Norden's analysis provides not only the incentive to study the passage in a new light but also what remains the basic approach to the structure of the hymn. The two stanzas are vv. 15-18a and vv. 18b-20. The German scholar E. Käsemann agrees with the analysis of Norden, except he asserts that Paul added material distinctive to his theology to a preexisting hymn.[62] Particularly, he says, the two phrases "the church" and "through the blood of his cross" are Christian additions to a previously existing Gnostic hymn.[63] Käsemann, thus, sets a precedent for studying the hymn and extracting from it specifically Pauline or Christian elements. Others, such as Lohmeyer, agree with the two basic stanzas analysis but suggest that three lines were inserted.[64] Still others suggest a structure of three stanzas.[65]

Despite the structural confusion, the hymn has two clear thematic divisions. One section presents Christ's relation to the created world. Paul answered basic questions about the origin and purposes of creation. The other section presents Jesus' relationship to the redemption of what he created. Paul reminded the readers of the redemptive purposes of God in and through Christ.

THE STRUCTURE OF THE HYMN. Scholars have devoted considerable attention to the structure of the hymn, with little agreement. Some who deny this is a pre-Colossians tradition see the entire section as one unit and do not concern themselves with further structural analysis. Others are convinced that the hymn has two stanzas; some of these scholars acknowledge a refrain between the two. Still others find three verses. Each of those who divide the hymn into verses suggests that Paul inserted his own theology into the hymn at certain points. He did this either to make the hymn personal, a reflection of his own

---

[60]Here these elements are: "image of God" (1:15), "visible" and "invisible" individually and in contrast to each other (1:15,16), "thrones" (1:16), "dominion" (1:16), "be established" (1:17), "beginning" (1:18), "preeminent" (1:18), "making peace" (1:20), "dwell" (1:19), and "reconcile" (1:20).

[61]See E. Norden, *Agnostos Theos, Untersuchungen zur Formengeschichte religioser Rede* (Darmstadt: Wissenschaftliche Buchgesellschaft, 1956), 250-254.

[62]E. Käsemann, "A Primitive Christian Baptismal Liturgy," *Essays on New Testament Themes* (London: SCM, 1964), 149-68.

[63]Ibid., 150-53. He argued that the rest of the hymn makes good sense apart from a Christian interpretation.

[64]E. Lohmeyer, *Die Briefe an die Philipper, und die Kolosser und an Philemon* (Göttingen: Vandenhoeck, 1953), 40-68.

[65]E.g., Martin, *Church's Lord*, 44-49.

theology, or to apply the hymn specifically to the false teachers at Colosse. The following discussion presents the alternatives generally.

Two-Stanza Arrangement. Those scholars who accept a two stanza arrangement divide the hymn irregularly. They explain that the portions which break the rhythm are additions. The two-stanza approach basically divides the hymn as follows.

Strophe One

He is the image of the invisible God
　　　The first-born over all creation.
　　For by him all things were created
　　　things in heaven and on earth
　　　visible and invisible
　　　　　whether thrones
　　　　　or powers
　　　　　or rulers
　　　　　or authorities
　　all things are created by him and for him.
　　He is before all things,
　　　and in him all things hold together.

Strophe Two

And he is the head of the body, the church
He is the beginning and the first-born from among the dead
　　　so that in everything he might have the supremacy
　　　for God was pleased to have all his fullness dwell in him
　　　and through him to reconcile to himself all things
　　　　whether things on earth
　　　　or things in heaven,
　　　　by making peace through his blood shed on the cross.

Three-Stanza Arrangement. Scholars who see three stanzas in this passage make the middle portion a stanza unto itself. In a general way, their format is as follows.

Strophe One

He is the image of the invisible God,
　　　the first-born of over all creation
　　For by him all things were created:
　　　things in heaven and on earth
　　　visible and invisible
　　　　whether thrones or powers or rulers or authorities
　　All things were created by him and for him.

Strophe Two

He is before all things
> And in him all things hold together.
> And he is head of the body, the church.

Strophe Three

He is the beginning and the firstborn from among the dead
> so that in everything he might have the supremacy
For God was pleased to have all his fullness dwell in him
> and through him to reconcile to himself all things
>> whether things on earth or things in heaven
> by making peace through his blood shed on the cross.

Likewise, most of these interpreters find insertions which break the rhythm of the stanzas. This is particularly true of Strophes One and Three, which they argue must conform to the meter of Strophe Two. Nevertheless, these division points should help orient the interpreter to the difficulties of hymnic analysis in the New Testament.

THE AUTHORSHIP OF THE HYMN. The question of the authorship of the hymn naturally arises. Since there is no break in the textual tradition at this point, clearly Paul included it at the time of writing the epistle. The question is whether it was original with Paul.

Two factors must be considered. First, the meter seems to break the flow of what surrounds the hymn. Although Paul led into it with majestic and poetic language of his own, the hymn has a different flow in its basic structure. Its literary style so differs from what comes before and after that it seems quite likely that Paul incorporated a preexisting piece of literature into the epistle. The second consideration is the content of the hymn. Several ideas are not typical of Paul. Parallels of most of these may be found in the Pauline corpus, however, so care must be taken in this line of reasoning.[66]

Which is correct is a difficult decision. The hymn would easily have referred believers to something they knew well and to a common theology. That would have served Paul's purposes of showing that what he wrote conformed to their understanding of the truth. Whether the hymn was original with Paul, he put his approval on it as though it were his own by including it in the letter. It is, therefore, in a general sense "Pauline." Any suggestion that the hymn was inserted later has significant difficulties to overcome. The hymn appears to be the foundation for many of the ideas found in the letter and is, thus, interwoven through it.

---

[66]E.g., Ephesians has many parallels of the lordship of Christ applied to the church, yet they are not in hymnic structure.

If the hymn were not composed by Paul for this occasion, other insights arise. First, the hymn would not be reflective of the problem Paul addressed in the epistle. The concepts of the hymn had an independent circulation. The theology certainly applied well to the new context, however, so that it readily answered the Colossian situation. Second, the hymn would reflect a high Christology held generally in the church. These ideas about the lordship of Christ were commonly accepted and understood. This understanding went beyond the church at Colosse. Third, the reason for Paul's incorporating it into this letter must be explored further. Since he did not know this church firsthand, it served his purpose well to remind the members of what they held in common and to build much of his argument on it.

THE CONTENTS OF THE HYMN. The hymn to Christ has two uneven stanzas, but their themes are consistent. The first relates Jesus to creation; the second, to redemption. The first considers the created world, including the material creation and supernatural beings. The second considers the reconciliation of these various created elements which have gone astray. Therefore, Paul contributed to the two main themes of the Bible: creation and redemption. Together, the two stanzas make a strong case for the supremacy of Christ. He is Lord over creation, and he is the Lord of the new creation.

The hymn expresses another significant theological theme of Scripture. Every area of life touched by sin also must be touched by grace. To leave an aspect of creation in the grasp of sin would allow sin to triumph over grace. Such a thought is unthinkable. Although sin dominated over the created world, bringing eternal repercussions, sin does not rule totally, forever, over any aspect of creation. That is the burden of this section. Jesus' lordship is seen by virtue of both his position in creation and his position in redemption.

Jesus: Lord of Creation (1:15-17). The structure of the passage provides a guideline for analysis. In this first stanza of the hymn, the structural analysis reveals two assertions about the person of Christ (v. 15) that are followed by a reason for the assertions (v. 16) and a summary statement expressing Jesus' prominence (v. 17).

1:15 Two assertions set the direction for the entire discussion. They are: "He is the image of the invisible God," and "[He is] the firstborn over all creation." Two important matters emerge from the first assertion: the idea of the image of God and how the image is a revelation of God. In the Greek world, the word "image" (*eikōn*) conveyed one of two nuances of meaning. Both elements were always present, but one tended to dominate the other. The first is that of representation. The image represented and symbolized what the object pictured. This usage occurred often in the contexts of an image on a coin or a reflection in a mirror.[67] If this emphasis were primary, Paul would have said

---

[67] C. Vaughan, *Colossians and Philemon, BSG* (Grand Rapids: Zondervan, 1973), 38.

Jesus was the symbol of deity. Paul would have meant that Jesus exactly symbolized God.

The second element of meaning in the word "image" (*eikōn*) was manifestation. When the term was employed, it meant that the symbol was more than a symbol. The symbol brought with it the actual presence of the object. Thus J. B. Phillips translated it, "visible expression," and by it Paul meant that Jesus brought God into the human sphere of understanding. He manifested God. The terminology is similar to Heb 1:3, where the writer stated that Jesus is called the "exact representation" of God, and John 1:18, which states that Jesus "has made him known." The point is that in Christ the invisible God became visible. He shared the same substance as God and made God's character known in this earthly sphere of existence. The revelation of God in Christ is such that we can actually see him, even with all of our limitations.

This points to a significant truth about the uniqueness of Christ. The Old Testament forbade images made in the likeness of God (Exod 20:4-6). No person was to design a likeness of God and use it for worship. To do that confined the concept of God to the mental image conveyed by the symbol. God would always be conceived of in terms of the specific symbol which pictured him to people. This was inadequate because God was bigger than that and because the people were to think the highest possible thoughts of God. On the other hand, the Old Testament clearly stated that persons were created in the image of God (Gen 1:27, where in the LXX the Greek word *eikōn* is also used). Paul argued that concept at Corinth when the women apparently were violating proper authority structures within the church (1 Cor 11:7). He also related Adam to Christ in a unique manner (1 Cor 15:45), a theme which deserves some contemplation.[68] In this passage, he stated that Jesus was unique in that he manifested the image of God. Thus, for Paul, Jesus bore the image of the earthly, Adam, and the image of the heavenly, God. He was the unique manifestation of both God and man, always embodying the best of both wherever he was. In choosing the word "image," Paul stressed that God was present wherever Jesus was. He was the personal manifestation of deity.

The second assertion about Jesus expresses his relationship to all of creation. This is found in the term "firstborn." History reveals that this term has had various definitions. In the fourth century, Arius, a preacher from Alexandria, Egypt, taught that Christ was a created being. He was greater than the rest of the creation but lesser than God himself. Arius hoped this position would protect Christianity from the charge of polytheism. This position was condemned in the church in A.D. 325. Even so, Arius's position has refused to die and lives on in several sectarian groups. He understood this text to teach that

---

[68]E.g., the development of this theme in H. Ridderbos, *Paul: An Outline of His Theology* (Grand Rapids: Eerdmans, 1975), 78-86.

Jesus was the firstborn (part) of the creation (whole).[69] Even though Jesus was unique among created beings, he was still created. According to Arius, Jesus occupied the strange position of being "created creator."

The Greek word "firstborn" comes from two words which mean *to bring forth, or beget* and *first*.[70] The word is seldom used outside of biblical materials, and its use in extra-biblical sources has limited value to biblical meaning. It occurs 130 times in the LXX, normally with the primary meaning of *primogeniture*. Used this way, it expressed the first birth of men or animals. The word, however, also developed a second use in the LXX. It often expressed a special relationship with God the Father, one of privilege.[71] This is certainly the meaning in such passages as Ps 89:27, where David is called the "firstborn" among the kings of the earth. In the New Testament the word occurs only eight times. It is clearly used literally of primogeniture only once.[72] The rest of the occurrences are figurative, and they are far removed from any idea of birth. Finally, the Fathers also used the term figuratively. Polycarp, for example, referred to an enemy of the church as the "firstborn of Satan."[73]

The Jewish concept of the birthright also influences the meaning of the word. As Lightfoot pointed out, the term "firstborn" referred to a rite (ritual) that accorded the first son a special place in the family. The term soon lost the meaning of the first in time and developed the meaning of first in priority. Following this reasoning, Paul stated that Jesus "is His Father's representative and heir and has the management of the divine household (all creation) committed to Him."[74]

The meaning of privilege predominates in the passage. Three lines of argument support that conclusion. First is the lexical significance of the term as it was used in the biblical materials. Second is the idea of birthright, which figured so prominently in Jewish life. Third is the problem of mixed metaphors. If Jesus were a created being, the figure of birth is hardly appropriate. Birth and creation are not to be equated here. The point of the metaphor is to distinguish Jesus from creation, not to tie him to it by placing him within it. Michaelis

---

[69] This would be a partitive genitive, in which the part is a portion of the whole.

[70] The terms are πρῶτος ("first") and τέτωκα, perfect of τίκτω ("to bring forth").

[71] This is confirmed first by the use in the LXX of such passages as Exod 4:22 and Jer 31:9, in which the stress is on the idea of privilege rather than birth. Second, the Hebrew בְּכוֹר is the word translated by the Greek πρωτότοκος 111 of its 130 occurrences in the LXX (with 6 more from this word group, and 5 have no equivalent). The Hebrew term "might become increasingly remote and even detached altogether from the idea of birth or the whole question of origin" (W. Michaelis, *TDNT*, 6:873). Certainly the term often stresses the idea of privilege. See the article by K. H. Bartels, *DNTT*, 1: 667-669.

[72] The eight are Luke 2:7; Rom 8:29; Col 1:15,18; Heb 1:6; 11:28 (plural); 12:23; Rev. 1:5. The one time it occurs with a literal sense is Luke 2:7, and that is a questionable usage. For a thorough and valuable discussion of this data, see Michaelis, 6:865-882.

[73] Polycarp, 7:1.

[74] Vaughan, 39.

pointed out "that Adam, though not born but created, can be called the 'first-born of the world' in Nu. r., 4 (141c)."[75] Recognizing this usage, we can see that the term must refer to the unique place of Jesus in relation to creation.

The definition of "firstborn" provides understanding for the statement translated "over all creation." As previously noted, some have wanted to take the statement in a partitive sense, as the "firstborn part of the whole creation." This is impossible with the sense demanded of the word "firstborn." The NIV translation correctly states that Jesus is "over all creation." The term "firstborn" distances Jesus from creation rather than subsumes him under it. Therefore, the point is that Jesus is the firstborn (preeminent) with reference to the creation, just as later Paul argued that Jesus was preeminent "out of the dead."[76]

Thus two assertions are made regarding Jesus. In his work toward us as revealer of God, he manifests God to us. In his work toward creation, he is prominent over it.

1:16 In this verse Paul provided the reason for asserting the supremacy of Christ over creation. The three phrases "by him" (v. 16a), "by him" (v. 16b), and "for him" (v. 16b) indicate the relationship. In actuality, three different ideas are expressed by these phrases. The first of these is the Greek expression translated literally "in him."[77] It should be understood as *in his mind* or *in his sphere of influence and responsibility*. Practically, it means that Jesus conceived of creation and its complexities. Creation was his idea. Hendriksen illustrated the term by saying Jesus is the cornerstone from which the whole building takes its bearings.[78] The illustration is limited, however. The phrase points to Jesus as the "detailer" of creation.

Theologically a clear distinction is to be made between the work of the Father and the Son. The Father, of course, has a significant relationship to creation. He is presented as the architect; he determined to bring creation into existence. The Son, Jesus, actually brought the plans into existence. Through his creative imagination and power, the created order exists. He is, in a sense, the foreman of the construction. The Spirit, finally, does the actual work of applying the plans in a hands-on relationship to creation. This statement about Jesus, therefore, speaks to Jesus' originating the details of creation and bringing them into existence by his own creative energy.[79] The second informative phrase is that creation came into existence "through him."[80] The NIV says "by him." This phrase means that creation came to be through his power and ability.

---

[75] Michaelis, 6:876, n. 30.

[76] This takes the genitive construction as a genitive of reference.

[77] The Greek is ἐν αὐτῷ.

[78] W. Hendriksen, *Colossians and Philemon*, NTC (Grand Rapids: Baker, 1979), 73.

[79] In another sense, of course, the Scriptures speak of the unity of deity in all tasks, including creation and redemption. Yet there are fine divisions of responsibility which are regularly maintained by a number of different biblical authors.

[80] The phrase is δι᾽ αὐτοῦ.

He is the effective agent of creation. In this Paul spoke consistently with other biblical writers. In John 1:1ff., John affirmed emphatically that everything created owes its existence to Jesus. In Heb 1:1-3, the writer pointed to Jesus' creative and sustaining power in relation to all material things.

Finally, the passage affirms that creation exists "for him." The literal expression is "unto him."[81] This means that Jesus is the goal of all creation. Everything exists to display his glory, and ultimately he will be glorified in his creation. Paul's argument in these verses may be illustrated by an artist who produces a sculpture. Originally the idea and details of the sculpture come from the mind of the artist. He builds the proportions, the perspectives, the figures, and the emphases desired from the statue. Then, the sculpture is constructed by the artist as he and he alone can "see" it. Finally, those who admire the finished work think of the artist who imagined, planned, and accomplished the work of beauty. As long as the sculpture stands, people remember and appreciate the artist. In the same way, Jesus is the central point of all of creation, and he rules over it.

When discussing Jesus' work in creation, Paul expressed the dimensions of creation. They are "things in heaven and on earth, visible and invisible, whether thrones or powers or rulers or authorities" (1:16). The series begins with two contrasts between two dimensions of life set against each other. They are universal in scope. A chiastic arrangement reveals that they are one unit of thought.[82] In a chiasm, the outside members receive emphasis. Thus the unseen world receives emphasis, expressed here as "heaven . . . things invisible." The seen world receives secondary emphasis, expressed as "earth . . . visible."

The two dimensions are dimensions of creation. Some modern readers are prone to understand "heaven" as the term which describes the timeless future destination of believers. Others see it as an unending time, an eternal realm. Sometimes the term does refer to the state of eternal bliss, but neither explanation is correct in this context or in this epistle. Paul used the word for another dimension: the unseen but created reality. This meaning is demonstrated by the immediate context and the context of both Ephesians and Colossians. The immediate context sets heaven and earth apart from each other, but attributes their existence to the creative energies of Jesus. If heaven were understood as the place where God lives, it could hardly have been created by Jesus in the way Paul discussed it here. Second, the Epistle to the Colossians uses the term "heaven(s)" similarly to Ephesians.[83] Actually, the term is used in two ways in these epistles.

---

[81] The Greek is εἰς αὐτόν.

[82] Here, the chiasm is (1) heaven, (2) earth, (3) visible, and (4) invisible. Two groups emerge: (1) and (4) refer to the same general thing, and (2) and (3) do also. There is a slight emphasis on the heavenly, invisible dimension of creation.

[83] Generally the term "heaven" is plural, "the heavens" (οὐρανοῖς).

On one hand, it may have reference to the heavens as a place above the earth (Col 1:23; 4:1; Eph 4:10; 6:9). This is the more common designation. On the other hand, it may refer to a place where spirits dwell and where the Christian is placed spiritually at the time of his salvation (Eph 1:3,20; 2:6; 3:10). This is also the place of the evil spirits against whom the Christian wars (Eph 6:10ff.).[84] Since in the conclusion of this verse Paul referred to spirit beings primarily, it may well be that he had in mind the home of spirit beings, a different dimension of existence. Probably, however, Paul spoke of the earth and heaven as created realities. Here the heavens are the locale of the spiritual warfare in which Christians engage.

The thought of the two dimensions of creation, however, soon gives way to the spirit beings who live there and who concern the Christian. These are identified as "thrones or powers or rulers or authorities." Paul may well have referred here to the same kind of pre-Gnostic *plērōma*, although nothing specific in the text demands such interpretation. The assumption may be made that these categories continue the twofold categories of heaven/invisible and earth/visible. In fact, the terms may be used in that fashion, capable of designating human political rule (thrones, powers, rulers, authorities). The chiasm has ended, however, clearly indicating that the twofold categories are over.[85] This is a new list which identifies a new perspective within the scope of creation, but different from heaven and earth.

There is a general consensus among scholars that the terms used here refer to spiritual beings. Some, such as Theodoret and several of the Fathers, seemed to understand them as good spirits. They have been given the task of supervision. The "thrones" are the cherubim; the "authorities" "rulers," and "powers" are the guardian angels of the nations.[86] Little evidence exists to determine whether these are good or bad. They are simply higher classes of angelic beings. In light of 2:8-3:4, however, they probably refer to fallen beings who oppress the Christian. In Ephesians, the terms definitely refer to enemies of the gospel (Eph 6:10ff.). They may have been the focus of the Colossian teachers since evidently they taught the necessity of intermediaries between God and man.[87] These terms may refer to separate classes of beings rather than designating one type. F. F. Bruce points out that "the highest angel-princes, like the rest of creation are subject to Christ as the one in whom, through whom and for whom they were created."[88] Although little biblical evidence exists on which

---

[84] Some patterns of usage seem to exist regarding οὐρανός, but they defy clear analysis. Also, Paul seemed to use οὐρανοῖς almost interchangeably with οὐρανός. Thus the specific context must determine the precise meaning.

[85] Chiasms mark the beginning and end of a specific section.

[86] Taken from Moule, 65-66.

[87] E.g., Martin, *Church's Lord*, 40.

[88] Bruce, 198.

to base the conclusions about spirit hierarchies, Moule was certainly correct in stating, "The cumulative effect of this catalog of powers is to emphasize the immeasurable superiority of Christ over whatever rival might, by the false teachers, be suggested."[89]

These spirit beings occupy a significant place in the epistle. The special attention they receive suggests considerable preoccupation regarding them. Indeed, they are the object of much discussion here and in 2:8-3:4. Paul seems to have felt a need to note that these spirit beings are created by the power of Christ and conquered by the power of the cross (2:15).

1:17 The summary includes two statements of significance to the readers. The first is, "He is before all things." Clearly this comment has a time orientation, and it teaches that before creation Jesus existed. Since for the ancients priority in time often meant priority of person, this argument not only stresses Jesus' role in creating but also gives him a prominent position with respect to creation. The second statement is, "In him all things hold together." The work of creation included the continual sustaining of what was created. Looking to the present, ongoing routine of creation, therefore, Paul stated that Jesus keeps things in order. The Creator has not forgotten the creation. He daily maintains a balance in the universe.

Jesus: Lord of the New Creation (1:18-20). As creation and redemption go together in theology, so Paul tied them together in the second stanza of the hymn. Here, Jesus is praised for his role in the new creation. In the new creation, every aspect of creation touched by sin will be touched by grace. This does not mean that every element affected by sin will be redeemed into a state of grace. It means that every category of creation will be restored and that those areas left in a state of sin will be put into their proper place by the power of Christ. The structure of this stanza parallels the first. There are two assertions (1:18) and reasons for the assertions (1:19-20).

1:18 As in the first stanza, two statements made about Jesus set the direction for the stanza. They relate to Jesus in his role of Redeemer. The first is, "He is the head of the body, the church." In this statement, "church" is in apposition to "the body," thereby explaining both elements. This is an organic concept of church. The metaphor of the church as "the body" was commonly used by Paul and adapted easily to many different aspects of the church's life. It may stress the interdependency of the various parts of the body (cf. 1 Cor 12:12-26),[90] the dynamic aspect of the body as it strives for maturity (Eph 4:15-16),[91] the

---

[89] Moule, 65-66.

[90] In 1 Cor 12:12-16 Christ is not one part of the body, but rather permeates the whole. The entire body *is* Christ. The point to be made here is the organic and functional interrelationships that the "body" metaphor implies.

[91] In Eph 5:15-16, the goal of the rest of the body is to grow to the stature of the head, Christ. Clearly, the dynamic, maturing nature of the body is in mind.

redemptive role of the head for the body (Eph 5:23),[92] or the hierarchy of the parts of the body, the head being superior to the rest (Col 1:18). These diverse applications of the illustration point out the adaptability of the concept. Perhaps the emphases overlap on occasion since the metaphor is pregnant with possibilities. The common element in all is that of organic interrelationship. Each aspect of the body really is a part of the others.

On other occasions, Paul used the organizational model of the church rather than the organic. Stressing authority relationships, the organizational model suited some purposes well. For example, it well described pastor/deacon relationships. Both the organic and the organizational models are appropriate, depending on the emphasis desired. In Col 1:18 the authority and direction-giving aspects of the head over the body receive the focus.

In interpreting this picture, some important truths emerge. First, the organic picture illustrates the unity of the head and body. Although clearly Christ can and did exist without the church, the imagery chosen lends itself to expressing the concept that the head is incomplete without the body. Similarly, the body is incomplete without the head. This is more fully developed in Eph 1. From an earthly perspective, the church is necessary since it is the visible body of Christ. Most of what the world sees of the whole body, it sees not in the head, but in the body, the church. Thus the idea of corporate personality, so prevalent in the Old Testament, may emerge here as well.[93]

Another truth emerges in this statement. As Paul began to enumerate the areas of Jesus' lordship over what is redeemed, he focused on the church. Indeed, redemption and reconciliation pertain primarily to the church since the fallen spirit beings and creation are not reconciled in the same way. Instinctively Paul's thoughts turned to the church when he contemplated redemption.

The second assertion is that he is the beginning. The term has two possible applications, both of which have been understood here. First, at times the word means temporal primacy. As such, it refers only to being first in time. References such as Matt 19:4,8; Heb 1:10; 2 Pet 3:4 employ this sense. At other times, the word means primacy in authority or rule. As such, it refers to the unique one who rules with appropriate authority. References such as Rom 8:38 ("principalities," KJV; "demons," NIV) and 1 Cor 15:24 ("rule," KJV; "dominion," NIV) reveal this aspect of the term.[94] The interpretive question, therefore, is whether temporal or positional language best suits the context. Although

---

[92] A natural tendency in "body" relationships is reversed in Eph 5:23. Generally the rest of the body will sacrifice itself for the head. The imagery pictures the radical nature of the work of Christ in providing for the body.

[93] See, e.g., C. F. D. Moule, *The Origin of Christianity* (Cambridge: University Press, 1977), 47-96, and O'Brien, *Colossians, Philemon*, 50, for a further discussion of these aspects of the imagery.

[94] The masculine form of the word ἀρχή used here is ἄρχων, which means "ruler." The same root idea, therefore, can be used easily to refer to either.

some may argue for the temporal setting on the basis of the word "firstborn," authority is the better understanding. When "firstborn" is understood as seems to be demanded in 1:15 (and 1:18), the temporal element is removed. The entire force of the hymn points to the supremacy of Christ by virtue of his person. Therefore, the positional terminology is to be preferred over the purely temporal. This does not mean, however, that temporal ideas are completely lost. The fact is, the age of redemption came at a specific point in time, at the resurrection of Jesus. That event marked the conclusion of the redemptive work of Jesus.

The age of redemption was initiated by a specific person, Jesus, who is the Redeemer. Because redemption took place in a time framework, the temporal element enters the discussion. From the human perspective, historical sequence forms the framework for understanding. Nevertheless, the primary concern is positional. Jesus became the Lord of redemption and the firstfruits of those who belong in that redeemed company (1 Cor 15:20-23). God determined that a new order would be built around the person of Jesus, and that is the focus of this second portion of the hymn.

The term "beginning" is explained by the word "firstborn" (1:18). Actually, the NIV translates incorrectly at this point. In order to emphasize clarity of thought, it states, "He is the beginning and the firstborn from among the dead." The translators have inserted the word "and" to tie these two descriptions together, as though they were two separate items. The Greek text simply places the two descriptions side by side. The second interprets the first so that "firstborn" actually restates the idea of "beginning." Thus it should be translated, "He is the beginning, that is, the firstborn out of the dead." This translation captures two elements found within the original: The appositional relationship between "beginning" and "firstborn" is maintained, and the tie between the two uses of the word "firstborn" is stressed (1:15; 1:18). Balance is achieved in the poetic and rhythmic elements of the hymn.[95]

The phrase "from among the dead" sets the direction for the new phase of the lordship of Christ. Clearly the phrase notes the supremacy of Jesus in his resurrection. The "dead" may be used spiritually (Eph 2:1) or physically (1 Thess 4:15). Here the real sense is conveyed, i.e., that Christ actually died but rose from the realm of the dead into a new life. Even so, the spiritual connotations subtly remain. Death infected humanity because of sin, and thus death depicts the plight of sinners who bear the consequence of sin.[96] It recalls the fact that Jesus entered the world of sinners, endured their punishment, and rose victorious with the power of the Spirit. Thus, in Christ there is a new order of

---

[95] Some argue that the two assertions are "beginning" and "firstborn" and that "head of the body" goes with the verse.

[96] An important side note in this regards calls to mind Rom 5:12-14 where Paul made significant contributions to the nature of sin in the world. There his argument allows for the fact that some who did not sin in the way Adam did still die. It opens the door to the discussion that one who did not sin could still die because he entered the human condition and took on him the penalty of sin.

existence. It is a resurrection existence. It is an after-death existence that is guaranteed by the fact that Jesus, who died as any die, rose in resurrection to redeem those who trust him.

The purpose of the resurrection is stated here as "so that in everything he might have the supremacy." In light of this context, the word "everything" must be understood as the creation, over which Jesus reigns as king, and the order of redemption, over which he reigns as head. He is the central figure, therefore, in both domains. Just as creation depends on him for its existence and order, redemption depends on him, and he is the primary figure in it. Jesus is both a model and an integration of the two realms. The integration occurs because of Jesus' central place in creation and redemption. He ties the two together in his person. The model is that he embodied both the old order, in a physical body, and the new order, in a resurrection existence. Both dimensions owe their existence to him, the preeminent one.

Two reasons that support the assertions made in 1:18 are given in vv. 19-20: "For God was pleased to have all his fullness dwell in him, and through him to reconcile to himself all things." The first has to do with Jesus' person; the second, with his work.

1:19 Paul's first claim about Jesus was that God's fullness dwelt in Jesus. The description cannot be understood apart from the context of Colossians. Many have pointed to the Gnostic or pre-Gnostic use of the term "fullness."[97] In the Gnostic schemes in general, the term "fullness" (*plērōma*) referred to the totality of the emanations from God. The emanations, or "aeons," were spiritual and separate from the material world. Although these emanations came from God, they were not considered part of God.

Two basic problems arise with interpreting *plērōma* this way. First, Gnosticism was basically second-century movement, and no real evidence supports a widespread Gnostic-like understanding of *plērōma* so near the middle of the first century.[98] Second, this interpretation requires that Jesus be distinct from God, being an "emanation" from God. Strictly speaking, Paul would have to have meant that Jesus is the totality of these emanations from God. Paul hardly used the term with that meaning since he was convinced otherwise about the person of Jesus. The other use of the term in Col 2:9 supports a non-Gnostic interpretation.[99] The most that could be reasonably asserted in this relation is that the technical use of the term may have been in the early stages

---

[97] The Greek term is πλήρωμα.

[98] See, e.g., the discussion by E. Yamauchi, *Pre-Christian Gnosticism: A Survey of Proposed Evidences* (Grand Rapids: Eerdmans, 1973). See also the updated reprint by Baker, 1984. His work concerns Gnosticism in general but is helpful in this regard.

[99] Lohse states, "Since, according to Valentinian teaching, the 'plērōma' is indeed the heavenly fullness to which, however, God does not belong, this understanding of the word 'plērōma' cannot contribute anything to the explanation of Col 1:19—for there can be no doubt that in the Christhymn, God himself is called 'plērōma' " (57).

of development and that the hearers would have listened intently upon hearing the word read.[100]

In contrast to this more technical usage is a nontechnical definition. The term may express simply "totality." As modified in 2:9, the term means "the full measure of deity," and 1:19 must bear the same sense.[101] Therefore, it expresses that Jesus was completely God. Everything that God is, Jesus is. As the following section reveals, however, God is more than Jesus. God includes the Father, Son, and Spirit. Jesus is only one aspect of God, but he is every bit God. Paul could easily state that God and Jesus are in some sense different, while at the same time stating that they share the same essence.

The interpreter faces both lexical and grammatical problems when seeking to understand the Pauline concept of "fullness." The Greek text does not provide a subject for this statement. The NIV supplies the word "God" to make sense of the construction: "For God was pleased to have all his fullness dwell in him" (1:19). This insertion properly clarifies the construction. In the Old Testament, the term is used to show God's pleasure with right actions and displeasure with evil.[102] In the New Testament the term expresses God's pleasure with his Son at his baptism (Matt 3:17) and transfiguration (Matt 17:5). Although neither of these specific occasions lies behind this text, clearly there is a precedent in Scripture for the phrase to be used with God as the subject. Here Paul stated that the Godhead determined that the human Jesus would be God, sharing all the properties, characteristics, and prerogatives of God himself. Of course, the movement in the incarnation was that God took flesh, not that a human was elevated to deity. The statement actually means that God was pleased to take human form in Jesus. He was no less than God,[103] and he continues to be fully divine ("dwell" is present tense stressing an ongoing reality).

Another factor to consider in this statement is that Paul attributed everything to the Father. The context stresses the work of God the Father on behalf of Christians. The motif continues here. There is perfect harmony in the plan of salvation, for God the Father initiated the deliverance of his people (1:12-14), and God the Father delighted in the fact that Jesus was fully and completely

---

[100]For surveys of the issue of the term and its "Gnostic" associations, see Lightfoot, 257-73, and G. Delling, *TDNT*, 6:299-300.

[101]*BAGD*, 672.

[102]The LXX uses the same Greek verb, εὐδοκέω, in expressing this pleasure in Pss 147:11; 149:4 as examples of a more pervasive usage.

[103]For clarity, it is perhaps good to comment on Paul's use of the term "God" in this epistle. Without a context, the term may mean the totality of God, i.e., all three persons of the Trinity of God. It may also represent the Father in distinction from the Spirit and Son. To this point in Colossians (and generally in the epistle), all uses of the term "God" have referred more precisely to the Father, the architect of all things (1:2,3,6,9,10,15). Often the two "persons" of deity are contrasted with each other in this chapter (1:3,10,15).

God (1:19). There is no depreciation of the person and work of Jesus, but there is a heightened appreciation for the involvement of God the Father.

1:20 At this stage, Paul took up his second concern, which was the work of Jesus. Like the previous statement, this has God as the subject: God delighted in Jesus' central role of redemption. Thus his person (truly and fully God) and work (reconciliation) occur in complete harmony with God the Father and fulfill the divine plan precisely. The nature of the reconciliation may be understood in considering its scope, its goal, and its means.

The scope of reconciliation includes the material creation, the animal world, humanity, and spiritual beings. It may be tempting to think of reconciliation as affecting humanity only; the text goes far beyond that: He reconciled "all things, whether things on earth or things in heaven." No doubt this more succinct expression intends to call to mind the more extended statement of 1:16. There Paul included supernatural, spiritual beings specifically as the things in heaven. In using the term "reconciliation," Paul assumed that something had gone wrong. All of creation was touched by sin. The world was out of order and needed a correction. This was provided in Christ.

As a helpful digression, some discussion of the biblical view of this disorder will clarify Paul's thought. There are three specific concerns: the spirit world, the human world, and the material world. Each has been alienated and stands in need of correction. The spirit world suffered a fall when many of the angels rebelled.[104] The human fall is recorded in Gen 3 and its theological implications explored in Rom 5:12-21. The material world was affected as a result of the fall of Adam and Eve, as recorded in Gen 3:17ff.[105] The various situations explain the spiritual battles between demons and God/angels, the moral dilemma faced in the human condition, and the natural disasters and difficulties in the material world. Thus, sin affected every area of creation, and the work of God in redemption extends likewise to every area of creation. That is the subject of this portion of the hymn. Nothing lies outside the realm of Christ's reconciling work.[106]

The goal of reconciliation is important to consider. Paul spoke of being reconciled to God (2 Cor 5:20), but here he spoke of reconciliation to Christ. This emphasizes some significant points of Pauline theology. Since Christ

---

[104] Fallen spirits are recorded in Jewish literature in 1 Enoch x-xvi; xxi; Apocalypse of Baruch lvi.12f; Jubilees v.6; 6QD ii.18-21, and elsewhere. The Old Testament seems to refer to the fall of angels in Isa 14:12ff. and Ezek 28:11-12, where the prophet addressed the historical kings and the "spirit" which motivated them to be anti-God. This is particularly pronounced in Ezek 28:13 where the prophet said, "Thou wast in Eden, the Garden of God" (ASV) when obviously the King of Tyre of Ezekiel's day was not that old.

[105] This account explains the turmoil of the creation which is also expressed by Paul in Rom 8:19-23. These texts also demonstrate an expectation that redemption will affect the earth as well.

[106] That, of course, does not mean that everything is brought into a proper, "saving" relationship with God.

reconciled things to himself, this statement clearly assumes the deity of Jesus. The sin that affected all creation was primarily against God. The reconciliation must also be toward God. Paul spoke in broader terms here, however, by saying that the reconciliation is to Christ. Thus the way to reconciliation with God is to be reconciled to Christ. He is the intermediary between God and all things.

According to 1 Cor 15:20-28, because of the resurrection, Jesus brings into reality the blessings of the new age. These two passages are complementary in that they include both the resurrection of Jesus and the organizational structures that come because of the resurrection. First Corinthians describes Christ as the one who subdues hostile and opposing parties. He also reorganizes all of life, making harmony out of chaos. Jesus himself is the focal point. He has been given the task of making right what has gone wrong. By his power and authority, he will correct every aspect of creation. Ultimately he will present this properly arranged universe to God who will be glorified in all. Thus everything that exists is organized around Christ.

In Col 1:20 the common understanding of reconciliation must be broadened. At the most basic level, reconciliation means the restoring of a broken relationship. Typically in Scripture it involves persons because the Bible was written to transform human life. Reconciliation usually involves two prerequisites: Both parties must have a willingness to be reconciled, and there must be an occasion that brings them together. God has demonstrated his willingness and provided the occasion by taking the initiative to send Jesus as reconciler. The willingness is produced by the work of the Holy Spirit. A felt need, often prompted by circumstances of life, provides the occasion. Thus reconciliation is normally voluntary and volitional.

Here, however, reconciliation involves more than a voluntary movement. The natural creation was subjected to sin "not by its own choice" (Rom 8:20), and its reconciliation will be of God's choosing in his time. Regarding the spirits, in Col 2:15 Paul employed the language of warfare in stating that the spirit powers will be subdued by Christ.[107] Their ultimate destiny was settled when they chose either to rebel or submit to God's glory in eternity past.[108] Now, God offers no possibility of renewal to those who rebelled, presumably because they had a full knowledge of God when they chose sin.[109] Now they live in an

---

[107] The setting of that text is drawn from the language of battle in which Christ is seen as the conqueror disarming and pacifying his enemies.

[108] The theme of fallen spirits permeates first-century Jewish literature (see note 104). It makes its way into Scripture in the New Testament in such passages as 1 Pet 3:19 and Jude 6.

[109] When Adam and Eve sinned, they had a precise and accurate knowledge of God, but it was not the same as the spirit beings who saw God with clear, "spiritual vision." If God's grace toward humans can be explained by reason (which is highly unlikely), perhaps this is the way. The sinful act of humans was not as insightful as the rebellion of spirit beings. Therefore, it was not a final act in the same sense. God offers to humans a chance of renewal.

intermediate time in which they exercise limited powers of rebellion. Some day, however, that will cease. The work of Christ's death will be applied completely to them.

As regards the human world, there is the possibility of a voluntary reconciliation; but for those who are not reconciled to Christ there is the sentence of death (2 Cor 2:14-16). Thus reconciliation may be effected by voluntary submission to Jesus, which brings the blessings of salvation, or by involuntary submission, being conquered by the power of his might. Reconciliation must be defined in this context, therefore, as all things being put into proper relation to Christ. Those who respond to his voice will be brought into a relationship of grace and blessing. Those who oppose and reject him will receive eternal punishment involving removal from God's blessings and the active outpouring of his judgment. In the end, everyone and everything will be reconciled in this sense.[110] Everyone and everything will be subordinated to Christ.[111]

The means of reconciliation is described in another rather strange expression for Paul, "by making peace through his blood, shed on the cross" (1:20). The Greek text has a more direct statement, "through the blood of his cross." Several aspects of this statement demand attention. First, the blood of the cross points to the theology of the blood atonement which runs throughout Scripture and speaks of the radical death of Jesus (blood actually flowed from the body). Second, it identifies the substitutionary aspects of the death of Christ by recalling the blood sacrifices of the Old Testament, which were substitutionary in nature. Third, the expression identifies blood with the cross. Paul did not often put blood and the cross together. For him, they were synonymous: Each stands for the other. Although Rom 3:21-31 reveals that the two may occur together, to find the two in one statement emphasizes Paul's thought. The use of "blood" dramatically pointed to the blood which was shed at Christ's death. The emphasis is no doubt physical and theological. It is physical in that the terms "blood" and "death" point to the real experiences of human beings. It is theological in that Paul calls to mind the history of the blood tradition in Israel.

The peace achieved through the death of Jesus is an objective peace. It is the peace of relationships, not feelings. Although the human heart cries for feelings of peace, the deep need is for a relationship of peace. When relationships are correct, feelings follow. Here, as generally for Paul, the peace brings order and harmony into what is otherwise chaotic and distorted. The reconciliation of all things, as interpreted here, suggests that the peace is the restoring of harmony

---

[110]For a helpful study of this aspect of reconciliation, see P. O'Brien, "Col. 1:20 and the Reconciliation of all Things," *RTR* 33 (1974): 45-53, and *Colossians, Philemon*, 53-57. Of the many ideas suggested by scholars, the position above is in harmony with the conclusions of O'Brien who quoted Lohse approvingly that the "universe has been reconciled in that heaven and earth have been brought back into their divinely created and determined order . . . the universe is again under its head and . . . cosmic peace has returned." (*Colossians, Philemon*, 56; Lohse, 59).

[111]Note the parallel in Phil 2:5-11. Every knee will bow and every tongue will confess.

to all things, the many dimensions of existence ("things on earth or things in heaven"). Paul identified restored order often as a result of the work of Christ. It applied to individuals in Rom 5:1, where the peace *with* God is the immediate result of justification. It applied corporately in relationships in Eph 2:11ff., where peace between races is a result of the work of Christ. Here, Paul expressed the cosmic aspects of the harmony effected by the cross.

Significantly, an act in time and space had repercussions beyond both time and space. Jesus' death at a specific point in time and in the physical dimension of life affected beings outside of time who live in the spiritual dimensions of existence. Thus there is a unity of the two worlds, physical and spiritual. They are reconciled in an act of time, and peace is forever established.[112] From a theological perspective, therefore, there is a unity between the two. Unity is effected by divine creation, observed in God's intervention into the world through miracles and the incarnation, and solidified in redemption. Creation is the handiwork of God, and the Christian should understand the unity of all things in Christ. Elsewhere Paul reflected on this theme in 1 Cor 15:25-28 and Phil 2:9-11. These cosmic dimensions are as much a part of the gospel as are the personal.

In this discussion of reconciliation, Paul had two basic reference points. First was the beginning of restoration, which occurred at the cross. The death of Christ provided the objective basis upon which all else followed. Thus Paul looked backward in time, resting his hopes on what was done in Christ. Second was the culmination of reconciliation which will take place in the future. Paul expressed by faith this necessary outworking of the death of Jesus. Thus Jesus died not only to provide individuals with salvation but also to restore a harmony to the universe. That harmony is an assured aspect of redemption.

Christians are wrong to wait only for the new cosmic order. Because of this expectation, Christians must have an ecological sensitivity. The world belongs to God. When creation is damaged or creatures become extinct, the world loses a picture of God. With each of these, less of God is known and, therefore, less knowledge is available through natural revelation. Equally, since creation is destined to glorify Christ, Christians must work to encourage that now. Wise care and use of physical resources are in harmony with the Christian world view.[113]

The hymn to Christ has a much broader application beyond the Colossian situation. Grand themes are addressed which provide a theological overview within which readers can find themselves. The contextual key that opened Paul

---

[112]This has a bearing on what the philosophers call the empirical or phenomenal and numinal or spiritual dimensions. No matter what identifying term is used, they are viewed here as a harmony and the work of Christ spans both realms.

[113]Other applications grow out of this world view as well. For example, this means that there is an integration of all of life so that a Christian should enjoy nature and use it as God intended. The theological principle has far-reaching ramifications.

to this lofty description of the person and work of Christ is vv. 12-14, the description of the kingdom of Jesus, the "Son he loves," and the believers' place in that kingdom. All Christians may legitimately see themselves exactly as the Colossians did: as sharers in the kingdom of God. By virtue of belonging to the King, the blessings of the kingdom are available. The specific application to the Colossian church will be made in the verses which follow.

Before departing this passage, an identification of the major theological themes will summarize the section well. First, God's will is known because of and through the work of Christ on the cross. Second, God has caused Christ to rule. He has enthroned him. He rules supreme over creation and redemption, over the world and the church. Third, all of existence is united in Christ. There is unity and order in creation and redemption. Paul laid the foundations of a Christian view of ecology. Fourth, Jesus is the central figure in creation and redemption. Fifth, ultimately, redemption means that Jesus will present a restored and ordered creation to God the Father. The function of the second person of the Godhead is to administrate the affairs of earth and to subdue those who resist. Finally, Jesus is the God-man and the mediator between man and God. There is no need for another (this argument is clear in 2:8ff.).

(4) The Salvation of the Colossians (1:21-23)

²¹Once you were alienated from God and were enemies in your minds because of your evil behavior. ²²But now he has reconciled you by Christ's physical body through death to present you holy in his sight, without blemish and free from accusation— ²³if you continue in your faith, established and firm, not moved from the hope held out in the gospel. This is the gospel that you heard and that has been proclaimed to every creature under heaven, and of which I, Paul, have become a servant.

Having spoken of the universal and cosmic nature of the work of Christ, Paul applied it specifically to the church at Colosse. The content resembles Eph 2:1-11, where many of the same terms, phrases, and ideas are employed.

In applying the work of Christ, Paul used a historical sequence of their lives before and after salvation. In the Greek text, these ideas are expressed in one long sentence, demonstrating the unity of thought found here. The NIV separates the sentence into three sentences which correspond to the basic flow of the Greek.

THE COLOSSIANS' FORMER CONDITION (1:21). Paul reminded the Colossians of the blessings of reconciliation by recalling their condition before salvation. Two descriptions provided insight and focused their thoughts.

1:21a This context deals with reconciliation. When Paul used the term "alienation," it obviously meant that at one time the Colossians had been outside the sphere of God's blessing. In Eph 2:12 Paul used the same term and form (perfect passive participle) to express the relationship to the "commonwealth of Israel" (NASB). No doubt the same meaning applies here. The

Colossian Christians were alienated from the hope of Israel. Israel looked for the hope of salvation through a Messiah. The Gentiles had no such expectation. Thus the wonder of God's working is expressed. Israel was the focus of God's redemptive plan as his covenant people. Now, through Christ, the Gentiles also became participants in these covenant blessings. The spiritual meaning is more significant than the political metaphor. The Colossians "were once continuously and persistently out of harmony with God."[114]

1:21b   The Colossians also had been "enemies in your minds because of your evil behavior" (1:21). Paul identified both the source and effect of their disposition toward God. Three key terms present a package revealing their former situation. "Enemies," while a strong term, occurs in Scripture to describe the contrast between God and those who do not do his will (Rom 5:10; Jas 4:4). The word has an active connotation. They made themselves enemies.[115] The second significant term is "mind."[116] In the LXX the term is usually translated "heart,"[117] and the terms in the New Testament speak of a person's disposition. Actions naturally arise from the disposition, which is a matter of the mind/heart. Paul explicitly stated as much in Rom 1:18-32, where he wrote that inaccurate thoughts about God produce ungodly conduct. The disposition may be good or bad, and the context in which it occurs determines the attitude the writer wishes to convey. Here in Colossians the disposition is negative, anti-God, and counter to the best interests of the individuals themselves. The third important idea is "evil behavior." Although the NIV translates the phrase "because of your evil behavior," the causal element requires explanation. Paul characterized the mind (disposition) as evil, and the evidence he used was their evil works. The cause of their sinfulness was not their evil deeds; their evil deeds came from their sinfulness. That seems clear enough here and in Eph 2. Evil works simply reveal the heart of the matter, which is the mind/disposition. Before becoming Christians, the Colossians were enemies of God because their mind/disposition was to do evil. An axiom of Scripture is that "by their fruit you will recognize them" (Matt 7:16); so here the mind produced the fruit of actions.

The former condition was desperate. These Gentiles were far removed from the promises of God's blessings. Further, their minds were opposed to God, their actions were evil rather than good, and they willingly assumed an anti-God posture. They were God's enemies. In such a condition, the possibility of

---

[114] O'Brien, *Colossians, Philemon*, 66. The perfect passive verb with the present of εἰμί, a periphrastic construction, provides this meaning.

[115] In contrast to R. Bultmann, *Theology of the New Testament* (New York: Scribners, 1952), 1:286. A good discussion of the term occurs in W. Foerster, *TDNT*, 2:814.

[116] The Greek is διάνοια. Here it is a dative of reference so that the text is "with reference to the mind, by their evil works."

[117] Cf. Gen 8:21; 17:17; 24:45; 27:41; and others which are documented by J. Behm, *TDNT*, 4:965.

reconciliation seemed remote. They would not naturally choose another course of action. That was their former condition. God took the initiative to change all of that. The simple reminder of who they used to be served to bring adoration and renewed commitment to the Lord who changed their lives.

THE COLOSSIANS' PRESENT CONDITION (1:22-23). The present condition is one of reconciliation: they were reconciled.[118] In 1:12 God the Father initiated their salvation; here God the Son does. The Colossians owed their salvation to the initiative of God in their lives. Paul stated that by virtue of their faith in Christ they had already experienced reconciliation. They had voluntarily responded to the lordship of Christ and experienced peace with God. In that sense, they participated in the new order of redemption, as firstfruits along with Jesus himself. They had new values, motivations, and outlooks.

Paul discussed in these verses two related matters which continued the thought of previous sections. These are the means of the reconciliation of the Colossians and the purpose of their reconciliation.

1:22a Paul naturally and easily moved from the discussion of salvation to the means of achieving it: "by Christ's physical body through death." This common expression reveals the importance of the death of Christ for Pauline theology. The terminology is similar to that of the hymn, but the language is more expressive. There can be no doubt that he was making direct application of the previous discussion of reconciliation in the second stanza of the hymn (1:20).

Paul used sacrificial terminology to describe the way reconciliation occurred. First, reconciliation involved a physical sacrifice: "by Christ's physical body." Resuming and applying the language of 1:20, Paul expressed the truth that moral and spiritual changes come because of the death of Christ. In 1:20 Paul spoke of the reconciliation of all things through Christ's death. Here, he spoke of the reconciliation of individuals through Christ's physical body. Perhaps arguing against those who claimed that Jesus had no physical body, Paul explicitly spoke of the physical nature of the sacrifice.[119] What was done redemptively was done in the body and through the body.[120]

---

[118]There is a textual variant here between the aorist active and passive verb "reconcile." The difference is whether or not "he" (Christ) or "you" (Colossians) is the subject and point of reference. The data is difficult to determine, although the active form seems to fit the context well. Ultimately the thought is unaffected, but the emphases are different. The NIV follows the active reading.

[119]Those who see an incipient Gnostic setting will note that the argument counters the Gnostic claim that Jesus only appeared to have a body. Regardless of whether there is a Gnostic orientation, this particular wording stresses the importance of the flesh in the sacrifice of Christ.

[120]The literal phrase "body of his flesh" is no doubt a Hebraism as was commonly used in Qumran, as Lohse, 64, n. 20, supported convincingly. As to the word "body" (sōma) in Paul's use, the work of R. Gundry, *SOMA in Biblical Theology with Emphasis on Pauline Anthropology* (SNTSMS 29; Cambridge: University Press, 1976) should be consulted. He makes a strong case for the term having a physical meaning in Paul's usage.

Reconciliation involved not only a physical sacrifice but also a total sacrifice. Paul's phrase "through death" emphasizes the reality and totality of the sacrifice. The death of Christ is as necessary to the gospel as the resurrection. Together, the "physical body" and "death" reveal the physical suffering of Christ in redemption. Flesh, blood, and death express the total nature of the sacrifice.

1:22b Paul always kept the purpose of reconciliation in mind: "to present you holy in his sight." Rather than focusing on the doxological purpose, that of bringing praise to God's glory, as in Eph 1:6,12,14, Paul envisioned the completeness of character appropriate to those who trust Christ. The two ideas, of course, are complementary. God is best glorified among those who have cooperated with his working and whose lives reveal true Christian character. The latter emphasis countered those who would lapse into careless Christian living. This was a real danger that threatened the Colossians.

Paul expressed the time for presenting these converts to Christ in eschatological terminology. The future time will be the time of the Parousia, when Christ returns to the earth. At that point in time, Paul hoped the Colossian believers would have true Christian character. The future aspect of this is confirmed by the conditional statement "if you continue" (v. 23). Paul saw a time lapse between the present and the future time of presenting his converts to Christ. The dual historical reference points in Paul's theology emerge again. The past, the cross, must be viewed in light of the future, the reconciliation of all things. Similarly, the past for Christians, their salvation, must be viewed against the backdrop of the future, their meeting God after the course of history has been run.

In addition to the future time element of this event, Paul's thoughts turned to the character expected of the believer. Three statements describe it: "holy in his sight," "without blemish," and "free from accusation." Scholars have taken Paul's language in three ways: sacrificially, judicially, or generally. The first two statements of the verse recall the language of animal sacrifice. Every animal offered to God had to be holy and without flaw. (This terminology led some scholars to think in terms of a sacrificial setting for the entire passage.[121]) Such terms as "present," "holy," and "blameless" support this conclusion. If that analogy is correct, Paul thought of Jesus as the great examiner who will inspect the Christian to determine his suitability for sacrifice. However, Paul's use of sacrificial language has present implications rather than future. This is clearly seen in Rom 12:1-2 where Paul commanded believers to present their bodies as living sacrifices. That is the natural response to the mercies of God. In this context, the language looks forward to the return of Christ.

---

[121] E.g., Lightfoot, 160-61. Other passages, such as Rom 12:2, support Paul's use of sacrificial terminology.

Other scholars have suggested a judicial setting for this idea. They point out that the phrase "free from accusation" overrides and interprets the others. "Free from accusation" is a judicial term. It pictures a judge declaring a person innocent. This is a better understanding because Paul clearly taught that each believer would stand before the judgment seat of Christ to give account. He lived with an expectation of that day. Nevertheless, there is little to commend the judicial idea in the language of this particular passage.

Rather than pressing the sacrificial or judicial ideas, it seems better to take the words in a general sense. Lohse interpreted the words in this way. He stated that Paul considered "the Christians' present lives are lived in God's presence. ... God's act of reconciliation has already accomplished everything; perfection is thus not to be gained by one's striving. Rather, perfection is there to be received as God's gift and to be verified in the life of the Christians."[122] He correctly noted the impact of the completed work of Christ. Two other factors must be considered.

1:23 First is the future aspect to the text.[123] Second, the conditional clause which follows in v. 23 suggests an interval between the time of their reconciliation and their presentation to God. In fact, Paul considered three time perspectives here. In the past, they were reconciled. In the future, Paul expected purity. In the present, they were to continue until the day of the Lord.

Paul addressed the responsibility of the Colossians in the interval between reconciliation and Christ's return. He stated, "If you continue in your faith, established and firm, not moved from the hope held out in the gospel" (v. 23). His words, "if you continue," are significant. They are part of a first-class conditional sentence in Greek.[124] Some have suggested that the construction implies an element of doubt.[125] However, there is no doubt about the outcome of the condition.[126] Paul fully expected them to continue in the faith.

Two factors support Paul's optimism in this context, one grammatical and the other theological. The grammatical element is the force of the first-class condition. The first-class condition presents a *logical* relationship which should best be translated "assuming that (the protasis) is true, then (the apodosis)."[127] This passage should be translated "assuming that you continue. . . ."

---

[122]Lohse, 65.

[123]This in spite of Lohse's contention that κατενώπιον does not refer to the future day of the Lord.

[124]The construction is εἴ γε in the protasis which includes both positive ("continue") and negative ("not moved") aspects.

[125]J. B. Lightfoot, *The Epistle of Paul to the Galatians* (Grand Rapids: Zondervan, 1957), 135.

[126]Three other cases of this construction contain the same force and cannot be understood as doubtful. These are Gal 3:4 (but see ibid.); 1 Cor 15:2; Eph 3:2.

[127]See the instructive study by J. L. Boyer, "First Class Conditions: What do they Mean?" *GTJ* 1 (Spring, 1981): 75-114. Sometimes elementary students of Greek grammar learn to translate the first-class condition as "since." That would make the passage read "since you continue in the faith." But only one third of the first-class conditions can fit into that pattern of assured reality (e.g.,

The theological matter concerns the doctrine of the perseverance of the saints. Paul taught that those who know the truth will continue in the truth. They will not fall away. Indeed, the personal commitments made at conversion naturally produce a positive, lifelong commitment to Jesus. P. O'Brien correctly states, "If it is true that the saints *will* persevere to the end, then it is equally true that the saints *must* persevere to the end."[128]

There are three possible interpretations about why Paul used the first-class condition. The options are: that Paul actually placed a condition on the believers so that they might lose their salvation if they did not continue in the faith; that the clause refers to the "blameless" presentation of the believers at the day of the Lord; or that Paul assumed all believers would continue in the faith and that was an evidence that they were, in fact, genuine in their commitment.

The first position suffers because Scripture does not teach that one can lose salvation, and the direct statements of the apostle contradict that.[129] The second position is a distinct possibility in light of the exhortations to purity of life and work. If some would not be blameless at the second coming (a logical conclusion from Paul's writings), perhaps the conditional clause here relates to the "blameless presentation" at that time. The problem is that Paul spoke of the departure from the faith in strong terms. He called it apostasy. The (hypothetical) problem addressed was not moral, in the arena of Christian living, but confessional. The Colossian Christians were addressed as moving away from the hope of the gospel itself! This second category, therefore, hardly pertains. The third position is the most likely. The exhortation was a true exhortation. They were encouraged to continue in the faith. There was no doubt that the genuine believers would continue. Even more, the fact that they did continue evidenced the reality of their commitments.

In concluding this section, Paul took the theme of the gospel and again brought it to its universal significance. The gospel was the same message they heard, which, in turn, was the same gospel preached to every creature and was the message which had captured the energy of Paul. The literary pattern moves from the cosmic nature of Christ's work to its application in the lives of the Colossians. It then moves from the message heard by the Colossians to that heard by all of creation. The movement, therefore, is from the general to the specific and from the specific back to the general.

Another exegetical problem in this verse is Paul's statement that the gospel "has been proclaimed to every creature under heaven." The Greek text differs from the NIV in the expression "to every creature." In Greek it literally is "in every creature." The point is that the place of the preaching is the creature

---

Matt 12:27, which cannot). Most sentences of this type are logical assumptions for the sake of argument.

[128] O'Brien, *Colossians, Philemon*, 69.

[129] Such passages as Rom 8:28ff. reveal that for Paul the believer could not lose salvation.

("in"), and "every creature" should be understood as "all humankind."[130] Paul hardly meant that every person had heard the gospel. That would defeat the point of his mission and his intense desire to preach where Christ had not been proclaimed. The point is that the gospel is the same gospel that was proclaimed from city to city. There is thus a universal aspect to the gospel which, as Bruce said, "is a token of its divine origin and power."[131] Wherever the gospel has been preached, it is *this gospel* which has been proclaimed; there is no other. This, no doubt, stands in contrast to the sectarian views being propagated among the Colossians, which were both of recent development and specific to the geographic territory around Colosse.

Finally, Paul stated that he was a servant of that same universal gospel. Perhaps it was of significance to those who were changing the gospel from what it was originally to what they wanted it to be. Paul had no proprietary interest in the gospel—it was not his.[132] Rather, he was privileged to be servant to it. Paul used the term "minister" (NASB; *diakonos*) rather than "bond-servant" (NASB; *doulos*), the common term for his relationship to Jesus Christ (see, e.g., Phil. 1:1, though the close relationship of these terms should be noted since the NIV translates both as "servant"). He was subject to the gospel and privileged to be a part of its propagation. This identification with the gospel served to remind the church that he, and it, had a stewardship responsibility with the things of God. Paul provided a twofold reminder and confirmation of the truth of the gospel: It was the same one preached throughout creation, and it was the one which Paul propagated.

The central element of the gospel is the person and work of Jesus. In applying the hymn to his readers, Paul stressed this centrality both cosmically and redemptively.

2. Paul's Place in Christ's Kingdom (1:24-2:7)

Paul's greeting and thanksgiving of Col 1 led to an extensive discussion of the kingdom of Christ and its application to the Colossian Christians. Paul's ministry involved the promotion of the kingdom. Since these believers had not seen Paul personally, he included an extended section on the nature of his ministry. Although passages such as this occur rather frequently in the Pauline corpus, they seem to be interjections. They clarify the ministry of Paul in order to

---

[130]Cf. the same statement in the commission recorded in Mark 16:15 and the discussion by Foerster, *TDNT*, 3:1029.

[131]Bruce, 213.

[132]There are, of course, passages where Paul identified with the message and claimed personal involvement with the gospel. His general attitude, however, is expressed here. See also the notes on Phil 1:12ff. and the text of Gal 1:6-17. Particular references which use the expressions "my gospel" are in connection with theological affirmations about Jesus (Rom 2:16; 16:25; 2 Tim 2:8).

address more significant theological points.[133] The inroads of heresy demanded a response, and the response included a defense of his ministry.

From a literary perspective, the passage unfolds in two major sections (beginning in 1:24; 2:1). The sections are introduced in the first person, effectively changing the point of reference from Christ to Paul and the churches. The end of the second section is more puzzling. Some end it after 2:5; others, after 2:7. Two factors influence this question. First, the application of 1:21-23 is somewhat parallel. Paul concluded his description of the work of redemption with an exhortation to remain firmly built on the foundation of the gospel. In 2:6-7 the same kind of exhortation occurs, indicating what may be a similar transition point.[134] Second, Paul employed the construction "as therefore" (2:6).[135] Although the construction may indicate a new section loosely related to the previous by drawing a logical inference, it may also be an effective application of what was just presented. In this epistle, Paul judiciously used the construction for an application of his subject matter. There are only five occasions of the term "therefore" (*oun*), and each functions in that manner.[136] With all of this in mind, it is best to end the section at 2:7 rather than 2:5.

In this section, one idea logically gives way to another, even though there are significant changes of thought between them. The first connecting link is the term "servant," which occurs in 1:23 and again in 1:25. Paul's servanthood to the gospel brought him into service to the church. The second connection is the term "struggling," which occurs in 1:29 and 2:1. Paul's general striving to bring people to perfection in Christ caused him to strive for those in Colosse and Laodicea. The third connecting link is the term "faith," which occurs in 2:5 and 2:7. Paul's desire to know the nature of their faith brought an exhortation to continue in the faith. Significantly, these word connections (or associations) end at 2:7 and do not begin again in the same way until 2:20ff.

The semantic associations reveal a pattern in the writing. A concept is presented followed by a specific application to the Colossians. That occurs in 1:15-20 (larger concept) and 1:21-23 (application). It occurs again when the

---

[133]This is the case most precisely when the nature of the gospel is at stake, as it is here. E.g., Paul's defenses of himself in Gal 1-2; Eph 3:2-13; Phil 3:1-16; 1 Thess 2:1-16.

[134]The words are not the same, even though the metaphors used in both places are. The five terms employed are certainly to be understood in the same semantic field and are, thus, synonymous. They are: 1:23, "founded" (θεμελιόω), "firm" (ἑδραῖος), "not removed" (μὴ μετακινούμενοι), and 2:7, "rooted" (ῥιζόω), and "build upon" (ἐποικοδομέω). The semantic field is close enough to reveal a legitimate parallel.

[135]Ὡς οὖν (2:6).

[136]These five are 2:6; 2:16; 3:1; 3:5; 3:12. Two of these clearly apply the theological principle at hand. Colossians 2:16 and 3:1 apply 2:8-15 and 2:20-23 respectively. Two others apply the heart of the ethical commands in the following fashion: 3:5-11 applies 2:20-23 and 3:12ff. applies 3:1-4. These last two are major division points so that they mark off an application section of the epistle. This pattern influences the understanding of 2:6, which should be seen as applying the previous teaching of 2:1-5.

concept presented in 1:24-29 is applied in 2:1-7 to the specific churches in Paul's mind. In a broad sense, the cosmic picture of Christ demands a faith response from people. The apostolic ministry of Paul brought about that response. His ministry included theological dialogue and debate with those who opposed his message and ministry. That scenario, so common in gospel proclamation, found expression here.

(1) Paul's Ministry to the Churches (1:24-29)

²⁴Now I rejoice in what was suffered for you, and I fill up in my flesh what is still lacking in regard to Christ's afflictions, for the sake of his body, which is the church. ²⁵I have become its servant by the commission God gave me to present to you the word of God in its fullness— ²⁶the mystery that has been kept hidden for ages and generations, but is now disclosed to the saints. ²⁷To them God has chosen to make known among the Gentiles the glorious riches of this mystery, which is Christ in you, the hope of glory.

²⁸We proclaim him, admonishing and teaching everyone with all wisdom, so that we may present everyone perfect in Christ. ²⁹To this end I labor, struggling with all his energy, which so powerfully works in me.

In this summary statement of Paul's ministry, two focal points emerge. The Greek text contains one long and cumbersome sentence which the NIV conveniently breaks into five sentences. These are subgrouped into three and two. The natural emphases occur at the repetition of the root word "fill" (*plēroō*) which occurs in 1:24-25. In v. 24 the developed form is translated, "I fill up [*antanaplērō*] in my flesh what is still lacking in regard to Christ's afflictions." In v. 25 it is, "to present to you the word of God in its *fullness* [*plērōsai*]."[137] This lexical pattern provides the insight to recognize that Paul here conceived of his mission in two dimensions: suffering and completion of the word of God.

TO COMPLETE THE AFFLICTIONS OF CHRIST (1:24). **1:24** The first aspect of Paul's ministry involved suffering. Perhaps Paul reflected here on the words of explanation at his conversion experience. God told Ananias that Paul would learn how many things he must suffer for Christ's sake (Acts 9:16). From the beginning of his ministry, Paul and others knew that unique suffering would be his lot. That knowledge came through direct revelation from God. Perhaps, further, Paul reflected on the fulfillment of that prediction in the various experiences of suffering in his ministry. Even at the time of writing, Paul was suffering in house arrest for the sake of Gentile churches. In a unique way, the apostle was granted the privilege of suffering for the Messiah.

Suffering for the Colossians. Paul suffered because of the specific ministry God called him to do. He planted churches in Gentile, pagan territory, and that

---

[137]This latter translation seems both awkward and incorrect. As will be seen, the basic idea is that of prediction/fulfillment rather than full presentation. It also softens the impact of the Greek construction.

brought reactions from Jews and Gentiles alike. Three terms explain Paul's suffering for them. In v. 24 he used the phrases "for you," "for the sake of his body," and "which is the church." In what sense was Paul's suffering for the church, particularly the Colossian church which Paul had never seen? Colossians 1:25ff. explains the unique theological insights God gave Paul. He preached a message of inclusion: Gentiles were included in the work of God. This meant that the Christ could be—indeed was—resident among the Gentiles. The message was broadly messianic and offended many Jews who did not want the blessings of the messianic kingdom to go to Gentiles. It also caused a reaction among Gentiles who saw a threat to their religious practices and economic livelihood.[138] Paul suffered in two ways. He suffered the attacks of those he sought to reach with the gospel, and he suffered at the hands of the Jews who sought to stop the advance of the gospel. His suffering related to the Colossians in that his personal difficulties came because of his attempts to convince the Jews to accept the Gentile believers. Details of that interpretation await the section on Paul fulfilling the word of God.

Suffering for the Christ. This passage contains a unique teaching about suffering. Paul stated that his call involved "filling up . . . Christ's afflictions" (NASB). The statement has produced thousands of pages of discussion and many theological interpretations. Only an overview can be provided at this point.

Paul used an unusual term for "fill up," occurring only here in all of Scripture. The basic root means "to fill," as to fill in substance or content. The preposition "again" (*ana*) is prefixed to the root, and another Greek preposition, "in place of" (*anti*), is added to it. Together, the word literally conveys the idea of "completing in place of" or "complete for someone else."[139] The word seems to demand the ideas of exchange or vicariousness and repetition.

Many suggestions have been made as to the meaning of Paul's expression.[140] They may be divided into three categories based on whether the interpreter understood the sufferings as atoning, mystical, or eschatological. First, some may read the passage and assume that Paul meant that Christians must suffer to accomplish their own atonement.[141] While not denying the atoning work of Christ, this view depreciates it by suggesting that the work of Christ was insufficient and that believers must contribute to their own salvation. Paul

---

[138] Frequently the temples were major sources of income for a community. E.g., in Acts 19:17-41 the gospel produced a riot for these reasons.

[139] *BAGD*, 72-73.

[140] The most helpful history of interpretation is by J. Kremer, *Was an den Leiden Christi noch mangelt, Eine interpretationsgeschichtliche und exegetische Untersuchung zu Kol, 1,24b*, BBB 12 (Bonn: Hanstein, 1956), 5-154. Interestingly, Hendriksen provided a good survey of several current possibilities but omitted some of the more recent and likely interpretations (*Colossians*, 91-98).

[141] This view was held by H. Windisch, *Paulus und Christus: Ein biblisch-religionsgeschichtlicher Vergleich*, UNT 24 (Leipzig: Heinrich, 1934), 236-50.

specifically countered both of these in Col 2. As Lohse states: "Paul and all other witnesses in the New Testament unanimously agree that the reconciliation was truly and validly accomplished in the death of Christ, and that no need exists for any supplementation."[142]

Two other commonly accepted interpretations are mystical, building on the "in Christ" theme so prominent in Paul. The first builds upon the identity between Paul and Christ. The church and Christ exist in a closely personal relationship so that what one endures the other endures. Advocates say that the apostle, reflecting on his identification with Christ, spoke of participation in Christ's sufferings.[143] Two major problems occur between this interpretation and the context of Colossians. First, Paul distinguished himself from Christ and Christ's work. He called himself a servant rather than an equal. Second, the question of the lack of Christ's sufferings remains. In what sense would there be any lack in what Christ did? This mystical interpretation fails to satisfy the details of the text.

A second mystical interpretation builds on the relationship between Christ and the Christian in the Christian's sufferings. Support for this interpretation occurs in the statement of the risen Lord in Acts 9:4, "Saul, Saul, why do you persecute me?" Obviously Saul thought he persecuted misguided people, particularly Jews, but the Lord took it personally. Paul actually persecuted Christ.[144] This interpretation comes nearer to the point of the passage, but it also seems inadequate. It does have the advantage of moving from the idea of redemptive suffering which the others contain incorrectly.

The most fruitful route of interpretation considers the Jewish apocalyptic setting of Paul's ministry and is eschatological. This section of the epistle particularly reflects a Jewish eschatological orientation by using such terms as "mystery" (1:26, 27; 2:2), "kingdom" (1:13), and "tribulation" or "affliction" (1:24, NIV). The Jews expected the Messiah's coming to be preceded by a time of tribulation, but the time of tribulation had fixed limits (Mark 13:19-20). The kingdom could be entered only through tribulations (Acts 14:22), which would give way to the glory that would follow. Since in this passage Paul used the term "tribulations" of the Christ rather than "sufferings" ("afflictions," NIV), he wrote in an eschatological framework. It is significant that the word "tribulations" is never used of Christ's redemptive work. Instead the word regularly used is "suffering."[145] Further, in this interpretation the phrase "the Christ" has its full messianic significance. It is not simply an alternate

---

[142]Lohse, 69.

[143]E.g., A. Deissmann, *Paul: A Study in Social and Religious History*, trans. W. E. Wilson (London: Hodder & Stoughton, Ltd., 1926), 162ff. in various places. Some support may come from Matt 20:23: "You will drink my cup."

[144]This must mean, of course, that Christ lives in Christian people.

[145]The Greek word "sufferings" (πάθημα) gave rise to the English word "passion."

designation for Jesus.[146] The eschatological context, the choice of the word "tribulations," and the article with Christ all point to a time of tribulations associated with the Messiah.

These Messianic Age sufferings are both personal, for Paul, and corporate, for the entire church. The word implies a vicarious element to these afflictions. Some become sidetracked in their thinking, focusing on the statement that these are "Christ's afflictions." They identify them with the cross. However, that interpretation finds no support in this passage or elsewhere. The substitutionary element is explained in the remainder of v. 24, where Paul stated that they are "for the sake of his body, which is the church." Thus the afflictions are neither for Jesus nor for Paul and his salvation. They are related to the church. Paul's afflictions were endured for the sake of the gospel to the Gentiles. They were a part of the reaction of unsympathetic hearers—Jews and Gentiles—to the message of the gospel.

The context contains two other ideas. First, the afflictions of Christ had a lack. The word "lack" suggests that Paul thought of a fixed number of tribulations, some of which remained unfulfilled.[147] Perhaps Paul meant that the inauguration of the age of salvation could not be completed until the universal implications of the gospel appeared. All those who contributed to that understanding suffered (e.g., Stephen), and Paul suffered uniquely because he was the apostle to the Gentiles. In a real sense, then, when his work was completed, the implications of the gospel as a message for all people would be clearly known.

Second, Jesus' afflictions became Paul's sufferings. Paul carefully distinguished between the two. He suffered in his body ("in my flesh"), and there was a real struggle. The text reveals some parallels between Jesus and Paul. Both suffered in the flesh; both suffered vicariously; both suffered for the gospel; and both suffered for the church. Many differences between them occur, however. Paul did not suffer redemptively. Jesus completed the work of redemption for all people. Paul's task was to open the door for a universal proclamation of the gospel. At the least, he hoped to convince all people of the validity of the gospel and its application to all persons, Jew or Gentile.

TO COMPLETE THE WORD OF GOD (1:25-27). **1:25** The second aspect of Paul's ministry involved the word of God. He stated that God called him to "present to you the word of God in its fullness" (1:25). Again, Paul's use of a word built on the Greek word "fill" reveals the importance of his argument. But in what sense could Paul claim to fill the word of God?

---

[146]The article with the word "Christ" is significant here in this regard, especially in an eschatological and messianic context. Paul emphasized it was tribulations of *the* Christ.

[147]G. B. Caird, *Paul's Letters from Prison: Ephesians, Philippians, Colossians, Philemon,* *NClarB* (London: Oxford University Press, 1976), says, "It is almost as if he is thinking of a fixed quota of suffering to be endured" (184).

The Role of Paul. Paul saw his role as a servant (*diakonos*) of the church. *Diakonos* speaks to the true servant role rather than some position of authority or leadership that might be inherent in another term. Even the term "slave" (*doulos*) sometimes carries the idea of authority, similar to the Old Testament "servant of the Lord." "Servant" (*diakonos*) does not. The service fulfilled a part of the divine plan which God foresaw long ago, but which he clarified through the course of events in Paul's life. In fact, not everyone understood the working of God as Paul did. In the administration of God (*oikonomia*; lit., "household management"), God selected Paul to complete what was lacking in understanding and fulfilling the Old Testament predictions of the future. Colossians 1:25-27, like v. 24, are filled with eschatological language. Terms like "administration" ("commission," NIV), "mystery," and "now revealed," look to the Messianic Age of the fulfillment of Old Testament prophecy. They call for a careful analysis. Paul, as the apostle to the Gentiles, served the church by alerting them to the meaning and significance of many obscure Old Testament passages. By his divinely appointed ministry, Paul encouraged a fulfillment of prophecy related to the Gentile mission. Until his day, these texts had been a mystery.

The Revelation to Paul. **1:26** Paul's role in the administration of God's plan related to the "mystery that has been kept hidden for ages and generations, but is now disclosed to the saints" (1:26). In Pauline terminology, a mystery was a truth which lay hidden in the pages of the Old Testament, and its explanation awaited another day.[148] The day of understanding came with the death and resurrection of Christ, and the mystery was revealed to the saints (believers). The language and themes call to mind Eph 3:1ff., where Paul explicitly detailed his calling in God's redemptive plan. There was no sense of pride. God selected Paul for this special service of theological disclosure.

1:27 The content of the mystery is "Christ in you, the hope of glory" (1:27). This particular statement does not occur in the parallel passage in Ephesians. Three interpretations have emerged. Some take the expression to mean "Christ within you." These interpreters equate this to a statement about the indwelling Christ who is resident in the hearts of believers.[149] While this truth is clearly taught in Scripture, the context does not develop the theology of the indwelling Christ. Others, therefore, have understood this text to mean "Christ

---

[148] His terminology parallels that of the Qumran community which developed a *raz-pesher* hermeneutic. The רז (mystery) was generally equivalent to the Pauline μυστήριον. It was a truth unexplained in the Old Testament which awaited another day for clear explication. The explanation was a *pesher*, a term common among the rabbis for the interpretations they derived from the biblical text. This hermeneutical motif found its most similar use to Paul's in the Qumran community as the Teacher of Righteousness interpreted Scripture. E. E. Ellis, *Paul's Use of the Old Testament* (Grand Rapids: Eerdmans, 1958), and F. F. Bruce, *Biblical Exegesis in the Qumran Texts* (London: Tyndale, 1960).

[149] Hendriksen, 89; C. Vaughan, "Colossians," *EBC*, said, "The context requires that one understand the phrase as referring to an inner, subjective experience" (11:192).

among you (Gentiles)."[150] Understood this way, the passage speaks to the blessings of Israel—specifically the Christ—promised to all the world through the work of Christ. These blessings are available to non-Jews because the Christ was actually among them.[151] Paul could have had both ideas in mind so that the Christ actually indwelt the Gentiles![152] In light of the context, one of the last two options must be correct.

Christ was also their "hope of glory" (1:27). The expression means that Christ was their hope of receiving and participating in glory. Because of what he did—his death and resurrection—the Gentiles could expect to share in glory. Here again Paul stated that the only hope of glory is Christ. Gentiles, like Jews, must rely on him for their salvation.

PAUL'S MESSAGE, METHOD, AND PURPOSE (1:28-29). **1:28** Paul's message was Christ. Clearly Paul conceived of the hope as Christians resting in a person. The gospel is not a system, hierarchy, or set of regulations. It is the person and work of Jesus, which is, indeed, the message. Paul's method is stated by two verbs in the sentence: admonishing and teaching. "Admonishing" in Scripture has the connotation of confronting with the intent of changing one's attitudes and actions.[153] Here the term speaks to the task of calling to mind a correct course of action. It encourages people to get on with what they know to do. "Teaching" complements "admonishing." "Teaching" is the orderly presentation of Christian truth for converts so that they may know how to grow.[154] Paul's methods called for both confronting and instructing. Paul's purpose was "to present everyone perfect in Christ." Three emphases emerge in this purpose. First, three times in the Greek text of this verse Paul referred to "everyone."[155] Clearly he could not rest until all Christians lived up to what God expected. Second, Paul had an eschatological perspective. When he stated "to present" every person, he thought in terms of the return of Jesus and the desire to see each Christian mature in the Lord.[156]

---

[150]So Lightfoot, *Colossians*, 168; Martin, *Church's Lord*, 66; Lohse says, "Christ preached among the nations" (76).

[151]In the Old Testament, the Jews tended to think in terms of "Jews among Gentiles" as the hope of Gentile glory. The perception was that all the world had to worship as the Jews did to be right with God. Such worship would only come as the Jews spread the knowledge of the truth to the Gentiles. This statement, then, contrasts with that one. Now—in the Christian era—it is Christ among the Gentiles.

[152]Hendriksen, 89, seems to take this position.

[153]The term νουθετέω was used by Paul in the following representative contexts: 1 Cor 10:11 (to new Christians), Eph 6:4 (regarding training children), 1 Cor 4:4 (in ministry to the churches), Titus 3:10 (in relation to heresy).

[154]This term, διδάσκω, commonly expresses the task of the pastor to provide an orderly and organized presentation of Christian truth. See Eph 4:11.

[155]The NIV fails to pick up this emphasis by translating only one of these occurrences. The Greek reads, "admonishing every man and teaching every man . . . to present every man." Obviously that is somewhat awkward in English, but it makes the strong point Paul wished to make.

[156]This theme predominates in the Pauline Epistles. See 1 Thess 2:12, 19-20.

1:29   Third, Paul willingly exerted himself toward that end. The term "struggling," which occurs here and in the next verse (2:1), was used of athletes who painfully pursued athletic glory. Paul claimed, however, that his struggle was accompanied by God's energy which energized him. The repetition of the term "energy" stresses the inner strength supplied by the Lord.[157] Thus, utilizing athletic imagery, Paul looked forward to the day of the second coming, realizing his goal was to present mature Gentile Christians to the Lord at that time. If that were to be accomplished, it would be done through the power of Christ which effectively worked in him, in spite of the stresses of this life.

Paul's ministry fulfilled God's word in that way. The Old Testament predicted a Gentile response to the Lord. For generations few, if any, knew how this would be accomplished. God revealed it to Paul, however, who saw that the Gentiles could know Christ among them as their hope of participation in glory. Although there were struggles in the ministry, this revelation from Scripture motivated Paul to spread the message of salvation to the churches, a task which brought with it so many personal sufferings on their behalf.

(2) Paul's Ministry to the Colossians (2:1-7)

[1]I want you to know how much I am struggling for you and for those at Laodicea, and for all who have not met me personally. [2]My purpose is that they may be encouraged in heart and united in love, so that they may have the full riches of complete understanding, in order that they may know the mystery of God, namely, Christ, [3]in whom are hidden all the treasures of wisdom and knowledge. [4]I tell you this so that no one may deceive you by fine-sounding arguments. [5]For though I am absent from you in body, I am present with you in spirit and delight to see how orderly you are and how firm your faith in Christ is.

[6]So then, just as you received Christ Jesus as Lord, continue to live in him, [7]rooted and built up in him, strengthened in the faith as you were taught, and overflowing with thankfulness.

As Paul applied his ministry to the Colossians, he began with the struggle. In 2:1 he stated, "I want you to know how much I am struggling for you and for those at Laodicea, and for all who have not met me personally." This struggle was emotional rather than physical (as was the case in 1:24). The use of the same word to describe it, however, demonstrates Paul's total involvement with them.

The New Testament does not record the founding of every church. In addition to Colossians, Paul mentioned the sister church in the neighboring town of Laodicea (cf. 4:16). The Apocalypse reveals that several strong churches existed by the time of its writing (see the seven churches addressed in Rev 1-4

---

[157]The Greek text actually reads with a double emphasis: "struggling according to his energy which energizes me in power." Two different words for power are used, and the interpretation above attempts to capture the spirit of the Greek expression.

and note that Colosse is omitted), but that is the first mention of them. By the time of the writing of Colossians, the church apparently already had considerable maturity. It also had a close relationship to the apostle Paul. There was a mutual interest between them. The best suggestion regarding the church's founding is that it occurred while Paul was at Ephesus in the mid-50s and that his converts or disciples reached out to the neighboring towns with the gospel message.[158] Since none of them had seen Paul's face, these "Pauline" congregations had matured through another of Paul's team.

THE OBJECT OF PAUL'S CONCERN (2:1). **2:1** Paul struggled because he wanted to see the Colossian Christians.[159] While on the surface the statement may seem arrogant, in light of the context it makes good sense. Paul was realistic enough to recognize that people bring movements. He also remembered his commission from God (1:25) and knew it would be advantageous for them to meet him. Additionally, Paul was serious about accomplishing the task God gave him. He wanted opportunity to know and encourage all Gentile believers personally. His emotional struggle, therefore, had spiritual dimensions. He desired to be faithful to his calling, and that could best be accomplished by a face-to-face meeting.

THE PURPOSE OF PAUL'S CONCERNS (2:2-3). In these verses Paul presented his purpose with three statements introduced in the NIV by "My purpose is," "so that," and "in order that."[160] The three are progressive, but each expresses various aspects of the one hope. They may be understood as the purpose, the intermediate goal, and the ultimate goal.

2:2 The purpose was that the Colossians might be encouraged in heart. The term "encouraged" might be translated equally well "exhorted," and the flow of the sentence suggests at least an element of exhortation is present. Their encouragement grew out of a genuine love which formed a tie stronger than a merely physical one. The Greek text reads, "that you may be encouraged since you are knit together in love," or possibly, "by your having been knit together in love." The word for "united in love" (*symbibasthentos*) occurs often in the Septuagint, always with the sense of "instructed."[161] The connotation is logical

---

[158] Paul taught in a school of Tyrannus for two years, which would have given ample time for his students to reach out to these cities. The cities were all in the same general area of Asia and on the same main road.

[159] The Greek term for "struggle" is ἀγωνία, which emphasizes the emotional difficulty of some hardship.

[160] The Greek text makes clear that the first statement introduces the other two and that they are to be considered as aspects of the first. The first is introduced by a conjunction, ἵνα, showing purpose, and the other two are introduced by the preposition εἰς. The three are, nevertheless, progressive so that while the three are part of the one statement, there is a logical movement toward the last εἰς statement of knowing the mystery of God who is Christ.

[161] C. Vaughn, *Colossians*, BSG (Grand Rapids: Zondervan, 1973), 65, but he did not take this position in his later commentary in *EBC*.

as well since the process of uniting in love is a process of being instructed by love as to how to live properly. Teaching, however, does not occur in this context, and the connection between instruction and love is awkward. If Eph 3 is a proper parallel to this passage, the love identified here is the love Christ had for them all. Surely that undergirded Paul's thoughts here as it did so often in other contexts. Christ's love for them provided a basis for unity and formed a common bond between them. Christian growth is a group task! The individuals of the church needed each other. The parallels in Eph 3:17 make this clear by employing another metaphor, "being rooted and established in love."

The intermediate goal develops the idea further. Paul's encouragement envisioned a full understanding. He called it the "riches of complete understanding." Here Paul spoke of the benefits of a full understanding. There were spiritual riches reserved for those who encourage each other and have a strong commitment to the body of Christ.

The ultimate goal, for Paul, was to "know the mystery of God, namely Christ" in the fellowship of the church.[162] The statement is comprehensive, involving a complete knowledge of Christ.

In 1 Tim 3:16 Paul used a similar expression, the "mystery of godliness." In both texts there appears to be something hidden—the mystery. In 1 Timothy, it is the mystery of being godly; in Col 2:3, it is the mystery of God himself.[163] The hidden God appeared in Christ—he reveals him; he explains the mystery. Therefore, if the question is, What is God like? The answer is, Christ.

2:3 Paul naturally moved to an expression of the resources of God in Christ. Since Christ is God manifest, all real wisdom originates in him. The false teachers focused on wisdom; Paul focused on Christ. God in Christ is the perfect storehouse of real knowledge, and that knowledge supremely appears in Christ. The precise meaning of this statement is difficult to determine. It could mean that Christ *is* the wisdom, therefore they needed no other, as taken in the interpretation above. Conceivably, Paul could have meant that Christ discloses God's wisdom. In this case, Christ is the key to the storehouse of all God's resources. The former view fits this immediate context better, although clearly Paul asserted that faith in Christ brought the resources of God.

Paul knew that the Colossians had begun the pilgrimage which would lead to maturity. In light of Eph 3:14-19, this goal was a full understanding of the treasures of knowledge found in Christ. Thus, as the group interacted with each

---

[162] Many variant readings occur here (the UBS text has eleven). The question seems to be whether God is included equally with Christ (several variations), or whether Christ is the location of all the treasures of God. The last is most preferred, as the NIV and many newer translations make clear, based on the principle that the shorter reading is preferred. The context also explains that Christ reveals God, and therefore the shorter is most likely.

[163] In 1 Tim 3:16 Paul stated that godliness is Christ. The mystery is explained in terms of a hymn extolling the proclamation of Jesus. That is where "godliness" centers.

other in love, each and the whole would experience a deeper understanding of
Christ. No doubt this understanding was a knowledge of how God works
uniquely in the lives of each one so that they saw the application of Christ's
love in their lives. Sharing in the experiences of others enriches personal experience and deepens the corporate understanding. The people of Colosse were
seeking knowledge. However, the heresy threatened to substitute a pseudo-
knowledge for the riches of the treasures of wisdom found in Christ. If they
were to find real knowledge and, as some taught, salvation through it, they had
to find it in a commitment to Christ. Their common commitment to Christ and
to each other would lead them in love to a more mature understanding of God
and his ways in Christ.

THE REASON FOR PAUL'S CONCERN (2:4-5). Paul expressed his reasons for
concern in a twofold way.[164] There are theological and personal perspectives.

2:4   Theologically, he was concerned that the Colossians not be deceived
by "fine-sounding arguments." The real threat was that they might be deceived
by a fast line or by smooth talk. The church had to learn to see beyond the fine-
sounding language of the heretics to the empty and damning arguments they
were presenting. Thus, it was to grow in the knowledge of Christ to avoid the
deceitful traps of heretical arguments. These heretical arguments came in the
appearance of deeper theology. In reality, they were subtle inroads of heresy.

2:5   Paul also had a personal reason for his concern. He could not be with
the Colossians in person, but he felt a strong spiritual tie to them. They were
his spiritual children, though they were not directly his converts. Paul delighted
in the nature of their Christian commitment. It was orderly and firm. Some
point out that these are military terms. If so, they suggest the camp was in order,
the defenses in place. They had begun well. The combination of terms reveals
that the false teaching had not had good success to this point. Now Paul wanted
to see their faith develop equally.

THE APPLICATION TO THE COLOSSIANS (2:6-7). In making specific application of these things to the Colossians, Paul's primary concern was that they
continue to grow in Christ. Three statements provide understanding of the
nature of the Christian experience of the Colossians.

2:6   First, they had already received Christ Jesus. Paul reminded them of
this basic truth but called them to consider more, "as you received . . . continue." They were to reflect on *how* they had received him, and that was to be
a model for their present lives.[165] "As" (*kathōs*) draws attention to the relation-

---

[164] The "this" (τοῦτο) refers back to 2:1-3, which it can do in Paul's writing when no explana-
tory content is provided after it. The ἵνα is purpose.

[165] Some interpreters may see this clause in a slightly weaker sense than a comparison clause
of explanation, as is understood here. If the clause is explanation, it provided a model for the continued growth. If the clause is simply emphatic, it called them to remember *that* they were Christians and that they were to live consistently with that prior commitment.

ship between receiving and continuing. Although Paul did not state precisely the point of comparison, the context surely called them to a focused faith in the all-sufficiency of Jesus in salvation. They were to remember the nature and content of their faith at the time of their salvation, and that was to guide them throughout their Christian lives as well.

These believers had received "Christ Jesus as Lord" (NIV) or more literally "Christ Jesus the Lord." Here the construction and the meaning need comment. The construction, with "Lord" at the end introduced by an article, does not occur elsewhere in the Pauline Epistles.[166] If Paul had written "Lord Jesus Christ," attention would focus on the office of Jesus—his lordship. This calls for a different analysis. The word "Lord" is in apposition to "Jesus Christ," and the article in the Greek accentuates his point (the Greek reads "Christ Jesus the Lord"). The statement means *you received Christ Jesus, the one who is the Lord*. This construction recalls the longer discussion of the hymn, for example, and graphically relates it to Christ. Jesus is that Lord.

The meaning goes beyond other similar passages. This is the only place in the Pauline Epistles where the verb "received" has a personal object. Elsewhere it occurs with "teaching" (1 Cor 15:3; Phil 4:9), with the "gospel" (1 Cor 15:1), and with the "word" or the "teaching" (1 Thess 2:13; 2 Thess 3:6).[167] The distinctive use has led some to conclude that Paul referred to accepting a message about Christ.[168] That would fit the context. On the other hand, the strong impression from the text is that they actually embraced *him*, not simply the message. This accords with the complaint about the heretical teaching that it was not "holding fast to the head" (2:19, NASB). The statement means, therefore, that they received Christ *as Lord*, the Lord discussed in the hymn of 1:15-20. The threat of the false teachers was that they would undermine that understanding of Jesus as the Lord of all.

2:7 The second statement describes the nature of their experience: "rooted and built up in him . . . strengthened in the faith." Two metaphors combine to express their initial growth in Christ: "rooted" and "built up" in the faith. The one metaphor pictures sinking the roots of faith into the soil of Christian truth. The other calls to mind building on the foundation of faith. Although one metaphor comes from agriculture and the other from construction, together they make a strong point. This church had a firm basis for its faith and had built well upon it. The words recall 1:23 even though synonyms occur there, not the exact terms. Paul continued the description with another participle in Greek,

---

[166] This construction, using two articles in this way, does not occur elsewhere in the New Testament.

[167] The only two exceptions to this pattern are Col 2:6; 4:17. Outside the Pauline Epistles the combinations are broader.

[168] *BAGD*, 619. It states "accept *Christ Jesus*, i.e., the proclamation of him as Lord."

"strengthened." This points to the continued growth of the church, similar to "built up in him," but with a distinct emphasis.[169] The strength is related to its faith. Probably, as throughout this section, Paul did not mean the experience of faith, or "personal faith," even though the Colossians' personal faith was strong. The attack was against "the faith," the system of Christian truth and its ramifications in life. The church was commended for its growing strength in Christian truth.

The third statement describing Colossian Christians is that they were "overflowing with thankfulness." Paul frequently employed thankfulness as one of the litmus tests of Christian health. He assumed that Christians would live in an attitude of thankfulness for the many blessings bestowed upon them. By contrast, one of the first indicators of departure from God is a lack of thanksgiving (e.g., Rom 1:21ff.). The deep roots of the faith evidence themselves in an attitude of gratitude for both the initial experience of salvation and the continued sustaining of life. Faith and the nature of a Christian foundation are often invisible, but thanksgiving is a visible response to the grace of God in their lives. It was an important quality for Paul to identify. A significant variant in the Greek text affects the interpretation of this section. Some manuscripts read, "abounding in faith in thanksgiving."[170] More likely, however, Paul commended them for their thankfulness during the growth process. In terms similar to 1:9-11, Paul praised them for the evidences of knowing the will of God in their lives. Thus, throughout their Christian experience, they had been thankful.

This section functions in two vital ways in the progress of the epistle. First, it ties Paul to the Colossians, identifies his tribulations with their faith, and brings them more closely into the Pauline fold. Second, this autobiographical section serves to introduce the real problem at Colosse, the heresy that tended to undermine the faith. Significantly, Paul first addressed the heresy from personal and ministerial perspectives. He shared his heart with them before moving to theological persuasion to equip them to evaluate the devastating effects of the new heresy.

---

[169] Actually four participles modify the verb "as you received." They are: "rooted" (ἐρριζωμένοι), "built up" (ἐποικοδομούμενοι), "strengthened" (βεβαιούμενοι), and "abounding" (περισσεύοντες). The first two are joined by "and" with the preposition "in him" going with both. The third is a present participle joined to the other two by "and," but clearly recalling the same idea since the word definition forms a semantic field with the other two. The last has no "and" and appears to be by itself, modifying all of them in a complementary way. Thus there are three groups: 1 and 2, 3, and 4, which actually break down to two ideas, 1-2 and 3, and 4. The last becomes the basis of the next section, Paul's third statement to them.

[170] The variant reading has "in it (αὐτῇ)" which must have the feminine "faith" as antecedent. While manuscripts are equally divided, the shorter reading appears best here in light of the parallel of 1:12.

3. Paul's Defense of the Faith (2:8-3:4)

Colossians 2:8-3:4 presents the theological heart of the epistle. The heresy is exposed and discussed. Paul provided theological answers which formed a basis for Christian living (2:8-19). He also laid a foundation (2:20-3:4) for the ethical commands which follow in 3:5ff.

Before discussing the contents, an overview of the section is in order. Colossians 2:8-3:4 divides naturally into two sections: 2:8-19 and 2:20-3:4. The transition is marked by both literary and ideological features. First, the literary features of the section point to these divisions. In 2:8-19, three matters demonstrate the relationship. Paul employed his characteristic "therefore" to tie the two paragraphs together into one (2:16). Further, he addressed in order the two concerns identified in 2:8-15, the dominance of supernatural powers and enslavement to the law. Both of these subjects continue in 2:16-19. Finally, the commands which form the second paragraph (2:16-19) complete the theological section (2:8-15) by identifying proper action on the basis of the teaching of the section. Throughout, the specific teaching of the heretics occupied Paul's thought.

At 2:20 a change of patterns occurs. There is a symmetry of organization so that two subjects are introduced by parallel clauses (first class clauses in Greek; "since," 2:20, NIV; cf. 3:1) and completed by commands (2:20a-23; 3:1a-4). The change of pattern from what preceded indicates a new segment in the argument.

Second, the content of the sections indicates a natural division. In 2:8-19, Paul addressed the heresies' twofold concerns of the spiritual powers and the law. These points are considered throughout the section. In 3:5, however, the content moves from the specifics of the heresy to instructions on how to implement more positive aspects of sanctification. Sandwiched in between these two, Paul spoke to the theology of Christian practice. The two sections of this second argument (2:20-23; 3:1-4) develop the theology of the death (2:20) and resurrection (3:1) of Christ. Theological patterns, therefore, reveal the structure. Considering these matters as well as those suggested below, it seems best to divide the passage into theological concerns (2:8-19) followed by practical concerns (2:20-3:4).

In this portion of the epistle, Paul was preoccupied with the arguments of his opponents. Both the theological content of the passage and the vocabulary suggest that. A number of words occur either one time or less than five times in the New Testament. In the epistle, Paul used 33 words which are used only one time in his writings. In these verses (2:8-3:4) 15 occur, which represents 45 percent of these words. The next highest single section of the book contains 5 words, representing 15 percent of the *hapax legomena*. Similarly, a higher number of rare words occurs here than elsewhere in the epistle. Paul used 64 words in Colossians which are found less than 5 times in the New Testament.

Of these, 21 occur in 2:8-3:4, representing 33 percent. The next highest single section of the book contains 14 words, representing 22 percent.[171] These statistics suggest an unusual Pauline vocabulary. Although the subject matter influences the use of specific words, it is also possible that Paul employed some of the terms the heretics used.

(1) Against the Theological Threat (2:8-19)

[8]**See to it that no one takes you captive through hollow and deceptive philosophy, which depends on human tradition and the basic principles of this world rather than on Christ.**

[9]**For in Christ all the fullness of the Deity lives in bodily form,** [10]**and you have been given fullness in Christ, who is the head over every power and authority.** [11]**In him you were also circumcised, in the putting off of the sinful nature, not with a circumcision done by the hands of men but with the circumcision done by Christ,** [12]**having been buried with him in baptism and raised with him through your faith in the power of God, who raised him from the dead.**

[13]**When you were dead in your sins and in the uncircumcision of your sinful nature, God made you alive with Christ. He forgave us all our sins,** [14]**having canceled the written code, with its regulations, that was against us and that stood opposed to us; he took it away, nailing it to the cross.** [15]**And having disarmed the powers and authorities, he made a public spectacle of them, triumphing over them by the cross.**

[16]**Therefore do not let anyone judge you by what you eat or drink, or with regard to a religious festival, a New Moon celebration or a Sabbath day.** [17]**These are a shadow of the things that were to come; the reality, however, is found in Christ.** [18]**Do not let anyone who delights in false humility and the worship of angels disqualify you for the prize. Such a person goes into great detail about what he has seen, and his unspiritual mind puffs him up with idle notions.** [19]**He has lost connection with the Head, from whom the whole body, supported and held together by its ligaments and sinews, grows as God causes it to grow.**

The theological threat concerned two major tenets of the Christian faith. These were soteriology, the person and work of Christ specifically related to the cross, and sanctification, the application of the cross to the development of personal purity. In this portion of the epistle, Paul addressed the theological

---

[171]This chart presents the actual numbers (approximate percentage):

	used one time		used less than five times	
passage	number	percent	number	percent
1:1-8	1	3%	1	1%
1:9-23	5	15%	14	20%
1:24-2:7	3	9%	6	9%
2:8-3:4	15	45%	21	33%
3:5-17	5	15%	11	17%
3:18-4:6	2	6%	9	14%
4:7-18	2	6%	2	3%

foundations of both of these subjects. Thus the text presents the *theology* of salvation (2:8-15) and the *theology* of sanctification (2:16-19). In the next section, Paul addressed the same subjects from a more pastoral perspective. Paul responded to the particular points of attack brought by the opponents. Since he responded to the specific problems at Colosse, some matters of interest to later Christians were not addressed. Paul's discussion was one-sided and confined to the main points of his opponents. Nevertheless, the theology is some of the richest and deepest in the New Testament.

There is a theological unity in these verses. Although Paul spoke of sanctification in these verses, he rooted his discussion in the conversion experience. Typically Paul did not separate the death and resurrection of Jesus. At 2:20-3:4, however, he dissected a unified, historical, and theological truth for the purpose of precise analysis. From a comprehensive perspective, salvation includes conversion, sanctification, and glorification. Further, sanctification and glorification grow out of justification. From another perspective, these may be separated for purposes of discussion and analysis. Since the false teachers attacked Paul's teaching regarding both conversion and Christian growth, Paul discussed each doctrine; this outline reflects that approach. It would be incorrect to assume that sanctification is a second and separate transaction. Even in this discussion, Paul related it to the death and resurrection with Christ. The text makes that point by beginning with an assumption that they died with Christ (2:20), by continuing with implications of their resurrection with Christ to a new life (3:1), and concluding with a reminder that all of it is because of their death with Christ (3:3). Thus, though the commentary seems to separate salvation (conversion) and sanctification (Christian growth), it does so for practical purposes. Christian living is possible because of both the death and resurrection of Christ and their implication together and separately in a believer's life.

To the Doctrine of Salvation (2:8-15). The attack of the heretics struck at the heart of the Christian faith. If they were correct, Paul was wrong and his work pointless. Their position was no flawed theory of how to work out salvation; this was a direct attack on the doctrine itself. Paul addressed it with directness and forthrightness.

Two concerns are addressed in this passage: the worship of angels and the practice of the law. The two themes occur in a chiastic pattern. In vv. 9-10,15 Paul referred to the supernatural powers which concerned the false teachers. In vv. 11-12,13-14 he addressed the concerns of the Jewish law. In this organization, two points may be seen. First, since chiasms emphasize the "outside" members, Paul primarily focused on the supernatural powers and their relationship to Christians, even though the discussion of the law occupies more space. Second, the supernatural powers relate to the law. Paul moved easily and freely from one to the other, so his readers would see his connection without difficulty or question. It is correct to assume, therefore, that the law and supernatural powers went together in the minds of the opponents at Colosse. They sought to get the church to submit both to the authority of supernatural powers and to the requirements of the law. Perhaps the connection between the two is the statement Paul made that these are "elementary" (2:8). Paul evaluated both the approach to the law (cf. Gal 4:3 and context) and the worship of angels as elementary. Therefore the "philosophy" had two seemingly diverse teachings which came to the church the same way.

The Nature of the Threat (2:8). **2:8** Paul saw this influx of heresy as a planned, organized attack against Christian theology. He warned against anyone taking the church captive.[172] The situation was real. The approach was both deceitful and ensnaring. It was not an attack from a misguided Christian. This was a purposeful attempt to draw Christians away from their moorings. Paul's metaphor implies that the church was unwillingly being taken ("captured") by these intruders. This does not suggest that they did not choose to follow the false teachers. The term accentuates the spiritual warfare involved. Perhaps it also stresses the deceitful methods used. In discussing the system, Paul spoke of the medium of the teaching and its measurement.

The false teaching made inroads through a medium that Paul called "hollow and deceptive philosophy." This is the only time Paul employed the term "philosophy," although it was a common enough term in the Greek world. Perhaps Paul chose the term because the heresy actually had philosophical roots rather than theological; that is, it may well have come from secular sources rather than religious.

The terms used to define this movement are all closely connected. In Greek, one article connects the terms "hollow and deceptive philosophy" or more literally "the philosophy and empty deceit." Both the article and the connection between the terms are important. The article points to a specific philosophy, rather than philosophy in general. Although Paul probably had little to say about the positive aspects of philosophy, no evidence in this verse indicates that he opposed the discipline. However, he certainly opposed this particular philosophy. The connection of the two terms also reveals that Paul saw it as an empty and deceitful philosophy. It had no substance. Following it led to nothingness. It was devoid of truth and, therefore, impotent. Strangely, there is little apart from this passage to define the teaching, and it has remained a puzzle for centuries.[173] Whatever it was, it was the medium for destructive heresy which threatened the very life of the church.

---

[172] The use of a singular participle to identify these persons reveals that Paul saw this as a series of attempts, a characteristic way of acting. The entire verse is active and dynamic in its force in Greek.

[173] The introduction to this commentary provides a survey of interpretation and issues involved.

Paul described the philosophy in terms of three characteristics which provide a standard of measurement. The parallel statements[174] indicate that the philosophy was human, elementary, and non-Christian.

First, the philosophy was human. The actual wording is that it "depends on human tradition." Basically, this teaching represented man's attempts to arrive at the truth. It was, therefore, a nonrevelational attempt to solve ultimate questions of life. Of course, there is nothing wrong with tradition. Paul used this same term in positive ways elsewhere.[175] History has shown many values of tradition. This particular tradition, however, was human in origin, lacking divine truth. That was the destructive element.

Second, it was elementary. Here Paul used the term "basic principles" (*stoicheia*), which has a long history of interpretation. Originally, the term referred to the four basic elements of the world: earth, fire, wind, and water. These were often seen in conflict with each other.[176] The term was later used of the basic elements of words, the alphabet. The construction of the alphabet allowed the formation of words and communication of ideas. The word later came to mean the "ABC's" of something, i.e., the basics. In some teachings, the "elements" were the signs of the zodiac and the powers that occupied the planets. These powers supposedly exerted their influence over the world and its activities. In Jewish circles, the term "elements" often applied to supernatural beings who ruled over people. Some considered them demons. Paul used the term in Gal 4:9, where he confronted false teachers who urged Christians to worship the elementary things. Paul opposed them as "no-gods," undeserving of worship. Even so, the Galatians were in danger of turning to them.

How did Paul use the term here? Most probably he employed a variation of Jewish terminology since most other elements of the heresy make sense when approached from that perspective (see the introduction to this commentary). He may have referred to angel powers, which were incorrectly perceived as being in authority over the world.[177] Whatever the specific interpretation, the elements were inferior. Christianity brought a higher and better system of worship to its believers.

Third, the philosophy was non-Christian. Perhaps more than the other evaluations, this one points to the heart of the danger. The philosophy was not "according to Christ." It was incompatible with Christ and contrary to the work he did on the cross. This reason alone would be enough to invalidate the teaching, but collectively the three descriptions decisively expose the nature of the philosophy.

---

[174] Each begins with the Greek preposition κατά, used to present a standard by which it may be measured.

[175] The term is παράδοσις which occurs, e.g., in 1 Cor. 15:1ff. in defining the gospel.

[176] See Delling, 8:666-87.

[177] There is no clear use of the term in this sense in the New Testament. It is used in the sense of "elementary" in Heb. 5:12 and 2 Pet. 3:10, and that makes good sense here.

The most serious error of the false teachers at Colosse was that they went about their spiritual lives with only natural insight. They did not go to God to learn of him, nor did they learn from the revelation of Christ that was available to them.

The Answer to the Threat (2:9-15). In answer to the teaching of the heretics, Paul focused on the person and work of Christ. Throughout the section, the two points of reference for the heretical teaching remain the supernatural powers and the law. The work of Christ relates to both of these.

Paul taught that there is a strong spiritual connection between Christ and believers. What Jesus did in providing redemption, believers did with him in God's mind. They are in Christ, and he is in them. This relationship brings many spiritual benefits. Paul emphasized the importance of this relationship by employing the "in him" phrase or a similar expression frequently in vv. 9-15.[178] Paul saw the false teachers as a threat to the work of Christ and the union of believers with Christ. To counter them, Paul described Christ as the sufficient Savior (2:9-14) and Christ as the sovereign Savior (2:15).

Beginning with Jesus, the sufficient Savior, Paul logically progressed from Jesus' work in relation to the law to his domination over other spiritual beings. Colossians 2:9 introduces all of these ideas. It relates to the law in that Jesus' work is useless without an understanding of his person. Primarily, however, it relates to his unique place in relation to created beings. This means that vv. 9,15 belong together logically and vv. 10-14 form a unit which presents two aspects of Jesus' work. Nevertheless, the order of the text will be followed in the exposition, even though the thematic arrangement follows the chiasm.

2:9 Jesus is completely God. The first concern of the section is the translation of v. 9, "In Christ the fullness of the Deity lives in bodily form." The NIV translation takes the most direct approach to the Greek text, which solves the most problems and creates the least. "The fullness" is the subject of the verb "lives." Some translators supply "God" as the subject and translate, "God has caused the fullness to live in him." There is no need to insert what is not in the text, however, when the text is clear enough.

The greater question here is whether "the fullness" is used in a technical sense, possibly expressing the ideas of the philosophy. If it is, the term "fullness" describes the totality of the emanations from deity which were a part of the Gnostic and possibly pre-Gnostic system of thought. The proponents argue that wherever the term occurs it has Gnostic associations. They contend that this context supports that conclusion. If this were the case, Paul's arguments would effectively diffuse the philosophy. The context, however, does not demand Gnostic definitions. It would be as difficult to conceive of all the emanations of deity residing in Jesus bodily as it would to consider him divine, as

---

[178]These may be the prepositional phrases "in him" and "with him" or the verb compounds with some preposition.

Paul did here. Further, for Gnostics, the emanations were progressively "less divine," until one emerged that was able to create the material world. The Gnostics would hardly consider that the higher and lower could coexist in one being. The basic difficulty is that Paul argued for the deity of Jesus, and to understand *plērōma* in a Gnostic way would mean that Jesus is separate from God. No matter how great the beings of the "aeons" were, they were less than and other than God himself. There are, therefore, significant problems in taking a technical, philosophical understanding of the term.

Paul meant that the fullness of deity dwells in Christ. The expression is unusual, but the God-man relationship cannot be expressed well in human language.[179] The fullness of deity was Paul's way of stating that Jesus is every bit God. On the other hand, Paul avoided modalistic language. The fullness refers to the completeness of the divine nature, but it does not mean that Christ is all there is of God. In fact, the word for God chosen by Paul expresses deity, not divine nature.[180] Jesus is every bit God but does not exhaust the dimensions of deity. Father and Spirit are equally divine.[181] Finally, Paul identified the location of this fullness. It is "in bodily form." This expression, like the others, has given rise to multiple translations and interpretations.[182] The point of tension is that the verb "lives" occurs in the present tense so that Paul stated that Jesus *now* has the fullness of deity in bodily form. Many, therefore, have taken the expression "bodily" in a spiritual or metaphorical sense. They say it means something like "totally."[183] The problem with that is that Paul generally used the word "body" (*sōma*) for the real body. Thus, with Lightfoot,[184] it seems best to understand that the fullness of God lives in Jesus in bodily form. In the "form" of Christ we have the reality of God. The tie between God the Father and Jesus Christ is that they share deity. This expresses some of Paul's high Christology.

---

[179]Thus the church councils of history had difficulty describing the hypostatic union (the two aspects of Jesus' person, God and man). Often they could state what it was not better than they could state what it was.

[180]Significantly, Paul used the term "deity" (θεότητος) rather than divine nature (θειότης).

[181]The term "the fullness of the deity" is chosen rather than a simpler statement, such as "he was totally God," which is open to more misunderstanding than the expression chosen. Jesus is, of course, completely God, but so are the Father and the Spirit. Therefore, there is more to God than Jesus is, in that God emerges in three modes at the same time. On the other hand, Jesus has the essence of deity and contains in himself everything that any of the other "persons" of the Godhead have.

[182]Some of these are: "completely" (Jerome), "really, not as a phantom" (Augustine), "essentially" (Hilary), "in essence" (most Greek Fathers), "the physical body" (Lightfoot). These are representative of the exegetical difficulties here.

[183]Hendriksen quotes Ridderbos approvingly and states "the indwelling essence of God is thus completely concentrated in Christ" (112).

[184]Lightfoot, " 'in bodily wise,' 'with a bodily manifestation' " (182).

2:10 Anticipating the thoughts that follow (vv. 13-15), Paul stated that "you have been given fullness in Christ" (2:10). The same root for the word "fullness" occurs here and in v. 9 (the "fullness" dwells in him). Although this is an obvious play on words, it is equally obvious that Paul did not mean the Colossian Christians were elevated to the same stature as Jesus. Nor did he mean that any one Christian became deity. He rather picked up the generic use of the term to state that, just as Jesus was fully God, believers are fully complete in him. Nothing lacks in salvation. The understanding of salvation may grow, and the appropriation of the blessings of salvation may increase; but in Christ, they had all there was, the "fullness" of salvation.[185]

The support for this statement follows in the second portion of the verse. The truth is rooted in Jesus' position as head over powers and authorities. Calling to mind 1:16 (see the notes there), Paul used the term "Head" to express Jesus' relationship to these powers. Scholars debate whether the term "Head" implies primarily the source of the powers' and authorities' existence or Christ's position of authority. Although the term may have application to either, there is normally a blending of the two so that the terms are not mutually exclusive. Thus, while it is true that principalities and powers owe their existence to Jesus, it is equally true that they are subject to him. Paul explicitly stated that in v. 15. There was no reason for any allegiance to other supernatural beings. Since the Colossian believers were complete in Jesus, and he is greater than these beings, the believers had no relationship to spirit powers. Paul returned to this discussion in 2:15. It was enough for him to anticipate that later discussion here by stating that since Jesus is God, he surpasses all created beings. Those related to him by faith share in his lofty position. They have a complete salvation.

They were completely saved (2:11-14). These four verses contain two subjects relevant to the Jewish audience Paul addressed: the covenant, which was symbolized by circumcision, and the law.[186] These two reference points stand for all the requirements of the law. There is a logical relationship between the two. One recalls the entrance to the legal system; the other recalls the continued life it expects. These aspects form the basis for Paul's discussion of the Christian life. There is an entrance (baptism into Christ) and a continuing (life by faith). Using Old Testament imagery, Paul explained that God took care of the old life at conversion (2:11-12) and that he provided for the new life at the same time (2:13-14). These two aspects of Christian living are compared

---

[185] Interestingly, Paul used a periphrastic verbal construction for this statement. The perfect participle with the present of the verb "to be" stresses the dynamic of the state of existence. Thus, this could be read, "We have reached and enjoy a state of fullness."

[186] Circumcision and law were Paul's main reference points in arguments against Jewish opponents. By arguing that in Christ the spiritual aspects of these were fulfilled, he effectively demonstrated that the requirements no longer apply. See the discussions in Rom 2:17ff.; Gal 3:15ff.; and such passages where the pattern is clear.

respectively to circumcision (2:11-12) and the law (2:13-14).

2:11 The first requirement of the law, circumcision, introduced a Jew to all of the law's obligations. Conversely, the Jews taught that no one could keep the requirements of the law without having been circumcised. Every Jewish boy was circumcised, and it was the first responsibility of a male proselyte. Paul defined circumcision in v. 11 and related it to baptism in v. 12. His discussion is Christological and spiritual, rather than physical and legal.

Paul's definition of circumcision included three elements: spiritual circumcision, putting off sinful nature, and the circumcision of Christ. First, he spoke of spiritual circumcision, defining the believer's circumcision as "unhandmade" ("not . . . done by the hands of men," NIV).[187] Three times the word "unhandmade" occurs in the New Testament; twice it was used by the apostle Paul. In Mark 14:58, it describes the temple Jesus would raise up after his death. He referred to a spiritual temple not built by men. In 2 Cor 5:1, Paul referred to the body ("building") of heaven as unhandmade. He contrasted the natural earthly body ("handmade") and the supernatural, heavenly body ("unhandmade"). In the reference from Jesus in Mark, the word described spiritual rather than physical temples. Further, "unhandmade" implies "of divine working" rather than human. Both of these references contain the same idea. The third use is in Col 2:11, where Paul contrasted the circumcision of the body ("handmade") and a circumcision which is not on the body ("unhandmade"). This, like the other two occurrences, points to a spiritual reality. It is a spiritual act done by God himself.

The concept of spiritual circumcision began in the Old Testament and continued in Paul's writings. The longest discussion occurs in Rom 2:17ff. (esp. 2:29) where Paul contended that God desires the circumcision of the heart, not the body.[188] The Old Testament had stated as much earlier (Deut 30:6). Physical circumcision had value only when the heart was also committed. The Old Testament spoke of this circumcision, a circumcision beyond the law, which the law's circumcision pictured. Two streams of thought developed. Some took it literally and became legalistic. Others, like Paul, understood the spiritual nature of the law.[189] They assumed the spiritual reality

---

[187]The suggestion that this was addressed to Gentile believers is interesting but not determinative. Surely the Jewish believers would have needed a proper spiritual circumcision as well. It runs counter to this passage to think that Paul wanted Gentiles to be free from physical circumcision and yet put spiritual value on Jewish circumcision. The most that may be said is that the message may have been promoted by Jews and that Gentiles might have been made to feel inferior. Paul's message applied to them all.

[188]There he further argued that surely God would grant circumcision to one who kept the entire law but was not circumcised; conversely, a circumcised person who did not keep the law could not expect any benefit from circumcision. He rather painstakingly pointed out that God is concerned with the heart more than with the body.

[189]See, e.g., Rom 7:14, where Paul argues for the spiritual quality of law contrasted with his own carnality.

which circumcision symbolized. Since it was a matter of the heart, not the body, it had to be spiritual.

The second element in the definition of circumcision is translated by the NIV as "in the putting off of the sinful nature" (2:11). Literally the phrase reads, "the putting off of the body of flesh." Typically for Paul, the term "body" referred to the physical body. He did not use the word metaphorically, meaning something like "the mass of flesh." In contrast, however, Paul did use the word "flesh" in a moral sense. The word usually identified the moral principle which characterizes humanity (flesh). Thus, the statement here refers to putting off the fallenness that guides people naturally, i.e., apart from the moral insight that comes from the Holy Spirit.

Some interpret this passage as continuing the strong Christological focus, rather than having a focus on the believer. They say that the "putting off" refers to Christ's death, at which time he put off his physical body. Further, the "circumcision of Christ" may refer to his death, when the spiritual circumcision was effected. Several arguments speak against that. First, the subject of the passage is the Colossian believers ("you"). The most natural reading is that they were the ones to whom this happened. Second, the parallels to Rom 6 suggest that Paul meant this to refer to the believer. Third, it would be an awkward way for Paul to refer to the death of Christ. If it did refer to Christ, the term "flesh" must be understood literally as "physical body" rather than the "sinful nature" of the NIV (which is a poor translation at any rate). Fourth, 2:15 states that Christ "disarmed the powers and authorities." This is hard to see as parallel to 2:11. Surely the parallel is in 3:9 in reference to the believers who had "taken off [their] old self." It is best to see Paul as speaking to the Colossians and their "circumcision."

Paul used similar terminology in Rom 6, where he stated that the "body of sin should be paralyzed" or "done away with" (6:6). Both passages are set in the context of the believer's baptism, both refer to the morality that characterizes non-Christians, and both speak to new possibilities for the Christian. The body is the instrument of sin and righteousness (Rom 6). Before conversion, sin dominates. After conversion, the body progressively adapts to new purposes and functions. The body is a primary focus of Christian commitment (Rom 12:1). Therefore, the phrase "body of flesh" refers to the fallenness that rules in and through the physical body. That principle has been put away at baptism.

The NIV translation may confuse the English reader by calling the state of pre-Christian existence a "nature." In fact, the term "nature" is an awkward one since it seldom communicates effectively. If the term "nature" means *a characteristic way of acting*, the translation "nature" is correct. At conversion, a believer begins to act a new way, giving evidence of a new nature. The term, however, is confusing because of the way it is often used by modern Christians. Many refer to an old nature and a new nature which are co-resident within the believer. Such an understanding confuses this passage. The old nature has been put off at the believer's circumcision, and it is no longer present. This subject becomes a primary concern in 3:5ff. The third element is the statement "with the circumcision done by Christ." The Greek text says simply the "circumcision of Christ." However, the use of the term "unhandmade" earlier calls for an understanding of someone who is able to construct without hands, (i.e., without human involvement). Sometimes that person is God himself; here it is Christ. Therefore, the circumcision is done by Christ as he operates on the hearts of believers to separate them from the world. This phrase can hardly be interpreted as the circumcision Christ endured, even though association with Christ permeates the passage. In summary, circumcision is defined as spiritual, affecting the moral principle of flesh, and performed by the Lord himself.

2:12 Paul related the concept of circumcision to baptism. The primary stress lies on the spiritual experience of believers in their union with Christ. The three points of identification with Christ are death, burial, and resurrection. The many references to "in him" and "with him" demonstrate that this is done vicariously, as believers accept the work of Christ on their behalf. Clearly, it is at the time of salvation that this spiritual circumcision was performed.

The believer's death with Christ is foundational to this context, as it is to Paul's thought in general. This "death by identification" satisfies both the demands of the law and the penalty brought by sin. Here, Paul omitted any discussion of death with Christ directly and spoke only of burial with him. Burial incorporates in it the idea of death because only the dead are buried. A parallel account, 1 Cor 15:3ff., defines the gospel in terms of the truths that Jesus died, was buried, rose again, and was seen by many. Paul identified the two focal points to the gospel: the death and resurrection of Jesus, each accompanied by its own kind of proof. Death was proved by burial; resurrection was proved by the witness of many who saw him alive. Thus when stating that they were buried with Christ, Paul stressed the reality of their death, evidenced by the burial.

The term "burial" is appropriate because of what it pictures. The Christian's baptism is a burial. It pictures placing the believer in an environment incapable of sustaining life. For Christ, that meant the grave. For the believer, water symbolizes the grave. It also pictures the resurrection to a new environment of life. The reference to baptism, therefore, calls to mind the practice of immersion because immersion best pictures these truths.

In the only other Pauline context that discusses baptism in this manner (Rom 6:1-4), Paul identified the baptism as "into Christ." The spiritual aspects, not the symbolic, were uppermost in his mind. It is the same here. It is a baptism with him into the grave ("burial"), representing a death to the old life. Paul was not, however, addressing the event of water baptism; he was addressing the spiritual meaning that undergirds it. No one is baptized into the grave with Christ. Rather, believers are incorporated into the work of Christ at salvation. When Paul used the term "baptism" in a soteriological context, it was spiritual rather than physical. These soteriological passages are Rom 6:3,4; 1 Cor 10:2 (of baptism into "Moses' system"); Gal 3:27; Eph 4:5; Col 2:12. In one context Paul spoke of physical baptism, claiming he did not baptize anyone (1 Cor 1:13-17). A pattern emerges. In soteriological texts, the spiritual reality predominates. In solving a problem at Corinth, he mentioned the ordinance. Although some see an overlapping of the two uses in Scripture (so that baptism into Christ actually occurs at water baptism), there is no evidence for such a conclusion. The distinction Paul made was between the theology of salvation, which is expressed by "baptism into Christ," and the picture of that experience, which is the act of baptism. This passage certainly speaks to the theology of salvation.

It is possible to explain the text as having two focal points: circumcision and resurrection. Those who do so note the parallelism between the "in whom also" or "in him also" of v. 11 and the "in whom also" or "and raised with him" of v. 12. Both refer to identification with Christ, and the primary statements are balanced. Each has an explanation. Circumcision is explained by burial in baptism; resurrection is explained by the working of God. The parallelism is attractive and corresponds to the major points of Jewish concern (circumcision and law). Against it, however, is the association of death and burial in the "baptismal" section. Most naturally, death and resurrection went together in Paul's thought.[190]

The question is, Whose circumcision was it? Did Paul mean to point his readers to the death of Christ primarily and to their participation in it? Both sides present good arguments secondarily. The NIV translation clearly interprets the text to refer to the believer's participation in Christ, rather than Christ's experience. The corollary is that "body of flesh" is translated as sinful human nature rather than Christ's body. Although parallels with Eph 1:19-23 (of Christ's experience) and 2:4-7 (of the believer's identification) and the grammatical structure of the passage commend an understanding that refers to Christ, it is probably better to emphasize participation with Christ. The believer's salvation is, thus, in view. This fits the natural flow of the text, the theological parallel of death and resurrection, and the parallel passage in Rom 6:1-11.[191]

The believer's burial with Christ is effected at his spiritual baptism, and his resurrection with Christ depends on God's power ("the working of God," NIV). Specifically, through faith in "the working of God" a spiritual resurrection occurs. God alone produces life after death. The resurrection of Jesus is both a

---

[190] See G. R. Beasley-Murray, *Baptism in the New Testament* (London: MacMillan, 1962), 153-54.

[191] This is a difficult decision. Either understanding is possible. Ultimately, the same theological truths surface. The difference is a matter of emphasis and detail in Jesus' or the believer's life. O'Brien, *Colossians, Philemon*, 101-20, has an excellent discussion of the issues and differs with the commentary interpretation.

model for our faith and the basis for it. Paul continued a parallel between the believer and Christ. Jesus committed himself to God, trusting he would raise him up. That faith was rewarded. Knowing that God raised Jesus, believers know that he will also raise others from the dead. The resurrection depends on the power of God to effect a new life, and at baptism the symbolism of trust is carried out. Paul specifically mentioned faith. The resurrection life of the believer is effected by faith in the power of God who alone can bring it about. In the text, this truth is reinforced by the use of passive verbs which, grammatically, call for the subject to be acted upon by another. God does the work. Believers simply trust God to act as he desires in accordance with his good and perfect will.

Christian faith has two dimensions. First, it is an identification with Christ, specifically with his death. This occurs at the time of conversion, of baptism into Christ. Second, it is an expectation of resurrection to new life because of the power of God based on the resurrection of Jesus. In this text Paul stressed two aspects of our spiritual experience which correspond to the two basic truths of the gospel (1 Cor. 15:1ff.). Believers participate in the death and burial of Christ in a personal spiritual way.

Three comments regarding the relationship of circumcision and baptism are in order. First, Paul connected circumcision and baptism.[192] Primarily, he paralleled circumcision and burial into Christ. Nevertheless, many see a direct relationship between the two here. Some use this passage to support baptism of infants which, they say, corresponds to circumcision.[193] Here, however, the salvation experience corresponds to circumcision. Circumcision and baptism are two illustrations of salvation. There is, of course, a mental picture conveyed by the two illustrations. In drawing parallels between the two, the logic of the passage demonstrates that Paul relates circumcision to baptism, rather than baptism to circumcision. That is, a circumcision takes place at a Christian's spiritual baptism. He developed the meaning of the Christian's circumcision by appealing to baptism, rather than defining baptism in terms of the Old Testament circumcision. In this comparison a New Testament truth is illustrated by the ritual of circumcision. There is no evidence that baptism fulfills a necessary correspondence to the Old Testament system.

The second concern here is the meaning of baptism. Although this certainly relates to the practice of baptism, the meaning of the term impacts interpretation. There can be no doubt about the fact that Paul's primary reference in the

---

[192]Care should be taken here. The context is spiritual rather than physical. O'Brien warned, "Baptismal statements are not developed in the passage" (*Colossians, Philemon*, 119). Nevertheless, the following comments are legitimate.

[193]This may be found, e.g., in the theology of J. O. Buswell, Jr., *A Systematic Theology of the Christian Religion* (Grand Rapids: Zondervan, 1973), 2:259-65, who attempted to show grammatically and syntactically how this relationship is formed. His presentation fails to take account of the flow of the passage and tends to read into it.

employment of the term "baptism" was to spiritual baptism, what he called "baptism into Christ" in Rom 6:1-3. The water ritual may lie in the background of thought, but the spiritual meaning is primary. It is nevertheless important to remember that spiritual baptism brings to mind the picture of physical baptism. Spiritually, it is the point of time when a person identifies with the death of Christ and, through faith, anticipates the new life which God will bring to him. This passage calls for an intelligent, active response on the part of the believer. That can hardly be equated to the entrance into a covenant community (as was true of circumcision) and related to the parents' faith (as is true of infant baptism). The entire context points to the time of conversion.

The third element has a bearing on the mode of baptism. Although physical baptism is somewhat removed from the statements of Paul here or in Romans, theologians have always taught that the mode of baptism should picture the meaning. The meaning of baptism is related to a believer's personal faith, to death and burial with Christ, and to the resurrection to new life. The Christian mode of baptism, therefore, will be the one that best pictures a situation of burial and resurrection. The meaning calls for a picture based on a personal and active faith, which represents the theological truths of the salvation experience (death and resurrection). Immersion best pictures that event.

In this passage, Paul described Christian experience in the terms of the Old Testament legal system. Circumcision is no longer required or desired. In the Old Testament, physical circumcision represented the first requirement of the law, but God always desired spiritual circumcision. Christians are spiritually circumcised when they are united with Christ by faith at the time of salvation. God took care of the first of the Jewish requirements, therefore, in salvation. By this picture, Paul compared the initial entrance to two contrasting systems. Circumcision brought the legal system. Salvation brought a relationship of freedom by faith.

Paul turned to the second aspect of the legal system, the law, in vv. 13-14. There he spoke of the law and its obligations.

2:13 The starting point for discussion is salvation. Paul stated that God made the Colossians alive *while* they were unbelievers. He did this in Christ. Clearly, salvation is God's action on behalf of sinners while they are still sinners. God saved them while they were spiritually uncircumcised. Paul used the terms "dead" and "uncircumcised" to describe their former condition. Like Eph 2:1-10, the terms appropriately relate to the discussion at hand. Death calls for a resurrection, which believers have in Christ. Uncircumcision calls for circumcision, which believers also have in Christ. In these equations, "dead" and "uncircumcision" form a semantic field so that they refer to the same condition. They both confirm the fact that believers' circumcision occurs at salvation and reaffirm that the "unhandmade circumcision" corresponds to being made alive.

2:14 Paul discussed the Christian's relationship to the law because the teachers at Colosse attempted to bring Christians under obligation to the Commandments. Paul knew such obligation was enslaving and legalistic. Legalism is any philosophy or movement that assumes God's blessing comes from keeping the law, whether Jewish Law or human law. It assumes a contractual relationship whereby in one's thoughts God can be bought by human effort. Legalism is an ever-present danger for Christians. Both Christians and non-Christians confuse it with real religion. Some of Paul's most instructive teaching against Christian legalism occurs here. Yet, it should be noted the term law (*nomos*) does not occur in this book.

Two metaphors express the heart of what Christ did for believers: the handwriting of ordinances being removed ("the written code") and nailing the accusations to the cross ("nailing it to the cross"). The first is the more complicated to interpret. Literally, the handwriting is a certificate of indebtedness written in one's own hand.[194] Taken this way, this means that there is a pronouncement that the personal note which testifies against us is canceled. Twice the word occurs in Tobit (5:3; 9:35, LXX) in a request for payment of a loan.[195] The word and the idea it expresses must be interpreted in connection with its modifier, "in regulations."

Several views have dominated the history of this interpretation.[196] First, the "written code" is viewed as a heavenly book which contains God's secrets or man's misdeeds. This, however, seems unrelated to this context.[197] Second, it is said to refer to a covenant between Adam and the devil. Some of the early Church Fathers took this position, but there is no hint of any such covenant, and the idea of regulations counters this. Third, it refers to the law of Moses. The Jewish application is obvious here. It would account for the "regulations," and the parallel of Eph 2:15 suggests that this is the law. Against this view, however, is the fact that Paul never spoke against the law. The failure of persons is not in the law, but in the weakness of the flesh (Rom 8:4). Fourth, it has been understood as a certificate of debt from humans to God—an I.O.U. Many point to Phlm 19 as an example of the kind of situation envisioned.

The best resolution lies in understanding the different aspects of the Mosaic law as Paul addressed them in the New Testament. The word "regulations" (*dogmasin*) naturally refers to an organized and purposely arranged list of laws—a code. It refers to the law of Moses.

---

[194] *BAGD*, 880.

[195] E. Lohse, *TDNT*, 9:435.

[196] W. Carr, "Two Notes on Colossians," *JTS* [NS] 24 (October, 1973), 492-500. See also among many articles, Lohse, *TDNT*, 9:435-36; O. A. Blanchette, "Does the Cheirographon of Col. 2:14 Represent Christ Himself?" *CBQ* 23 (1961), 306-12; H. Weiss, "The Law in the Epistle to the Colossians," *CBQ* 34 (1972), 294-314; and the extended bibliography in O'Brien, *Colossians, Philemon*, 101-33.

[197] A. J. Bandstra, *The Law and the Elements of the World. An Exegetical Study in Aspects of Paul's Teaching* (Grand Rapids: Eerdmans, 1964), 158-63, draws attention to this setting.

The handwriting refers to the indebtedness related to the law. Paul commonly spoke of two aspects of the Mosaic law. One is the condemnatory nature of the law (1 Cor 15:56; Rom 7:13ff.; Gal 3:10; Deut 27:26). Clearly the law condemns, but the law also reveals God's standards and the human failures related to it. The revelatory aspects of the law are beneficial, and Paul acknowledged their helpfulness (Rom 7:13ff.). The text states that the code that was against them was canceled. Paul meant that the condemnatory aspects of law were removed.[198] The Christian still profits from the revelation of God's character that the law embodies.

The condemnatory aspects of law are "canceled." The word used often signified the wiping (scraping) of the papyrus sheets so they could be used again.[199] If this analogy applies, the slate of human lives was soiled with an I.O.U. that stems from the law and its requirements. Paul stated that once it stood against the Christian, but these regulations no longer obligate. They were removed by the work of Christ. Paul never stated that the law was done away. He did affirm that believers had no relationship to law because of the work of Christ. Paul's most significant terminology in this regard is in Rom 7:1-6 where he stated that the believer died and could be married to another husband. The law continued alive, but believers engage in a "resurrection" marriage with Christ which frees them from the demands of the former "husband" ("the law").

The second metaphor is "nailing it to his cross." Interpreters differ as to the exact meaning Paul had in mind. Most likely it referred to the indictment hung over the prisoner's head when he was crucified. By such action, the criminal's debt to society was canceled since he paid for the crime.[200] The New Testament evidences this use in Matt 27:37 and John 19:19, where the Jews placed the charge against Jesus above his head. Perhaps Paul used this terminology because the gospel story contained it and he found it a useful way to describe the spiritual aspects of the vicarious suffering of Jesus. This interpretation most effectively captures the spirit of the context, but some see the metaphor as an act of triumph. They say that the symbolism refers to an act of defiance or triumph.[201] Some support may be garnered from the fact that this approach anticipates v. 15.

By these metaphors, Paul presented his theological conclusions regarding

---

[198] See Martin, *Colossians, NCB*, 83-84. J. Callow, *A Semantic Structure Analysis of Colossians* (Dallas: Summer Institute of Linguistics, 1983), 147, says that it refers to a serious document drawn up by God listing the charges against us. He reflects several commentators but misses the dual function of the law as recorded in Rom 7:13ff.

[199] Hendriksen objects to this literal use. He says that what is meant here is "the complete destruction of the law, regarded as a code of rules and regulations" (*Colossians*, 121, n. 91).

[200] E. F. Scott, *The Epistles of Paul to the Colossians, to Philemon and to the Ephesians*, MNTC (London: Hodder & Stoughton, 1930), 47, is one who points this out, although Moule questions it.

[201] Bruce, *Colossians*, 239-40.

the law and the work of Christ. God forgave, canceled the condemnatory aspects of the law, and paid the accusation in full. He did not say that the law passed away, nor did he intimate that God would use another standard besides law to judge. He did affirm clearly that believers have no obligation to the law. In his death, Christ satisfied the law's demands. The Colossians who listened to the false teachers may have been guilty because they remembered that they did not keep the law, but the truth is that the law's demands were kept. Forgiveness comes from God's taking initiative in Christ to satisfy the law. Thus both God's justice and mercy combine to devise a way to uphold the law as a divine standard and yet pardon the sinner. The result is freedom for the believer.

2:15 Having discussed the question of law, Paul moved to the subject of spirit beings. This returns to the last portion of a chiasm (see 2:9-10). The point of the discussion is that God in Christ triumphed over these beings. The sovereignty of Christ is evidenced in his relationship to other spirit beings. They were disgraced; he deserves honor.

Another graphic picture describes the work of Christ. To understand it, several issues demand interpretation. They are: the subject and meaning of the verb "having disarmed," the definition of the "powers and authorities," and the significance of the cross. Paul used the verb meaning "having disarmed" in parallel with the preceding verbs of vv. 13-14. The subject there was God the Father, though some understand it of Christ.[202] Similarly, the verb most likely means "he stripped them" rather than "he divested himself."[203] Another question related to the meaning of the verb is whether it should be applied to the military setting, thus meaning "disarming," or to the political realm, meaning "disgracing." The NIV prefers the military, but the political fits better in light of the discussion of lordship.[204] The text means that God disgraced the powers.

The other two questions remain. The "powers and authorities" may be either all spirit beings, good and evil, or evil spirits alone. Although the immediate context provides no clue, it would be difficult for Paul to resume a discussion which he already began without the identical words referring to the same beings (see 1:15-20). Further, it would hardly be necessary to disgrace (or disarm) those angels who worshiped God and contributed to his glory. This must refer to evil spirit beings.[205] Finally, the cross was the time and occasion of this

---

[202] See the discussion in Lightfoot, *Colossians*, 189-91, who made the most convincing case for the middle voice of the verb as well.

[203] This takes the middle voice as deponent (an active translation). That makes the best sense of the passage, contrary to Lightfoot (see note 202). See the discussion in Lohse, *Colossians*, 111-13, and Hendriksen, *Colossians*, 122-23. An excellent brief discussion of the subject and meaning of the verb appears in N. T. Wright, *Colossians and Philemon*, *TNTC* (Grand Rapids: Eerdmans, 1986), 115-18.

[204] Eleven translations favor the military usage.

[205] See Wright, 115-16, for the suggestion that these referred to the gods of the nations. Few accept his observation.

action. A paradox occurred. Jesus hung naked and disgraced, dying publicly for sinners. The evil forces assumed they had triumphed. In reality, through this act of both sacrifice and triumph, God disgraced these evil beings. The tables were turned. God triumphed in the redemptive work of Christ.[206]

Paul ended this section on a triumphant note. His arguments countered his opponents at every point. The sovereign Savior disgraced his enemies on the cross, exposing them to public shame. Clothing was the visible distinguishing mark of an authority figure. He could afford the best clothing, and he was obligated to wear the best to represent the people subject to him. When defeated or demoted, the first symbolic act was to remove the royal garments. The image Paul used here portrayed that action. God stripped his enemies of their "royal facade," exposing them for what they really were. No one should follow them. They were defeated, disgraced, and powerless because of the work of Christ. The passage recalls the kingly rule of Christ presented in the Christ hymn. Jesus is a sufficient Savior (2:9-14), and he is a sovereign Savior (2:15).

To the Doctrine of Sanctification (2:16-19). In these three verses, Paul focused his attention on the implications of his teaching for Christian living. The major themes are the same as in the soteriological section (2:8-15). Here Paul discussed the Colossians' relationship to the law (2:16-17) and to the supernatural powers (2:18-19) which were so much a part of the false teaching. The tone changes in these verses. Two commands predominate (vv. 16, 18). They form the two reference points for discussion. The first section concerns asceticism (2:16-17); the other, angel-worship (2:18-19).

Concerning Asceticism (2:16-17). At this point Paul addressed the practical outworkings of the "hollow and deceptive philosophy" (2:8) at Colosse. The philosophy appreciated the law but advocated ascetic practices in hopes of conquering the flesh. The setting appears to be both Jewish and separatist.

Before answering the threat, Paul described the nature of the asceticism. It was distinctively related to matters of the law. However, the attitude of some believers in the church had to be addressed as well.

2:16a Some members of the congregation were critical and dominating. Paul addressed this first because of the persuasive power of these attitudes. Obviously these people held strongly to their beliefs and were convincing in their propagation. Paul's basic command confronted the entire congregation: "Do not let anyone judge you." It is an awkward statement. No one can control the attitudes or actions of another. The individual responses to those who judge could be controlled, and that was Paul's real concern. He warned the church to make sure it did not give in to the persuasion of this philosophy. It was not to be brought under bondage to these teachings by willingly submitting to regulations which seemed spiritual. Such a critical spirit was exactly contrary to the freedom for which Paul fought so energetically. It violated the agreements of

---

[206]This excellent observation comes from ibid., 116.

the Jerusalem Council a dozen years earlier (Acts 15), and it was devastating to Christian living. The false teachers attempted to enforce regulations on the group which were foreign to the spirit of Christ and unnecessary to Christian faith. Their message was non-Christian. It reflected matters of personal choice and had little to do with one's relationship with Christ.

2:16b The substance of the false teaching was the ritual observance of the law. The two concerns identified frequent battlegrounds in the early church. They were diet ("what you eat or drink") and days ("religious festival, a New Moon celebration or a Sabbath day").[207]

The question of diet was an emotional issue in the first century. It took two distinct forms. Both grew out of the Jewish conscience, but one had more direct relation to the Jewish law. The first matter concerned the application of the Old Testament laws. The dietary laws of the Old Testament required careful discrimination between clean and unclean meats. This issue had been settled *in theory* by the time of the missionary journeys of Paul. Jesus addressed the issue so clearly that Mark could apply Jesus' statement to the matter of meats (7:19). Peter, the charismatic leader of the early Jerusalem church,[208] came to believe in the freedom to enjoy all meats through a very real and dramatic, though highly symbolic, vision of unclean animals lowered in a sheet from heaven (Acts 10:15).[209] Peter faced the reality of virtually everything in his religious and cultural heritage being replaced by Christ, and he passed the test. Later, he had a slight lapse of practice, but not theology (Gal 2:11-21). Even though the mainstream of the Christian movement had settled these questions, pockets of resistance existed. Indeed, the Judaizers who followed Paul attempted to bring his converts back under these kinds of laws.

Dietary practice was questioned from another perspective. In 1 Cor 8-10, Paul addressed the question of meats offered to idols. Some Christians taught energetically that it was against Christian principles to eat any meat that had been offered to idols.[210] Other equally devout Christians believed that meat was undefiled regardless of how it had been "dedicated." Emotions were equally strong among both groups. Although the Jewish aspect is less pronounced in the Corinthian conflict, the principles they used to argue their

---

[207] Many texts refer to them. Note especially Rom 14:1-15:6; 1 Cor 8-10; Acts 15. The specific issues of these passages differ, but they all deal with food and holidays.

[208] James was the administrative leader and bore the primary responsibility for the direction of the Christian movement in Jerusalem. Peter, however, remained a leader by virtue of his natural talents and spiritual gifts.

[209] The primary lesson from this vision was clearly that Gentiles, who were formerly considered unclean, were acceptable to God. That is clear from the location and development of the Book of Acts. However, it is impossible to miss the vehicle of communicating the message. Peter had to face the question of diet. It was a lesson from the lesser to the greater.

[210] A common practice in that culture was to offer meat to idols for the perpetuation of their temples. The excess meat was sold in shops which sometimes advertised the fact that the meat had been given to the gods.

points come from the Old Testament concept of the uniqueness and holiness of God.

At Colosse the Jewish nature of the philosophy predominated. It seems, therefore, that the question dealt with matters of Jewish law, that is, the eating of clean and unclean meats as forbidden or condoned in the Old Testament. The ascetics added to the Old Testament regulations and made them more intense than the Old Testament required. Paul did not handle the issue in Colossians as he did in 1 Corinthians.

The second issue of asceticism concerned special days. Again two aspects of this issue surfaced in the first century. Some believers in more Gentile settings concerned themselves with whether to worship on the Sabbath or on Sunday. They also debated the question of participation in pagan holidays.

The Jewish concern over special days grows out of the Old Testament. Certain religious days were to be observed: feasts (Lev 23), new moons (Num 10:10; 28:11), and Sabbaths (Exod 20:8-11; 31:14-16). These occasions were more than legal requirements found in an ancient document. They helped establish a national and ethnic consciousness that represented all that was distinctively Jewish. Perhaps, therefore, the issue was theological and cultural. The Jews believed that God had given their culture as well as their theological beliefs.

Paul strongly forbade the Colossian Christians to come under these regulations. Such things may appear spiritual, but spiritual life is a matter of relationship with Christ and the heart's commitment to him. To consider these matters as necessary to the Christian life would undermine the work of Jesus. If human effort is effective, the work of God is unnecessary.

2:17 Paul answered these teachers by explaining the relationship between these practices and Christianity (v. 17). Their regulations were called a shadow of things to come.[211] As a shadow relates to its substance, these regulations related to Christ. The terminology reinforced the interpretation that these were aspects and outworkings of the Jewish law. The Jewish system can easily be understood as "vaguely resembling" the truths of the New Testament.

A shadow is less significant than the object which causes it. A shadow is temporary, lasting until the substance arrives in view. A shadow is inferior in that it imperfectly resembles the object. No one prefers the shadow to the substance. Thus the reality is of more significance and value than the shadow. The shadow is anticipatory. In historical sequence, the "the old covenant" shadow came first and provided a representation of the "new covenant" object. Although vague, it was enough to point people to the reality so that when they saw the object itself they could recognize it for what it was. As Paul employed this terminology, each aspect was appropriate. The law, Paul argued elsewhere,

---

[211] A similar use is in Heb 8:5; 10:1.

was temporary and inferior (Gal 3:19-20). Inasmuch as it was a revelation of God's character, however, it was a representation of Christ.

The shadow is caused by the body ("reality"). The nature of the body has been the subject of considerable discussion. Many commentators take the word to mean the actual body of Christ, i.e., his physical body.[212] While the term "body" (*sōma*) normally does refer to the physical body, it is difficult to see how this interpretation answers the questions here. Is the law set against Jesus' body?[213]

The best suggestion is that the term "body" simply contrasts and completes the common shadow/body distinction.[214] The reality to which the shadow points is "of Christ."[215] Christ and the new age he inaugurated (i.e., his things) complete the image of the shadow. Thus, Christianity completes, fulfills, and corresponds to the matters of the shadow.[216]

Concerning Angel Worship (2:18-19). These two verses repeat the pattern of the previous two. They begin with a command, continue with a description of the problem, and end with some suggestions as to how to counter the false teachers. There are many interpretive difficulties in this section.

2:18 Paul began this section with a warning which the NIV translates "do not let anyone . . . disqualify you." The word "disqualify" builds on the word which means *to umpire* or *award the prize.*[217] If this meaning applies, the idea is that the Colossians were in danger of losing the prize of their commitment to Christ. Other commentators understand the word to mean *put you under judgment.* Thus it is a synonym for the word used in v. 16. Although the two occur in an almost synonymous relation, there are differences in them. Paul's point was that following such teaching would lead to a loss of the joy and spiritual

---

[212] Among the many who interpret it this way, see Lohse, 117; Moule, 103; and Martin, *Colossians*, 91-92.

[213] Similarly, suggestions that this is metaphorical and refers to the body of Christ in a larger sense than the physical are also difficult to interpret. See Lohmeyer, 123.

[214] Most commonly the metaphor was "shadow/icon" (σκία/εἰκών), but on occasion the word "body" could be substituted. It may be legitimately argued that Paul deliberately chose the term "body" rather than "image" for conceptual/theological reasons. However, the reason is unclear.

[215] The genitive construction may be possessive: "belonging to Christ" (Lightfoot, 195; Vaughan, *Colossians*, 204); associative: "with Christ" (Hendriksen, 124); appositional: "Christ's body (Martin, *Colossians*, 91).

[216] Some have pointed to the Platonic nature of this discussion (Martin, *Colossians*, 91). In Platonic thought the things of earth were simply shadows of what existed in the real world of thought. The dualism of Platonic thought, however, was static: The two existed at the same time. For Paul, they were sequential: One gave way to the other. Further, in Platonism the two dimensions remain in separate realms of existence. For Paul, the body as well as the shadow appear on earth and that is the primary place of their existence. Finally, the Christological distinctive always separates Pauline thought from other philosophies as it does here.

[217] The word is βραβεύω, and its compound form καταβραβεύω is found here. It is a rare word and lends itself to two possible connotations. (E. Stauffer, *TDNT*, 1:637-39).

benefits of the relationship to Christ who is the head. The attack was serious. It could have led to a spiritual disqualification.[218]

Four modifying clauses explain the specific philosophy. These are translated as "delights in false humility and the worship of angels"; "goes into great detail about what he has seen"; "his unspiritual mind puffs him up"; and "he has lost connection with the Head."[219] The first three phrases speak of the specific claims of the false teachers;[220] the last is Paul's evaluation of the seriousness of the doctrine.

The first characteristic explains a joyful commitment to the spiritual rigors which claim to produce a higher form of worship. The term "delights in" seems to be the best translation of the Greek "willing in."[221] Thus the false teachers joyfully committed to these practices.

The terms "false humility" and "worship of angels" have had several possible interpretations. Some commentators have taken them to mean a false humility (as translated by the NIV) since the adherents willingly worshiped angels rather than Christ.[222] Others have suggested they refer to the practice of being ready to serve the organized religious system of the false teachers. For these interpreters, the terms relate to the cult rather than to the individuals within it.[223] More recently some have been persuaded that the terms are associated with religious fasts and relate to the practice of depriving the desires of the flesh so that unusual spiritual experiences take place.[224] This third view has much to commend it, but the resolution depends, in part, on the meaning of "worship of angels."

The worship of angels occupied a central place in the false teachers' appeal. The primary question is whether the expression is objective (worship given to angels) or subjective (worship with angels).[225] Which would be more likely? If the situation reflects a pre-Gnostic and Gentile context, worship directed to

---

[218] On the one hand, this does not necessarily refer to a loss of salvation. It refers to a failure to grasp the nature of Christian freedom. On the other hand, there could be a corporate loss.

[219] The four are participial clauses which are presented in parallel. The grammar differs slightly, however, because the first three are identical, but the word "and" (καί) occurs before the last one. Perhaps this suggests that the last, "not holding fast the Head," is really a part of the answer to the teaching.

[220] O'Brien (*Colossians, Philemon*, 145) and others suggest that the first two of these were slogans of the false teachers. Whether they were direct quotations, they certainly encapsulate the interests of the teachers. The third statement also seems to relate to the characteristics of the teaching. It involves a puffed up mind. The fourth, however, inaugurates Paul's criticism of this position.

[221] Θέλων ἐν seems to be equivalent to the Hebrew בְּאַהֵפֵץ.

[222] Lightfoot, 194.

[223] Lohse, 118.

[224] This is discussed at some length in the introductory materials. In addition to that discussion, see O'Brien, *Colossians, Philemon*, 142.

[225] Strictly speaking, the subjective genitive would call for the worship *produced by* angels. This, however, seems out of the realm of possibility.

angels makes good sense. This, in fact, is the biggest obstacle to seeing the false teaching as completely Jewish. Nevertheless, Francis presents ample evidence that the phrase could be better understood in a context of a rather esoteric Judaism, such as at Qumran.[226] Since most of the characteristics against which Paul spoke in this epistle can be comfortably placed in a Jewish setting, the weight of evidence must go in that direction. Thus the objective genitive seems best.

This first characteristic, therefore, describes a commitment to what was perceived as a higher form of worship. Consistent with the Jewish traditions that the angels were higher than humans and that they worshiped and served God, the false teachers seem to have developed a procedure to induce a higher spiritual experience equivalent to the angels' experience. To effect it, however, required severity to the flesh. Through ascetic practices, they taught that the mind and spirit could be sensitized to higher spiritual realities. These became an evidence of spiritual superiority.

The second characteristic of this worship has been equally debated. It appears that the phrase "goes into great detail" is the key to the expression.[227] As noted in the introduction, the phrase has been variously interpreted. In brief, the interpretations may be considered under two categories. Dibelius represents the first. He made famous the view that the term "entering" ("goes," NIV) was used in the technical sense of entering into a sanctuary to worship. Thus it had the significance of an initiation into a cult or one of the mystery religions which later grew to such prominence in the Greco-Roman world.[228] Perhaps the most devastating aspect of this teaching was that some in the congregation were claiming a spiritual superiority because of their supposedly higher spiritual insights. Others interpret it differently. They have pointed out that the technical use of the term should not be applied here. They suggest that the term was used of "detailed investigation"[229] or of actual possession of some spiritual truth.[230] The latter approaches appear to fit the context better. These teachers attempted to get their converts to "possess what they have seen."[231]

Some textual variants make this statement negative, but they do not have serious attestation. Taken that way, the text reads, "entering what they have not

---

[226] See the introduction and the evidence given and accepted by O'Brien, *Colossians, Philemon*, 142-43.

[227] Greek ἐμβατεύω.

[228] M. Dibelius, "The Isis Initiation in Apuleius and Related Initiatory Rites" *Conflict At Colossae*, ed. F. O. Francis and W. A. Meeks, 2nd ed. SBLSBS 4. (Missoula, Mont.: Scholars, 1975), 61-121. See also the introduction of this volume.

[229] H. Preisker, *TDNT*, 2:535-36.

[230] F. Francis, "The Background of EMBATEUEIN (Col 2:18) in Legal Papyri and Oracle Inscriptions," *Conflict at Colosse*, ed. F. Francis and W. Meeks (Missoula, Mont.: Scholars, 1975), 197-207. He points out that generally the term was used of physical or geographical possessions but that it could denote the heavenly possession.

[231] The interpretation "investigate in detail" would not greatly alter the conclusion since thorough investigation may well be the first step to, or a synonym for, possession.

seen." This interpretation makes easy what is an otherwise more difficult statement. Therefore, the negative is unlikely, following the textual principle that the more difficult is to be preferred. They did not attempt to "enter what they have not seen." This interpretation suggests that they were seeking to gain spiritual experiences which they did not know firsthand. They were always seeking new insights and experiences beyond what they knew to be reality. This reading came from an attempt to discredit visions and other ecstatic experiences, but such experiences were commonly induced. The best explanation is that the false teachers were inducing spiritual experiences and hoping to make them the norm for worship. Such a "spiritual orientation" is a treadmill. The seeker of these experiences can never be satisfied, and the experience becomes the hermeneutic and the authority behind spiritual life. So-called spiritual experience is everything.

The third characteristic, "his unspiritual mind puffs him up with idle notions," points to the false teachers' empty high-mindedness. The mind (*nous*) responds to moral and spiritual insight. The mind of the flesh, as the Greek literally says, is the natural mind unaided by the Holy Spirit. This way of thinking puffs up the worshiper without cause. It produces a false pride which leads to a haughty disposition. Such religious experiences seem (to the natural mind) to be genuine spiritual insight. They even set a standard for measuring all of life's experiences, but they lack authenticity and integrity. This third stage was probably the outworking of the previous two. A progression seems likely. The worship with the angels led to the full possessing of these spiritual experiences. These experiences, in turn, produced a way of thinking which prized false religious insight and perpetuated the entire process.

2:19   The final characteristic of the "deceptive philosophy" (2:8) bridged the gap to Paul's severe criticism of this position, which would come later.[232] Paul considered this teaching so far removed from Christian truth that it was actually a sub-Christian worship experience. It was seeking to enrich the religious life without the source of that life, Christ himself through the Holy Spirit. Theirs was a "headless" religious movement.

These four characteristics reveal the progressive seriousness of the false teachers' worship goals. The hermeneutic of experience predominated. One experience led to another, and the hunger for such experiences was fed by the mind of the flesh which so delights in experiential religion. Paul called for an experience based on Christ and the gospel and suited to the building up of the whole body. Individualistic experience-seekers fell far short of God's will.

Employing one common metaphor, the body, Paul suggested two reasons this teaching would not suffice. First, it was disconnected; second, it would starve spiritually. Paul had employed the metaphor of the head and body rela-

---

[232]The NIV begins a new sentence with this participle. While that violates the grammar of the text, it may capture the sense.

tionship in 1:18 and of principalities and powers in relation to Christ (the head) in 2:20. Here he used it of the church and Christ. In ideas reminiscent of the two stanzas of the hymn in 1:15ff., the metaphor is adaptable to two different realms: creation and the new creation. Before, the ideas of authority and source of creation merged, but authority by virtue of origins received the emphasis. Here the two also combine, but clearly Paul thought of the energy supplied by the head to the body.

The church would readily accept the head/body terminology. It was frequently employed.[233] This picture expressed a treasured union with Christ which formed the basis of all spiritual blessings in Christ. Swiftly and skillfully, Paul pointed out that the teachers were not even Christian. From the Gnostic perspective, this was not simply a matter of being severed from the highest of supernatural beings because Gnostic teaching did not appreciate Christ in that way. This meant the participants were being severed from one of the essential beings through whom it was necessary to ascend to the higher ones and ultimately to God. From Paul's perspective, the worship of angels was to be severed from God who is embodied in Christ.

The rest of the metaphor explains the seriousness of being severed from the head of the body. Paul employed medical terminology of that day to point out that the body could not grow without the head. The head was absolutely essential. Two emphases occur. First, the whole body received nourishment from the head. There is no other source of strength for anyone in the body. This means that whatever growing the church would do, it would do because of its connection to Christ. The false teaching threatened to sever that relationship. Second, without Christ, the Head, any growth that might take place would be misdirected. The goal is to grow with "God's growth." Any suggestion of spiritual growth apart from Christ is a false spirituality. The Christian is to be energized and empowered by Christ the head so that genuine spiritual growth can take place. This means, of course, that spiritual experiences like those advocated by the false teachers in Colosse have no lasting value and do not promote real spiritual growth. Thus it is a serious matter for the body to be dislocated from the Head.

In these verses, Paul discussed the theology of Christian growth with two specific reference points that were the foundations of the false teaching. The first was asceticism. Regarding practices related to the law and/or strict observances, the Christian has been forgiven and thus has satisfied the law's demands. No person should succumb to the critical and dominating spirit which prevailed in those circles. The second was angel worship. Regarding ecstatic and esoteric spiritual experiences of worshiping as the angels do, Christians should realize that they need only Christ. Whatever one experiences,

---

[233] See the data at 1:18.

the objective tests of truth must prevail. Christ, rather than experiences, determines spiritual reality.

(2) Against the Practical Threat (2:20-3:4)

[20]Since you died with Christ to the basic principles of this world, why, as though you still belonged to it, do you submit to its rules: [21]"Do not handle! Do not taste! Do not touch!"? [22]These are all destined to perish with use, because they are based on human commands and teachings. [23]Such regulations indeed have an appearance of wisdom, with their self-imposed worship, their false humility and their harsh treatment of the body, but they lack any value in restraining sensual indulgence.

[1]Since, then, you have been raised with Christ, set your hearts on things above, where Christ is seated at the right hand of God. [2]Set your minds on things above, not on earthly things. [3]For you died, and your life is now hidden with Christ in God. [4]When Christ, who is your life, appears, then you also will appear with him in glory.

This passage continues Paul's thought by presenting the practical outworking of the theological foundations. The content is similar to the previous passage because of the close connection between the issues involved. Theology and life intermingle, and theological heresy normally works itself out in life as well. The two theological reference points of salvation and sanctification continue to provide the structure here. Paul spoke concerning salvation (the believer's union with Christ in death) in 2:20-23. He spoke regarding sanctification (the believer's union with Christ in resurrection) in 3:1-4.

This theological theme undergirds all of Paul's teaching on Christian living. In many passages he made it explicit (i.e., Rom 6:1-14). In other places, it lay in the background. In these verses, Paul made the connection as clearly as anywhere. Because of believers' death with Christ, some things have no relevance. Because of resurrection with Christ, other things occupy Christians' minds. In the process of growth these things become clear.

This passage contains one teaching about Christian living. This teaching, however, unfolds in two logical units. The structural unity can be seen in the fact that each unit begins with a conditional idea which the NIV translates "since." The exhortations to Christian living grow out of a systematic understanding of Christian truth and Christian experience. The readers would identify with what happened for them, and they were to build their Christian lives on it. A semantic unity can be seen in fact that the same words occur in each unit. Most notably, the phrase "with Christ" ties the two together.

TO THE DOCTRINE OF SALVATION (2:20-23). Paul looked back to the time of the Colossians' conversion, which he called their death with Christ. The false teachers failed to understand the full meaning of that spiritual experience, and the reason they made such inroads into the church was the immaturity of the Colossian Christians. They did not fully understand the significance of their salvation, either. In that kind of situation, accurate theology would have prevented heresy.

As Paul called them to remember their past experience, he also pointed to the present. They continued to live with the same life view that characterized non-Christians. They were preoccupied with this world. Paul's teaching reveals that any preoccupation with this world and its ways sidetracks Christians. Too often, Christians let the practical issues of the world become reference points for their spiritual development. This may happen in two radically different ways. Christians may become preoccupied with this world by indulging in its activities. Lives of luxury, licentiousness, and lust destroy spiritual insight and growth. Christians also easily become preoccupied with this world by measuring their Christian growth in terms of this world and its reference points. Thus they look to their separation from the world as evidence of their Christian maturity. In this, their spiritual road signs are the things of this world, rather than the things of Christ. This latter situation was the problem at Colosse. They were looking to worldly wisdom to measure spirituality. When this occurs within the church, the church is misdirected and lives are powerless. Paul countered this by discussing the nature of the false teachers' attacks and by providing reasons Christians should not submit to them.

The Nature of the Attacks (2:20-21). The false teachers brought with them definite ideas about religious life. They had an organized system which forbade certain practices. Generally, these issues reflected the religious issues of their day. Paul's discussion in vv. 20-21 both defines these practices and reveals their character as enslaving and legalistic.

2:20 Paul first exposed this system as enslaving. He asked why the believers "submit to its rules." The Greek has one word which would better be translated why "are you coming under the dominion of this dogma" (*dogmatizesthe*). The word "dogma" was used then in much the same way as it is today. It represented an essential part of a particular teaching. "Being dogmatized" meant to come under the rule of this particular dogma. Since the dogma was non-Christian, it was particularly devastating to Christian growth. The problem at Colosse was the people willingly embraced a system of thought contrary to Christianity. The system was enslaving.

2:21 Paul quoted the particular rules of this dogma: "Do not handle! Do not taste! Do not touch!" The NIV correctly places these in quotation marks, as though they were slogans from the false teachers. Frequently in this type of argumentation Paul quoted his opponents. For example, in 1 Corinthians many slogans were quoted and analyzed for the congregation. Two of them provide insight into this procedure. In 1 Cor 7:1 the text says, "It is good for a man not to marry." Probably this came from a "spiritual" segment of the church (the Christ party?) who reasoned that sexual abstinence was a mark of Christianity. They argued that the truly spiritual would not succumb to the sexual desires of the flesh even if they were married! Paul quoted them in order to provide a reference for the discussion which followed. There he modified their position.[234] Another example occurs in 1 Cor 10:23 where Paul cited a slogan from the libertine party in Corinth: "All things are lawful" (NASB). They realized their Christian freedoms and flaunted them before other Christians. Again, Paul agreed with the truthfulness of their position, but modified it. He agreed as a general reference point that "all things are lawful." He modified their position, however, by saying that "not everything is constructive." Specific individual freedoms must not harm the individual or other Christians. In both of these illustrations, Paul agreed with the basic truth of the statements but modified them in light of the abuses within the church.

Corinth was different from Colosse. At Corinth Paul corrected a tangential Christianity by bringing the various groups into harmony. They were correct in essence, but they rode a "hobbyhorse" which fragmented the fellowship. The problem at Corinth was lack of genuine spirituality. Paul was, therefore, less harsh and brutal in his words to them.

Paul's harsh attacks against the system at Colosse exposed it for what it really was: a heresy. It threatened to undermine the very heart of the gospel, and those who followed it did so to their spiritual shipwreck. The style of argument, however, is the same. The words were taken from the opponents themselves. They represented theology in microcosm, and Paul's use of catch words called the entire system to account. It was a system of do's and don't's about earthly things. These systems run contrary to the nature of the gospel and the freedom found in Christ.

Reasons Not to Submit (2:22-23). In this passage, Paul provided two reasons Christians should not submit to false teachers. The first reason is the nature of the conversion experience. Paul's introduction to these verses served as the first reason not to submit to these teachers. He stated, "You died with Christ to the basic principles of this world, why as though you still belonged to it do you submit." The term used, *stoicheia*, already has been discussed (cf. 2:8). It may suffice here simply to reinforce its usage. Christ's death delivered believers from these basic elements of the world. They had left that domain. Their attraction to them, therefore, represented an attraction to a pre-Christian way of thinking and living. The basic principles of human religion became the reference points for Christian experience.[235] That should never happen. They wanted to measure their Christian progress by things of this earth. This represented a backwards glance, judging the present in terms of the distance from the past! As will be seen in the next section, the Christian life is measured by

---

[234] He said that as a general reference point it is good not to touch a woman, but not in the context of marriage. Sex is commended for married couples.

[235] Although "elements" (στοιχεῖα) does not refer to a religion by itself, the teachings came dressed in religious clothing. It was nothing more than natural insight applied to religious outlook. In that sense, it was "elementary."

always looking to the things of Christ. This first argument reminds the readers of two important truths: their death with Christ delivered them from the concern about worldly things, and this was a worldly religion regardless of the theological terminology that accompanied it. They were never to go back to such an outlook.

The second reason is the character of the things to avoid. Paul's next point appealed to the foolishness of building Christian experience on things which typify this world. Two statements reveal the imperfection of the system. One is found in each of the verses in this section.[236]

2:22 First, the objects of this system were consumable (2:22). The Greek text is graphic. These things would perish with use. The warning suggests that the focus was limited to this world and that which passes away. Such things are the objects of human commands and teachings, which contain no more insight than the world of which they are a part. Since the Christian's life is never-ending, the Christian should focus on what lasts. These things pass on in time and, for many of them, in a short time. Using them or not has little significance to the broad spectrum of time and eternity. Like so many other similar religious systems, this one substituted the temporal for the eternal, making food and observances the center of its practice. This is both foolish and unnecessary for the Christian.

2:23 Second, the objects of their concern had no value in sanctification. This verse is one of the most complicated in the epistle. Interpreters differ on the words themselves (semantics), the word relationships (syntax), and the basic thrust (interpretation). The NIV translation captures the spirit of the text well: "Such regulations indeed have an appearance of wisdom." The Greek text actually says, "which is a word having wisdom." The singular "word" (*logos*) points to the entirety of the system, but it specifically represents the catchwords of v. 21. The question at this point is whether Paul spoke "tongue in cheek" or seriously. If he were serious, he granted that this system did, indeed, contain an element of wisdom, but not nearly what is offered in Christ. Because the entire passage takes a strong negative attitude toward the system, the context reveals that Paul was diametrically opposed to it. It seems better, therefore, to understand him as speaking in irony. The false teachers claimed wisdom, and their claim appealed to some. In reality, however, they had only an appearance of wisdom, a wisdom of this world which the world approves as true religion.

The appearance of wisdom was "with their self-imposed worship, their false humility and their harsh treatment of the body." Again the NIV translates the spirit of the passage well. It reveals three characteristics of this "appearance of wisdom." The first characteristic is that it was "self-imposed worship." The Greek text actually says that this "wisdom" is "in will-worship." The word

---

[236]Each verse begins with a relative pronoun which characteristically defines the noun it modifies. This is a typical restrictive use of these forms.

implies that it is a voluntary submission of the will to the worship advocated by this system. Earlier, Paul addressed the practice of "worship of angels" (2:18), and apparently the same practice is addressed here. Some maintain, therefore, that this is voluntarily accepting a lower object of worship, angels, as an act of humility. They willingly worshiped lesser beings rather than Christ. However, the context suggests a self-imposed ritual that brought an emotional and experiential lift. With that precedent in the epistle, the NIV translation fits better.

The second characteristic of this appearance of wisdom was "false humility." The Greek says literally "humility." Some commentators place this directly with "will-worship" so that the humility is that identified with a humble, voluntary worship.[237] More likely, Paul used the term to refer to physical humility, i.e., fasting, which was practiced by many early Christians. With the evidence for that identified earlier, it seems best to take this as a false humility, which is one aspect of self-induced religious experiences. This humility refers to a false characteristic of abasement, primarily in reference to the body.

The third characteristic was "harsh treatment of the body." All commentators understand this as the asceticism connected with religious ritual. The major question is whether it was a part of the other two or distinct from them. In light of the previous argumentation, it seems best to take this as a part of the inducement of religious experience. After lengthy physical stress, the body responded in unusual ways which they interpreted as religious experiences.[238] Perhaps this stage of involvement was more intense than the "catchword" stage of v. 21, but it is probably the same in kind.

These three forms of denial of the flesh appeared to contain wisdom. They recalled the questions of John the Baptist's followers to Jesus' disciples regarding fasting (Matt 9:14). Everyone expected religious people to fast. Since that was how religion was done, it seemed wise to follow that pattern. Some may even have applauded the discipline and intensity of commitment of those who practiced such things. Often the world praises people with misguided religious practices more than those who follow the truth. The translation of the NIV, therefore, best explains Paul's thought. Paul was not commending these people for their actions. He spoke in irony, pointing out the foolishness of these extremes.

---

[237] It is noteworthy that the Greek text joins "will-worship" and "humility" by the conjunction "and" (καί). This argues that the two go together. There is further confusion. The third characteristic joins the other two without a conjunction (the UBS Greek text inserts one in brackets). This probably argues for joining all three into one type of religious exercise rather than two opposed to the other. This is further confirmed by the introductory preposition "in" (ἐν) which unites all three descriptions.

[238] Such practices are common in many societies where fasting, prolonged rhythmic dance, and other inducements produce an emotional/spiritual experience.

The NIV translates Paul's final statement in this regard as "but they lack any value in restraining sensual indulgence." The Greek says literally, "not in a certain value toward satisfying the flesh." The options here are diverse. Some interpreters contend that Paul meant that the inferior wisdom of this system and its practices did not satisfy the flesh. This implies that the cravings of the flesh can only be satisfied in a relationship with Christ. This seems unlikely. Paul never spoke of satisfying the flesh, nor did he say that Christ satisfies the desires of the flesh. The flesh is to be denied and conquered by the Spirit (Gal 5:21ff.). The better interpretation is that the false wisdom and practices did not curb the desires of the flesh. They only spoke to the environment, not the heart.

Paul taught that only God can conquer the flesh. In Gal 5:21ff. the Holy Spirit battles the flesh and keeps the flesh from fulfilling its lusts. In Rom 7:14ff. the mind and the flesh are contrary to each other. The deliverance comes from the Lord Jesus Christ. Further in Romans, in a discussion of amoral practices, Paul stated that some think the freer Christian will fall into sin more easily (Rom 14:4). The power to stand against the sins of the flesh, however, comes from the Lord who effects victory in a Christian's life.[239]

Asceticism only changed the environment.[240] The flesh could not be conquered through such practices. Therefore, the entire system was flawed. The teachers devoted themselves to ascetic practices and physical torture, hoping to produce a higher spiritual state. In the end, their approach was misguided at three points. It was only a product of this world. It focused on perishable (earthly) objects, and it did not offer a means of conquering the desires of the flesh. What, then, did Paul offer in its place?

To the Doctrine of Sanctification (3:1-4). Paul turned his thoughts to a more positive aspect of Christian living in this section of Scripture. The foolish attempts at sanctification found in 2:20-23 often entrap Christian people. The real issue is the outlook found in 3:1-4. Here Paul explained the nature of the Christian's higher calling (3:1-2) and the reasons to seek this higher calling (3:3-4). Although this section focuses on the Christian's new values, clearly these values are rooted in conversion. Conversion includes a radical change of mind which produces the desire for separation from the world.

The Nature of the Christian's Higher Calling (3:1-2). These two verses begin like the last section. A "since" clause provides the foundation for the theology.[241] Paul discussed the Christian's resurrection. In a spiritual but real sense, Christians have left this life and its loves. They have moved to a new domain where Christ lives. That brings new understanding.

---

[239] Of course, this passage speaks to Christians and amoral practices. The tie here is the sins of the flesh. Paul realized that God conquered the flesh.

[240] Sometimes environments need changing. The mistake is in thinking that holiness is a product of one's environment rather than the power of the Lord.

[241] Like 2:20, this is a first-class condition in Greek which sets up a logical relationship. It should be "assuming you have been raised with Christ, then. . . ."

Two commands form the essence of this calling. They define a Christian perspective, and they call people to action. The imperative format urged the readers to get involved in what Paul said. They were to learn the theology in mind and life.

3:1-2 The first command is, "Set your heart on things above" (3:1). The second command parallels it: "Set your minds on things above" (3:2). The primary difference is the difference between "mind" and "heart." In actuality, the Greek has no word here for "heart"; it is an inference from the translators. The word "mind" is actually a part of the verb used in the second command, "be minded about things above" (*phroneō*). Although these are presented in a parallel structure, they are not synonymous. There is a contrast in the two commands. They speak to two aspects of a person's being. The verb "be minded" occurs often in Paul's writings. It occurs in Rom 12:3 where Paul stated that Christians should have a proper mind about themselves and their gifts.[242] More frequently, however, the term occurs in Philippians, where the paradigm is the mind of Christ which should be in believers (Phil 2:5). The term implies more than a way of thinking; it includes values and loves as well. It could well be translated "delight in things above." In contrast with this second command, which speaks of values, the first command refers to desires. Since basic desires proceed from the heart (Jesus' words in Mark 7:15), the NIV correctly inserts the word "heart." The first concern is moral; the second, mental.

The command to continue seeking things above, the essence of these two verb forms, follows a typical pattern in Scripture. Two realms of existence often were designated as above and below by biblical writers. This is illustrated in the account of Jesus with Nicodemus (John 3:12-13), where the discussion follows the pattern of the earthly contrasted with the heavenly. As is typical for John's Gospel, Jesus claimed to be from above (3:13) and on a mission to the earth below. That Paul accepted such terminology is confirmed in Phil 3:14, where Paul expressed his desire to gain "the upward call" of God. Although the imagery comes from the athletic field, specifically the awarding of a crown, Paul's thought went further. He thought of the upward call as the prize from Christ Jesus, calling Paul to go to where Christ was. The imagery served Paul's purpose well. In Gal 4:26 he used the term again, this time of the "upward city," Jerusalem, which is free. Developing an allegory between Hagar and Sarah and their offspring, he spoke of a figurative Jerusalem. In reality, the Christian belongs there; it is of the heavenly realm.[243]

The higher things, those above, are defined in Col 3:1 as "where Christ is seated at the right hand of God." This imagery calls to mind the enthronement

---

[242] The root word occurs four times in that verse as Paul warned about "high-mindedness" (ὑπερφρονεῖν) and urged "soberness" (σωφρονεῖν) in their appraisals of themselves (φρονεῖν, twice). He defined soberness as in accord with the "measure of faith."

[243] Each of these texts uses the word "above" (ἄνω) in a contrast.

of Christ, and Paul based his thought on Ps 110:1:

> The Lord says to my Lord:
> "Sit at my right hand
> until I make your enemies
> a footstool for your feet."

For the early church, the passage demonstrated the deity of Jesus. Their insight was given by the Lord himself (Matt 22:44; Mark 12:36; Luke 20:42). In dialogue with the Jews, he asked, "What did David mean?" There were two Lords here, David's Lord and the Lord who spoke to him. Following Jesus' pattern, the early church used the text as one of the primary Christological passages from the Old Testament to indicate the deity of Jesus Christ.

The New Testament writers applied the text consistently, although Paul rarely used it.[244] The metaphor of "right hand" has two possible meanings. First, it meant *power*. Perhaps Mark 14:62 provides the insight to understand this metaphor. There Jesus told the high priest, "You will see the Son of Man sitting on the right hand of power, and coming in the clouds of heaven." The association of right hand with power translated the metaphor. The right hand was a place of power, and Mark alone translated the image for his readers. The term also may refer to a position of privilege. In the Gospels the disciples aspired to a privileged place with Christ in the kingdom. Jesus replied it was not his place to grant such wishes (Matt 20:23; Mark 10:37). F. F. Bruce, referring to the conceptual parallels of Phil 2:10ff. and Eph 4:10ff., says, "Because He has been elevated to the position of highest sovereignty over the universe, He pervades the universe with His presence."[245] This latter interpretation fits the context of Colossians. Paul argued that Christ was the preeminent one over all of natural creation and redemption (1:15-20). He argued later that all portions of the body were supported by the Christ and depended on him (2:19). Although the ideas of privilege and power merge to some degree, the idea of the rule of Christ predominates.

This command called the Colossians to focus on matters related to the rule of Christ in the world. Since he is the sovereign one, his concerns should occupy the Christian. Here, as much as anywhere, the twofold perspective of believers appears. They lived in two domains: the fallen order and the redeemed order, a division Paul had already used in 1:15-20. While being a part of the fallen order, they were not to let that environment occupy their thoughts and minds. Their values were to be different. Creation will pass away; the

---

[244] It occurs three times in the Pauline Epistles (Rom 8:34; Eph 1:20; Col 3:1) and five times in Acts (2:25,33,34; 5:31; 7:55,56). The most occurrences in the epistles are in Hebrews, where the psalm is quoted or referred to five times (1:3,13; 8:1; 10:12; 12:2). Of course, the Gospel writers employed it as well (Matt 22:44; 26:64; Mark 12:36; 14:62; Luke 20:42), recording it from the lips of Jesus.

[245] Bruce, *Colossians, Philemon*, 259.

things of God will remain. Before they pass away, however, they will again reflect the glory of Christ, their Creator. The Christians had the responsibility of seeking ways to make that happen here and now. Believers' values and loves were to be focused on the rule of Christ, and consecrated energies were to be devoted to making that rule a reality on earth. In practice, this meant that the believers could not succumb to teachings which limited the focus of Christianity to this earth and its rituals. The task of the Colossian church was to call people to Christ and away from earthly things. It was to call people to life.

Reasons to Seek the Higher Calling (3:3-4). Paul presented three reasons Christians should seek things above. The theological incentive behind these reasons in found in v. 1. The three reasons are: the resurrection with Christ (3:1), the new life source (3:3-4), and the future manifestation of glory (3:4).

This entire section presents the nature of the resurrection life, but in v. 1 Paul called them to recognize the reality of it. Paul's logic emerges in 3:4, as he recalls the believer's death with Christ: If the believer died with Christ, how does he now live? He lives in resurrection as a new creation of God.

3:3 The question may well be asked: If I died with Christ, how do I continue to live? Paul's answer was that Christians' lives are "hidden with Christ in God." Although some may understand the point of this statement to be the safety of believers, Paul used it to refer to the source of believers' lives. The new life source, that which sustains Christians, is Christ. Paul clearly stated as much in the next verse. Just as Christ is now hidden from the eyes of the world, the Christian's life in Christ is also hidden. Christians appear as dead to the things of the world, but very much alive with a source of life that goes beyond this world and what it can provide. The new life is Christ. His life energizes Christians, enabling them to be and do what they should.[246] The life Christ provides encourages believers to seek the things identified with that life.

3:4 The believer's life, which is hidden in Christ, will be revealed. At his return each person will see him and, perhaps for the first time, be confronted with the magnificence of his person. The theme of hidden/manifestation occurs here.[247] The Christian's life is hidden now, but it will be obvious to all when Christ is manifest to them. The second coming of Christ will be a time of glory (*doxa*).

In Col 3:4 Paul communicated this glory. Believers will appear in glory with Christ. Christians will share in Christ's glory, and Christians will contribute to his glory. The present time is a time of death. Often Christians suffer for their faith, but they continue with a life source unknown to those who do not know Christ. Someday, however, Christ will be revealed. When he is, the source of

---

[246] It should be emphasized that Paul did not say, "Christ provides life," though, of course, he does, and Scripture attests to it. Here he stated, "Christ *is* life." That is the point!

[247] The terms suggest that what is unknown now will become openly known later. Κεκρύπτω is contrasted with φανερόω, forming a thematic/semantic pattern which holds the verses together.

Christians' lives will become apparent to all persons. The reason Christians have had the values, outlook, and service to God and others will be clear. The hidden life will be manifested.

The values and goals of Christians will also be vindicated. The glory of Christ will captivate the minds of unbelievers as well as believers. Unbelievers will know that Jesus is Lord (Phil 2:10), and they will know that they based their lives on the wrong principles. They will also see that Christians built their lives correctly. Their lives and ambitions were energized by Christ through the Spirit, and they sought to contribute to the concerns of Christ on earth.

Until then, the Christian life remains hidden. Christians are misunderstood, belittled, and persecuted. Unbelievers attack both Christians and the Christ whom they love and worship. Someday, however, that will change. The King of glory will return and become the preeminent one in creation and redemption, as Paul wrote in 1:15-20. Christians will share in that great day.

For these reasons, Christians should seek higher things. The concerns of the false teachers caused misguided Christian living. Christians had a greater destiny than earth. They were to prepare for heaven. They were to call the people of earth to consider the things of heaven and of Christ's rule. They were to work for the reconciliation of all things—natural and human—in the spirit of 1:15-20. In this, any preoccupations with the things of this earth sidetracked the real concerns.

While Paul spoke so pointedly against preoccupation with earthly things, he spoke equally challengingly about the earthly nature within Christians. The world is one thing, the heart is another. Both the outlook and the heart must conform to the higher things identified with the rule of Christ in the universe. Paul turned to that subject in the next section.

The strictly theological portion of the epistle ends here. Paul began with a prayer for a real knowledge of God's will. He ended with a call to live in accord with that will. All personal resources should contribute to the rule of Christ. Significantly, Paul ended this section with the believer's hope—the revelation of Christ. The Christian virtues Paul so appreciated in the Colossians were based on hope (1:3-8). The instructions Paul issued made sense only in light of this hope—the manifestation of Christ's glory and the vindication of Christian living.

SECTION OUTLINE

III. THE PREEMINENCE OF CHRIST
IN CHRISTIAN LIVING (3:5-4:6)

With the doctrinal foundations in place, Paul addressed the false teachers and exposed their errant positions. The apostle turned his thoughts more directly to the specifics of Christian living. If Christians were not to succumb to such a system as the false teachers proposed, what were they to do? Might they live in disregard of personal purity? Might they do their own thing without regard for others? Did it mean anything to follow Christ? Each of these concerns was handled in proper theological order. The Christians' hearts were to be in submission to the lordship of Christ who is, indeed, Lord of creation and redemption. Equally, the Christians' focus was to be on the concerns of their Lord. "Things above" were to occupy believers' thoughts and energies. These two foundations work their way into life. Paul never excused careless living. He was supremely concerned with holiness and purity, and this section of the epistle develops these concerns with reference to individual Christians and the church.

The second part of the epistle falls into three logical groupings. Although uneven in both number of verses devoted to them and the lasting significance of the message, they each contribute to Paul's thought uniquely. The first section describes individual and corporate responsibilities (3:5-4:1). The second section exhorted the Colossians to be careful witnesses (4:2-9); and the third, finishes the epistle with miscellaneous greetings (4:10-18).

From a structural perspective alone, separate groupings are difficult to distinguish. From 3:5-4:6, Paul issued a series of commands, all of which seem to have equal weight. Thereafter, he sent various greetings. The command section contains at least fifteen commands. Four of these, based on the grammatical constructions of the passages, urged the Colossians to stop practices which were ongoing (3:5; 3:8; 3:9; 3:21), and eleven encouraged the cultivation of Christian attitudes in the individual or community. From a thematic or logical perspective, however, distinct groups of commands emerge. First, some encourage personal spiritual growth. These are: "put to death" (3:5), "put off" (KJV) or "you must rid yourselves" (3:8), "do not lie" (3:9), and "put on" (KJV) or "clothe yourselves" (3:12), "bear with each other and forgive whatever grievances you may have against one another" (3:13), "forgive" (3:13), and "put on love" (3:14). Paul used two pictures to organize these commands: death to life, and changing clothes.

The second group of commands is directed to the church (3:15-17). Twice Paul referred to characteristics that should always be present. In v. 15 Paul said, "Let the peace of Christ rule in your hearts"; and in v. 16 he said, "Let the word of Christ dwell in you richly." This smaller section describes the order God desires in the church.

The third group of commands concerns the family (3:18-4:1). These commands inform and encourage church members to submit to God's order in their homes. Ephesians 5:22-6:1 is similar to Col 3:18-4:1 and helps explain the Colossians passage.

Finally, a fourth group of commands relates to the ministry of the gospel (4:2-6). Although this group begins with Paul's desire that the church pray for him, it clearly stresses the collective witness in the world. Paul would have his opportunities for service; so would they. Although the format is the same, the subject changes from their *being* what was proper in God's economy to their *doing* what was proper in Christian witness. For that reason, 4:2-6 has a distinct place of its own.

1. Order in the Christian Life and the Church (3:5-4:1)

Here Paul's primary ethical concern surfaced. If the Colossians were not to live like those around them, how were they to live? In response to God's grace, they had specific duties. Three matters concerned Paul as he wrote this section of the epistle. He began with the personal dimensions of Christian order in the church. Soon his thoughts clearly had corporate meaning and application, and the personal aspects of Christian living were subordinated to the corporate responsibilities. The corporate aspects may be anticipated in vv. 13-14, but these responsibilities were developed in vv. 15-17. The third concern evident here is the family. Individual Christians must have Christian relationships in the home. There are interesting movements in these verses. Paul moved from theology to practice and from the individual to the group.

(1) The New Person (3:5-17)

⁵Put to death, therefore, whatever belongs to your earthly nature: sexual immorality, impurity, lust, evil desires and greed, which is idolatry. ⁶Because of these, the wrath of God is coming. ⁷You used to walk in these ways, in the life you once lived. ⁸But now you must rid yourselves of all such things as these: anger, rage, malice, slander, and filthy language from your lips. ⁹Do not lie to each other, since you have taken off your old self with its practices ¹⁰and have put on the new self, which is being renewed in knowledge in the image of its Creator. ¹¹Here there is no Greek or Jew, circumcised or uncircumcised, barbarian, Scythian, slave or free, but Christ is all, and is in all.

¹²Therefore, as God's chosen people, holy and dearly loved, clothe yourselves with compassion, kindness, humility, gentleness and patience. ¹³Bear with each other and forgive whatever grievances you may have against one another. Forgive as the Lord forgave you. ¹⁴And over all these virtues put on love, which binds them all together in perfect unity.

¹⁵Let the peace of Christ rule in your hearts, since as members of one body you were called to peace. And be thankful. ¹⁶Let the word of Christ dwell in you richly as you teach and admonish one another with all wisdom, and as you sing psalms, hymns and spiritual songs with gratitude in your hearts to God. ¹⁷And whatever you do, whether in word or deed, do it all in the name of the Lord Jesus, giving thanks to God the Father through him.

Paul's ethics grew out of a carefully constructed theology. In this first ethical portion, the theme of death and resurrection continues. As before, 2:20-3:4, Paul emphasized death with Christ as the beginning of change in a Christian's life (3:5). He then discussed the implications of being alive and involved in a living Christian community, the body of Christ. The implications of spiritual death and resurrection apply to specific life-styles which Paul explained with the metaphor of changing clothes. The new person deserves a new look. Two ideas, death/life and old/new, form the skeleton of this passage.

DISCARD VICES (3:5-11).   These verses specifically develop the theme "put to death." The theme seldom occurs in the Pauline Epistles, but it does occur in foundational passages. Along with its counterpart, the resurrection, it forms the basic theological underpinning for all ethical concerns of the Christian. The specific words "put to death" (*nekroun*) do not occur in any other Pauline passage.[1] They were no doubt used here because of the emphasis on death (2:11-12; 2:13; 2:20; 3:5).

The command to "put to death," thus emphasized, appears unnecessary. In the previous places in this epistle, Paul stated that the Christians did die with Christ and that reality becomes a part of the believers' experience at the time of salvation. Two matters emerge as interpretive concerns: Why did Paul give the command, and to what did it refer? As to the former, the command was necessary because of the nature of the death with Christ. It is a spiritual reality, but the experiential and psychological aspects of the believers' position in Christ must be worked out. Although the believers died with Christ, they seemed to be unaware of the specific implications of salvation and, therefore, unable to live the consecrated life so desired. That is the burden of Rom 6, the clearest parallel to Paul's thought here.

In Rom 6, the new situation of the believer is argued in detail. Beginning with identification with Christ in baptism (6:3ff.), Paul explained the way Christians overcome sin in their lives. For Paul, being dead to sin did not mean that persons did not sin. Three aspects of this truth speak to a life lived as dead to this world. They are logically identified in Rom 6. The first aspect is knowledge. Paul laid the foundation for Christian experience in knowledge. In regard to sin, the foundation is the knowledge of what Christ's death means regarding sin. When a believer accepts Christ, a death takes place. In the spiritual reality, the believer "went to the cross" with Christ, was buried with Christ, and arose a new person. That ended any obligation to sin and its demands. The first aspect of victory over sin is to know the reality of the Christian experience. Death with Christ is the foundation.[2]

Paul used experiential terms to explain the believer's death with Christ in Rom 6:5ff. The old self was crucified in order that sin might be rendered ineffective in the believer's life (Rom 6:6). Thus, the experiential aspects do not necessarily flow from knowledge of the truth. Paul continued the discussion by stating that a believer must present his members to Christ.[3] The fact is, persons

---

[1]Related terms, of course, do occur. Bultmann is perhaps correct in his assessment that the adjective occurs in the idea of baptism, and Paul's employment of it is for emphasis, attracted to the adjectival form. A related word, θανάτου, does occur (Rom 8:2). See R. Bultmann, *TDNT*, 4:892-94.

[2]There are, of course, many aspects and applications of the fact that Christians died with Christ. The one developed here and in Rom 6-8 is experiential. It confirms Paul's tendency to move from theology to Christian experience.

[3]The same term, "members," is used in the two contexts. They are used in different ways, however.

serve whom they obey (Rom 6:16). Naturally, Christians will be urged by the Holy Spirit to follow their conversion experience with such consecration, and for Paul and others in the New Testament, Christian growth verified the claim to be in Christ. Nevertheless, the steps of such commitment need explanation. The second aspect of Christians' death with Christ, therefore, is the experiential one. It is a stage of volition and commitment. The knowledge foundation calls for an action of the will. Christians must *choose* to live consistently with their spiritual experience.

The third aspect of experientially understanding the Christian's death with Christ is ability. Paul's theology moved to one more dimension of this subject. In addition to knowledge and will, there must be power. Committed, knowledgeable Christians need divine help to live differently. In Romans Paul spoke of the Holy Spirit who provides divine help for believers (8:1-11).[4] The Holy Spirit is not discussed directly in Colossians. The power comes from the church ministering effectively to itself: members serving and encouraging other members (3:15-17).

This brief overview of Paul's view of the doctrine "dead with Christ" clarifies the first question related to the command to "put to death." Why was the command necessary? The command was given because, though believers had died with Christ, the death of unchristian behavior was not necessarily an experiential reality. The theological aspects of the doctrine of dying with Christ were presented earlier (2:9-3:4). The practical aspects had to be explored.

Completely Kill Your Sinful Actions (3:5-7). Paul applied the doctrine by identifying lists of sins and Christian graces. These often are called vice and virtue lists. The first list of vices encompasses vv. 5-6. Paul identified five vices (v. 5) and reasons to leave them (v. 7).

3:5 Several scholars point out that moralists commonly used lists of fives to identify their moral concerns.[5] Some even point out further that the same sins are often mentioned by the secularists and the writers of Scripture. Christians are always called *at least* to the standards of morality of those who live around them. Their morality should exceed it. Paul's organization of thought was definitely Jewish in origin, the outworking of serious reflection on the Old Testament. Three lists of fives occur in this section, vv. 5,8,12.

In the first list of vices, Paul identified five sins which relate to personal actions. Four of them consistently refer elsewhere to sexual sins, to which he

---

[4] In following Paul's argument in Rom 5-8, it is particularly important to understand that Rom 6 speaks of the commitment process and the necessity of it. Romans 8, however, speaks of the effecting of the power actually sought. It is the Holy Spirit who accomplishes these matters in a Christian's life.

[5] See, e.g., E. Lohse, *Colossians and Philemon, Her* (Philadelphia: Fortress, 1971), 137. Perhaps too much is made of the parallel to the Iranian "Pentaschema" by many scholars. Whether it was a common convention of speech, Paul would certainly have organized his thoughts. There are many examples of that in his writings.

added a fifth, covetousness. He located these sins in the "members" (KJV; "whatever belongs to your earthly nature," NIV). The term "members" (*melē*) occurs more in the Pauline Epistles than in the rest of the New Testament.[6] The rabbis taught that there were 248 members (*melē*) of a person's body which were related to the 248 laws of the Torah.[7] In the LXX, the term occurs eight times and primarily describes the bodily parts of a sacrificed animal.[8] Each of these uses the term for physical parts of a whole body. In this type of ethical context, Rom 6 provides a paradigm. In Rom 6 the word refers to the parts of an individual Christian's body, the focus being on the physical body as an instrument of sin. In picturesque and graphic language, Paul warned about sin dominating in the body. Here, however, the word cannot be a reference to the physical body. These are actions, attitudes, and appearances. The word seems to cover more than the sexual sins listed. It refers equally to the sins identified later. Here, as elsewhere, Paul seems to have been referring generally to all facets of a person's being, identifying them as members. The unifying idea between the physical and attitudinal definitions of the term is that the members are agents through which persons express themselves. Their motivating force (sin or righteousness) finds expression through their members. Certainly people sin through the vehicle of the various parts of their make-up. Paul located sin within the individual and commanded that it be stopped there.

The five sexual sins always occur first or second in Paul's lists. They are first in 1 Cor 6:9; 6:18; Gal 5:19; Eph 5:5; 1 Thess 4:3. If another type of sin is named earlier in the list of vices, as in Rom 1, that sin is some form of idolatry. Paul's thought, therefore, moved from idolatry to immorality. Perhaps his thinking followed the two tables of the law. Positively, love for God and neighbor encapsulated the two sets of five commandments. Negatively, idolatry and immorality encapsulated these commandments. Certainly idolatry is the antithesis to having no other gods, and immorality is the blatant disregard of love for the neighbor. Lohse suggests that Paul mentioned sexual sins because they were the particular weakness of Gentiles. The typical Jewish polemic was that all Gentiles were idolaters and, thus, engaged in every vice.[9]

Although the four sins identified are sexual, they convey different ideas. "Fornication" ("sexual immorality," NIV; *porneia*), always first in Paul's lists of sexual sins, refers to illicit sexual intercourse. Sometimes it was used as a synonym for adultery, but different emphases are found. "Adultery" identifies sexual intercourse as the breaking of a covenant of marriage. The violation of an agreement makes the act even more distasteful and disrespectful.

---

[6]In actuality, μέλη occurs thirty-four times in the New Testament. It occurs twice in Matthew, three times in James, and twenty-nine times in the Pauline Epistles.

[7]J. Horst, *TDNT*, 4:559.

[8]*HatRed* 2:909.

[9]Lohse, 138. He quotes approvingly an insightful article by B. S. Easton, "New Testament Ethical Lists," *JBL* 51 (1932): 1-12.

"Fornication" generally refers to the act itself, without immediate regard for the contractual or promissory agreements.

Fornication was consistently forbidden in the Bible. It was the will of God that his people abstain from sexual immorality (1 Thess 4:3) since no one whose life-style was characterized by sexual immorality would inherit the kingdom of God (1 Cor 6:9). It was the legitimate cause for divorce (Matt 5:32; "unfaithfulness," NIV). Apparently it came first in Paul's lists because it not only expressed an intensely personal sin of self-indulgence but also became the focus of a group of sins with which it normally occurs. Such is the case here.

"Uncleanness" (KJV; "impurity," NIV; *akatharsia*) often follows fornication. It refers to a general impurity. In its normal sexual context, it seems to refer to the defiling that comes in connection with fornication. "Uncleanness" was also common in the Gentile world. Many religious teachers in the first century sought women converts for sexual reasons. Once, Paul defended the source, content, and motive of his message and action against a charge of uncleanness (1 Thess 2:3-4). That same spirit was to characterize the Colossians.

The next two words belong together. "Lust" (*epithymia*) and "passions" (*pathos*) or "evil desires," as translated in the NIV, generally refer to strong desires gone bad. Although the word can, on occasion, be used of an honorable desire (1 Tim 3:1), the normal use is negative. It refers most often to the misdirected fulfillment of bodily appetites, usually sexual appetites. A passion is uncontrolled and habitual lust. When lust goes unchecked, a passion for what is forbidden arises. Habits are formed which feed each other. Lust encourages passion, and passion produces more perverted lust.

The clearest Pauline relationship between the two words occurs in Rom 1:24-26. Enumerating successive stages in pagan movement away from God, Paul began with lust (1:24). God gave them up in their lust to unlawful and irregular affection. The second stage is more intense. There Paul stated that "passions" dominate (1:26). The sins he described there he associated with more intensive sexual lust. When this passage in Colossians is compared to Romans, it seems clear that passions are the second, more intense stage, and lust is the first.

The last member of the first list is "greed" (NIV) or "covetousness" (KJV; *pleonexia*). At first sight, it seems to be out of place for two reasons. First, it is not a sexual sin. Second, it is modified by a clause and none of the others are. These two indications make it remarkable in this context. It is the longing for something that belongs to someone else or placing supreme value on something not (yet) possessed. As used in this context, it is a serious sin; and Paul no doubt included it because it is, in kind, the same as sexual sin. It represents a strong movement of desire toward something out of God's will at the time.

The modifying clause identifies "covetousness" as idolatry. Two aspects of the construction modify the word. It is introduced in the Greek text with the definite article, and it has a relative clause following it ("which is idolatry"). Some have pointed to the article before "covetousness" and drawn the conclusion that Paul referred to a specific kind of covetousness, i.e., the kind which is idolatry. That opens the door to manifold suggestions as to which kind of covetousness he had in mind. Nothing in Paul's writing or the New Testament generally helps distinguish one covetousness from another. The article is employed because it identifies. The article often is found in situations where modifying clauses further define the noun.[10] Both the clause ("which is idolatry") and the article in the Greek text (though left untranslated in NIV and other English translations) build a case for the definiteness of the noun.

Paul never subdivided covetousness into smaller categories. That seems strange since Exod 20:17 explicitly explains what not to covet.[11] Covetousness is the only commandment so explained. Perhaps this was done in the Old Testament because covetousness is a basically undefined sin—each person could be left to his own interpretation. Here Paul defined the nature of the sin, but he did not explain it by application as Moses did. He stated it is idolatry. Thus greed places something or someone (see Exod 20: "neighbor's house," "neighbor's wife," etc.) ahead of God. That is not likely to be done overtly since society frowns upon it, but subtly and easily other things take the glory God demands for himself.

The identification of covetousness with idolatry reveals an important Pauline perspective regarding the law. While writing this list, he seems to have had the Ten Commandments in mind, mentioning most of the last five. Covetousness is number ten. Significantly, number ten equals number one, having no other gods beside God. Although the ten are divided into love for God and love for neighbor,[12] little distinction can be made between the two lists. If number ten, covetousness, is actually a violation of number one, idolatry, they are all of the same character. None is to be perceived as a purely physical act toward another person. They are all spiritual. Thus for Paul, the Commandments instructed about relations with neighbors. Breaking a Commandment toward a neighbor is, in reality, breaking a commandment against God himself.[13]

These five, therefore, are sins of personal aggression. The individual who commits them thinks more of himself than he does of others. For Paul, sexual

---

[10] See BDF, 258, 1. They argued that the relative clause calls for the article defining the noun. The preceding noun is thus made definite.

[11] There five types of covetousness are identified: the neighbor's wife, house, servants, asses, and anything that is the neighbor's. Even the Old Testament, however, does not subdivide for purposes of identifying different kinds of covetousness. It subdivides for clear application since this is in many ways the most undefined of sins.

[12] By Jesus, Jews before Jesus, and Paul.

[13] Other Scriptures warn about this practice. James at least twice warned that speaking against a neighbor or criticizing a neighbor speaks against the law (Jas 4:11). He went even further. He stated that such activity speaks against God who both made all persons in his image and gave the law for the sanctity of life.

sin harmed the individual himself—it was a sin against one's own body (1 Cor 6:18); it ruins relationships; it contributes to autonomy—the anti-God spirit; and it represents a lack of self-control. These all characterize the old self.

Paul gave two additional reasons Christians should never practice these sins. They bring the wrath of God (v. 6), and they characterized the former life (v. 7).

3:6 Paul warned that such sins incur the wrath of God. The NIV phrase "because of these" picks up the Greek text clearly.[14] It recalls the list of sins which Paul called "members" and which he instructed them to put to death. The reference to wrath called to mind the future judgment day which, in the spirit of the prophets, Paul identified as already coming. It was, and is, in process. Consistently in the New Testament the day of eschatological judgment is in view.

God's wrath is a theme which occurs in both the Old and New Testaments. Some scholars, in the spirit of Marcion of the second century, claim that wrath is an unworthy description of God. They say it is an Old Testament concept associated with God the Father rather than the merciful Christ. L. Morris, however, points out that the concept of God's wrath is a frequent New Testament theme.[15] The clearest description of it occurs in Rom 1-3; 5:6-11. It is not primarily an emotion, though emotional elements surface since all of God's being is set in motion in the expression of each attribute. Primarily, his wrath is the active reaction of his nature against all that is contrary to his nature. It is a recoiling of God's entire being. It has logical and volitional elements and primarily expresses God's judgment on people. Significantly, it generally occurs at the end of the sin lists in Paul's writings.[16]

In recent times, much discussion centered on where Paul learned his lists of sins. Some interpreters see Paul's lists as evidence that lists circulated in the first century and that they were modified by Paul for specific situations.[17] Others have pointed out that the lists in Paul's writings are far too varied to follow any specific pattern.[18] Most likely G. Cannon is correct in stating that the common tie is the tendency for making lists.[19] Of the many lists of vices

---

[14] The Greek is διά plus the plural accusative.

[15] L. Morris, *The Apostolic Preaching of the Cross* (London: Tyndale, 1955), 179-84.

[16] E.g., 1 Thess 4:3-6; 1 Cor 5:10-11; 6:9; Rom 1:18-32.

[17] Thus F. D. Gealy, "The 1st and 2nd Epistles to Timothy and the Epistle to Titus," *IB*, who states, "The list was a floating list of vices currently available and easily adaptable to the writer's purposes, a whiplash of stinging words of the sort that any orator of the time well understood where to get and how to use" (497-498). Lohse relates Paul's lists to the Iranian "Pentaschema" so well-known to all philosophers of the day (137). Easton, 1-12, indicates that this was a list modified to fit concrete situations.

[18] See, e.g., N. McEleney, "The Vice Lists of the Pastoral Epistles," *CBQ* 36 (1974), 204; E. F. Scott, *The Pastoral Epistles*, MNTC (London: Hodder & Stoughton, 1936), 119; and G. Cannon, *The Use of Traditional Materials in Colossians* (Macon, Ga.: Mercer, 1983), 58.

[19] Cannon, 59.

and virtues in the New Testament,[20] Eph 4:31; 5:3-5 parallel Col 3:5-11. Significantly for Paul's discussion here, the most common evils Paul identified in these lists are fornication (eight times) and idolatry (five times).[21] These sins were regarded by Jews as typically Gentile sins. These two sins best represent the unlawful lists of the two tables of Commandments, idolatry toward God and fornication toward persons.

3:7 The second reason not to sin is that such sins represent a non-Christian outlook. These sins used to characterize the Colossians. Now different attitudes and actions should characterize them. Paul's commendation of their current situation affirmed who they were in Christ and provided a reason not to continue in sin. They were Christians. They should do better. Although Paul expected them to do better, he realized that even as Christians they could sin.

Completely Conquer Your Sinful Attitudes (3:8). **3:8** Paul's attention turned to the Colossians themselves.[22] His address included a further description of particular sins.[23] The sins are mentioned in a group of five. In contrast to the former list, this list is more social in nature. These sins destroy social relationships and are more expressive of attitudes than specific actions. The five are: "anger" (*orgēn*), "rage" (*thymon*), "malice" (*kakian*), "slander" (*blasphēmian*), and "filthy language" (*aischrologian*). Perhaps Paul assumed that the Colossian Christians would have conquered already the temptations regarding sexual sin in v. 5.[24] At least they had a conscience. Since the new life is to be lived corporately with all Christians, positive Christian social relationships are mandatory. These five, then, are mentioned not so much because they are more typical of Christians than of non-Christians, but because they are necessary to harmonious relationships in the body of Christ. Respect for all persons should characterize all Christians, but there must be a special regard for the church.

Completely Control Your Sinful Appearances (3:9-11). Lying was the next matter Paul addressed. Typically, Paul presented his concern and included a reason for it. Although the pattern consistently occurs, this last example differs in that only one sin is mentioned, lying. Perhaps it is sufficiently grievous in

---

[20]The lists of vices includes: Rom 1:24,26; 1:29-31; 13:13; 1 Cor 5:10,11; 6:9-10; 2 Cor 12:20; Gal 5:19-21; Eph 4:31; 5:3-5; 1 Tim 1:9,10; 6:4,5; 2 Tim 3:2-5; Titus 3:3; 1 Pet 2:1; 4:3,4; Jude 8,16; Rev 9:20,21; 21:8; 22:15. The lists of virtues includes: Matt 5:3-11; 2 Cor 6:6,7; Gal 5:22-23; Eph 6:14-17; Phil 4:8; 1 Tim 3:2,3; 6:11; Titus 1:7,8; Jas 3:17; 2 Pet 1:5-7. These lists exclude Colossians. They come from ibid., 54-60.

[21]Ibid., 59.

[22]This section is reminiscent of Eph 2:1ff., where Paul identified the readers with the sins he denounced.

[23]His introduction to v. 8 is "but now" (νυνὶ δὲ), reminiscent of Eph 2:13 where it marks a contrast between the former life and the present. In Colossians, it serves to make this contrast but continues to identify an attitude of the new person, the one converted from the old ways to the new.

[24]This may be a reasonable assumption, but the evidence from Corinthians and Thessalonians may lead to a different appraisal.

itself to be mentioned alone. Further, unlike the other lists which include various groupings of the Ten Commandments as the rationale, this one addresses only one Commandment, the Fifth. Even further, this sin represents the ultimate violation of trust. No community can exist without its members telling the truth.

This particular command seems to continue what has preceded and to introduce what follows. Its form differs from the previous commands, which were simple prohibitions: "put to death" (3:5) and "put away" (3:8, KJV). This one, however, is to stop a practice. It comes with the insertion of the negative so that it reads "do not be lying" to one another. Thus, the grammar of the text suggests something different about this sin.[25] A further distinctive is that it introduces a lengthy rationale about why such behavior is inappropriate. There is a new self in Christ, and a new value system prevails. This command introduces a slightly new direction of thought.

At the same time, the command continues the thrust of the passage. Paul presented two lists of sins to avoid, and he continued with this one major concern. Surely it is as characteristic of the old life as the other ten. Paul stated as much in his rationale which, in essence, developed the rationale of v. 7 to new insights. Here, as in the previous verses, Paul presented a basic command and a reason for the command.

3:9a Understanding how this command, as it stands, related to a Christian group is difficult. Was lying a particularly prominent sin at Colosse? If so, about what were they lying? The passage gives no specific information about these matters. The command seems to speak to more than verbal lying. It recalls all falsehood, whether by actions or words. Perhaps the church had a hypocritical or deceptive element in it. Perhaps the false teachers employed a tactic of deception regarding Paul and the gospel of grace. Perhaps the command is always appropriate for Christians without regard for specific situations which prompt it. In the command, two matters are clear. First, this command is of singular importance in the way it is expressed. Second, the Christian community is to be characterized by truth and truthfulness. All lying belongs with the old self who is gone.

The reason for this command has two aspects, although they occur as one part of the text. The basic reason is the Christian's new character, the new self. The presence of the new self has broad implications for all of life, particularly to personal values. Here Paul had a specific characteristic of the new self in mind. In v. 11 Paul described the new self as a place "where" there are

---

[25] The first two commands of the section are aorist imperatives; this one is a present imperative. This command also has the negative, placing it in a different class grammatically and perhaps, therefore, in Paul's mind as well. Paul's three groups of vices are paralleled by three groups of virtues. The virtues get progressively shorter, ending with one—the primacy of love. Perhaps in Paul's mind they contrast, lying uniquely representing the negative; love uniquely representing the positive Christian attribute.

no distinctions among persons. Therefore, the two sections are the Christian's new character, vv. 9b-10, and the Christian's new values, v. 11.[26]

3:9b-10   Three verbs in these verses describe Christian character. The first two look back to the time of salvation; the third looks to the present process of renewal. In the metaphorical language of changing clothes, Paul explained that the old self had been put off, the new self had been put on, and the new self was in process of growth toward a new goal. The three dimensions presented describe a Christian's standing before the Lord. Several aspects of this demand comment: the definition of old self/new self, the time of the change from one to the other, the process of growth, and the ultimate goal.

The definition of the old self and the new self is crucial to a proper understanding of Christian experience. Sometimes interpreters understand them as synonymous with an old nature and a new nature. Actually, there is little in Scripture about the "natures" of a Christian person, though there are many descriptions about the Christian's new actions, desires, and values. To equate the terms old self/new self with natures goes beyond acceptable evidence. The terms are never used psychologically at all. They are historical. The old self and new self are never described as coexisting in anyone. One replaces the other. Finally, the old self is never a proper description of a believer. A believer is a totally new person.

Paul used the terms old self/new self in three important texts: Eph 4:20-24; Col 3:9-11; Rom 6:6. The closest parallel to this passage is Eph 4:20-24, although the actual constructions which express the concept vary somewhat. The Romans passage contains the most extensive explanation of the relationships between the two. It is worth noting that the term for "old" in "old self" (*palaios*) occurs in all three passages, but there are two different terms for "new" (*kainos*, Eph 4:24; *neos*, Col 3:10; omitted in Rom). The term "old" (*palaios*) basically means "old in years, or belonging to the past."[27] The terms for "new" mean *new in time* (*neos*) or *new in quality* (*kainos*). The distinction between them fades in specific contexts, and there seems to be significant overlap between the two terms in Ephesians and Colossians.

The use of the terms helps determine the meaning. First, the time element helps. In Rom 6:6 Paul explained that the old self was crucified at the time of salvation. That parallels Col 3:10, which says that they put off the old self. Ephesians uses a different grammatical construction,[28] but the meaning

---

[26]From a structural perspective, only one reason is provided. All of this section is subordinate to the participle "having put on" (ἐνδυσάμενοι). From a thematic perspective, however, the adverbial clause beginning with "where" (ὅπου) provides a second reason by describing an essential attribute of the Christian's person.

[27]*BAGD*, 605-06.

[28]In Col 3:10 Paul used aorist participles, showing an action antecedent to the time of the main verb, which is present. Clearly since both the putting off and putting on are both past, it seems Paul stated what he did in Romans. Ephesians, however, employs aorist infinitives, in which the

remains the same. Second, the exclusive nature of the terms helps. In each of the three primary passages, both the old self and the new self stand alone. The old goes so the new can appear. Since the new replaces the old, they do not coexist.

This usage points to a clear definition. The old self is the pre-Christian state. The new self is the Christian state of the believer. The terms are descriptive and historical, not psychological. In other words, Paul used the term "old self" as synonymous with unregenerate, while "new self" pointed to conversion and regeneration. The psychological definition seeks to attribute sin in the life of the believer to the old self. Those who take that view tend to speak of both old self and new self as present together. They say that people sin because of the domination of the old self over the new. Paul did not use that terminology. Consistently for him, the old self did not exist in the believer. The believer will sin, but that is not attributed to the old self. Sin happens because of the imperfect process of growth in the new self.

The second concern was the *time of the change* from old to new. According to Rom 6:6, the change occurred at the time of baptism into Christ, conversion. Ephesians and Colossians suggest the same time sequence. The task for believers is to stop living like the old self and to develop actions in accord with the new self.

The third concern is the *process of growth*. Paul wrote in both Ephesians and Colossians of the new self being renewed. In Ephesians, the order of presentation is: having put off the old, being renewed, and to put on the new (4:20-24). In Colossians, the order is: having put off the old, having put on the new, being renewed. The difference is one of perspective. Paul stressed the initial introduction to Christianity to the Ephesians. They learned that they would grow into a new person, and the putting on of the new self was seen as the culmination of growth. In other words, they would look like the new self. They would have maturity.[29] Paul took the Colossians back to their conversion experience, where the change he described had already occurred. They were in a process of growth in the new self.

In both passages, Paul used the term "renewed" (NASB). It describes the process of change in the salvation experience. In Col 3:10 he made it clear that the goal of renewal is the image of the Creator. What was lost in the fall into sin is gained through the application of grace. Through this process of renewal, individuals corrupted by Adam can gain what Adam lost for himself and his offspring.

---

antecedent time frame is not clear. The context shows that Paul expressed the same concept. It points the Ephesian Christians *back* to the time they learned Christ, recalling what they knew at that time. They learned then "to put off" the old and "to put on" the new. It was a part of their initial orientation to Christ. Thus, in all three passages, there is agreement in the time of this action.

[29] Paul stressed maturity in Ephesians, especially in chpt. 4.

The next concern is the *goal of growth*. Paul described it in 3:10. The goal is knowledge. Knowledge was a preoccupation of the false teachers. Paul stressed knowledge (*epignōsis*), genuine knowledge attained through Christ in the process of renewal. This is progressive, not instantaneous. It comes through Christ, not some other flash of insight as, perhaps, the false teachers were saying at Colosse. This genuine knowledge is of the Creator. Paul used the language found in the creation accounts. Specifically, the term "image" is significant. People were created in the image of God. That image was marred when they sinned. Through conversion and growing in Christlikeness, believers are renewed "according to the image" of God. The measurement of growth is the restored image of God in people.[30]

Paul stated in 3:10 that Christians grow in the image of the Creator. According to Gen 1-2, God the Father is the Creator. According to this epistle, Christ is the Creator (1:16; see also John 1:1-2; Heb 1:1-3). The witness of Scripture is that God the Father planned creation and God the Son brought it into existence. Creation may be attributed to both or either. A second matter related to the creation is whether Paul spoke of the creation of humanity or the creation of the new self. In Eph 4:24, he stated that the creation was in righteousness and holiness. Although that may refer to the creation of new creatures, the church, the terms most naturally call to mind the creation of the world. Genesis 1-2 speaks of the original creation as holy and able to walk and talk with God, though the exact terms of Ephesians are not found there.

Who, then, is the object of growth? Paul normally explained that Christ is the measure of the Christian's growth. In the parallel account, Eph 4:24, God is the one who created. In Ephesians, Christ is the measure of the fullness of stature (4:13). Further, Paul stated in Col 1:15 that Christ is the image (*eikōn*) of God, and here he stated that the goal of renewal is to be in the image (*eikōn*) of the Creator. The goal is to be like God, and that is accomplished by being like Christ.[31]

One final concern in the passage is the prominence of knowledge. Paul explained that the knowledge was of the renewed image of God in the believer. Knowledge is essential to the process. This statement recalls the frequency of references to the mind in Scripture. One of the clearest statements of it is Rom 12:1-2 where Paul located the growth of a Christian in the "renewing of the mind." Thus, knowledge is a significant component of Christian growth. Knowledge is produced as one walks in the will of God (1:9-11), is transformed by the power of God, and is the restoration of the image of God once distorted by sin.

---

[30] From a grammatical perspective, it is significant that the phrase here is κατ᾽ εἰκόνα, suggesting a standard of measurement.

[31] Cf., e.g., Rom 8:29 where the goal of God's working in the believer is to be like God's Son.

3:11 Paul moved from character to values. This section is still governed by the command to stop lying to one another. In contrast, the church was to accept each other regardless of the artificial distinctions imposed by an earthly perspective. These distinctions typified the old self's way of thinking. The new self thinks differently.

Paul identified several categories of artificial distinction. The first is national or ethnic pride: Gentile versus Jew. The division between these two groups was common in the New Testament, especially where the church contained a large Jewish element. The division occurred in the argument of 1 Cor 1:22, for example, where the church was on Greek soil. But why was the word "Greek" used in reference to church members in Asia? Apparently the division was generally accepted in the Greco-Roman world, as is evidenced by Paul's employing it in his letter to the Romans (1:16-17, NASB). The second category speaks to religious heritage or the lack of it: circumcision versus uncircumcision. Apart from the fact that the circumcision issue became the distinguishing element of diverse theologies (e.g., Galatians), the reason for identifying people in this manner must have been to call to mind their religious backgrounds. The third category is culture: Barbarian and Scythian. These two were particularly noted for cruel behavior and generally uncivilized actions. Since both groups were known for their similar behavior,[32] this is a point of comparison, not contrast. The final category is economic: slave or free.[33] The Colossian church apparently had both slaves and free in its composition, if both Onesimus and Philemon were members.

In contrast to these artificial, earthly distinctions, Paul said, "Christ is all, and in all" (3:11b). The new distinction is Christian/non-Christian, rather than nationality, race, religious background, or economic distinctions. This is the only time in the Pauline literature that the phrase "all and in all" occurs. Three times, however, the phrase "all in all" occurs, either with God or Christ as the subject. In 1 Cor 12:6, Paul spoke of the administration of spiritual gifts. Noting the differences of operations, he stated that God is the one who works "all in all." It seemed to be his way of saying God is totally in charge. In 1 Cor 15:28, Paul described the end of this age. Christ will subdue everything, then "God will be all in all." Paul meant that everything will be focused on God himself, whereas previously each member of the Godhead has had his own focus. In heaven there will be a collective adoration of God. In Eph 1:23, the church is called the "fullness of him who fills everything in every way." The one who fills "all in all" is Christ, and the description relates to his totality of presence.

---

[32] See Josephus, *Antiquities* II:269, who identified the Scythians as especially cruel barbarians.

[33] The Greek text makes clear divisions between the first two categories by inserting an "and" (καί) between them. The last four, however, are separated only by commas. Paul's cryptic style surfaces here. It seems best to understand that he conceived of the four as in two contrasting groups. The definitions support that.

Here in Col 3:11 it speaks of Christ being the total concern, preoccupation, and environment of the Christian. Like the other occurrences of the phrase, it speaks to the totality of his presence, in contrast to the other distinctions of purely human designation.

DEVELOP VIRTUES (3:12-17). Continuing the metaphor of changing clothes, Paul turned to the new look of the believer. The introductory command uses the word "put on" (NASB) or "clothe" (NIV), which is the same word found in 3:10 (*endyō*). Paul had said the believers had put on the new self. Now he said they were to put on specific characteristics of the Christian; presumably these are characteristics of the new self. This represents the tension between the position and practice of the believer. The Christian is a new self, but he must learn to act like it.

Three commands form the structural backbone of this text. The first, found in 3:12, is clothe yourselves with Christian characteristics. The second, in 3:15, commands the church to let the peace of Christ rule in it. The third, in 3:16, urges the church to let the word of Christ dwell in its midst. Paul moved from the individual and personal characteristics to corporate commands. He began with individuals, but he spoke to the church at large before the end of these verses.[34] The three commands call for three divisions of thought corresponding to them. First, Paul addressed social relationships in the church (3:12-14). Second, Paul spoke to harmony in the church (3:15). Finally, he called for the freedom for the word of God in the Christian community (3:16-17).

Social Relationships in the Church (3:12-14). Every social group has its problems, and the church is no exception. Paul, therefore, called the Colossians individually first and then collectively to be characterized by Christian graces which enhance their relationships. He began with individual qualities (3:12), moved to interpersonal qualities (3:13), and concluded with one indispensable quality (3:14).

3:12 The new clothing of the Christian begins with personal attributes: compassion, kindness, humility, meekness, and patience. Their inclusion suggests the need for long-suffering with others in the group. The entire context is slanted toward harmony in the church. Since the letter does not reveal a problem in the church, either these are always appropriate or they addressed a problem otherwise unknown to the modern reader. Significantly, Paul focused on the individual who is to have patience, rather than the one who caused a problem. The place to begin in any group tension is with oneself rather than others.

---

[34] On the one hand, v. 12 seems clearly to be directed toward individuals in the congregation. On the other hand, v. 16 is clearly to the group. Paul built a case from the individual to the corporate entity. Like all collective commands, since the group only functioned when the individuals did, all commands had both personal and corporate application.

3:13 These five attributes are followed by two others of the same type: enduring ("Bear with each other," NIV) and forgiving. Enduring speaks to the practice of other Christian characteristics. Some believers in the church were being offended by the actions of others. The terms called the believers to a high standard of personal action when offended. "Enduring" is putting up with others even when they fail or act differently from what is expected. "Forgiving" is based on the root word for "grace." It carries the idea of a free forgiveness, perhaps because of grace. These two qualities were linked in Paul's mind as they often are in practice.

They are especially appropriate when one is offended. The text says, "whatever grievances you may have against one another." It obviously speaks to the offended party, not the offending one. It may be that the offending person had little, if any, awareness of what he had done. The offended should take initiative in enduring and forgiving, rather than waiting for the offender to apologize. By enduring and forgiving, the conscience is cleansed and the matter forgotten. The burden is lifted, and the offended can think and act like Christ even toward the offender. Harboring resentment and ill will toward another does little good, and to do so is beneath Christians. Anyone can hold grudges, but the mark of Christians is that they do not. They forgive regardless. The pattern for this behavior is Christ's forgiving the believer. The term used here for forgiveness, *charizomai*, is the same that occurs in the command to the believer. Many parallels may be drawn. Most importantly, however, Paul spoke of the gracious act of Christ by which he initiated forgiveness of sins before confession occurred. The model stands as a constant challenge to believers.

3:14 Paul singled out one characteristic above all others: love. The term chosen is the most frequent in the New Testament, *agapē*. Consistently it describes God's love, as well as the love Christians should have for God, the world, and each other. Like the Old Testament and Jesus, Paul advocated love as the fulfillment of the Mosaic law. It contrasts with the immorality of 3:5, which characterizes blatant lawbreakers.

Two qualifications reveal the primacy of love. First, Paul urged the Colossians to put on love above all these other things. It was uniquely important to their social well-being. Perhaps he had in mind a specific expression of love since he used the definite article (in the Greek text, but not translated in NIV) with it, which would otherwise be unnecessary.[35] Second, Paul stated that love uniquely tied them together. The NIV says, "which binds . . . all together in perfect unity" (3:14). The expression means that mutual love would bring the group to perfection. In parallel of Eph 3:14-19 (esp. vv. 17-18), Paul expressed his conviction that the many dimensions of love could be understood only by

---

[35] The definite article serves to specify that the quality is one of a specific type. The attribute could stand alone, as do the others previously listed (except covetousness). The others are anarthrous.

observing its operation in the group. By this expression Paul meant that the love would bind them together unto completeness.[36]

Harmony in the Church (3:15). **3:15** The second command called the church to harmony. The peace of Christ was to rule in the believers' hearts. Peace is a common expression in the Pauline literature. It occurs regularly in prayers and the opening salutations of Paul's epistles. When employed, it carries with it all of the meaning of the Hebrew *shalom*, a general sense of well-being and prosperity. It is the quiet disposition which arises when people are committed to the lordship of Christ in their midst. Although the peace is generally an individual matter, in this case the church was addressed. Paul advocated that peace guide all its collective activities. Thus, rather than a command for personal peace, this one stresses harmony in the group, as the rest of the verse demands. The basis of this peace was the work of Christ, as Paul made clear in Eph 2:1-10.

Significantly, Paul urged the Colossians to let the peace "of Christ" rule in their midst. Perhaps recalling the words of Jesus (John 14:27), Paul extended the meaning to its social dimensions. Normally when Paul discussed peace, he prayed for peace in the believers' experience. Most of the time, the prayer for peace occurred in the Pauline salutations. All the letters contain it. In all but two of the salutations, Paul stated that peace came jointly from God and the Lord Jesus Christ.[37] Four other times he spoke of peace coming from God without a reference to Christ.[38] This is the only place that Paul spoke of the granting of peace as an activity of Christ alone.[39] The usage clearly reveals that Paul conceived of God the Father and Jesus as having the same level of authority. It reveals his high estimation of Christ, who does what God does. Even though he is not present physically on this earth, faith in him continues to be the answer to a troubled disposition as it was when he was on earth (John 14:1). Though

---

[36]The word "completeness" is τελειότητος in Greek and has the basic idea of bringing things to an appropriate and logical end. The interpretation given takes the form as an objective genitive, i.e., bond that is directed toward perfection, with which many agree (see, e.g., W. Hendriksen, *Colossians and Philemon*, NTC [Grand Rapids: Baker, 1964], 158-159). Others understand this as a genitive of description, meaning something like "the perfect bond." F. F. Bruce takes the expression to mean the bond that ties the list of virtues together perfectly (*Commentary on the Epistles to the Ephesians and the Colossians*, NIC (Grand Rapids: Eerdmans, 1957), 281). In light of the Ephesian parallel, however, it seems best to take it the other way. Additionally, Paul never stated that love was a binding force between virtues such as this.

[37]The references are: Rom 1:7; 1 Cor 1:3; 2 Cor 1:2; Gal 1:3; Eph 1:2; Phil 1:2; 2 Thess 1:2; 1 Tim 1:2; 2 Tim 1:2; Titus 1:4; Phlm 3. The two Pauline Epistles that do not associate peace with God the Father and Jesus Christ jointly are 1 Thessalonians and Colossians. As might be expected, each of these has a variant reading which includes Christ. These, however, are not as well attested and may be explained as accommodations to the typical Pauline pattern.

[38]These passages are: Rom 5:1; 1 Cor 7:15; Phil 4:7; Col 1:2.

[39]The genitive expression could mean "the peace appropriate to Christ," that is, "a Christian peace." If so, that would be unusual for Paul. He probably means a peace from him should guide the worship functions of the church (including decision-making).

Paul did not begin this epistle by stating that Jesus gives peace, this is the only time it occurs apart from identifying God with it.

The peace is to "rule" in the congregation. The term for "rule" is often translated "umpire." That was its original use and may well be the meaning here. However, the term became associated more broadly with any judgment to be made.[40] The fact is, the congregation was to do nothing without the peace of Christ as the environment which overshadowed the action. Such peace also gave a sense of validation to the activities of the church. The specific place of rule was in the believers' "hearts." In typical fashion for the Old Testament and often for the New, the term signifies the general core of one's being. It is the decision-making and valuing aspect of persons.[41] Since the term is plural and distributive, the heart of each member is implied. The individual hearts had to be at peace for the congregation to be at peace.

The reason for such peace is that the believers were called into one body. The corporate interpretation, therefore, makes sense. The spiritual environment of each believer is the one body which they all share. Paul's rationale for peace was "since as members of one body you were called to peace."[42] Apparently the body is the body of Christ (1:18) in which each believer is placed at conversion. Often Paul spoke of the centrality of love in the congregation (Phil 1:9-11; Eph 3:12-17), now he spoke of peace. Apparently the work of the false teachers posed a threat to the thinking and the harmony of the congregation itself. Paul believed that the peace of Christ would keep them on the proper path in their quest for the truth.

Paul ended this exhortation with the command to become thankful. Colossians contains many references to thankfulness.[43] This particular word, however, does not occur elsewhere in the New Testament. The Colossians were to become thankful persons. The combination of thankfulness and peace is a logical one. Generally a lack of peace results from self-seeking or dissatisfaction with things as they are. Thankfulness points one to the realization that all things are provided in Christ. There is no room for ill will or bitterness if thankfulness prevails. The epistle provides ample reasons for thankfulness.

Freedom of the Word of God (3:16-17). The structure of this final command of the section parallels the previous verse advocating harmony in the church. Each verse has a primary verb. The conjunction "and," which seems to be more of a connective than a conjunctive idea, joins the two verbs. The rich indwelling of the word of Christ is parallel to the statement that everything should be done in the name of Christ. The rather lengthy explanation of the word of Christ indwelling parallels Ephesians and may be subdivided into two groups. The

---

[40] *BAGD*, 146.

[41] J. Behm, *TDNT*, 3:611-13.

[42] C. F. D. Moule, *The Origin of Christology* (Cambridge: University Press, 1977), 76.

[43] The verb is found in 1:3,12; 3:17. The noun occurs in 2:7 and 4:2. This is the only occurrence of the adjective εὐχάριστος in the entire New Testament.

prepositional phrases "with all wisdom" and "in grace" ("with gratitude," NIV) introduce these two groups.[44]

3:16 The word of Christ was the focus of the congregation. Some understand the phrase "word of Christ" to refer to the word that comes from Christ. The parallel with 3:15 suggests that possibility.[45] Since peace comes from Christ, the word that comes should also be from him. There are, however, few parallels to the word of Christ as a continuing dynamic force in the church. The Colossians were to look back to the words of Christ, not within or ahead to the words Christ would speak. This phrase is best understood as the word *about Christ*.[46] The community was constantly to recognize the reason for its existence by a continual concern for the gospel message and its implications in the congregation. While some understand this to refer to the indwelling of the word in the individual life, the text moves to a corporate expression in the modifying statements. This most likely refers to the words "in you," although individuals certainly had to make sure it was in them as well.

Colossians and Ephesians differ in this context. Because of the close parallels between Col 3:16-17 and Eph 5:18-21, the two passages speak to the same general concern. Colossians says, "Let the word of Christ dwell in you," whereas Ephesians has, "Be filled with the Spirit." Both of these result in the same or similar activities which follow in both texts. Therefore, Colossians should be interpreted in similar fashion with Ephesians, even though the terminology differs. If these are two sides of a coin, so to speak, the focus on the gospel message equals the importance of the filling of the Spirit, and they both result in the same things.[47] The entire context points to the freedom of the word

---

[44] Punctuation variations in the Greek text and the correlating translations influence this last point. In support of the interpretation given here for "in all wisdom" are: NGT, ASV, RSV, among others. Among those who see the phrase as completing what preceded are: WH, KJV, RV, and TR. In support of the interpretation of "in grace" are: the KJV, RV, and ASV. Those who make no clear choice here are: TR, NGT, RSV and others. The reasons for taking the phrases as introducing the following participles are primarily the balance in the text as this occurs; the parallel with Eph 5:19ff., which places commas before the primary verbal ideas which parallel Colossians; and the parallel expression in Col 1:28 in which the phrase "in all wisdom" clearly goes with these words.

[45] Among them, Bruce, 283, and J. B. Lightfoot, *St. Paul's Epistle to the Philippians*, reprint ed. (Grand Rapids: Zondervan, 1953), 222.

[46] So, Hendriksen, 160, says, "The objective, special revelation that proceeds from (and concerns) Christ—"the Christ-word"—should govern every thought, word, and deed."

[47] Ephesians contains ample evidence to suggest that Paul was not speaking of the filling of the Holy Spirit in the believer's life. While he might have been speaking of such filling, several factors suggest otherwise: the construction differs from all the other occasions of describing the filling of the Spirit (which all occur in Luke and Acts); many doubt whether the Holy Spirit is designated in Eph 5:18; and, the parallel in Colossians says nothing about the Holy Spirit. Commentators who take that position argue that the human spirit is to be filled by the activity of the group in encouraging each other. At the least, there is no reason the Ephesians passage should be considered normative over the Colossians passage in Christian experience. As noted in the text, because of the parallels, it seems Paul had the same goal and means in mind.

to determine the actions, motivations, and decisions of the group. It, like the peace of God, becomes a measure of church life. Before every activity, the church should answer two questions: Is the peace of Christ present in the congregation at this point? and Is this consistent with, and will it promote knowledge of, the word of Christ?

Certain activities encourage the freedom of the word of Christ. These occur in two descriptive statements introduced by the prepositional phrases discussed above. First, "teaching and admonishing one another with all wisdom, and as you sing psalms, hymns, and spiritual songs. . . ." The statement naturally divides into three parts: the importance of wisdom, the activity of teaching and admonishing, and the matter of the songs themselves.

The concept of wisdom occurs frequently in this epistle.[48] Obviously the church expressed some concern over it; it was, without doubt, the subject of the false teachers. In 1:9 Paul told the believers to pray for the wisdom of God. In 2:3 he stated that the wisdom was in Christ. Now he urged them to be wise in the employment of the various exhortations to each other. Wisdom in this epistle always has a spiritual dimension and is related ultimately to the mind of God. Paul encouraged them to express their corporate worship in real wisdom, which centers in and promotes Christ. Thus as they grew in their understanding of spiritual truth, they were to encourage others in the context of real wisdom. Among other aspects, wisdom means that there are proper means to an end, and those means will be employed.

The word of Christ became prominent by the exercise of spiritual gifts. The spiritual gifts identified here are teaching and exhortation. Paul was particularly fond of these terms in Colossians, using them of himself and his ministry in 1:28. Teaching is the orderly arrangement of truth and effective communication of it. Teaching is mentioned as a spiritual gift in Paul's writings (Rom 12:7) and is closely associated with the role of the pastor (Eph 4:11). Here, however, the church members teach each other in the ways of God. Similarly, admonishing frequently became the task of the Christian leader (Rom 15:14; 1 Thess 5:12; Col 1:28), although on occasion it refers to various members encouraging others (here and 1 Thess 5:14).[49]

Admonishing differs from teaching. Admonishing has the element of strong encouragement. It is generally practical and moral, rather than abstract or theological. It is the way teaching is reinforced in the lives of the hearers. Such orderly arrangement of truth and strong practical encouragement are to be done in wisdom. Among other things, that means the person exercising these gifts will understand, in the will of God, how to exercise them appropriately. It also means that their exercise will be distinctly Christian in motivation and method.

---

[48] See 1:9; 1:28; 2:3; and 4:5 along with this verse.

[49] The Pauline use accounts for eight of the nine occurrences of the word: (Acts 20:31); Rom 15:14; 1 Cor. 4:14 (2); Col 1:28; 3:16; 1 Thess 5:12,14; 2 Thess 3:15.

The specific vehicle for teaching and admonition is song. Christians have always sung their faith, and here is a biblical basis for it. Three terms provide insight into the nature of early Christian singing.[50] Although there is a consensus that the terms have significant overlap and cannot be distinguished sharply, there is some help in seeing where they most differ. "Psalms" are, no doubt, the psalms of the Old Testament.[51] The word "hymn" occurs only twice in the New Testament, here and Eph 5:19. It may describe a "festive hymn of praise."[52] Recent studies have addressed the presence of hymns in the New Testament and found them in many places, such as Col 1:15-20 and Phil 2:5-11. In Scripture, however, they are never called hymns, and the use of the term reflects modern church worship more than is necessarily true of the first century. "Spiritual" songs seems to describe other musical compositions, perhaps like gospel songs.[53] Whatever they were, Paul cautioned that they must be spiritual, not secular. Together, these three terms address the entire scope of musical expression in early church worship.

The passage instructed the Colossians on the proper use of music in the church. Music is a vehicle through which a message is delivered. Interestingly enough, the New Testament says little about musicians assisting in worship, even though they appeared frequently in Israel's worship, as described in the Old Testament. Paul did not identify music as a spiritual gift, but he omitted other talents as well. This passage teaches that the spiritual gift is not music, but music may become an effective vehicle for the exercise of a gift. The gifts are teaching and admonishing. The medium of music, therefore, must remain secondary to the message it conveys. Music is legitimate only when it is a medium pointing beyond itself to the exhorting and encouraging of other believers and the evangelization of unbelievers. Christian musicians must give primary attention to what is communicated and secondary attention to how it is communicated. Singing effectively teaches and encourages. In 3:16, the pastoral function Paul claimed for himself in 1:28 is broadened to include the entire congregation and the medium of music. Few activities have such ability to teach, prompt recall, and encourage, and they have always been a vital part of Christianity.

The second descriptive statement modifying teaching and admonishing is "with gratitude in your hearts to God." The expression may parallel the previous one, or it may be subordinate to it. Commentators are divided at this

---

[50] Here the forms of these three are considered locative, giving the sphere in which these activities of teaching and admonishing occur. In contemporary church worship, most pastors do not sing their messages through these vehicles!

[51] Although this is generally true, it is difficult to see how 1 Cor 14:26 ("each one has a psalm") fits this definition.

[52] So O'Brien, *Colossians, Philemon*, 209.

[53] Hendriksen says that it means "ode," a term which is derived from the Greek root (162).

point.[54] On the whole, the parallelism is probably better.

Christian singing is to be in the realm of grace. Some have interpreted the construction to mean something like "singing gratefully" unto the Lord.[55] However, in light of Paul's insistence on the realm of grace as the believer's hope of salvation, a better interpretation is that the phrase refers to hearty Christian singing, singing with an understanding of grace because of the working of grace in the life. Grace reminds singers that the message and not the singers bring salvation. It further reminds them that everything good about which they sing comes because of God's grace. There is no room for self-praise, ambition, or high-mindedness in the realm of grace. Those who sing do so because they have felt the transforming power of God in their own lives, and they sing with an awareness of that grace.

The location of the song is the heart. Paul's point does not contrast the heart and the mouth, as if to say that there should be silent singing rather than vocal. Consistent with the previous uses of "heart," it carries the Old Testament idea of the totality of the motivating and valuing aspect of persons. Paul urged the Colossian believers to have their entire beings involved in the song. The song should come from a thorough and consistent commitment of life to the Lord. Nothing else pleases God. Nothing else teaches and admonishes others as well as the heartfelt, enthusiastic singing that comes from those who know personally what grace means.

These two modifiers explain how the word of Christ is able to dwell richly in the congregation. They were to teach and admonish each other with a mutual involvement in the lives of others. They were to accomplish this through songs of various kinds. These songs, in turn, were energized by the freedom of the word of Christ so that an ever new song of grace appears.

3:17 Paul summarized the paragraph in v. 17. It fittingly complements v. 16, but its implications extend back to v. 12.[56] All of life is addressed with the words "whatever you do" and "in word or deed." The division parallels both the rabbinic concern about behavior matching confession and the Pauline concern of consistency of commitment. The two realms of speech and action encompass every area of life. A truly Christian commitment incorporates them both.

The "name of the Lord Jesus" provides the proper atmosphere for life. The Colossian believers were not only to come to God through Jesus and to worship Jesus but also to live their lives conscious of his authority and reputation. To

---

[54]The parallelism is suggested by the two prepositional phrases which introduce the statements. The subordination is suggested largely by the repetition of terms for "song" and "singing." It seems that the word for singing, ᾄδοντες, picks up and continues the idea of ᾠδαῖς in the previous statement.

[55]O'Brien, *Colossians, Philemon,* 210.

[56]In a real sense, it summarizes 3:5-17; since the positive commands occur in vv. 12-17, it is best to link it with these verses alone.

invoke his name at this point no doubt called to mind their baptism, which was done in the name of Jesus (Matt 28:16ff.). Further, it reminded them of the blessings of salvation which come in the name of Jesus (John 14:26) and the power available for service (Luke 10:17).[57] The person of Jesus was everything to them, and, because of grace, all of life was to be a contribution to him. His authority and reputation concerned them. They were to do nothing apart from his direction, approval, and purposes. Living in accord with his name means "in harmony with his revealed will, in subjection to his authority, in dependence on his power."[58]

This section ends with a return to the idea of thanksgiving. "Giving thanks to the Father" occurs in 1:12, which introduced the many reasons thanksgiving is appropriate. They relate to salvation. Now, after the lengthy theological and practical discussion since that passage, Paul characterized a Christian's thanksgiving as going *through Jesus* to the Father. Thus God is to be thanked for delivering believers from darkness and placing them in the kingdom of his Son through the work of the Son. Paul made explicit in this epistle the fact that God comes to the world through Jesus and the world comes to God through him as well. The believers had access to God because of the work of the Son of God. Their thanks was to rise to the ears of God through his Son.

(2) Family Relationships (3:18-4:1)

18Wives, submit to your husbands, as is fitting in the Lord.

19Husbands, love your wives and do not be harsh with them.

20Children, obey your parents in everything, for this pleases the Lord.

21Fathers, do not embitter your children, or they will become discouraged.

22Slaves, obey your earthly masters in everything; and do it, not only when their eye is on you and to win their favor, but with sincerity of heart and reverence for the Lord. 23Whatever you do, work at it with all your heart, as working for the Lord, not for men, 24since you know that you will receive an inheritance from the Lord as a reward. It is the Lord Christ you are serving. 25Anyone who does wrong will be repaid for his wrong, and there is no favoritism.

1Masters, provide your slaves with what is right and fair, because you know that you also have a Master in heaven.

Christian commitment affects every area of life, including the family. It was natural, therefore, for Paul and other writers to specify the Christian's

---

[57]These specific books may not have been known, but surely the traditions which underlay them were circulated early and the significance of the name would have been understood by all Christians.

[58]Hendriksen, 164. The change from the rather consistent use of "Christ" for the name of Jesus to the "Lord Jesus" is striking. It may have reference to the historical Jesus, as the name "Jesus" would suggest in contrast to "Christ," the title of his mission. Perhaps Paul wanted to use the title "Lord" in this context because of its appropriateness to the subject matter. That would lead him to prefer "Lord Jesus" rather than "Lord Christ." The latter combination rarely occurs, but it does in Col 3:24.

responsibilities in these areas. Several matters of introduction will help put these commands in their proper perspective.

Paul presented another list of instructions, which Luther called *Haustafeln*. The term has received almost universal acclaim. The New Testament contains several passages of lists which address domestic relationships (Eph 5:22-6:9; 1 Tim 2:8-15; 6:1,2; Titus 2:10; 1 Pet 2:12-3:7). Other moralists and philosophers had similar lists.[59] The question arises, therefore, as to how Christian this list is.[60] Certainly it captures the spirit of Jewish theology and ethics, and similar expectations occurred in the Gentile world. This particular formulation, however, along with Eph 5:22-6:9, has distinctively Christian elements. It speaks to accepting the proper order of home and society for Christian reasons, "as unto the Lord." None of the other lists were motivated in this way, nor was their ultimate goal the glory of the Lord.[61]

In the Roman world, the household included all those who were the responsibility of the head of the house; therefore, the original readers would have included servants. The broad perspective that included servants suggests servants and masters were members of the Christian community at Colosse. The fact that Paul included servants often in his ethical lists points to the fact that there were actually people to whom the teaching applied. These rules were not simply theoretical discussions. At the church of Colosse, probably both Onesimus, the servant, and Philemon, the slave-owner, worshiped in the same fellowship.

The passage resembles Eph 5:22-6:9. Both the basic content and the order of presentation are the same. Colossians is much shorter in the first two sets of relationships, husband/wife and parent/child, but more extended in discussing the master/slave relationship. In each case Colossians presents the heart of the matter, but both Ephesians and Colossians interpret the other.

The order of the text is significant. The text moves logically from marriage to family to extended family concerns; the movement is from the most intimate circle outward in couplets of relationships. There is also a pattern in the way each couplet is introduced. In each case, the one who submits comes first. This subtle way of emphasis suggests that Paul spoke primarily to the three groups of people who submit and secondarily to the others. Even though at times more is said to those mentioned second, the ones mentioned first receive more emphasis.

---

[59] See Lohse, 154-56, for a brief discussion of other similar lists in the Hellenistic world.

[60] Scholars vary in their appraisals of the list. Lohse, e.g., says, "These rules for the household are not, insofar as their content is considered, 'a genuinely Christian creation' and thus they cannot, without further ado, be considered to be 'applied kerygma'" (154, n 4). There is a lengthy and adequate discussion of various source theories for the list in O'Brien, *Colossians, Philemon*, 215-18.

[61] Hendriksen notes that the list is distinctively Christian in three ways: its power to carry out the commands (the grace of God), its purpose (the glory of the Lord, 3:17), and its pattern (Christ the bridegroom) (167).

The consistency of presentation in the New Testament domestic lists reveals a further truth. God has a definite order for his economy on the earth. Since the order is God-ordained, Christians have a responsibility to accept it and live within it. The question of the abiding nature of these commands cannot be discussed fully here.[62] Some suggest they are culture specific. They say that the words only relate to the culture in which they were given and that they must be altered significantly to apply to another generation.[63]

This conclusion poses many difficulties. Only a few can be identified here. First, nothing in the passage itself suggests even remotely that this was a temporary command for a specific situation. If it were, a relative position would be easier to accept. Second, the appeal to the culture of the day is fraught with difficulties. By what standard is the culture to be measured? Is the twentieth-century cultural pattern the norm, or could it be that the Bible intends to correct the modern scene at this point, as it does at many others? The argument most often used against the universal nature of these commands is that the culture accepted such an order for the family, but when the position of women and slaves changed, the biblical mandates had little meaning. If this is the case, the real meaning of the command is "to let the order of society be true in the church." That principle will not work. Similar statements could possibly be said of any ethical position that is out of character with the New Testament. The end result is an authority (the Bible) which is no authority since at any place where the culture differs with express biblical commands the Bible will be perceived as secondary to culture.

Third, Paul explained that the order for husband and wife was distinctly beyond cultural aspects like this when he argued similarly in 1 Cor 11:2-16. There he accepted the order of creation as one evidence of the timelessness of the pattern. Further, in that passage Paul explained that the pattern for the home is the Trinity itself. There is a functional subordination within the Godhead! Thus, before creation and the fall, there was an order of relationships. Fourth, the principle of culture-specific application only does not work with all of these commands. While it is true that Paul advocated that slaves accept their position and adjust to it, it is equally true that he sowed the seeds of emancipa-

---

[62] The exegetical and hermeneutical literature on this issue is as extensive as any in the New Testament, and it grows daily. The issue is theological, exegetical, hermeneutical, ethical, and, of course, each of these areas is easily affected by bias and emotion.

[63] Lohse, e.g., says: "They do not offer timelessly valid laws, nor do they endow a particular social order with ageless dignity. As times change, so does the general estimation of what is fitting and proper. Christian exhortation, however, must constantly impress on new generations the admonition to be obedient to the Kyrios. How this obedience is to be expressed concretely at any given time, will always have to be tested and determined anew" (157). H. Conzelmann, in H. W. Beyer, P. Althaus, H. Conzelmann, G. Friedrich, and A. Oepke, *Die kleineren Briefe des Apostles Paulus*, *NTD* 8 (Göttingen: Vandenhoeck, 1965), 153, agrees. In reaction to this, it should be noted that nothing in the text identifies how to update what is provided, nor does anything suggest it stands in need of such update; there is no word from the Kyrios as to how and when this task must be done.

tion here and in the Epistle to Philemon, which no doubt the church at Colosse read. There is no equivalent passage for the husband and wife or parent and child.[64] Even more difficult, the principle of "cultural acceptability" hardly works with the parent-child relationship, and whatever principles apply to one of these three must be equally applicable to all three. The Pauline command for children comes directly from the Ten Commandments, and no one advocates its reversal in society. Children are always expected to obey their parents as a pattern of life.[65]

The point is that this order of relationships appears to be a universally applicable Christian distinctive. Paul's message was that whenever these relationships exist, the people in them are expected to act as Paul commanded through the Spirit of God. When servants are servants (and masters are masters), these guidelines pertain. When children are children (and parents are parents), these guidelines remain. Likewise, when a woman is a wife (and a man is a husband), this is the order God expects. Of course, when other situations occur, such as when servants/slaves are freed, a different set of guidelines are appropriate. Most of these situations were addressed by the writers of Scripture.[66]

Two final introductory comments must be made. First, this presents an order for domestic relationships. It is a part of the divine economy as it pertains to this earth. In heaven things will change. Each of the situations addressed has some comment about the commands being appropriate "in the Lord." Rather than thinking of these guidelines as "house rules," as is commonly done, it is better to think of them as rules which govern specific situations of life for Christians. Second, each of these follows the same pattern. Paul addressed the "submitting" party first. Then he provided a motivating statement, calling them to accept their specific responsibility in the Lord. Finally, he followed these

---

[64] Some scholars argue that Gal 3:28 lays the seed for such a change when it says "neither male nor female." That passage is complicated by the use of rare words: "male" ($\mathring{\alpha}\rho\sigma\epsilon\nu$), used only nine times in the New Testament; and "female" ($\theta\tilde{\eta}\lambda\upsilon\varsigma$), used only once. The word $\mathring{\alpha}\rho\sigma\epsilon\nu$ may have a "strong emphasis on sex" in the passage where is occurs most frequently (Rom 1:27) (*BAGD*, 109-10). If that is the reason for the *hapax legomena* $\theta\tilde{\eta}\lambda\upsilon$ (to emphasize sex) in Gal 3:28, the passage should read something like "in Christ . . . there is neither sex." However it is interpreted there, the passage is soteriological in nature and context, explaining the work of Christ. Since Paul consistently kept this order of instruction in the domestic passages, there must have been no inconsistency in his mind between this text and Gal 3:28.

[65] There are, of course, elements of society which do advocate the freedom of children from their parents. Most, however, recognize that anarchy would be the result. The situation does illustrate the point being discussed. Whose cultural norm judges Scripture? Can any subculture establish its own morality, picking and choosing the elements of Scripture that it advocates as authoritative and discarding the others? There must be some workable, biblically consistent principle to guide in such difficult matters as these.

[66] Two most notable places where this occurs are in 1 Cor 7, where Paul argued in detail about the various relationships that should be maintained regarding sex and marriage, and the Pastoral Epistles, where there are specific guidelines.

with a command to the other party as to how they are to act in fulfilling their Christian obligation.

WIVES AND HUSBANDS (3:18-19). *Wives (3:18).* **3:18** Starting with the most basic of domestic relationships, Paul addressed the wives' behavior. The wives were to submit to their husbands. The command occurs consistently in the New Testament guidelines so that there is a uniform attitude on the matter. The term means "to subject or subordinate."[67] The verb form occurs thirty-eight times in the New Testament, twenty-three times in the Pauline literature, but only one time in Colossians. There appears to be a difference in the specific nuance of the term according to the voice in which it occurs (active or middle voice).[68] When it occurs in the active voice, the power to subject belongs to God himself. This is evidenced in 1 Cor 15:24-28 (Christ subjecting all things); Phil 3:21; Rom 8:20; Eph 1:21-22. In the middle voice, it describes a voluntary submission which resembles that of Christian humility. It may describe Christ's submission to God (1 Cor 15:58), church members to one another (Eph 5:21, a parallel context to this one), believers submitting in the exercise of their prophetic gifts (1 Cor 14:32), or the proper order for wives (Eph 5:22ff.; Col 3:18). This latter use appeals to free agents to take a place of submission voluntarily. The term does not suggest slavery or servitude, and certainly never calls for the husband to make his wife submit. If he could, her heart would not be in it. Besides, Paul addressed wives here, not husbands. In this context, the word differs radically from the word which describes the role of children and slaves who are to obey (*hypakouō*).

In comparing this command with Eph 5:22ff., a more holistic picture emerges of the relationship Paul advocated. It has been suggested based on Eph 5:21-22 that there is a mutual submission of husband and wife. While that idea contains an important relational principle of mutual consideration, the text speaks against that. Ephesians 5:21 introduces domestic relationships by the participial form of the verb "submit." It is an evidence of the filling of the Spirit. As the text develops, however, only three of the six receive the command to submit: wives, children, and slaves. It seems clear, as some point out, that the husband submits to the wife by loving her and caring for her needs; but, it should be noted, Paul did not directly call that submission. Admittedly, Ephesians needs clarification, and that occurs in Colossians. In Col 3:18 Paul directly called upon the wives to submit, and the text does not use the word in relation to the husband at all.[69]

---

[67] *BAGD*, 847-48. The middle means to subject oneself.

[68] This distinction is recognized in *BAGD*, 847-48, where it is called active and passive, but most explicitly in M. Barth, *Ephesians, Translation and Commentary on Chapters 4-6, AB* (Garden City, N. Y.: Doubleday, 1974), 709-15.

[69] The point is that consistently in Scripture the wife is to submit to the husband. The only passage which could be interpreted to suggest "mutual submission" is Eph 5:21ff., which many have allowed to become the standard for interpreting all others. The others, however, do not support that

A second matter to note is that in each passage the wife's submission is different from the others. Children and slaves are told to obey; the wife is not. Submission is voluntarily assuming a particular role because it is right. Obedience is not directly commanded. Submission demands obedience as a pattern, but there are times in which obedience to a husband may become disobedience to God.[70] By using the word "submit," Paul separated the kind of obedience expected by the wife from that expected of others. The wife has a very different relationship to her husband than children to parents or slaves to masters.

The motivation for voluntary submission is that it is a proper Christian attitude. The phrase "as is fitting in the Lord" identifies these concerns. The word "fitting" has the idea of proper as a duty.[71] By employing the statement, Paul made it clear that such submission is an outworking of the lordship of Christ. It is part of the Christian order.

As before, this phrase clarifies a common misunderstanding in Eph 5:22. The phrase "as to the Lord" sometimes bears the interpretation that the wife's relationship to her husband is to be patterned after her relationship to the Lord. Thus a husband may claim that the wife must obey him totally in the same way that she does the Lord. Conversely, some wives have claimed that the phrase means that they submit to their husbands only when their husbands act like the Lord. In times when the husband fails, it is not necessary for the wife to submit. Both of these interpretations miss Paul's point. Submission is a matter of Christian commitment. It comes with salvation. Voluntarily taking a position of submission is a matter of a wife's relationship to the Lord, not to her husband. It is "fitting in the Lord."

Naturally, some express concern about the wife having a seemingly inferior role. Such thinking is unbiblical and a misunderstanding of these passages. First, since Paul used the term of Jesus' attitude who is Lord of all (see 1 Cor 15:28), the term may be appropriately used of one with the highest office. Both wives and husbands must recognize that the term has nothing to do with personal worth and value. Second, Paul described a functional situation which reflects God's plan for families on this earth.[72] He was not speaking ontologically, that is, regarding the essence of personhood. There is a functional subordination, but an essential equality. Differences of roles to accomplish specific functions do not call for the categories of superior and inferior. It is better to speak of "suited for" and "not suited for." Such an economic division is found

---

interpretation. Each passage must be studied in harmony for a complete understanding of the others and for a complete understanding of proper Christian interpersonal relationships.

[70] E.g., such cases involve immorality, cruelty, and improper conduct. The guideline then is to obey God rather than a husband. Even then, however, the commitment must be to submission to God's plan as a pattern of life and the best order for society.

[71] The Greek is ἀνῆκεν. *BAGD*, 66.

[72] The term "functional" refers to the administration of affairs and the organization of tasks for proper operation.

in God, where the Father, Son, and Spirit each have different operations (functional subordination), but they are all equally divine (essential equality).[73] Thus Christian relationships on earth are patterned after those in God, and both husbands and wives should endeavor to understand their roles in that light.[74]

Husbands (3:19). The counterpart of the wife's responsibility is that of the husband's. In direct, simple, and clear terms, Paul expressed the duties of a Christian husband. The discussion is briefer than that of Eph 5:22ff., where the major portion of the instructions for marriage are directed to the husband's care for his wife. There the command to love was developed more fully. Here Paul simply stated it. He did add to the words found there, however, when he said that husbands were not to be bitter toward their wives. This verse naturally falls into two divisions: Husbands, love your wives; and do not be bitter toward them.

3:19 The simple, positive command is to love. The term *agapē*, used here, never occurred in secular household tables.[75] The command, therefore, appears to be a distinctively Christian element of the marriage relationship. It was common, of course, for husbands to love their wives sexually, but Paul advocated much more than that. In his description of the husband's love in Eph 5:22ff., he clearly stated that the husband was to love his wife sacrificially. Her inner beauty and self-fulfillment were to be his delight, and he would do whatever he could to promote her personal well-being and satisfaction. The model is Christ's love for the church.

Some have suggested that the husband's love for the wife is his submission to her.[76] He submits by leaving his own desires and taking her concerns as his own. While this dynamic helps define the husband's love, it should be noted that the text does not call the husband's responsibility "submission," nor does it state that Christ submitted to the church. The text calls it "love." In the dynamics of Christian relationships, a husband's loving, caring, sacrificial approach to his wife's well-being makes her responsibility of submission easier.[77]

---

[73] Scripture generally assigns different roles to the three persons of the Godhead. The Father plans, the Son accomplishes, and the Spirit applies. Each, however, is fully God.

[74] Lohse understands the passage to mean that Christian wives were to adapt to the prevailing social order of the day. He implied that the term "submit" was frequently used of marriage relationships outside the New Testament (157). O'Brien, however, disputes this assumption, claiming that there are only two instances of the word used for wife/husband relationships apart from Scripture (*Colossians, Philemon*, 221). Paul called the Christians to a standard and pattern of behavior which was not necessarily well accepted even for that day.

[75] O'Brien states, "They do not occur in any extrabiblical Hellenistic rules for the household" (223).

[76] They base this on the assumption that Ephesians calls for a mutual submission. This is difficult to derive from the text (see note 69).

[77] In light of this discussion, the husband's love or lack of it does not relieve the woman of her responsibility toward him. Nor does the wife's lack of submission relieve the husband of his responsibility toward her.

Paul followed the positive command to love with a negative one, "Do not be harsh with them." This term does not occur in other ethical lists.[78] The word is followed by the preposition "toward" (*pros*) which also is unusual.[79]

Since Paul issued the command here, he probably meant that the marriage relationship could become an irritant to the one who does not love properly. The husband was to take care to see that bitterness did not develop.

CHILDREN AND PARENTS (3:20-21). Moving from the innermost family circle, Paul addressed the parent-child relationship. As before, his cryptic comments express only the heart of what he provided in more extended fashion in Eph. 6:1-4.

Children (3:20). **3:20**   Again Paul spoke to the one who was to submit first. Because he addressed children, he must have expected children to be present when the text was read aloud in the congregation. The church meeting included people of all stations in life. Race, age, and economic standing paled in significance when people were in Christ.

Paul commanded children to "obey." The word "obey" (*hypakouō*) is stronger than the word "submit," used of wives earlier.[80] The text reinforces this by the use of the phrase "in everything." Obedience was expected. In Eph 6:2-3 Paul stated that doing so was a fulfillment of the Ten Commandments and qualified the children for the reception of a promise.[81]

From the two lists, Paul apparently was addressing young children here. Two factors inform this interpretation. First, the use of the term "children" rather than "young men" (or equivalent) shows Paul was addressing younger children.[82] Second, in Eph 6:4 fathers were told to "bring them up." The training process involved teaching children how to obey, and those who heard these words would respond properly. Nothing in the text suggests a specific age, however. The term "children" primarily describes children in relation to their parents, so the assumption is that they were at home and under the parents' supervision.[83]

The motivation occurs at the end of this verse: "for this pleases the Lord." Two parts of this expression stress the Christian motivation. First, the word

---

[78]The term is πικραίνω. It does occur elsewhere in the New Testament, but not in these contexts (e.g., Eph 4:31 and the noun in Heb 12:14).

[79]"Toward," πρός, means in the relationship, but several commentators have suggested it does not mean "with her" but "because of her," i.e., because of the marriage.

[80]This may be surmised from the definition of the two terms ὑποτάσσω and ὑπακούω, and from the use of the active voice here rather than the middle of ὑποτάσσω.

[81]There he quoted Exod 20:12 and Deut 15:16.

[82]This would have been strengthened if Paul had used the term τεκνία instead of τέκνα, as John did in 1 John 2:12, although there it appears to be a nuance of the word which is endearing rather than pointing to age. Paul used that term only once, Gal 4:19, when he addressed his spiritual offspring. John used the term "young men" (νεανίσκος), but it never occurs in the Pauline literature.

[83]*BAGD* states that the term is literally a "child in relation to father and mother" (808).

"pleases" almost always describes the relationship to the Lord. It conveys the thought of "well pleasing."[84] Second, the phrase "in the Lord" occurs. This means "since you are in the Lord." It calls the child to remember the state of grace and the responsibilities that grow from it.[85] Thus the children have a responsibility in the Christian family order. To be pleasing to the Lord as a Christians, they should obey their parents.

Parents (3:21). **3:21** In the Lord, parents have a mutual responsibility to children. There is a command and a practical reason. Parents are told not to embitter their children. Paul used the term "fathers" in addressing the parents. The term may easily encompass both father and mother, as it does here, but it also served to remind them that the fathers bore a primary responsibility for the children in the home. Paul meant that they should not embitter or irritate their children. The word "embitter" (*erethizō*) occurs only one other time in Scripture (in 2 Cor 9:2). This speaks of an irritation or even nagging. Parents embitter children by constantly picking at them, perhaps refusing to acknowledge their efforts. The fact that children might become discouraged suggests that the parents too easily reminded the children that they were not good enough. This activity had no place in the Christian home. If correction were needed, it should have been toward the behavior of the child, not the child's personhood, and it should have been enforced quickly. Discipline was not to be prolonged so that nagging occurred.

The reason for the command was to avoid discouragement. Constant nagging produces a situation where children are discouraged either because they cannot please those they love or because they feel they are of no worth to anybody.

In this case, Ephesians and Colossians complement each other by presenting two sides of the issue. In Ephesians, Paul exhorted the parents to raise the children in the nurture and admonition of the Lord. This suggests a positive, Christian environment in which children will appreciate the Christian commitment of the parents. In time, children should believe in the Lord and mature in the Christian life and world view. In Colossians, Paul warned parents not to discourage their children. Especially in the child-rearing process, fathers were to embody Christian principles and remember the equality of all persons in Christ. In God's sight, children and parents have equal worth, and parents were to treat their children with respect as persons.

SERVANTS AND MASTERS (3:22-4:1). The guidelines for slavery were more complex than any of the other relationships. At the same time, they reveal the heart of the matter that underlies these commands. They are perplexing because it seems that Paul should have written to undermine the institution of slavery

---

[84] Noted by the εὐ prefix to the word. One location of this is Rom 12:1-2.

[85] See N. Turner, *Syntax, A Grammar of New Testament Greek*, ed. J. H. Moulton (Edinburgh: T & T Clark, 1963), 263.

or at least to encourage the revolt of the slaves. On the one hand, to do so, would have caused significant difficulty in the first-century setting, and undue persecution would result. Besides, Christians could do little by force. On the other hand, the teaching of the apostle here and elsewhere clearly sowed the seed for the emancipation of slaves and the end of the institution. Paul did what he could in the best way possible.

Most slaves (*douloi*, sometimes translated "servants") found themselves in situations of hopelessness. Slaves were, generally speaking, victims of war. The slavery was political and economic, not racial. Similarly, virtually every class of person lived with the realization that war could cause them to lose everything and be sold into slavery. Those who revolted, seeking to use power to gain freedom, found themselves in a worse position than before. It simply would not do for Paul to advocate slaves walking away from their masters. That would endanger many innocent lives and frustrate the spread of the gospel.

This penetrates to the heart of the entire "house-table" section. How could slaves respond positively as Christians *within* their circumstances? Surely they could make a valid response to the gospel that would produce a better situation for them now and in eternity. Paul, in fact, presented the appropriate response. He called them to acknowledge and accept the fact that God knew their situations and that he rewarded them for how they acted in those situations.

Servants (3:22-25). Paul said more to the slaves than to any other group in this context. This may have been the result of several factors. First, there may have been a large number of slaves in the congregation at Colosse. Second, there may have been trouble among the slaves. Possibly some slaves were encouraged by the successful escape of Onesimus from Colosse to Rome. Perhaps he became a kind of folk hero, the idol of the downtrodden. Clearly, there is some reason so much attention is placed on Onesimus in Paul's writings.[86] Therefore, Paul may have been concerned to promote harmony in the church and the home. Third, Paul may have been troubled in general by the institution of slavery. His associations with Onesimus in Rome perhaps reminded him of the atrocities of the institution even when the slave had a Christian master. The Epistle to Philemon reveals that Paul advised Onesimus to return at some risk and, no doubt, only after a renewed consideration of the implications of his words. Such human relationships bring home the personal dimensions of an otherwise theoretical theology. Paul's emphasis on the Lord as the master surely reveals his dislike of human masters in any form.

3:22 Paul's guidelines about slaves' responsibilities were twofold: obey and serve genuinely. Regarding the obedience the Lord expected, Paul used the

---

[86] Although it is primarily in an obscure epistle to Philemon, the slave owner, it should be remembered that he was the only individual outside the Pauline team who received a now-canonical letter from Paul. If Colossians were written with an eye on Philemon, the space devoted to this man was considerably larger.

same term for the slave/master relationship that he had used to describe children and parents (another inescapable relationship). The word "obey" (*hypakouō*) occurs rather than "submit" (*hypotassō*). Further, slaves, like children, were to obey in everything. They had a complete responsibility to their masters.[87] Even here, Paul softened his words. The masters were only earthly masters. They were masters "according to the flesh." Paul subtly reminded the readers of a major theme of this section. There is an ultimate master reigning over both slave and master. Slaves of every age have rested their hopes of justice on that truth, and heaven has become a vital, hope-producing focus of life.[88]

The second portion pertains to slaves' service (3:22b-23). They were to serve genuinely. The tendency for all slaves was to work when the master watched, thereby easing their situations and, perhaps, qualifying them for favors.[89] Paul spoke against that. The slave was to do his work for the Lord, not for his earthly master. The all-seeing eye of the heavenly Master searched the motivations of the heart. This is the first reference to the heavenly Master as the object of all the slave's work. Since, in reality, he served the Lord, the work was to be undertaken with a spirit of reverence and fear.[90] All of life was to be lived with a conscious realization of the Master.

3:23 Paul continued the command to genuine service by urging slaves to work "with all your heart" (Col 3:23). Recalling the general admonition of 3:17 ("whatever you do, whether in word or deed"), Paul applied the principle to the slaves' work. The command involves the imperative form of the word "work." Even work for someone else was to be heartfelt. Literally, Paul stated they should work "out of soul."[91] The phrase occurs synonymously with the word "heart," but if there is a difference, perhaps it is in the fact that "soul" stresses the life principle and expended energy, rather than the pure choice which comes from the heart. Thus one may choose to work from the heart, but the actual work done comes from the life source itself.[92] The point is that the Lord concerns himself with the expenditure of energy and choices made with the life. He is the real Master.

---

[87] Like the other two relationships, however, this instruction probably assumed that a line could be drawn for immoral or illegal activities which might be encouraged by the master.

[88] Perhaps the slaves were most exemplary in their faith and love because of their hope. They had only a hope of heaven, but that was enough to live properly on earth.

[89] Some slaves held positions of trust. Some could earn private money. They sometimes could buy freedom, and some were given the right to own slaves of their own.

[90] Fear as a motive occurs seven times in all: Col 3:22; Eph 6:5; 1 Pet 2:17,18; 3:2,6; Eph 5:33 (see O'Brien, *Colossians, Philemon*, 227).

[91] Greek, ἐκ ψυχῆς.

[92] *BAGD*, 893-94, provides a survey of the range of meanings of the word. *BAGD* interprets this text to speak of the "feelings and emotions" with which the person works.

3:24　Three motivations for such service are given in vv. 24-25. The first appeals to the motive of reward, "You will receive an inheritance from the Lord as a reward." Paul introduced the idea by appealing to what they knew already. They knew the doctrine of rewards and punishments; now they were to count on it with their lives. As slaves, they could look forward to little on this earth. Perhaps some rewards were given for good work, but there was no inheritance. In speaking of rewards, Paul challenged them to consider the fact that their rewards were spiritual. Such rewards could not be taken away, and the real Master would pay them what really matters. The reward and inheritance seem to have involved the presence of the Lord himself. Thus, the motive was faithfulness to the Lord in the circumstances of life. Being a Christian meant that the concerns of heaven were to occupy the thoughts and energies of those on earth. This motivation strengthened many slaves on earth.[93] In it, those called to be slaves have taught the free that real freedom is internal, rather than external. They have also shown that real riches may be found in the midst of earthly poverty.

The second motivation was the sovereignty of the Lord: "It is the Lord Christ you are serving" (3:23b). The emphasis is clearly on the Lord. The rather unusual combination of "Lord" and "Christ" without the term "Jesus," points to two titles which were applied to the risen Jesus. "Christ" (*Christos*) referred to his messianic work; "Lord" (*kyrios*), to his sovereignty. Perhaps the combination served to remind the slaves of one of two truths, or both. The first was that they were to be conscious of their salvation, which came from the same one who was their Master. If he cared enough to save, he could care for all their needs. The second was that the combination stresses two aspects of the Lord's work which apply especially to slaves. His work of salvation was a total redemption. They knew that they served a Redeemer who is sovereign. He could deliver them in time, and he would deliver them in eternity. If, therefore, he allowed them to remain in slavery, he had some other plan for their lives. His plan temporarily overrode his deliverance. Whichever of these seem appropriate, the slaves were reminded that the Christian slave really serves the Lord.

3:25　The third motivation is given in v. 25: "Anyone who does wrong will be repaid for his wrong, and there is no favoritism." Here Paul reminded them of God's justice. Some commentators think Paul changed subjects in this verse and began his address to masters. They base the interpretation on the difficulty of conceiving that slaves could do such wrong, especially since it is heartfelt work that is the subject. Surely, they say, Paul warned the masters that God is also a God of vengeance and will repay justly. On the other hand, the principle of justice could have been a comfort for the slaves themselves. Some were mistreated, and their hope of vindication lay in the hands of God. Paul reminded

---

[93] It has given rise to some of the richest of music in the African-American spirituals which grew out of the slave era in America. The theme of hope beyond this life is beautifully presented.

them that God sees and judges according to perfect justice. A third possibility is that Paul had both parties in mind, and this general statement was applicable to all. If slaves did wrong, they would be punished by their heavenly Master. If earthly masters did wrong, they too would be punished by the Lord. However, the connective "for" (*gar*) makes this statement dependent on what preceded, and the flow of thought continues well without changing subject. On the whole, it seems that Paul comforted and motivated the slaves by appealing to God's justice.

The judgment of God occurs frequently in the Scriptures. Here Paul seems to have based his statements on the Old Testament law of "an eye for an eye,"[94] indicating that God would judge accurately. The justice of God is further indicated by the word "favoritism." The Greek term actually means "partiality,"[95] and three of the four times it occurs in the New Testament it refers to God's impartiality in judgment (Rom 2:11; Eph 6:9; Col 3:25). The other time it calls for believers to be impartial in their treatment of others (Jas 2:1). In each case, it suggests that judgments should not be based on external matters, but on what really is. One of those externals clearly identified is economic status (Jas 2:1). Here, then, the word applies to the master/slave relationship.

It may seem strange that the judgment applies equally to believers and unbelievers. Christian slaves took comfort in knowing that their unjust, unbelieving masters would face judgment day. The statement is almost proverbial. Surely Christian masters came under the judgment of God. God's righteousness demands that any injustice be punished.[96]

Masters (4:1). **4:1** No doubt these last words led Paul to address masters in terms of justice to their slaves. If they were to avoid judgment, they had to have a concern for fairness. Paul might well have inserted another proverb at this point: "The laborer is worthy of his hire."[97] Although slaves did not receive salaries, their basic needs were to be met in keeping with the value of human effort, time, and life. Such considerations would radically change the attitude of slaves to masters and of masters to slaves.

The motivation given to masters (4:1b) reminded them that they, too, were slaves. The heavenly Master rules over all. Since presumably they had read the words regarding the slaves' heavenly Master, Paul could speak briefly to the

---

[94] Although in that context the guideline called for just vindication so that excessive punishments would not be given, it became a standard for all punishment. God alone possesses the attributes necessary to judge perfectly, taking all factors into account.

[95] *BAGD*, 720.

[96] The Scriptures affirm that Christians as well as non-Christians undergo a judgment. Believers can never lose their salvation, so that judgment is settled. Christians face a judgment of their works, which determines their crowns to be cast at the feet of Jesus.

[97] In 1 Cor 9:7-12 Paul developed this principle in the matter of supporting Christian ministers. He handled it in such a way as to suggest they all agreed on the rightness of it. The actual statement is, "Do not muzzle an ox while it is treading out the grain" (9:9).

masters with a cryptic comment. He obviously meant that the heavenly Master was all-seeing, sovereign, and just. Thus, in reality, earthly masters were slaves and were to treat their slaves like they would like to be treated.

Two matters beyond the interpretation of the text call for comment. The first regards the institution of slavery. The second is the application of this passage to those for whom there is no slavery. Regarding the first, clearly Paul sowed the seeds of equality. While it was impossible for the slave to effect equality, other than by the hard work which he would expect if he were a master, masters had a responsibility to treat their slaves fairly. When Paul said they were to do what was fair and right, he called on a sense of morality which, in time, spoke against the institution itself. Treating others the way they wanted to be treated would mean the release of slaves. As discussed earlier, however, the Roman Empire was not ready for that message, and to preach that kind of rebellion in those circumstances would have hindered the message of the gospel. The deeper matters of fair dealing had to come from the heart anyway, and Paul spoke directly toward that end.

This passage has no direct parallel application outside of slavery. The binding relationship of slave to master forms the context for a deep trust in the sovereignty of God and the value of human effort. The fact that slaves were considered part of the household called for masters to care for slaves as they would family members. Those dynamics generally do not exist today.

Several applications are clear, however. First, the primary concern in the text is a Christian response to life's situations. If circumstances cannot be changed, Christians must respond with a sense of responsibility to God who has chosen not to alter their circumstances. No circumstance more dramatically presents that than slavery. Second, a theology of work emerges. Genuine service in honest vocation brings honor to God. God watches the stewardship of energy, time, and life. This passage teaches that work is honorable even if the profits do not accrue to the worker. Selfish gain should not affect Christians' work. They work in response to the Lord, realizing that God will ultimately supply the proper wages. Third, the passage clearly teaches the equality and dignity of all persons. Masters had a master, and slaves had a freedom when they realized that their labors were not confined to this life and the coffers of earthly masters. Ultimately, individuals are judged by personal responses to the Lord in each situation. These principles are adequately taught here. In contemporary life, the most probable parallel is the workplace, where these principles may be applied.

2. Prayerful Cooperation in Ministry (4:2-6)

Paul concluded the content of this epistle by reminding the church of some basic concerns: prayer (4:2-4), wisdom (4:5), and careful communication (4:6).

(1) Prayer (4:2-4)

[2]Devote yourselves to prayer, being watchful and thankful. [3]And pray for us, too, that God may open a door for our message, so that we may proclaim the mystery of Christ, for which I am in chains. [4]Pray that I may proclaim it clearly, as I should.

Paul ended his epistle as he opened it, urging his readers to prayer. The structure of these verses resembles the opening prayers of the epistles. The only direct statement in these verses is, "Devote yourselves to prayer." This statement is modified by two participles in the Greek: "watching" (v. 2) and "praying" (v. 3). The participle "praying" leads to Paul's concerns about his own ministry and the Colossians' part in it. Two specific concerns are revealed, both introduced by "that" or "in order that" in Greek.[98] The NIV fails to account for the complexities of these statements, and the meaning of the text is only generally conveyed. The command to pray concerned general watchfulness and Paul's ministry. Paul hoped for an open door to be faithful to his calling and for clarity in communicating the message.

In other epistles, Paul said, "Pray without ceasing" (1 Thess 5:17) or its equivalent. The same general tone occurs here. The specific word translated "devote yourselves" means "to persist in."[99] Though the word is different, the meaning is the same. Prayer was to characterize the Colossian church.

WATCHFUL PRAYER (4:2). The first characteristic of prayer is "watchfulness."[100] The term implies mental alertness. The Colossians' prayers were to be in tune with the times. Paul used the same word in 1 Thess 5:6-9 in parallel with the verb "alert" (*nephō*) so that two exhortations occur. The term "watch" has definite mental, perceptional associations, whereas the term "alert" implies a moral readiness. Since 1 Thess 5 is an eschatological context, some scholars suggest that the word carries a connotation of eschatological watchfulness. That conclusion, however, is unnecessary and, in this context, unlikely. Other verbs in Col 4:2-4 discourage the idea of eschatological watchfulness. The Colossians were to pray with mental alertness. Presumably, this meant that they were to know the circumstances of life, particularly those

---

[98]The style of the opening prayers is generally similar. There is normally one main verb, perhaps an understood verb, with several participles dependent on it and explaining it. In Col 1:3-6 the pattern is of one main verb, "we thank God," and two participles on which the rest depends, "praying" and "having heard."

[99]*BAGD*, 715.

[100]The word in Greek is a participle which complements the main verb, "devote yourselves to prayer" (προσκαρτερεῖτε). Another participle is parallel to it, "praying" (προσευχόμενοι). Some see these as imperatival participles, providing a second and third command to complement the command to prayer (e.g., Lohse, 164-65). The construction resembles the first prayer of thanksgiving (1:3-4) where the participles express attendant circumstances of some type. That is the best understanding here as well.

which affected the spread of the gospel. Informed prayer is likely to be more purposeful, personal, and powerful.

Paul added the statement "in thanksgiving." This term (*eucharistia*) is found frequently in this epistle. The literal expression is "being watchful in thankfulness," rather than the NIV translation "being watchful and thankful." Thankfulness is the environment for good praying, and it provides a safeguard for informed praying. Paul's circumstances could have been discouraging as he awaited trial for the gospel. To ensure a proper perspective, Paul urged that their prayer be offered in an attitude of thanks. This kind of prayer sees clearly the obstacles and difficulties but recognizes that God is able to work. The circumstances need not affect one's joy.

INTERCESSORY PRAYER (4:3-4). These two verses are structurally parallel with the exhortation to watchfulness. The term "pray" is actually another participle modifying "devote yourselves." The verb repeats the idea of "prayer" in the basic command of 4:2.[101] Thus by the repeated use of this term, Paul emphasized prayer and gave direction to the Colossians' prayers. Two specific petitions occur. The NIV notes this with the introduction of a new sentence in v. 4. Actually, it is an idea subordinate to the main verb "devote yourselves" and parallel to the petition "that God may open a door for our message."

First, Paul requested that they pray for an open door for the gospel (4:3). Paul always sought ways to communicate the gospel.[102] No one had better skills to turn any situation into an opportunity for witness. In these verses, Paul disclosed the reason for his success in witness as well as the reason he hoped to speak. His success was because he looked to the Lord to supply the wisdom for the opportunity. They were to pray that he would find an open door. The apostle lived for such opportunities that were often the redeeming virtues of his circumstances.[103] He knew, however, that God provided these doors of ministry.

Paul particularly hoped to proclaim the "mystery of Christ." The expression calls to mind 1:27ff. Paul's calling related to the mystery of Christ. It was, specifically, "Christ in you." That message brought the suffering and imprisonment Paul endured (1:24-26).[104]

---

[101] The words are cognates: the verb προσεύχομαι and the noun προσευχή. The repetition is for emphasis.

[102] Cf., e.g., his normal ministry of preaching in the synagogues, with the situation on Mars Hill (Acts 17:16-34), with the address at the riot in Jerusalem (Acts 21:17-22:29), with the reasoned defense before Jewish and Roman officials (Acts 24:1-21, 24-27; 25:1-11; 26:1-27), and even when natural disasters occurred (Acts 27:13-26; 28:1-10).

[103] See notes on Phil 1:12ff.

[104] The mention of chains brings the question of Paul's imprisonment. According to Acts 28:30, when Paul was in prison the first time at Rome, it was a house arrest. Chains were not needed. He endured a second, more severe imprisonment at Rome which, no doubt, included bonds and chains (2 Timothy was written then). The question of Paul's imprisonment has been a major concern of

The second petition occurs in v. 4: "Pray that I may proclaim it clearly, as I should." Paul asked for ability to walk through such doors as would open. Paul used the word "manifest" (*phaneroō*) rather than "proclaim" (*kēryssō*) as the NIV suggests. Consistently in Colossians, the term "manifest" refers to revealing what is hidden (3:4). Paul looked for new situations in which he could make the gospel known. On the one hand, Paul did not pray specifically for a "preaching point," as though that were the only approved means of spreading the gospel. On the other hand, v. 3 makes clear that Paul thought it imperative to speak the word. He hoped, therefore, for an oral ministry. He hoped further that he would do justice to the nature of the gospel so that the witness would be clear.[105]

(2) Wisdom (4:5)

5Be wise in the way you act toward outsiders; make the most of every opportunity.

Having discussed a door of opportunity in ministry, Paul turned his thoughts to wise conduct. The verb used, which is translated "be wise in the way you act," occurs frequently to identify proper conduct. Generally, translators use some form of the word "walk."[106]

Wisdom provides a proper environment for the Christian's walk. The theme of wisdom occurs frequently in this epistle, and that probably reflects a major concern of the false teachers as well. Literally, Paul said, "In wisdom be walking." Thus godly wisdom encompasses the life, as well as the words. At the beginning of the epistle, Paul prayed for the Colossians to know wisdom; here he prayed for them to live it.

Wisdom was necessary because of their Christian testimony. The "ones outside" (*exō*) needed examples of God's wisdom. The parallel passage in Eph 5:16 suggests that the reason for wisdom in the use of time is that "the days are evil." The eschatological setting of the first century enhanced the

---

scholarship. The situation resembles the atmosphere of Philippians, where Paul spoke of his chains as well (1:13). The word could be used as a reference for "confined, imprisoned" without the binding of actual chains. The word can actually be used of a marriage relationship that binds (1 Cor 7:27). The fact is, Paul was not necessarily speaking of literal chains. It may simply mean he was bound in jail, and that appears to be the case here. *BAGD*, 177-78, defines the term in these ways.

[105] Again, comparing this text to Philippians reveals some interesting parallels. First, Paul was pleased with the proclamation of the gospel even from preachers with the wrong motives. He stated there that Christ was being "proclaimed" (κηρύσσω and καταγγέλλω, 1:15-17). Second, his concern was to take advantage of any occasion for the advance of the gospel (1:12,18). Since the two epistles were written at approximately the same time, it must be assumed that Paul wanted a continued avenue for the gospel and hoped he would remain true throughout the entire ordeal of his trial.

[106] The verb is περιπατέω, which is found consistently in Paul's ethical contexts. It seems to express the rabbinic concern for the ethical walk to support religious talk.

prayer for wisdom. Although the passages have almost detailed parallelism (Col 4:5; Eph 5:16), Paul did not mention the evil day here. His concern was the non-Christians' response to the gospel and the attitude of Christians toward them. Divine wisdom results in a positive witness.

The expression "make the most of every opportunity" calls for some clarification. First, the verb "make the most" is structurally subordinate to the previous verb, "be wise in the way you act." The NIV translates it as though it were parallel.[107] The word continues the statement of the verse by describing a way to be wise in their walk. "Make the most" translates the verb *exagorazo*, which means *to buy back* in the active voice. It is middle voice in Greek here and conveys the idea of "make the most of the time."[108] The actual force is difficult to ascertain since it only occurs in these two passages. At the least, Paul called them to make the time count for Christian purposes.

The fact that the verb "make the most of" occurs with the statement to be wise suggests that there was an opportunity to take. When Paul stated that the wisdom was directed toward non-Christians ("outside"), he followed it immediately with the statement about time. He may have thought, therefore, in terms of making the most of time to win unsaved people to the Lord. Perhaps he reflected on his own limited opportunities as he awaited trial. The church should realize all of its opportunities to be of service to God and the world.

(3) Careful Communication (4:6)

[6]Let your conversation be always full of grace, seasoned with salt, so that you may know how to answer everyone.

In the give-and-take of life, both the content of words spoken and the method of speaking matter. Paul continued his exhortations to the believers by addressing their speech. Two statements illustrate the nature of Christians' talk: in grace and with salt.

The two descriptions challenge each person. "In grace" may be used in its full Christian sense of God's grace, in a generic sense of charming, or with a combination of both. The third option seems most likely. This use of the word may reflect an idiom that the readers would have understood as "charming."[109] However, Paul could hardly think of so grand a Christian word as "grace" and not fill it with Christian meaning. Like the salutation of this epistle (1:1-2),

---

[107] Some commentators and grammarians agree, calling the participle an imperatival participle, i.e., one that has the force of a command. They take the other participles of this passage in the same way (4:2-3). This is unlikely. The pattern occurs frequently in the Pauline literature. Imperatives are often followed by modifying participles. In this case, the participle is modal ("by buying up the time") or possibly generally complementary.

[108] *BAGD*, 271.

[109] See Lohse, 168.

Paul took a common expression and infused it with Christian meaning.[110] The result is something like: "Let your speech be always with the graciousness appropriate to Christians, i.e., those who live in a state of grace."

The second characteristic is that of salt. Again Paul's words were proverbial.[111] Salt had three uses at that time. It could preserve a food, "sterilize" a food (antiseptic), or season a food. Here Paul took the last meaning. Conversation was to be seasoned, i.e., acceptable and inoffensive.

Finally, their conversation was to be suited to each person. When confronting the masses of people as Paul and the others did, often someone took offense. Paul stated that each one should know how to answer each objector.[112] Sound answers offered with a positive spirit overcome many obstacles to the gospel. This text emphasizes the method of answering more than the content. It calls for Christian graciousness and sensitivity to the person and situation.

Paul ended the epistle with this call to Christian virtues. In a sense they parallel his beginning. There he prayed for wisdom to know how to walk worthily of the Lord (1:9-12). This wisdom involved growth, power for endurance and patience, and joyful thanksgiving. Here Paul urged them to pray for his witness, for their wisdom, and for their ministry in time and speech. That the epistle should end on a note similar to its beginning is fitting. It is also fitting that Paul should think in terms of reaching non-Christians with the gospel.

---

[110]This happens regularly in the salutation of Paul's epistles (see 1:2). See also R. Martin, *Colossians and Philemon, NCB* (Grand Rapids: Eerdmans, 1973), 128.

[111]Lohse cited a number of rabbinic sources that speak of the need for "salt" in a conversation (168-69, n. 39).

[112]The Greek is graphic. Two words combine to state "each one."

SECTION OUTLINE

IV. CONCLUSION (4:7-18)

   1. Those Who Journeyed to the Church (4:7-9)
     (1) Tychicus (4:7-8)
     (2) Onesimus (4:9)

   2. Those Who Sent Greetings (4:10-14)
     (1) Aristarchus (4:10)
     (2) Mark (4:10)
     (3) Jesus (Justus) (4:11)
     (4) Epaphras (4:12-13)
     (5) Luke (4:14)
     (6) Demas (4:14)

   3. Those to Whom Greetings Were Being Sent (4:15-17)
     (1) Laodicea (4:15-16)
     (2) Nympha (4:15)
     (3) Archippus (4:17)

   4. Final Greeting from Paul (4:18)

IV. CONCLUSION (4:7-18)

Paul concluded this epistle with a rather extended list of greetings. Since he had never visited Colosse, the people mentioned helped to establish and strengthen a firsthand relationship. Paul wrote another letter to a church he had not met, the Epistle to the Romans, in which he included a similar long list of persons. Both letters provide information on the nature of the Christian community in general and in Rome in particular. The list of names in 4:7-15 includes nine persons. All but one were male. This contrasts the list in Rom 16:1-16, which possibly includes ten women who labored with Paul.[1] Most of the names in Colossians occur with a lengthy description about the persons named. This, too, differs from most of the other epistles. Some information is disclosed here that is not contained elsewhere in Scripture. The list may be divided into three categories: those who journeyed to the church from Paul (4:6-9), those who sent greetings to the church (4:10-14), and those to whom Paul sent greetings through church members at Colosse (4:15-17).

1. Those Who Journeyed to the Church (4:7-9)

[7]Tychicus will tell you all the news about me. He is a dear brother, a faithful minister and fellow servant in the Lord. [8]I am sending him to you for the express purpose that you may know about our circumstances and that he may encourage

---

[1]This number includes Junia, who may or may not have been female.

your hearts. ⁹He is coming with Onesimus, our faithful and dear brother, who is one of you. They will tell you everything that is happening here.

In the first century, letters were often carried by personal messengers. The Roman government provided an adequate mail system, but personal couriers made the communication more meaningful. Often a particular situation occasioned such letters. In these verses, Paul identified both the courier and the immediate situation which prompted the letter.

(1) Tychicus (4:7-8)

The first person mentioned is Tychicus. Clearly, he functioned as a special messenger for Paul and carried this letter for him. He had a firsthand knowledge of Paul's circumstances and could give the recipients of the letter more information about Paul (4:7). Paul described him with three attributes of ministry: a loved brother, a faithful minister, and a fellow-servant.[2] Paul used the same terminology in Eph 6:21-22, with the exception of "fellow-servant." Likewise, he identified the same mission in both epistles. Tychicus traveled to both churches with news of Paul. This suggests that he had a special relationship with the churches of Asia. According to Acts 20:4, Tychicus came from Asia and later in Paul's life was sent to Ephesus (2 Tim 4:12) and Crete (Titus 3:12). He became prominent at the end of Paul's ministry, and Paul entrusted him with considerable responsibility, including the collection for the Jerusalem church (Acts 20:4). Since his home was Asia, he was well-suited to carry the letter and greeting to these Asian churches.

(2) Onesimus (4:9)

Onesimus accompanied Tychicus. Paul made two significant statements about Onesimus. First, he was a "faithful and dear brother." In this, Paul described Onesimus with the same terms used of the others in the group. Second, he was "one of you." Onesimus came from Colosse. Whether Paul meant he came from the church or simply was returning to it as a new Christian is not clear. Obviously, however, Onesimus belonged in the church fellowship at the time of writing. According to Phlm 10, Onesimus was a runaway slave. In Rome, that meant that he lost whatever respect he may have had previously and could have been severely punished by Roman law. For that reason, Paul urged the church to accept Onesimus. This became a test case for the instructions Paul issued regarding slaves and masters (3:22-4:1) and of whether Christianity could triumph over social and economic distinctions. The response Paul desired also included forgiveness of Onesimus's personal sin against Philemon. Paul expected Philemon to respond positively; apparently he did. The return of Onesimus to Philemon was the specific situation which prompted Paul's writing. The false teachers made significant inroads, and Paul needed to address

---

[2]These qualities represent the best in Christian growth. All three descriptions occur with one article before them all, and they are joined by "and." This is an emphatic way to indicate that all belong together in this one man.

them. The specific time to write, however, was largely influenced by this moral and ethical necessity. It may be that Paul sent Tychicus with Onesimus because of the uncertainty of how Philemon and the church would respond.[3]

2. Those Who Sent Greetings (4:10-14)

[10]My fellow prisoner Aristarchus sends you his greetings, as does Mark, the cousin of Barnabas. (You have received instructions about him; if he comes to you, welcome him.) [11]Jesus, who is called Justus, also sends greetings. These are the only Jews among my fellow workers for the kingdom of God, and they have proved a comfort to me. [12]Epaphras, who is one of you and a servant of Christ Jesus, sends greetings. He is always wrestling in prayer for you, that you may stand firm in all the will of God, mature and fully assured. [13]I vouch for him that he is working hard for you and for those at Laodicea and Hierapolis. [14]Our dear friend Luke, the doctor, and Demas send greetings.

Paul continued the closing by sending greetings from five men who were with him in Rome. They obviously had a close relationship with both Paul and the church. In some cases, the connection with Paul is clear, but history is silent on the connection with the church.

(1) Artistarchus (4:10)

Aristarchus was a native of Thessalonica and a traveling companion of Paul (Acts 19:29; 20:4). He probably became a Christian at Thessalonica (Acts 17:1-9) and enjoyed a quickly growing good reputation. When Paul took up the collection for the Jewish saints, Aristarchus was selected to accompany the money to Jerusalem (Acts 20:4). He remained with Paul on the journey to Rome (Acts 27:2). In Col 4:10 Paul called him a "fellow-prisoner," presumably in prison for the same reasons as Paul, and he was one of three Jewish believers who were with Paul at the time (4:11).

(2) Mark (4:10)

John Mark is one of the well-known persons of the New Testament even though there are few verses about him in Scripture. He was the cousin of Barnabas[4] and grew up in Jerusalem (Acts. 12:12). Like many people in the first century, he had two names. John was his Jewish name; Mark was his Roman name.[5]

Mark had a significant place in the early advance of Christian missions. He accompanied Paul and Barnabas on the first missionary journey (Acts 13:5). For some unknown reason, he returned home after the group entered Asia (Acts 13:13), and this became the occasion for division between Paul and Barnabas before the second missionary journey (Acts 15:39). Most likely, Barnabas, who

---

[3]More will be said in the Epistle to Philemon. See also the interesting discussion of Onesimus in F. F. Bruce, *The Pauline Circle* (Grand Rapids: Eerdmans, 1985), 66-72.

[4]The Greek word definitely means "cousin," *BAGD*, 66; see also Num 36:11.

[5]Bruce, *The Pauline Circle*, 74. His background suited him to Christian ministry since a church group, including Peter, met in his mother's house (Acts 12:12).

had discipled Paul in his early Christian years, discipled Mark from that point and saw him develop into an effective Christian minister. The Scriptures next speak of Mark in Rome, comforting Paul (Col 4:10,11; Phlm 24). F. F. Bruce suggested that Mark went to Rome after the edict of Claudius against the Jews was reversed sometime in the mid-50s.[6] He accompanied Peter and, perhaps, took up ministerial duties of his own.[7] When Peter wrote his first letter, Mark was with him (1 Pet 5:13). Later tradition indicates that Mark wrote the Gospel of Mark[8] and conducted a missionary endeavor to Egypt, where some think he founded the church at Alexandria.[9]

Paul thanked God for Mark. He became a "fellow-worker" and a comfort to Paul (4:11). In the last of Paul's epistles, written from a Roman prison, Paul requested Mark's presence (2 Tim 4:11). Any differences between these two saints were long passed. Paul mentioned the possibility that Mark would visit the Lycus valley, and the church knew to welcome him.

(3) Jesus (Justus) (4:11)

Jesus (Justus) occurs only here in the New Testament. He was one of the three Jews with Paul at the time of writing (4:11). He also comforted Paul in his trial. His two names were Jesus, which means *Joshua*, the Jewish name, and Justus, a Latin name.

(4) Epaphras (4:12-13)

In 1:7 Paul mentioned Epaphras as the one who brought greetings from the church to Paul. There Paul identified him as the one who brought them the gospel, a fellow-servant, and a faithful minister. In 4:12 Paul added that he was "one of them," a prayer warrior, and a diligent worker on their behalf. Epaphras's name occurs in Philemon as well. There Paul stated that he was a fellow-prisoner (Phlm 23).

Epaphras brought the gospel to Colosse. No doubt he was at least one of the evangelists of the Lycus valley. No one knows how or where he met Paul, but a strong friendship developed. Most likely, he met Paul while Paul taught at Ephesus, some one hundred miles west of Colosse, and returned home with the good news. At some point, he left Colosse and joined Paul in order to help him in his difficulties. The church probably sent him on its behalf since Paul inferred as much in Col 4:13. Since he worked diligently for three Christian communities (Colosse, Laodicea, and Hierapolis), they may have joined together to sponsor him as a tangible support for Paul.

At some point, Epaphras became a prisoner like Paul. Three times the text suggests that of him (Col 1:7; 4:12; Phlm 23). In the two references in

---

[6]The edict was in A.D. 49, and it was surely repealed by the accession of Nero in A.D. 54.

[7]Bruce, *The Pauline Circle*, 77-78.

[8]Eusebius, *Ecclesiastical History*, 3.39.15, who quoted a lost letter from Papias, *Exegesis of the Dominical Logia*, from the first quarter of the second century.

[9]Ibid., 2.16.1. There is some question about his founding the church there, but he probably did go to North Africa with the gospel.

Colossians, the word "slave" occurs. Epaphras was a "fellow-slave" with Paul (1:7) and a "slave of Christ." He is the only person other than Paul and Timothy about whom the term "slave" (*doulos*) is used. No doubt his slavery was to Christ, as was Paul's. In Philemon, however, Paul used a word which he reserved for actual prisoners (*synaichmalōtos*). This evidence reveals that Epaphras was a prisoner with Paul.

Epaphras "wrestled" in prayer for the Colossians. His commission was to represent them to Paul and to assist him in any way he could. As he fulfilled that commission, he carried a deep concern for the church he had established, and that concern became intercessory prayer. Specifically, he prayed for their maturity and assurance in the will of God (4:12). His prayer recalls Paul's prayer in 1:9-11. There is one additional element, however, and that is "full assurance." The term means *to complete, fill completely* (*plērophoreō*), and therefore may have come to mean "to be convinced fully."[10] Epaphras may have prayed for a complete understanding of the will of God. That parallels Paul's prayer that the Colossians would be filled with the knowledge of God's will (1:9).[11] Epaphras was commended for his hard work and intense prayer on their behalf. This was another way Paul thanked them for their contribution to him in sending such a one to him.

(5) Luke (4:14)

Luke had a significant role in the early church. Although Paul mentioned Luke only three times in the epistles (Col 4:14; Phlm 24; 2 Tim 4:11), he did more than any other person to enhance history's understanding of Paul.

Little is known of Luke's background. The best records suggest he was a native of Antioch, Syria, a Gentile, a physician, a writer, and a devoted Christian. The Anti-Marcionite Prologue to Luke, dating from the second century, states:

> Luke was an Antiochian of Syria, a physician by profession. He was a disciple of the apostles and later accompanied Paul until his martyrdom. He served the Lord without distraction, having neither wife nor children, and at the age of eighty-four he fell asleep in Boetia, full of the Holy Spirit.[12]

In the Book of Acts, three times the subjects change from "they" to "we" (Acts 16:10; 20:5; 27:1). Most likely this is evidence that Luke journeyed with Paul during those times. The evidence suggests Luke joined Paul at Troas and journeyed to Philippi with him (Acts 16:10); he remained at Philippi and rejoined Paul to take the collection to Jerusalem (Acts 20:5-21:8); and he joined Paul at Caesarea and journeyed with him to Rome (Acts 27:1-28:16). Later, at the time of Paul's second Roman imprisonment (ca. A.D. 65/66), Paul

[10] *BAGD*, 620.

[11] It is significant that a word on the same root, πληρόω, should be used in both the prayer and Paul's description here. Probably the two men prayed the same prayer for the church.

[12] F. F. Bruce, *The Spreading Flame* (London: Paternoster, 1958), 230ff.

wrote that only Luke remained with him as he awaited his trial (2 Tim 4:11). Paul called him the "loved physician," and Paul may have needed physical help as he grew older. He found it in this man who also knew the dynamics of spiritual ministry.

Obviously Luke was a writer.[13] Since Paul did not pen his own epistles, and Luke alone remained with Paul at the writing of 2 Timothy, Luke probably wrote that letter for Paul. The earliest traditions also indicate that Luke wrote the third Gospel and Acts, comprising about one third of the length of the New Testament. Acts provides more insight into the events of Paul's travels than any other book. Luke had many friends and among them was the Colossian church.[14]

(6) Demas (4:14)

Demas is mentioned only twice in Scripture, here and in 2 Tim 4:10. Although he accompanied Paul to Rome, later he "loved the world" and returned to Thessalonica, which may have been his home. No doubt Paul was saddened by this departure not only because of the loss to the gospel but also because of the loss of a personal friend and supporter. Paul's statement that Demas "loved this world" apparently means the pressures of Paul's situation and the lure of an easier life caused him to forsake the Lord.[15]

3. Those to Whom Greetings Were Being Sent (4:15-17)

[15]Give my greetings to the brothers at Laodicea, and to Nympha and the church in her house.

[16]After this letter has been read to you, see that it is also read in the church of the Laodiceans and that you in turn read the letter from Laodicea.

[17]Tell Archippus: "See to it that you complete the work you have received in the Lord."

Paul sent greetings to a final group of persons. The readers of the letter were instructed to greet them for Paul. Among other things, this reveals the closeness of the Christian communities in the area and the ease of communication from one to another.

(1) Laodicea (4:15-16)

Laodicea was located in the Lycus valley and was a neighboring city to Colosse. The church there dated from approximately the same time as the one

---

[13]This assumed that the Gospel of Luke and the Book of Acts were written by this same man.

[14]Luke is to be identified more closely with the Philippian church. He may have stayed with them during the years between the second and third missionary journeys and the "they/we" sections of Acts. Acts seems to indicate that he was in that region as a locale of ministry before Paul went to Philippi since he joined Paul at Troas. Some have even suggested that Luke was the pastor at Philippi.

[15]Paul did not say that Demas departed from the Lord. Paul's sharp criticism, however, could certainly be understood that way, and that is what most scholars have assumed about him. Not all who opposed Paul loved the world (see Phil 1:12-19).

at Colosse, and most likely someone other than Paul founded it. It apparently began as a vital, energetic Christian community, but by the end of the century suffered from lukewarmness and formalism (Rev 3:14-22). Paul took the time to write an epistle to the church, presumably at the same time he wrote Colossians, but the letter no longer remains. Paul also mentioned another city in the area of Laodicea and Colosse, Heirapolis (4:13). There was a church there, but, as far as can be determined, Paul did not write it a personal letter. The reason Paul wrote to the church at Laodicea and not to the church at Heirapolis may have been that Laodicea was located on the road to Colosse. Paul's courier had to travel through it, and its location encouraged frequent communication between these two cities. Heirapolis lies slightly north, off the main East-West road.[16]

(2) Nympha (4:15)

Since this is the only mention of Nympha, little is known about this person.[17] She lived in Laodicea, and the church met in her house. The New Testament often identifies a church meeting place by the woman's name, as in Acts 12:12 (Mark's mother), and Rom 16:5 mentions "their house" (Aquila and Priscilla). It appears that the female name has least difficulties and at least some other passages to serve as a pattern.

(3) Archippus (4:17)

Archippus appears in Scripture in two texts, both of which identify his work. In Col 4:17, Paul urged him to complete the work God gave him to do. No one knows what that involved. Perhaps he received a call to service, and Paul took the occasion to encourage him. In Phlm 2, Paul called him "our fellow soldier." That does not necessarily imply military service because Paul used the term of himself and his companions. Some take this to mean that he belonged to Philemon's family since Apphia, Philemon's wife, received greetings at the same time.

4. Final Greeting from Paul (4:18)

[18]**I, Paul, write this greeting in my own hand. Remember my chains. Grace be with you.**

The letter ends with a personal touch. Paul signed the greeting in his hand. This means that someone else penned the epistle, which happened commonly in the first century and with Paul's letters (e.g., Rom 16:22). Paul's eyesight prohibited his actually writing these letters (Gal 6:11). The authenticity, however, came from Paul's signature.

---

[16]See the excellent brief discussion of these three cities in Hendriksen, 6-14.

[17]There is some question about the gender of the name. If male, it could be a shortened form of Nymphrodorus, but the female Nympha (Νύμφαν) is fairly well attested. Some manuscripts mention the church at "his house" (D, K, are the strongest), and some mention "their house" (ℵ, A, C, P, are the strongest).

Two final reminders were given. They encapsulate the entire message of the letter. The first was, "remember my chains." The chains outwardly signified the value of the gospel for Paul. Were it not for a commitment to the gospel, Paul would not be under arrest, nor would he have faced the hardships he did. In Phil 1:13, Paul wrote another reason for the importance of the chains. They signified his relationship to Jesus Christ. His real slavery was to Christ, and that took him to Rome.[18] The chains constantly reminded Paul of the practical nature of his Christian commitment, and they also could have been an encouragement to others.[19]

Secondly, Paul reminded them of God's grace. He ended where he began. In a sense, the entire epistle argues for the principle of grace, that God supplies his salvation freely, that he requires nothing but a trust in the work of his Son, Jesus, and that grace sustains the Christians' life. If God's grace is with them, they need nothing else.

---

[18] See the discussion in Phil 1:12ff.

[19] That some others were encouraged is clear from Phil 1:15ff.

Philemon

──────── INTRODUCTION ────────

Christianity arose in a complex social setting. Many conflicting religions and philosophies contributed to a pluralistic environment where anyone could justify anything in the name of a personal god. Secularism rose to new popularity as Greeks and Romans often made only a token acknowledgment of the place of religion in society.

Christianity met these challenges. Christians claimed that faith in Christ brought a totally new way of thinking and acting. Everywhere Christianity spread, a sense of morality and social justice naturally went with it.

The Epistle to Philemon illustrates this truth. It is an informal letter addressed to a man converted to Christ by the apostle Paul. He was a slave owner of significant means, who apparently had some influence in the local church. Paul challenged his dear friend Philemon to consider the impact of Christ on the institution of slavery, the worth of all people, and the necessity of acting like God in forgiving and restoring those who fail. The epistle stands as a model of healed relationships in Christ and of Christian social justice.

This letter is a personal communication. It is warm, friendly, and Christian. It is the shortest of Paul's letters, containing only 335 words in the original Greek text. Paul wanted Philemon to accept and restore Onesimus, a runaway slave. His carefully constructed argument balanced three factors: his strong friendship with Philemon, his obedience to Roman law regarding runaway slaves, and his desire to help his new convert, Onesimus. This letter stands as a model for approaching social concerns which grow out of the transformed life of a Christian. Through its verses, many may see themselves in the position of Philemon, the person against whom someone had sinned. They may ask how God wants them to respond to a change of heart in the one who sinned against them. More may see themselves in the situation of Onesimus, who had sinned against someone. They, too, may profit from the letter. The message of the epistle survived, in part, because it vividly illustrates the believer's relationship with Christ. This picture of human reconciliation has crystallized a Christian understanding of proper human relationships. Further, in this passage Paul sowed the seeds of social reform based on unalterable truths which, when understood correctly, transform society.

1. The Authorship

Few scholars seriously question the Pauline authorship of this epistle. From the early Christian centuries, it has enjoyed almost unanimous acceptance in the Pauline corpus. The earliest collections of New Testament letters included Philemon without dispute.[1] The major objection to Pauline authorship came from the Tübingen School of F. C. Baur, who interpreted it as a second-century document instructing the church regarding slavery.[2] Today, virtually all scholars accept Pauline authorship.

2. The Place and Date of Origin

As with the other Prison Epistles, questions of place and date of origin interrelate. Three options have been suggested for the place of origin: Rome, Caesarea, and Ephesus. The supporting data for these imprisonments occur in the introductions to Colossians and Philippians. Clearly Paul was in prison at the time of writing (vv. 1,9,13,23). The traditional view identifies Rome as the origin of the epistle. Those who suggest Ephesus as the place of imprisonment and origin of the letter make two observations. First, Paul requested lodging for a proposed visit with Philemon (v. 22). Second, Onesimus was a runaway slave and probably would have run to Ephesus rather than Rome. Both arguments can be effectively countered, and they present no major obstacle to a Roman origin.[3]

---

[1] These are the Muratorian Fragment and Marcion's Canon.

[2] B. Weiss apparently considers this as one of Baur's greatest blunders. It shows how uniformly scholarship accepts the Pauline authorship. (Referenced in D. Guthrie, *New Testament Introduction*, rev. ed. [Downers Grove, Ill.: InterVarsity, 1990], 664).

[3] The introductions to Colossians and Philippians present an overview of the arguments pro and con.

The date of writing depends on the place of origin. Those who decide for an Ephesian imprisonment place it early, about A.D. 55. Those who accept a Caesarean hypothesis place the letter at about A.D. 58. The traditional dating from Rome places the epistle at about A.D. 61.

3. The Occasion

The letter makes clear the occasion for writing. Onesimus, slave of Philemon who was wealthy Christian convert in the Lycus valley, had run away from his master. After leaving his master, Onesimus became a Christian through his contact with Paul while Paul was in prison. He served Paul faithfully for a time (v. 13) but determined to return to Philemon to put his past life in order. Philemon was also converted to Christ by Paul, presumably while Paul was in Ephesus since Paul had not personally evangelized in the Lycus valley. A strong friendship developed, and Paul wrote to his good friend, urging him to forgive and accept Onesimus. Paul reminded Philemon of their relationship and suggested that his Christian commitment required such loving actions. Onesimus traveled home with Tychicus, one of Paul's companions (Col 4:7), and on the way they delivered the letters to Ephesus, Colosse, and Laodicea.

Several matters of interest remain obscured by history. First, no one knows why Onesimus ran away. Most commonly, scholars assume that he had stolen money and then absconded (v. 18). Others suggest that he only owed Philemon the value of the work that would have been done in his absence. A third view is that Onesimus was sent to Paul for a specific task and that he overstayed his time.[4] Paul knew that some restitution was in order, and he urged Philemon to hold him responsible for it rather than Onesimus. After his release from prison, Paul hoped to visit Philemon.

Second, no one really knows what happened to Onesimus and Philemon. History records no evidence of reconciliation. However, the fact that the letter survived and remains in the canon strongly suggests that they heeded Paul's desire. The church likely would not have preserved a letter of instruction had Philemon failed. After all, the letter belonged to Philemon. Perhaps Onesimus received a copy for his own records, but someone had to circulate the letter. Most probably, the letter accomplished its purpose of reconciliation and became Onesimus's "charter of liberty."[5] The sentiments of the Christian community would have turned against Philemon had he not responded positively.

Third, did Philemon release Onesimus and, perhaps, make him free to serve with Paul? Paul did not specifically request Onesimus's release, but v. 16 suggests it was the Christian response to the situation. History records an

---

[4] F. F. Bruce, *Paul: Apostle of the Heart Set Free* (Grand Rapids: Eerdmans, 1977), 400.

[5] Ibid., 406. Bruce also accepts the likelihood that Onesimus was the later Bishop of Ephesus mentioned by Ignatius.

Onesimus was bishop of Ephesus in the second century,[6] and some claim he was the same man.[7] However, Onesimus was a common slave name, and at least one other Christian of the second century bore the name.[8] Further, this would make Onesimus a very young man at the time of Paul's writing, and it is unlikely that the same man was still active some sixty years later. Since solid evidence is lacking, the better approach is to remain silent about suppositions.

4. The Purpose of the Letter

Paul wrote Philemon to implore him to forgive and receive his runaway slave, Onesimus (v. 10). No doubt when Onesimus determined to get matters straight at home, some fear entered his heart. Even though his master was a good man (vv. 4-7), as a runaway slave, Onesimus deserved punishment. If nothing else, he could be made an example to other slaves. Paul took the role of a mediator, imploring Philemon to have mercy on this new Christian. Perhaps the friendship between Philemon and Paul provided an avenue of approach.

A few commentators have challenged that purpose in writing. Some suggest that the real purpose was for Philemon to allow Onesimus to continue serving Paul. Thus, Paul really was asking for more than forgiveness and restitution: He was asking Philemon to read between the lines of vv. 13-14 and to donate Onesimus to Paul. This view does not fit well with the details of the text. First, Paul's statement of v. 21, "knowing that you will do even more than I ask," implies that his real request had been stated. What more could there be than sending Onesimus to Paul if that had been his concern? Second, in v. 15 Paul stated "that you might have him back for good." Onesimus was to remain at Philemon's house. Third, the four imperatives of the epistle speak to the reconciliation between Philemon and Onesimus, never to any benefit Paul might derive from the relationship.[9]

Some scholars point to the idea of *koinōnia* ("fellowship") as the central purpose of the letter.[10] "Fellowship" means *interchange*. In this, Paul first presented the close ties between himself and Philemon (vv. 4-7). Then, Paul developed the strong relationship between himself and Onesimus (vv. 10-14). In this,

---

[6]Ignatius, *Ephesians, I.*

[7]John Knox, *Philemon among the Letters of Paul: A New View of its Place and Importance*, rev. ed. (1935, Nashville: Abingdon, 1959).

[8]See J. B. Lightfoot, *St. Paul's Epistles to the Colossians and to Philemon*, reprint ed. (Grand Rapids: Zondervan, 1959), 311.

[9]The imperatives are: "welcome him as you would welcome me" (v. 17); "charge it to me" (v. 18); "refresh my heart in Christ" (v. 20); and "prepare a guest room for me" (v. 22). None of these explicitly suggest that Onesimus would have a future ministry with Paul. These insightful objections come from N. T. Wright, *Colossians and Philemon*, TNTC (Grand Rapids: Eerdmans, 1986), 169.

[10]E.g., M. D. Hooker, "Interchange in Christ" *JTS* 22 (1971): 360-61. Wright is supportive of this idea as well, 168.

both men had a debt of friendship to Paul, and both united "in Paul." Because of the close ties between Paul and each of them, close ties between Onesimus and Philemon were natural. This pictures believers and Christ. In different ways, both God and humanity have close ties to Christ.[11] The differing parties come together in Christ, who is the meeting place between them. The interpretation is attractive, and it may reveal why the epistle has been so loved through the centuries.

Finally, some have stated that the purpose was to destroy the institution of slavery.[12] If that were the case, however, Paul spoke too gently and acceptingly of the practice. Though Paul planted the seed of emancipation, his language was covert enough that slave owners have consistently appealed to it in support of their slave practice.[13] Paul's message was too gentle for that theme to be primary.

5. Approaches to the Epistle to Philemon

The Epistle to Philemon is a personal letter from friend to friend. Almost uniformly, scholars have treated it that way. The letter describes a real problem that did not need church intervention. A few have raised questions about the fact that it became public, and some have wondered if the letter has been interpreted correctly. Two alternate approaches represent ways of thinking which challenge a traditional understanding.

(1) Reconstructing the Circumstances of the Letter

A few scholars have attempted to reconstruct the circumstances described in the epistle. The most notable are the positions of E. J. Goodspeed and J. Knox. Although they approached the letter similarly, their suggestions vary at significant points. The position of Knox is as follows: Philemon was overseer of the Lycus valley churches who lived in Laodicea; Archippus, a patron of the church, lived in Colosse where the church met in his house; Archippus owned the slave Onesimus; Paul sent Onesimus to Philemon to gain support before going to his master, Archippus; Onesimus carried two letters to be read publicly; one was Colossians and the other was Philemon, which was identified as the letter to Laodicea (Col 4:16); Onesimus was released and appeared later in Ignatius's letter to the Ephesians, at which time Onesimus was bishop of Ephesus; Onesimus collected the Pauline corpus, and Ephesians became the cover letter for the group.[14]

---

[11] The teaching of Ps 8 may be recalled here. In Jesus, humanity achieved what it was promised by God. He brought humanity to new heights of honor.

[12] This was Baur's basic contention as he placed the epistle in the second century.

[13] Actually, the argument is that Paul did not forbid slavery in this book. At any rate, the message of freedom did not come through as strongly as some suggest.

[14] This outline is found in C. F. D. Moule, *The Epistles of Paul the Apostle to the Colossians and to Philemon*, CGTC, 15-16. Moule also criticizes the position incisively. See Knox.

The theory suffers severely, and scholars have almost universally rejected it. The letter places Philemon in the place of prominence, being the first one named, and there is no evidence that Philemon and Archippus lived in different towns. Similarly, the suggestion that Philemon was the letter to Laodicea has significant weaknesses. The theory raises more problems than it solves.[15] There has been little success in such theories.[16]

(2) Rhetorical Critical Theories

Rhetorical criticism has been applied to the epistle with some promise of exegetical fruit. Less radical than the other theories, these reconstruct the dynamics of the letter and do not necessarily call for a change of circumstances or a redefinition of persons. F. F. Church presents a helpful analysis which stimulates exegesis.[17] It serves as a good example of this discipline. Church understands that Philemon was constructed in a deliberative manner, with an exordium (thanksgiving, vv. 4-7), a proof (main body, vv. 8-16), and a peroration (closing, vv. 17-22). This analysis reveals the unity and integrity of the letter since its carefully constructed style contains similar words and themes throughout.

The exordium (vv. 4-7) accomplished three things. First, by praising Philemon, it established good will. Second, Paul stressed the qualities that were required for Philemon to respond as Paul desired. Third, Paul alluded to particulars which later would be adduced in the proof and underscored in the peroration. In the exordium, the basic elements of his arguments occur.

The proof develops Paul's argument (vv. 8-16). Paul opened with an appeal to *ethos* and *pathos* through a device of tautological parallelism, the repetition of ideas. Further, Paul established the motives of *utilitas, affectio,* and *honestas.* Unlike other orators, however, Paul added providence to his motive.

---

[15]Moule provides insight into his appraisal of this kind of reconstruction when he calls the position a "fascinating detective story" (14).

[16]See S. Winter, "Methodological Observations on a New Interpretation of Paul's Letter to Philemon" *USQR,* xxxix, No. 3 (1984): 203-12, and "Paul's Letter to Philemon" *NTS* 33 (1987): 1-15. Winter proposes a similar type of reconstruction based on Ricouer's hermeneutical "guess." The first article concerns hermeneutics and the second exegesis. She believes that the traditional "guess" is stagnant and proposes another to open up the meaning of the text. Her "guess" is that Paul wanted Onesimus as a Christian servant with him. Her reconstruction reassigns the traditional understanding of the roles of the various persons. However, she never answers the question of why her "guess" is better than the traditional "guess." She starts with the problem of "if Paul wanted Onesimus to be freed, why was he not more explicit about his intention?" (208-09). Her position fails at this point twice: first, that probably was not the reason for Paul's writing, so those scholars asked the wrong question to begin with; second, her question leaves the problem more pronounced (if Paul wanted to keep Onesimus *with him,* why didn't he be more explicit about that intention?). The fact is, Paul clearly stated what he wanted. Her exegesis is helpful, particularly in the second article, but her assumptions have no foundations.

[17]F. F. Church, "Rhetorical Structure and Design in Paul's Letter to Philemon," *HTR* 71 (Jan.-Apr. 1978): 17-33.

In the peroration (vv. 17-22) Paul fulfilled the four requirements of a closing. He stated his request (v. 17); he amplified his argument (vv. 18-19); he set the hearer in an emotional frame of mind (v. 20); and he secured the hearer's favor (vv. 21-22).

The analysis demonstrates the logic of Paul's address. The point, however, is that it appears to be a public, prethought letter, rather than a private correspondence between friends. Whatever conclusion may be drawn regarding that, rhetorical approaches have the value of stimulating exegesis. Nevertheless, two significant questions arise from these approaches. First, are they correct? All conversation involves rhetoric, and any letter could be subject to a critical appraisal about whether the author planned to use the conventions identified. Conventions simply chart the movement of the mind. Second, are the correct conventions identified? Beginning with the wrong model could radically affect the conclusion and, therefore, the interpretation of the letter itself.

Perhaps the most significant change of circumstance to come from rhetorical studies of Philemon is the nature of the letter. Throughout the history of interpretation, Philemon has been considered a personal letter. If Paul took the time to plan how to persuade Philemon of his will, perhaps the letter was not as personal as previously thought, or perhaps Philemon was not a good friend. Neither of these conclusions seems appropriate at this time.

6. Slavery in the First Century

The Roman world lived with slavery. From the earliest times, the government accepted and promoted the practice. By the first century, however, the institution of slavery was changing. Public sentiment decried harsh treatment of slaves, and many leading orators spoke against the institution itself. This caused many masters to free their slaves. Freed slaves found that they had been in a better social situation before their freedom.[18] The ethical issues were pronounced even then, and slavery became a primary concern.

Slaves were common at the time of the empire. Rome's military advances supplied most of the slaves. The armies brought back thousands of captives who were sold to increase the investments of private citizens who supported the army. Some reports indicate that often as many as ten thousand slaves per day were placed on the auction blocks in Delos. When Rome's military machine slowed, fewer slaves became available. The later days of the republic saw slavery at its zenith, but it diminished in the empire. In addition to wars, slave traders kidnapped people to sell. Some people became slaves because of crimes they committed, by birth, by failure to pay debts, or by choice. Initially, most slaves were barbarians, with little to offer other than physical strength. As Roman armies advanced, however, slave resources included the highly

---

[18] E.g., older slaves were sometimes freed because they could not work, and they could not support themselves in a free existence.

skilled and educated. These slaves brought a higher price and undertook quite responsible positions in the government or the home.[19] They were treated in accord with their value to the owner, and many lived quite well. Estimates of actual numbers vary, but it is reasonable to suggest that at least one third of the population of the city of Rome consisted of slaves. At Trajan's time, that amounted to approximately four hundred thousand.[20]

The Jewish situation was quite different. The Old Testament acknowledged slavery as an institution and had laws regulating it. Josephus recorded that Herod the Great tightened the regulations concerning slavery.[21] Jerusalem had a slave auction block, and the rabbinic literature mentions some who purchased slaves.[22] Generally slavery was limited to the cities and to Gentile influence in the land. Most rural families could not afford slaves and had little interest in the practice.

In the Roman world, treatment of slaves varied considerably. Strictly speaking, the owner had the complete right to do whatever he wished: Slaves were viewed as chattel. On one hand, an owner could sell, punish, torture, or even kill them. A series of uprisings in the first two centuries B.C. and the voice of concerned philosophers brought more humanitarian treatment, however.[23] Legal protection soon followed. At the beginning of the empire a *Lex Petronia* (law) forbade a master to give his slave to the beasts of the amphitheater without a judgment to do so. Claudius (mid-first century A.D.) decreed that abandoned sick slaves should be freed. Shortly thereafter, Nero instituted a legal procedure for hearing the complaints of injustice brought by slaves against their masters. Domitian (A.D. 83) forbade a master to castrate his slaves and set the penalty for doing so at half the offender's property. In the second century, reforms continued. Hadrian forbade the selling of slaves to the trainer of gladiators and also required a review of the death penalty for slaves before a master could enforce it himself. Finally, at the end of the second century, Antoninus Pius condemned as homicide the slaying of a slave by the sole order of his master.[24]

---

[19]Many public slaves belonged to various government bodies. Often the Greeks were highly sought because of their education.

[20]J. Carcopino, *Daily Life in Ancient Rome* (New Haven: Yale, 1940), 65. Trajan claimed to have 1,200,000 inhabitants in the capital city.

[21]Josephus, *Antiquities*, III:16.1f.

[22]J. Jeremias, *Jerusalem in the Time of Jesus* (London: SCM, 1969), 36. Tyre was the main center for the Palestinian slave trade, and most slaves entered through that route.

[23]The significant uprisings were primarily in southern Italy. They were in Eunus of Apamea (136-132 B.C.) and Spartacus (73-71 B.C.). The philosophical voice came primarily from the Stoic philosophers who believed in the equal rights of all people. See the discussion in H. Koester, *History, Culture, and Religion of the Hellenistic Age, Introduction to the New Testament* (New York: Walter De Gruyter, 1982), 1:61.

[24]These laws are reported and documented in Carcopino, 57-58.

On the other hand, there were always those who treated slaves well. Slaves of such masters were considered part of the family, and the master assumed their total care. Some were given high-level management positions in households; they were entrusted with the education of sons; they provided health care for their masters; and they handled delicate financial matters for the family. Valued slaves often were loved and protected. Some were allowed to marry, own property, develop financial resources, and will their estates to whom they would. Practically, slaves were an investment, and few could afford to abuse them.

The religions had a more consistent attitude toward the institution. The people recognized that slaves had souls, and all religions welcomed them into their fellowships. A slave could even practice a religion different from his master. To find slaves in the New Testament church, whether their masters chose to follow Christ, would be no surprise.[25]

In this social setting, the early church lived with slavery. It was a fact of life. Christianity recognized the evils of the institution and spoke against it mildly, but the religions in general had little to do with social change. "It would have been too much to expect these religions to have advocated the abolition of slavery as an institution (although some of the church fathers indeed demanded just that)."[26] Christianity arose in a real-life, tension-filled setting. The slave insurrections had already failed, causing significant injury, sorrow, and loss of life. On the positive side, "the social position of the slaves was not seen as a human disqualification."[27] Working within these tensions, however, the seed of abolition were sown. No epistle expressed that better and more powerfully than Philemon.

Many slaves took every opportunity to run from their masters. They normally fled to large cities, eating whatever they could and hiding from the authorities who might recognize them. Thus, freedom brought a worse life than they had had with their masters. In addition, the penalty for runaway slaves was severe. Although officially the government recognized the value of human life, many masters treated their slaves harshly. No doubt that was a fear in Onesimus's heart. Further, in Onesimus's case the matter was public, perhaps even common knowledge in the church.[28] A major social upheaval could have occurred, depending on how Philemon handled Onesimus. He would be a test case for the rest of the masters and slaves.

---

[25] See the discussion in Koester, 62.

[26] Ibid.

[27] Ibid.

[28] Interestingly, this personal and private epistle is written with more than one person in mind as well. This is seen in the interchange between singular pronouns of vv. 4-24 and the plural in vv. 3,25.

7. The Message of Philemon

This little epistle, largely neglected, contains a powerful and relevant message for contemporary Christians. Three major emphases occur: the teaching about slavery, Christian fellowship, and Christian living. These respectively relate to social change, communal life, and the mind of Christ.

(1) Paul and Slavery

The most obvious concern to contemporary Christians is the social institution of slavery. Many questions arise about the way Paul handled it. Why did he not forbid the institution? Why did he not recommend that Philemon release Onesimus? Why were his instructions so vague? For many, Paul moved too slowly in abolishing an evil institution.

The church lived in its own context. While slavery was accepted generally, many voices spoke against it during the first century. Some of these incited riot. Paul knew that the church could not be perceived as the instigator of rebellion leading to loss of life. The Roman Empire had within it the mechanism for effecting change, and that change had to come voluntarily from the individuals whose lives were changed by their Lord. Slaves could be freed by anyone, even if their freedom at times caused more problems than it solved.[29] Paul chose the theological route. If the theological seed were sown, a solid foundation existed for a permanent change that was more socially pervasive than one institution.[30]

Paul taught equality. Colossians 3:18-4:1 contains some basic principles (see the commentary notes there). Slaves served Christ in spite of their economic situation. Their owners were also slaves, only they were slaves to the Master in heaven. This equality was to lead the way to sympathy one for the other. Further, God called people to serve him in varied circumstances, and he judged impartially. The application of these principles would bring a *de facto* end to the institution.

In Philemon, Paul built his case on the relationships that emerge in Christ. It is a Christian defense against the institution. While others argued for the brotherhood of man,[31] Paul rooted his thoughts in the "in Christ" relationship. All "in Christ" were united, and they participated in a common task of knowing Christ. Right thinking people wish the best for their families, and right thinking Christians wish the best for their spiritual brothers and sisters as well. Thus,

---

[29] Specifically the problems involved the lack of resources to enjoy life and the amassing of a huge welfare state. These do not excuse the practice; they are mentioned to put the issue into perspective.

[30] E. Lohse, *Colossians and Philemon, Her* (Philadelphia: Fortress, 1971), well states the situation, "The question of the existing social order, in which there are masters and slaves, is not broached." In Christ the implications of human relationships have been "radically renewed so that slave and master are one in Christ." He equally insightfully states in a footnote: "For this reason, criticisms have been leveled against Paul that are as subjective as they are unjust" (205).

[31] The Stoic philosophers took that approach, and it is a valid argument. Its weakness is that Christians know more than that.

manumission of slaves logically proceeds from the message of the gospel. All persons are equal, and in Christ that equality can be freely expressed (Gal 3:28). "What this letter does is to bring us into an atmosphere in which the institution could only wilt and die."[32]

Paul's power was the power of the truth and faith in the Spirit of God. As he approached Philemon, he trusted Philemon to respond to the word of God in voluntary obedience. Paul did not speak against the institution; his theology spoke for him. Paul did not choose activism; he trusted the power of preaching. Paul refused coercion; he let God lead even his closest friends.[33] Thus, this small epistle does not forbid slavery overtly. Slavery was not even the issue it was written to solve: It was the occasion which provided the opportunity to address another matter. The issue was Christian relationships. Nevertheless, genuinely Christian relationships bring an end to such evils as slavery.

(2) Christian Fellowship

The primary message of this epistle is Christian fellowship. The term "fellowship" occurs at strategic locations in the epistle,[34] and the idea occurs elsewhere. "Fellowship" is participation in the lives of others. The NIV correctly translates v. 17 as, "If you consider me a partner." Partners' lives interrelate at the deepest levels, and partnership became the main avenue of appeal from Paul to Philemon.

This epistle addresses two two-way relationships. Paul converted Philemon at Ephesus, and a strong friendship grew. Later, Paul converted Onesimus at Rome, and an equally strong relationship developed. Because of the situation, however, a breach occurred between Philemon and Onesimus. The answer was Paul. He was the occasion for harmony between the two. He commended Onesimus for his new character and service, and he reminded Philemon of his Christian responsibility. Further, he willingly offered to assume Onesimus's indebtedness to heal the broken relationship.

Christian fellowship involves participation in the lives of others. On one hand, it means that believers fully acknowledge the circumstances which made others the way they are. It includes a realization that God can change them. On the other hand, it involves a willingness to become involved in making others' lives better. For Paul, that meant the risk of writing to Philemon. It could have meant financial loss and, potentially, the loss of a valued friendship with Philemon. Nevertheless, Paul knew he could encourage God's work in both friends, and he acted accordingly.

The epistle teaches practically what it means to be in Christ. Individualistic ideas and ambitions become secondary, and participation in the larger work of

---

[32] Bruce, 401.

[33] In the context of friendship, preaching a sermon about the evils of a friend's household hardly accomplished the desired goal. Paul gently urged him on.

[34] See the notes on vv. 6, 17.

God becomes primary. Christians must forgive. They must hope for the best. They must treat others as Christ treated them and as they hope to be treated. Paul promised Philemon that if he did what he should he would have Onesimus as a brother in the flesh and in the Lord (v. 16). Both relationships matter, but the spiritual relationship lasts forever. The call to Christ is a call to join in a fellowship with other Christians. That fellowship appreciates all others who are in Christ.

(3) Embodiment of the Christian Mind

A third powerful message from the epistle is expression of Christian thought in action. Some have referred to the fact that the epistle illustrates the theological principle of imputation, but that is only one part of a greater truth. The epistle is not an illustration. Paul expressed his own values, attitudes, and convictions. They were remarkably like his Lord's (Phil 2:5-11).

Expressions of Christian thinking permeate the letter. First, two people were in need of reconciliation, and Paul sought a way to accomplish it, just as Jesus did. Second, Paul pleaded the case of Onesimus, taking the side of the guilty in calling for forgiveness. Similarly, Jesus pleaded the case of sinners, bringing them to the Father. Third, Paul offered to pay the debt Onesimus owed, even though it was not Paul's responsibility. Jesus took the debt of sinners and paid it vicariously. Fourth, the reconciliation was, in essence, effected in Paul. He was the tie that brought Philemon and Onesimus together; through Paul, harmony was restored. Paul's consistent theme "in Christ" reveals that he thought the same way regarding the God-human relationship. In Christ, humanity and deity are reconciled.

Paul acted like Christ did. This epistle provides insight into Paul that no other does. Elsewhere he wrote about Jesus' willingness to act on behalf of sinners. Paul pondered the meaning of grace, the cross, and the nature of salvation. In other epistles, he wrote about the meaning of the cross for Christian living. In this epistle, he demonstrated that he understood the implications of the gospel. Apart from personal salvation, nothing equals Christlikeness in attitudes and actions. The gospel demands it. In the Epistle to Philemon, Paul demonstrated it.

--------- **OUTLINE OF THE BOOK** ---------

I. Salutation
    1. The Writers (v. 1a)
    2. The Readers (vv. 1b-2)
    3. The Greeting (v. 3)
II. Prayer of Thanksgiving for Philemon (vv. 4-7)
    1. Paul's Prayer (vv. 4-6)
        (1) Thanksgiving (vv. 4-5)
        (2) Content (v. 6)

SECTION OUTLINE

I. SALUTATION (vv. 1-3)
1. The Writers (v. 1a)
2. The Readers (vv. 1b-2)
3. The Greeting (v. 3)

I. SALUTATION (vv. 1-3)

Paul began this letter like his other epistles. He identified the writers, the readers, and sent a greeting. At the same time, this salutation is unique. Its brevity is noteworthy, but more significantly, Paul did not use his usual title in describing himself.

1. The Writers (v. 1a)

[1]Paul, a prisoner of Christ Jesus, and Timothy our brother

1a   The epistle identified two writers in the opening verse: Paul and Timothy. From the contents of the letter, Timothy was secondary, and one wonders why he was mentioned at all. He had a significant ministry around Ephesus both before and after this time.[1] The most likely reasons for including him are enumerated in the Colossians commentary. Yet perhaps there was a reason unique to Philemon. If Timothy ministered with Paul in Ephesus and that was where Paul introduced Philemon to Christ, Philemon may have known Timothy. Thus, although Timothy did not actually participate in the content of the letter, he was mentioned out of courtesy.[2]

Normally Paul used a title appropriate to his position in God's economy. Sometimes it was the title "apostle" because the situations he addressed demanded the authority which came with that office. At other times, he introduced himself as "slave," which seems to have been the title he preferred (see Phil 1:1). Some commentators call attention to the parallel with the Old Testament "servant of the Lord" and claim that it was a title vested with authoritative overtones. At any rate, Paul did not use either title here. Neither would have been appropriate. He wrote to a good friend, and to call attention to an office or authority in a private letter would be offensive.

---

[1] He was with Paul on his travels from the time of the second missionary journey, and he later pastored in Ephesus.

[2] E. Lohse, *Colossians and Philemon, Her* (Philadelphia: Fortress, 1971), considers the mention of Timothy as another way of pointing out authority since Paul softly reminded Philemon that he had people surrounding him in the work of the gospel. That suggestion does not appear likely. There is nothing in the letter to support the idea.

Paul did refer to his situation. He stated that he was a "prisoner of Christ Jesus." Some have suggested that even here Paul used a term of authority. Although it is a softer form, they say, it still speaks of superiority in Christ.[3] Some take a mediating position, assuming that the reference paved the way for his request. If so, Paul would have been saying something like, "In comparison with the *sacrifice* that I am making, is not the *favor* which I am asking you to grant a rather easy matter?"[4] Elsewhere when Paul used the term, however, he had no such motives (Eph 3:1; 4:1; 2 Tim 1:8). In light of these references and Phlm 9,10, the best understanding is that Paul used the words to speak of his location when writing.[5] If anything, perhaps it explains why he could not travel with Onesimus to ask Philemon personally for Onesimus's forgiveness.

2. The Readers (vv. 1b-2)

To Philemon our dear friend and fellow worker, [2]to Apphia our sister, to Archippus our fellow soldier and to the church that meets in your home

The text appears to address four readers. The letter makes clear, however, that Paul directed his comments to Philemon alone. The pronouns of the text parallel this pattern. In vv. 3,25, the salutation and conclusion, Paul used the plural pronoun "you." Some have suggested that the letter was actually written to a public audience based on this evidence and the fact that the letter survived publicly. In vv. 1-2,4-24, he consistently used the singular "you." The letter clearly addressed Philemon, and the subject matter discussed refers to him alone. Most likely, Paul included the others because they were part of Philemon's family and courtesy demanded it.

1b The first addressee was Philemon. Obviously Philemon was a man of some means since he had at least one slave and a house in which a church met. In the major cities, most people lived in rooms, rather than houses, and the fact that he had a room large enough for a meeting suggests he had above-average means. Paul called him a "dear friend" and "fellow worker." Paul used "dear friend" (*agapētos*) of groups (Rom 1:7; 1 Cor 10:14; 15:58; 2 Cor 7:1; 12:19; Phil 2:12; 4:1) and of certain individuals (Col 1:7; 4:7,9,14). He used the term "fellow worker" (*synergos*) of several close friends (Rom 16:9,21; 1 Cor 3:9; 2 Cor 8:23; Phil 2:25). The terms probably recall the time when Paul and Philemon served together in Ephesus, but no doubt Philemon continued his

---

[3]R. Martin, *Colossians and Philemon*, NCB (Grand Rapids: Eerdmans, 1973), 158, says they were a "mark of his apostolic authority" and called attention to Col 4:18.

[4]W. Hendriksen, *Colossians and Philemon*, NTC (Grand Rapids: Baker, 1964), 209. M. R. Vincent, *Critical and Exegetical Commentary on the Epistles to the Philippians and to Philemon*, ICC (Edinburgh: T & T Clark, 1897), 175, arrived at a similar conclusion.

[5]Interpreters have a tendency to read into the statement more than may be warranted. It has been taken metaphorically, figuratively, and religiously so that the phrase really means a prisoner to God rather than Rome. While Paul may have communicated a deeper imprisonment than was obvious, certainly he meant to state his literal imprisonment at this time.

service when he returned home to Asia Minor. These terms of endearment reveal the closeness between Paul and this dear friend and make Paul's request all the more remarkable. Perhaps he had known Onesimus before, and now, after his conversion, Paul willingly risked his friendship with Philemon to become an agent of reconciliation.[6]

2 The second addressee is Apphia, "our sister." The name occurs often in extra-biblical sources and was a distinctively Phrygian name.[7] She obviously had a Christian commitment since Paul called her a "sister." From the way he addressed her, apparently she was well-known to him also. Could she have served with Philemon and Paul? Apphia was probably Philemon's wife. Two factors suggest that: the warm, personal tone of the letter, which addresses house matters, and the close contextual connection with Philemon. Because women took charge of the house affairs, she probably had an interest in Onesimus. Although she may have been invited into the discussions regarding Onesimus, Paul handled the matter with Philemon.

The third person is Archippus. Because of the family context, many assume he was the son of Philemon and Apphia. Paul called him a "fellow soldier," applying a military metaphor to this Christian brother. He seldom referred to Christians at large by that designation.[8]

Finally, Paul addressed "the church that meets in your home."[9] In the major cities, social groups gathered in the homes of patrons who served as unofficial sponsors of the groups. Urban Christians followed the same pattern, hoping for a benefactor who had the resources to sponsor a church. Graciously, the Lord provided such people in most places, and Philemon was one of those.[10]

3. The Greeting (v. 3)

[3]Grace to you and peace from God our Father and the Lord Jesus Christ.

3 Paul's greeting was a Christianized form of typical greetings. The logical order preserves the way God works: Grace produces peace. These qualities come jointly from God the Father and Jesus. For Paul, Jesus performed the same activities as God. Particularly, he can supply grace and peace to the hearts of people.[11]

---

[6]Urging Onesimus to return could have further strengthened their friendship since losing a slave was a significant loss. From any perspective, however, Paul courageously intervened in a family matter, which could have cost him dearly.

[7]J. B. Lightfoot, *St. Paul's Epistles to the Colossians and to Philemon*, reprint ed. (Grand Rapids: Zondervan, 1959), 306. None of the inscriptions appear to be linked to this lady, however.

[8]See Col 4:10,17 for Paul's other descriptions of this man.

[9]The pronoun "your" is singular, indicating that Philemon was the primary one in Paul's mind.

[10]Probably Lydia functioned this way in Philippi. Note also Acts 20:7ff., where the church met in a third-story room.

[11]For further explanation, see the introductions to Colossians and Philippians.

SECTION OUTLINE

II. PRAYER OF THANKSGIVING FOR PHILEMON (vv. 4-7)
   1. Paul's Prayer (vv. 4-6)
      (1) Thanksgiving (vv. 4-5)
      (2) Content (v. 6)
   2. Commendation of Philemon (v. 7)

— II. PRAYER OF THANKSGIVING FOR PHILEMON (vv. 4-7) —

Paul began this letter by praying for the people to whom he wrote. The prayer includes a thanksgiving which resembles Col 1:3-14; the commentary notes there should be consulted. One unique factor of this thanksgiving is that it concerned an individual, Philemon. Because of this, the thanksgiving became a commendation of this man's character and Christian faith. Philemon embodied the good qualities Paul sought in all Christians.

1. Paul's Prayer (vv. 4-6)

4I always thank my God as I remember you in my prayers, 5because I hear about your faith in the Lord Jesus and your love for all the saints. 6I pray that you may be active in sharing your faith, so that you will have a full understanding of every good thing we have in Christ.

Structurally, the thanksgiving follows a typical pattern for Paul. The primary differences between this one and others are that this one is shorter and has some distinctive expressions. The thanksgiving revolves around the verb "I thank my God" (*eucharistō*). Two modifying expressions translated "as I remember you" and "because I hear about your faith"[1] continue the idea. These are followed by the specific content of the prayer, "I pray that you may be active."[2] Often Paul divided such introductions into two segments: thanksgiving for the readers and petition.[3] He followed that pattern here, but cryptically, both components occur in one sentence. It is best, therefore, to discuss this section in its logical (thematic) patterns of thanksgiving and prayer. This one long sentence in the Greek text captures both the spirit and the style of Paul's longer thanksgivings.

---

[1] Also typical of Pauline thanksgivings, these are predicate participles which modify the verb. The first is temporal and the second is causal. The NIV translates them well.

[2] This clause is introduced by the Greek conjunction ὅπως, an alternate for Paul's usual ἵνα showing content (non-final).

[3] See, e.g., Col 1:4-20, which divides into 1:4-8 (thanksgiving) and 1:9-20 (petition). Philippians 1:3-11 has the same structure of thanksgiving (1:3-8) and petition (1:9-11).

(1) Thanksgiving (vv. 4-5)

4a   When Paul thought of Philemon, he did so with joy and thankfulness. Some interpreters understand "always" as modifying the phrase "as I remember you" so that the construction reads, "I thank my God *every time I think of you.*" The Greek is capable of either translation,[4] but the stress most naturally is on *always* thanking God. Paul did not mean that he always gave thanks *when he remembered* Philemon. The expression does not mean that Paul did nothing but think of Philemon. He had many pressing matters on his mind. It does emphasize that Paul constantly remembered the Christian people who stood with him in ministry and the Christian life. They were a constant joy and occasion of thanksgiving.[5]

4b   The first modifier of "I thank my God" is "as I remember you in my prayers." The Greek construction is a participle with a temporal force. It means "while making remembrance of you," and it is followed by an expression of time, "as I pray." Both parts of the expression stress the fact that Paul actually thanked God for them. He remembered them in prayer (see Col 1:3; Phil 1:4).[6] Consistent with other passages, Paul gave the readers insight into his prayer life. He prayed with a thankful heart, and he prayed for Philemon with thankfulness.

5   The second modifier of "I thank God" is "because I hear." The present tense (I hear) rather than the past (I heard) suggests that Paul continued to hear a good report, perhaps from Onesimus and the others who surrounded him. It stressed the character of Philemon and, perhaps, his consistency.

The interpreter must make a syntactical judgment about the precise meaning of the words in v. 4b. What is clear is that Philemon was a man of faith and love and that he had a concern for both God and people. The NIV correctly interprets the text, understanding "faith" as a trust in the Lord Jesus and "love" as a quality directed toward Christian people. Some other translations keep a more literal wording. The Greek text is "the love and the faith which you have toward the Lord Jesus and unto all the saints." The statement has two possible interpretations. First, love and faith could be directed to both the Lord and the saints; however, this requires an awkward understanding of "faith." How could faith be directed toward the saints?[7] Further, the parallel in Col 1:4 clearly

---

[4] A comparison with Rom 1:8-10; 1 Cor 1:4; esp. Col 1:3-4 suggests that it goes with "giving thanks."

[5] The Greek idea is probably iterative, which preserves the continuous nature of the idea and its periodic aspects as well.

[6] The Greek participle is temporal, and the expression in Greek, ἐπὶ τῶν προσευχῶν, is a local phrase with temporal overtones. It means "while praying."

[7] M. R. Vincent, *Critical and Exegetical Commentary on the Epistles to the Philippians and to Philemon, ICC* (Edinburgh: T & T Clark, 1897), 178, accepted this construction. He argued that the statement "fellowship of faith" in v. 6 provides a good contextual reason for taking "faith" with "the saints." He translated v. 6 as "a 'communication' of faith to others." This idea has been almost universally rejected in favor of the other position.

relates the two qualities to the two different objects. Second, the faith could be toward the Lord and the love toward all the saints. This must be correct. The original construction is a chiasm.[8]

From this statement, two outstanding qualities of Philemon appear. First, he was genuinely Christian. His faith is described in present terms ("you have"), probably indicating a life consistent with his faith in Christ. Second, he demonstrated love for everyone. He possessed qualities which made him exemplary as a Christian, and these attributes made him sensitive to Paul's request.

The mention of faith and love anticipates a statement about hope. The triad typically occurs together, but hope is not discussed here. Since it is a major theme in Colossians in this connection (1:5-6), the omission seems strange. Perhaps two suggestions account for the absence, though one can never understand why something *is not* included.[9] First, this epistle has virtually no eschatological orientation. It deals entirely with a social/religious question. Second, and more importantly, this was a letter to a friend. There was little need to explain why Christian qualities emerged; friends understand such things. It served Paul's purposes well to identify the qualities, not explain them. Love is the more pronounced, as the "outside" member of the chiasm because of its importance to the letter (vv. 5,7,9). If Philemon really possessed a love for all the saints, he would act in love regarding Onesimus.

(2) Content (v. 6)

6 Although structurally Paul continued to modify "I thank God," the meaning changed direction. Recognizing this, the NIV begins a new sentence here. In a single sentence, Paul incorporated both thanksgiving and prayer for Philemon. Almost every part of this statement demands interpretation. It is "notoriously the most obscure verse in the letter."[10]

Four exegetical problems occur. First, what is the meaning of "participation of faith" ("sharing your faith," NIV; *koinōnia tēs pisteōs*)? Second, how is "in Christ" (lit., "into Christ") to be understood? Third, is "in Christ" to be connected with "effective," "good thing," or "knowledge"? Fourth, how should "in knowledge" be interpreted? These questions interrelate, so the difficulties multiply.

---

[8]The chiasm is a) the love, b) the faith, b´) toward the Lord Jesus, a´) unto all the saints. Colossians 1:4 makes this sequence of thought clear, and that close parallel should guide the interpretation of this verse as well.

[9]This is like proving the negative; it cannot be done. Ultimately no one knows why someone did not do something. It is surprising how much space is devoted to this type of reasoning in exegetical circles, however. It seems that many know what should have been included and was not or why something was not. It even becomes a criterion for integrity. Even with this expression of frustration with the procedure, some suggestions are offered. They are, of course, quite tentative.

[10]C. F. D. Moule, *The Epistles of Paul the Apostle to the Colossians and to Philemon*, CGTC (Cambridge: University Press, 1962), 142.

The phrase "participation of faith" uses two common words in the New Testament. "Participation," *koinōnia*, occurs frequently in Philippians, and the reader should see the discussions there. "Faith" expresses the heart of Christianity. Both words individually and together have various shades of meaning.[11] The NIV translation is highly unlikely because of what it communicates to many readers. It suggests evangelism, but that is far removed from any context supposed for this letter.[12] Paul was not encouraging Philemon to be an evangelist. Elsewhere, Paul acknowledged the importance of evangelists, but that has little to do with this epistle. The suggestion that *koinōnia* means a contribution because of being in the faith is more to the point.[13] Paul's words, however, depend on the deepest meaning of "fellowship." "Christians not only belong to one another but actually become mutually identified, truly rejoicing with the happy and genuinely weeping with the sad."[14] Philemon's "participation in the faith" would mean that he also participated in the good things that promoted the cause of Christ.

Paul prayed that this "participation in the faith" would work in the test case involving Onesimus. The other problems identified in this context may be resolved in harmony with that idea. The word "active" (NIV) translates the Greek *energēs*. The word means *activity*,[15] and the request was for the Christian faith to become active.[16] The phrase "in knowledge," ("full understanding," NIV) occurs often in similar prayers of Paul, and its meaning is clear (Eph 1:17; Phil 1:9; esp. Col 1:9-10). Paul realized that in the sphere of knowledge such activity would take place.[17] The Greek word "knowledge" (*epignōsis*) combines experiential and intellectual meanings, stressing a personal acquain-

---

[11]The complexities are noted by P. O'Brien, *Colossians, Philemon, WBC* (Waco, Tex.: Word, 1982), 279-80, who lists the following possibilities of interpretation: "the kindly deeds of charity which spring from your faith" (J. B. Lightfoot, *St. Paul's Epistles to the Colossians and to Philemon*, reprint ed. [Grand Rapids: Zondervan, 1959], 333); "the communication (to others) of your faith" (Vincent, 179); "your fellowship with other Christians created by faith" (E. Lohmeyer, *Die Briefe an die Philipper, und die Kolosser und an Philemon* [Göttingen: Vandenhoeck, 1953], 178); "communion (with Christ) by faith" (M. Dibelius, *An die Kolosser, Epheser und Philemon*, ed. H. Greeven [Tübingen: Mohr, 1953], 103; Lohse, 193); "the faith in which you participate"; and "the participation of other Christians in your faith."

[12]Further, κοινωνία "cannot mean 'sharing' in the sense of dividing something up and parceling it out." N. T. Wright, *Colossians and Philemon, TNTC* (Grand Rapids: Eerdmans, 1986), 176.

[13]O'Brien took this position, 280. It is similar to Phil 1:5, where the term is articular, as it is here, and Phil 4:14-15 (cognate and compound forms).

[14]Wright comments insightfully: "All are bound together in a mutual bond that makes our much-prized individualism look shallow and petty" (176).

[15]See F. Hauck, *TDNT*, 3:805.

[16]The subjunctive verb γένηται points to a potential activity rather than one already in progress.

[17]Some want to take ἐν ἐπιγνώσει as an instrumental idea, but the locative of sphere fits its other usages well. Paul may have tended toward an instrumental idea, but he still had the "thought environment" in mind.

tance with knowledge. Thus, knowing how to apply the faith to the matter at hand comes from experiential knowledge.[18]

The content of the knowledge is provided in the remainder of the verse. The words "of every good thing to us" modify "knowledge." Paul hoped that Philemon would come to a realization of everything good, "unto Christ." This phrase is not the same as "in Christ."[19] Perhaps the best parallel is Eph 4:12-13, where the leadership of the church is described as enduring "unto" the perfect unity. The English translators often make the phrase temporal, "'until' we all attain."[20] Thus, when Christians act in accord with the blessings they have in Christ, they grow closer to Christ.

Paul prayed that Philemon would use this knowledge to work out the implications of his faith in the matter with Onesimus. The "good thing" he knew to do was to forgive an erring and repentant brother who sinned before his salvation.[21] Such a reconciliation would have far-reaching implications in the whole church. It watched this test case with great interest. If Christianity could work in such tension-filled relationships, it could work anywhere. Paul, Philemon, Onesimus, the church, and all of Christianity had much at stake in Philemon's response. Paul prayed that Philemon would make the correct choice.

2. Commendation of Philemon (v. 7)

[7]Your love has given me great joy and encouragement, because you, brother, have refreshed the hearts of the saints.

After concluding the prayer for Philemon, Paul stated a reason he expected Philemon to respond.[22] In commending Philemon, Paul built on the expectations expressed in his prayer. He expected Philemon to do the "good thing" regarding Onesimus because Philemon was a man accustomed to doing "good things" for Christian people.

Paul rejoiced in Philemon's love. His love played a significant role in Paul's life and would move him to action (v. 9). The thanksgiving contains another chiasm on a grander scale. It begins in v. 5 where Paul praised Philemon for his

---

[18]See the notes on Paul's prayer for the Colossians (1:9ff.). "Knowledge" there is of the will of God and directed toward living in accord with that will. It, too, emphasizes the active nature of genuine knowledge.

[19]It is not paralleled in Eph 1:3-14, e.g., where the prepositional phrase ἐν Χριστῷ lists the blessings of salvation. This is "unto Christ," and Christ is the object of the good thing.

[20]This suggestion is made and supported by Wright, 176-77. The analysis makes good sense of the component parts with the least "reading in" of other ideas.

[21]Perhaps this is reinforced by the occurrence of "good" in v. 14. Ἀγαθόν occurs there as a description of what Philemon might do. The NIV translates it as a "favor."

[22]Phlm 7 is joined to v. 6 by γάρ, which provides a reason for the previous statement. It is a significant transition. Many warn against taking the γάρ with v. 6, stating it gives a reason for the thanksgiving of Paul in vv. 4-5 (Lightfoot, 336). It should be remembered, however, that the reason encompasses all of vv. 4-6 since Paul's thankfulness included them all.

love and for his faith. It concludes in vv. 6-7. In v. 6 Paul stressed Philemon's "participation in the faith." This corresponds to v. 5. In v. 7 Paul emphasized Philemon's love. It corresponds to v. 5 where he was commended for his love. Thus there is movement from the general to the specific in the passage. The faith and the love of which Paul spoke may be explicitly explained in vv. 6-7 successively.

7   The text makes clear that Paul was comforted by Philemon's love. Three expressions amplify that. First, he used the word "joy." Second, he modified "joy" by the adjective "much." Third, he used the term "encouragement." Paul multiplied his expressions to make his point. Further, these were all based on Philemon's love.[23] Many interpreters attempt to explain a specific occasion Paul had in mind, but no one knows how, when, or why Philemon acted as he did. Perhaps Paul simply identified a character trait in Philemon because he helped "the saints." Although the specific act remains unknown, it had significant effects. Paul used the word "bowels" ("hearts," NIV) to describe the way Philemon lifted the spirits of fellow Christians. The word identifies the seat of emotions, and Paul used it only when speaking directly and personally.[24] It occurs three times in Philemon (vv. 7,12,20). Whatever Philemon did, he brought joy to a desperate situation. When he acted, he lifted their spirits.[25]

In this thanksgiving, Paul set the direction for the remainder of the epistle. Most of the themes introduced here recur. The basic themes are love, faith, the Lord Jesus, saints, participation, good, joy, encouragement, and bowels of mercy. All appear later except faith, saints, joy, and encouragement.[26] Typical of Pauline thanksgivings, this one anticipated the resolution of a specific problem.

Paul also accomplished three important tasks through this thanksgiving.[27] First, he established goodwill between Philemon and himself. If there had been a lapse, perhaps because Philemon heard of Onesimus's location, Paul countered that misunderstanding. He genuinely praised Philemon. Second, Paul anticipated his case by stressing some of Philemon's good qualities which would affect his decision regarding Onesimus. He reminded him of the basis for Christian action. Third, he alluded to some particular matters that would be

---

[23] The Greek text uses the preposition ἐπί plus the locative case to make the point that the joy "rests on" Philemon's love.

[24] H. Koester, *TDNT*, 7:555.

[25] That Paul had some definite action or actions in mind seems clear by the use of the perfect tense to describe them (ἀναπέπαυται). This identifies the action as past, but it had continuing emotional lift. Probably the perfect tense means that the actions were over but Philemon gained the respect of all involved. Lohse, 195, calls it a gift of love, and some conclude that Philemon helped other Christians after the earthquake of A.D. 60.

[26] T. Mullins, "The Thanksgivings of Philemon and Colossians" *NTS* 30 (April, 1984): 289.

[27] These were identified by F. F. Church, "Rhetorical Structure and Design in Paul's Letter to Philemon," *HTR* 71 (Jan.-Apr. 1978): 22.

helpful to him later in summarizing his letter (v. 17). Some indicate that these came about as the product of forethought and that the letter is formal.[28] There is no doubt that, given the tensions inherent in the situation, Paul would have planned what to say to Philemon. It is doubtful, however, that he consciously thought in terms of manipulating a friend into accepting his desires.[29] Though he surely intended to influence Philemon.

---

[28] Church provides this as a model rhetorical letter, probably preplanned and masterfully produced. His analysis is extremely helpful.

[29] Such manipulation was the goal of the orators and, at times, the measure of their success. Capable orators could persuade any group of any subject under any circumstances without any forewarning. They did so by using various rhetorical devices. Paul's own testimony in 1 Cor 1-3, however, reveals his distaste for such an approach, and it hardly seems likely that he would employ these tactics on a friend. Some "devices" or "conventions" occur in common everyday conversation.

─── III. PLEA FOR ACCEPTANCE OF ONESIMUS (vv. 8-20) ───

At v. 8 Paul spoke to the subject at hand. The preceding verses occupy a disproportionate space, considering the length of this epistle, but they lay a good foundation. Now Paul turned to the situation with Onesimus which prompted the letter in the first place. There are three movements in this passage. First, Paul made his request (vv. 8-14). Second, he described God's purposes in the events (vv. 15-16). Finally, he appealed to his relationship with Philemon as an incentive (vv. 17-22).

1. Paul's Request (vv. 8-14)

Paul made his request in one long sentence in Greek. Structurally, it has three parts, which also provide the logical flow of this section. First two participles and their modifiers explain the manner of Paul's approach to Philemon ("I could be bold and order you to do what you ought to do," v. 8; "being an old man and now also a prisoner of Christ Jesus," v. 9). Second, Paul identified his request specifically by the repetition of the verb "I appeal" (vv. 9,10; *parakalō*). Third, Paul explained his relationship to Onesimus through three statements (vv. 10,12,13), each progressively more intense and personal.

(1) Paul's Manner (vv. 8-9)

8Therefore, although in Christ I could be bold and order you to do what you ought to do, 9yet I appeal to you on the basis of love. I then, as Paul—an old man and now also a prisoner of Christ Jesus

8 Paul preferred to speak gently to Philemon. Philemon was a man of Christian character, and Paul approached him out of love (v. 7). Two ideas reinforce that conclusion in these verses: Paul's refusing to use his authority and Paul's situation as an old and imprisoned man.

Paul chose not to use his apostolic and ministerial authority. He did not hesitate to appeal to his calling as an apostle when the need demanded, and on occasion he reminded people that they were brought into the kingdom through his efforts. Here, he hoped for Philemon to respond out of generosity. "Generosity ought to be spontaneous, not forced, and Paul does not want to interfere with the workings of Providence."[1] Nevertheless, he reminded him that he had the right to command. The phrase "I could be bold" (NIV) interprets the Greek concessively, "although I could be bold," but that may not be the correct understanding. Literally, it says, "having boldness in Christ to command you." Paul probably did remind Philemon of his rights which he refused to exercise.[2]

Paul could have commanded Philemon to "do what you ought to do." The word this translates, *anēkon*, occurs in Col 3:18 in speaking of the relationship of wives to their husbands. It speaks to what is proper because of the Christian order of things. The Christian realizes that God's economy differs from humanity's and certain things are inherently right. Treating a brother fairly and mercifully falls into that category. No Christian has the right to abuse another human being. Paul did not ask that Onesimus be released. He urged Philemon to respond to his Christian commitments and do what God expected. Paul subtly made his first point regarding accepting Onesimus.

9 Philemon was to act in a Christian manner, but even that could be coerced. For that reason, Paul based his appeal on love.[3] He had a specific love in mind, that of vv. 5, 7. Philemon's love should prove true in this case, as it had in so many others.

As a second approach, Paul reminded Philemon of his situation as an aged and imprisoned man. Paul probably reinforced one of two truths in this approach. On one hand, he might have appealed to sentiment. He was old, and his situation was precarious. On the other hand, Paul could have appealed to his authority as an elder and one who suffered for Jesus. Since Paul generally did not complain about his circumstances, but rather prided himself on his self-sufficiency (Phil 4:10-14), it is unlikely that he appealed to sentiment. His appeal was based on age and circumstance, not apostolic calling or ministry.[4]

---

[1]C. B. Caird, *Paul's Letters from Prison (Ephesians, Philippians, Colossians, Philemon)*, *NClarBib* (London: Oxford University Press, 1976), 221.

[2]P. O'Brien, *Colossians, Philemon*, *WBC* (Waco, Tex.: Word, 1982), 287-88, provided a whole range of options with this word. He opted for a translation "openness," stating that "Philemon's fine Christian character . . . meant Paul could speak openly and with affection."

[3]The Greek text reads διὰ τὴν ἀγάπην, "on account of the love."

[4]For the translation "old man" see *BAGD*, 700; G. Bornkamm, *TDNT*, 6:683; E. Lohse, *Colossians and Philemon*, *Her* (Philadelphia: Fortress, 1971), 199. Some disagree with this translation and prefer "ambassador" (πρεσβύτης). See J. B. Lightfoot, *St. Paul's Epistles to the Colossians and to Philemon*, reprint ed. (Grand Rapids: Zondervan, 1959), 336-37; and A. T. Robertson, *A*

This second aspect, therefore, humbly requested Philemon's response because of who Paul was *as a Christian* in these circumstances, not because of his position in God's economy.[5]

(2) Paul's Specific Request (v. 10a)

[10]I appeal to you for my son Onesimus

10a   Paul made his request with six short words in Greek ("I appeal to you for my son Onesimus," NIV). Twice the verb "appeal" occurs (vv. 9,10), and though it carries many shades of meaning, here it means *ask* or *beseech*. The most perplexing aspect of this verse is that Paul never made a clear request regarding Onesimus. Some take this as a sign that Paul did not seek Onesimus's release, and some believe that Onesimus was not even a runaway slave because Paul did not clearly state his request.[6]

The appeal coincides with the tone of the letter. Paul already stated that he did not want to be overbearing in his requests. Love would find a way to do right. Paul hoped that Philemon would restore Onesimus without penalty, but he trusted that Philemon would see that from the rest of the letter. Further, Paul had no specific request regarding Onesimus. If he had sought Onesimus as a servant, as some suggest, he would have asked. Paul had faith in Philemon and knew that the matter had to be handled between the slave and his master. In writing, Paul was beseeching *for* his friend, standing by him and urging his master to do what was right.

(3) Paul's Relationship to Onesimus (vv. 10b-14)

who became my son while I was in chains. [11]Formerly he was useless to you, but now he has become useful both to you and to me.
[12]I am sending him—who is my very heart—back to you. [13]I would have liked to keep him with me so that he could take your place in helping me while I am in chains for the gospel. [14]But I did not want to do anything without your consent, so that any favor you do will be spontaneous and not forced.

Three statements describe Paul's relationship with Onesimus. Philemon might have wondered how the two met, and certainly he would not know of the change in Onesimus's life. Paul explained these things in order to commend Onesimus, hoping that he would receive a favorable hearing from his master.

Grammar of the Greek New Testament in the Light of Historical Research (Nashville: Broadman, 1934), 201. W. Hendriksen, *Colossians and Philemon*, NTC (Grand Rapids: Baker, 1964), 217, strongly argues against this position, claiming it violates the context.

[5]This interpretation is not intended to downplay the overtones of authority which Paul often expressed. It is simply to state that Paul did not employ his major expressions of authority like he did at Corinth, for example.

[6]S. Winter, "Paul's Letter to Philemon" *NTS* 33:1 (Jan 1987): 1-15. That is one of her theses that she develops throughout the article.

For Paul, the new life in Christ made a radical difference; when he saw it in someone, he knew it would produce a continuing change.

ONESIMUS'S NEW LIFE (vv. 10b-11). **10b** First, Paul described Onesimus's new life. Somehow Onesimus came in contact with Paul while Paul was in prison. Perhaps he knew of Paul and sought him out. Paul revealed two facts about Onesimus's new life. First, Paul converted him to Christ. The Greek text actually says, "I begat in my bonds."[7] The relationship between Paul and Onesimus was strong, like a father and son. The rabbis often used that metaphor to describe their disciples, and it applied equally to such Christian relationships. The word "begot" is rare for Paul, especially in a spiritual sense.[8] He did not use the word "born again" for the new life. Jesus did use the term that way, and he was followed in that usage by John and Peter in particular. Paul's use of the metaphor simply refers to his part in Onesimus's conversion. The term "child" in v. 10[9] shows Paul's close relationship with Onesimus.

11 Onesimus had a change of character (v. 11). In describing that change, Paul used a double play on words. Once Onesimus was "useless"; now he was "useful."[10] The name "Onesimus" means *profitable*, and perhaps the play on words continues.[11] Some point out that Phrygian slaves were notoriously useless as a class[12] and that Onesimus proved that proverb to be true, but nothing in the text supports that conclusion. The terminology is appropriate for referring to anyone before and after conversion to Christ. At any rate, the new Onesimus was valuable. Paul knew Onesimus would make a good servant for Philemon, even if he had not been so before. Further, Paul saw a use for him in the service of the gospel (v. 13). There is, thus, an illustration of the change the gospel makes. Useless members of society can become valuable and productive.

ONESIMUS'S DESIRE FOR RESTITUTION (v. 12). **12** The second statement Paul made refers to Onesimus's desire to correct the wrong he had done. Paul said, "I am sending him to you." Paul could not have forced Onesimus to return to Philemon. He had run away before; he could do it again easily. Why, then, did Paul say he sent Onesimus? The wording stresses the change Paul saw in him. The fact that Paul sent Onesimus suggests a sensitivity to Philemon's property. Paul's strong ties with Onesimus were described as "bowels" ("heart," NIV), the word for strong emotions. Perhaps the change that took

---

[7] The word is aorist tense, first person singular.

[8] See *BAGD*, 155.

[9] "Child" is more common in Pauline writings: 1 Cor 4:17; 2 Tim 1:2; Titus 1:4.

[10] The Greek is clearer with its "sound alike" endings: ἄχρηστον/εὔχρηστον. These were common among the orators of Paul's day. Lohse, 200.

[11] N. T. Wright, *Colossians and Philemon*, TNTC (Grand Rapids: Eerdmans, 1986), 182, says that the root χρηστός would be indistinguishable from Χριστός, the name of Christ. That produces a "double pun."

[12] Lightfoot, 310.

place in Onesimus had particular significance to Paul. Was it a sign of his effectiveness in prison? Was it because he felt indebted to Philemon in some way and this would help repay him? No answer is available. This is another miracle of Christianity: a runaway slave and (possible) thief became the joy of the aged apostle. Paul's words convey a note of intensity. He sent him even though it was like sending Philemon his heart.

Some point out that the term "I send" connotes a legal environment.[13] The word often has the meaning of "send up" rather than "send back."[14] They suggest that the term fittingly described an appeal to a higher court or a higher authority. It fits well with the many financial and legal terms of the passage which, according to some, make the letter formal and legal. They conclude it was a public letter rather than a private correspondence between friends.[15] Two factors must be considered in light of that. First, Paul lived in a legal environment at this time. He was somewhat preoccupied with his own pending trial, and such legal terms were in the air of the praetorium. Naturally his vocabulary differed from letters written from other locations under different circumstances. Second, language borrowed from a specific milieu does not necessarily mean that the writer wrote from that perspective. Even among friends, Paul may well have used the language. Sometimes too much is made of such evidence.[16]

ONESIMUS'S VALUE IN SERVICE (vv. 13-14). Paul's third statement commended Onesimus as useful. Each of the three have progressively identified Paul's close relationship with the slave, and this last describes it even further.

13-14 Paul saw many ways Onesimus could be of service to him in his imprisonment.[17] Their fellowship was good, and he lifted Paul's spirits at a difficult time. Paul wished he could have kept Onesimus in Rome.[18] Some logic could have supported such thoughts. Knowing Philemon as he did, Paul knew he would be in Rome serving Paul if the opportunity presented itself. Further,

---

[13] The word is ἀναπέμπω rather than πέμπω.

[14] The word is rare in the New Testament. See *BAGD*, 59, where both definitions occur. *BAGD* prefer "send back" for this reference. The word occurs in Luke 23:7,15; Acts 25:21.

[15] See, e.g., Winter, 7, and John Knox, *Philemon among the Letters of Paul: A New View of its Place and Importance*, rev. ed. (1935, Nashville: Abingdon, 1959). Winter provides a comprehensive list of such words in her article, 2.

[16] That certainly is the case of Winter. She reconstructs the epistle's setting entirely based on a new supposition stemming from the vocabulary alone. The vocabulary and its context have been known for centuries, but the traditions regarding the epistle survived.

[17] The term for "service" is διακονῇ, a term with overwhelmingly strong Christian connotations. It seems fair to assume that Onesimus had gifts in the work of the gospel, and that caught Paul's imagination. To interpret this as some mundane or menial task to assist Paul in practical matters misses the New Testament associations of the word.

[18] The imperfect is voluntative, i.e., a wish that in reality is not the desire of the one who wished it. Yet it is more than a courtesy. When used, it suggests a deep tension, perhaps agony, in the mind of the user. See Acts 25:22; Gal 4:20; Rom 9:3.

such service appropriately expressed the father-son relationship, even if it were a spiritual one. Since Philemon could not be there, Onesimus could have served nicely—and appropriately—in place of Philemon. The thought had much to commend it.

Such a procedure would have destroyed everything about the impact of the gospel. Paul had no right to keep Onesimus; Onesimus needed to make restitution for his own sake; and the church needed the opportunity to see such an evidence of Christianity at work. In spite of these matters, Paul thought in terms of doing what was right in the proper way. Even seemingly proper ends must be brought about by proper means! Philemon also was a dear friend and child in the faith. Paul had to be true to both of his children and to the Lord.

As a further evidence of the power of the gospel, Philemon had to be free to decide what he would do. The choices varied, but Paul's trust in Philemon remained strong. Two expressions emphasize Paul's decision to urge Onesimus to return. First is a contrast between "I would have liked to keep him with me" and "I did not want to do anything without your consent." The first term, *eboulomēn*, means to "will,"[19] and the second, *ēthelēsa*, means "to wish."[20] Any difference in meaning, however, comes from the construction and context of this passage. There is a contrast in tenses: *eboulomēn* is imperfect; *ēthelēsa* is aorist. The tense contrasts an ongoing tendency with a decisive action,[21] and it impacts semantics. By the first word (*eboulomēn*), Paul meant a process of wishing; by the second (*ēthelēsa*), he meant an act of choosing.

The second expression is the contrast regarding spontaneity and forced responses. Paul knew the value of a Christian mind acting out of Christian conviction. Possibly he anticipated Philemon's response. He used the same word here as in v. 6, "the good" ("favor," NIV). No doubt Paul now made concrete what he prayed earlier, i.e., that Philemon would see the "good" and freely do it.[22]

---

[19] *BAGD*, 146.

[20] *BAGD*, 355-56. Lightfoot, 341, distinguished the two terms by stating that βούλομαι implies "a wishing," while θέλω implies simply "a will." That distinction is seldom maintained today, and little actually supports it.

[21] This is clear because of their juxtaposition in the same context. Apart from contextual proximity, any conclusions as to the precise force of the tenses is tenuous.

[22] F. F. Church, "Rhetorical Structure and Design in Paul's Letter to Philemon," *HTR* 71 (Jan-Apr 1978), took an opposing view based on his rhetorical analysis. He states that Paul offered up the motive of honor (Greek σεμνός). "Paul is literally forcing a point of honor. While ostensibly avoiding even the appearance of constraint, his argument is designed to do just that, yet without robbing Philemon of the opportunity to act on his own in a truly honorable fashion" (27). The point may be correct. Yet one wonders how anyone would write or speak a logical piece without being analyzed according to the conventions used in it. The process can be reduced to absurdity by assuming everyone prethought and arranged every conversation.

2. The Providence of God (vv. 15-16)

[15]Perhaps the reason he was separated from you for a little while was that you might have him back for good— [16]no longer as a slave, but better than a slave, as a dear brother. He is very dear to me but even dearer to you, both as a man and as a brother in the Lord.

15 In v. 15, Paul turned his thoughts another direction. Onesimus should have been blamed for his actions. They were illegal and unethical. However, rather than dwell on the past life, especially since it had been forgiven by God, Paul looked to the redemptive element. God constructed his plans in spite of, through, and above human events and circumstances. Paul knew that from personal experience, even as he awaited trial at Rome.[23] Paul never condoned Onesimus's actions, just as he never called evil good. Yet he saw how God could triumph over sin by grace. Onesimus evidenced that in his life. Paul took opportunity, therefore, to apply this understanding of God's providence to the situation at hand.

Dealing with providence has its own problems. No one knows why things happen as they do, and people can only guess about reasons. This is especially true in the case of evil, where many gaps exist in knowledge.[24] Many commentators point out the parallel between this statement by Paul and Joseph's comment in Gen 50:20 ("you meant it for evil, but God meant it for good"). Perhaps Joseph's life took on special significance to Paul because of his circumstances—Joseph served a prison term as well! Onesimus's case differed from Joseph's. Joseph suffered unjustly, and he remained innocent. Onesimus deserved punishment. The grace of God appeared, however, in that Onesimus did not get what he deserved. Rather, his circumstances brought him to a new life. God worked through them to accomplish his purposes *in spite of* failures, misunderstandings, and blatant sins. The gospel truly offers good news. Paul's introductory word "perhaps" (*tacha*) seems to warn that absolute knowledge about how and why things happen rests with God alone.

The redemptive side of the situation occupies the rest of the verse. First, a contrast exists between "for a little while" (lit., "for an hour") and "for good" (lit., "for the age"). Paul likely did not mean something as simple as "forever" with this statement. The word "age" (*aiōn*) was Paul's common term for "eternal," and that is consistent with the rest of the New Testament.[25]

---

[23]See his argument in Phil 1:12ff.

[24]Remember Job's friends who mustered all their spiritual insight only to be proven wrong in the final analysis. Their understanding of providence sadly lacked.

[25]This derives from the Jewish outlook that eternity was viewed with a time perspective, i.e., it was the future age. Normally, however, the word is plural when it speaks of eternity. Perhaps the singular word here reveals that Paul thought in terms of the remainder of this age and, by implication, into eternity. Paul knew the slim likelihood of a runaway slave willingly becoming a productive servant again.

In most cases, the relationship between servant and master suffered irreparable damage. This was different. Onesimus ran away, but now he would be a better servant—he would be more profitable and, therefore, an asset to Philemon in time, as well as a brother for eternity. Paul assumed what he taught in Col 3:22-4:1. Christian slaves were better slaves because they worked for their heavenly Master. It was a triumph of God's grace that a disgruntled slave ran away and then voluntarily returned a better person, willing to serve both his earthly master and heavenly Master for good.

16   The second contrast occurs between Onesimus's position as "a slave" and "a brother" (v. 16). Paul did not seek emancipation for Onesimus, nor did he assume it would be forthcoming. Paul looked beyond this earth and its relationships to other more important relationships. Onesimus was family—a brother. Before, his position as a slave meant that he was in the household, but he did not enjoy the privilege of sons. Now Paul introduced him as a brother— a full member of the Christian household. In doing this, he spoke to the spiritual realities that transcend earthly physical/economic situations. According to Paul's instructions, slaves and masters can coexist as Christians *even in undesirable economic arrangements*. Philemon was to recognize Onesimus as a Christian and, therefore, as a genuine brother. Their union had three dimensions. They were united in humanity, a brotherhood in itself. They were fellow-Christians and fellow servants of the Lord, a stronger brotherhood. Beyond these, they had the same spiritual parent, a closer brotherhood than most Christians experience with each other.[26] God supervises all of life—his providence was a foundation for Paul's confidence.

3. Paul's Relationship to Philemon (vv. 17-22)

[17]So if you consider me a partner, welcome him as you would welcome me. [18]If he has done you any wrong or owes you anything, charge it to me. [19]I, Paul, am writing this with my own hand. I will pay it back—not to mention that you owe me your very self. [20]I do wish, brother, that I may have some benefit from you in the Lord; refresh my heart in Christ. [21]Confident of your obedience, I write to you, knowing that you will do even more than I ask.

[22]And one thing more: Prepare a guest room for me, because I hope to be restored to you in answer to your prayers.

This last section of Paul's argument also has three stages. They are noted by predominating commands. The commands are "welcome him" (v. 17); "refresh my heart" (v. 20); and "prepare a guest room" (v. 22). The movements through these verses correspond to them.

---

[26]Paul's expression "both as a man and in the Lord" suggests the tie to humanity and the spiritual relationships which transcend it.

(1) Welcome Onesimus (vv. 17-19).

17   The idea of substitution predominates in this section. There is constant interchange between Paul and Onesimus. At times Onesimus represents Paul, and at times he appears "clothed in Paul." Paul used a favorite word, "partner" (*koinōnon*), in laying the foundation for this section. It is the common word for "fellowship," but had a much deeper meaning than *mutually satisfying conversation*. The NIV translates it well as "partner." Philemon and Paul participated in the same effort, getting the gospel to the world. They obviously took the relationship seriously. Now there would be a three-way participation with Onesimus's inclusion. If Philemon really fellowshipped with Paul, he would honor Paul's request.

The partnership meant two specific truths related to the situation. First, Philemon would welcome Onesimus as though he were Paul himself. The foundation for such action was laid in that Onesimus had been called Paul's child. Second, Philemon would forgive Onesimus as though he were Paul himself. This posed a deeper problem. The verse suggests that Onesimus stole from his master. For most interpreters that means both money and the labor Philemon had a right to expect from a slave. Forgiveness meant money, and money meant life. Paul asked Philemon to share his life with his runaway slave. Forgiveness also meant providing him the opportunity for a new start. Paul anticipated that in vv. 15-16.[27]

18-19   Would Philemon be able to accomplish such Christlike attitudes and actions? If not, Paul was prepared to pay (vv. 18-19). Again the language of the financial world surfaced as Paul used the words "charge," "account," "repay," and "writing this with my own hand."[28] Apparently, Paul owed Philemon nothing. His "account," therefore, meant that he was willing to assume an indebtedness for his newfound Christian friend. This assured Philemon that Paul fully expected him to forgive Onesimus his wrongs. He was prepared to get involved in the process financially, if necessary, for the reconciliation of the two men.

The thought of indebtedness reminded Paul of Philemon's spiritual debt to Paul. Paul had taken the gospel to Philemon. This reveals Paul's perspective regarding material and spiritual matters. Paul saw close relationships between each aspect of life, with the Lord in control of it all. Here that perspective surfaced again. Spiritual relationships predominate. If they were in order, other matters would take care of themselves. Even so, Paul was prepared to assume financial obligations in order to teach and live by spiritual truths. Reconciliation between Christians meant that much to him. Further, spiritual

---

[27] The language there sounds like Paul expected Onesimus to remain with Philemon as his slave.

[28] This is the equivalent of writing an I.O.U., which would be legally binding. It is the best example of the metaphor which underlies Col 2:14.

indebtedness (to the one who brought the gospel) could be handled in kind by material service. Paul easily and naturally conceived of the world as unified under the lordship of Christ. Jesus was Lord of everything—it all fit together in his economy.[29]

In this magnificent section of Scripture, one final truth emerges. Paul served as the agent of reconciliation. Perhaps in his mind his relationship to Christ demanded it. There is no better picture of what Jesus did for humanity than what Paul did and offered to do for Onesimus. He brought the offender to a point of reconciliation, and he embodied that reconciliation since both parties were intimately related to him. Paul practiced the mind of Christ in everyday relationships.[30] His study of Jesus' role in reconciliation of persons and God no doubt taught about reconciliation. Further, his service to Christ motivated him to reconcile persons to God and to each other. Christ demands this type of humble, Christlike service.

(2) Refresh Paul's Heart (vv. 20-21)

20 The second section in this passage called for Philemon to live up to his character. Perhaps again employing a play on words with the name "Onesimus," Paul asked for some "profit" ("benefit," NIV).[31] Word association may have guided Paul. Onesimus was in a position to "benefit" Philemon. Paul thought of a way Philemon could "benefit" him for all of his efforts. The benefit was not financial or material. Paul always sought the spiritual blessings, even when financial terminology rose to the foreground.[32] The benefit was to be "in the Lord." Paul lived on spiritual truths—they were the lasting treasures. Paul, thus, asked for a spiritual response from Philemon.

Paul asked for Philemon to exercise one of his strengths, refreshing. In v. 7 Paul praised him for "refreshing the hearts of the saints" (*anapepautai*). Here, he asked for Philemon to "refresh his heart" (*anapauson*). The same terms occur for "refresh" and for "heart" in both verses. "It is now Philemon's turn to be 'useful' to Paul—by doing for Paul what he is apparently good at doing for everybody else,"[33] refreshing people's hearts.

21 The refreshing is explained in v. 21. Philemon would do more than Paul asked. This has no specific reference to the emancipation of Onesimus.[34] Paul continued to leave that in the hands of the Lord and Philemon. His hope was that Onesimus would be treated fairly. Even so, Paul's joy was on a deeper level. He urged Philemon to refresh him "in the Lord," and immediately Paul asked for Philemon's obedience. Though Paul issued no specific commands,

---

[29] Colossians 1:15-20 expresses this in hymnic form as Paul presented Jesus' rule over the natural order and the spiritual.

[30] See the commentary on Phil 2:5-11.

[31] Onesimus means "profitable," and the name was important to the message of vv. 10-11.

[32] See, e.g., the notes on Phil 4:10-20.

[33] Wright, 189.

[34] Lohse, 205, makes this point strongly.

Philemon's actions were a matter of obedience. This cannot be, therefore, obedience to the apostle—that neither fits a context where no commands are given nor the phrase "in the Lord." Paul meant that he would be refreshed as his children walked in accord with the will of God. As he saw Philemon respond to a difficult situation, acting in accord with his Christian commitments under the leadership of the Lord and the Holy Spirit, Paul would be refreshed. In this, Paul sounds like the elder who wrote 3 John, "I have no greater joy than that my children walk in the truth" (3 John 4).

The final responsibility lay between Philemon and the Lord. Paul reminded Philemon of the implications of Christianity in such situations. He appealed to Philemon's Christian character and good reputation. He expressed confidence that Philemon would respond as a mature Christian should. Now it was up to Philemon. The case was finished. Voluntarily and spontaneously, Philemon must follow his Lord in doing what was right. Nothing brings greater joy than to see responsible Christian conduct.

(3) Prepare a Room (v. 22)

22 This section ends with one further command. It is almost like an afterthought, and it has caused more scholarly discussion than it merits. Paul asked for Philemon to prepare a place for him to stay. Although he was in prison, he was optimistic. Some have assumed that Paul threatened to come to see if his requests had been honored. The tone of this letter makes that unlikely. Friendship and fellowship predominate. Others have used this statement to point out Paul's fickleness in changing plans, and some use the information to reconstruct Paul's life and writings. In Romans, Paul wrote of his desire to go to Spain from Rome.[35] Six years after writing of his plans to go to Spain, Paul's plans could easily have changed. Perhaps he knew the value of Onesimus and longed to share with him again. Perhaps the long years of awaiting trial brought spiritual pressures and fatigue, and Paul longed to associate with a friend who had a gift of "refreshing the saints." Perhaps he simply needed to relive the ministry God had given him. At any rate, the letter closes where it began—with a warm touch of friendship between two who shared in a partnership in the gospel.

---

[35]This is a major concern in the discussion of the origin of the Prison Epistles. Earlier Paul expressed his desire to go from Rome to Spain (Rom 15:22ff.), and some want to place the Prison Epistles in an earlier time frame that would allow Paul to keep that desire. If so, Phlm 22 is a change of plans. To avoid that, some reconstruct Paul's life and writings (see the introduction to Colossians). The request for a lodging does not demand such reconstructions. Too much is made of Paul's travel expectations.

―――――――――――――― *SECTION OUTLINE* ――――――――――――――

IV. CONCLUSION (vv. 23-25)

―――――――――― **IV. CONCLUSION (vv. 23-25)** ――――――――――

[23]**Epaphras, my fellow prisoner in Christ Jesus, sends you greetings.** [24]**And so do Mark, Aristarchus, Demas and Luke, my fellow workers.**
[25]**The grace of the Lord Jesus Christ be with your spirit.**

23-24 The conclusion to the epistle includes greetings from some who were with Paul in Rome and a prayer for God's grace. The persons identified all appear in Colossians.[1] This gives evidence of the same origin and date for both epistles. Further, these men were well-known by Philemon and his house church, even as they were known at Colosse and Laodicea.

25 Paul ended the epistle with a prayer for God's grace. Paul commonly began and ended with God's grace. Particularly, if Philemon were to accomplish the task that lay before him, he would need a special portion of God's grace.

The grace was to be "with your spirit." Perhaps this is a part for the whole and, therefore, represents Paul's way of praying for the whole person. "The spirit" often identifies the person in communication with God. It is not a separate faculty but is a designation of a function of persons when they communicate with God, who is spirit. Paul, therefore, ended his epistle with a prayer that the channel for communication between God and people would be sufficiently clear that God's grace could be communicated. Further, this prayer asked that God's grace surround each individual of the church so that they might have the peace of God in their lives as well (v. 3).

―――――――――――――――――――――――――――――――――――――

[1]See the commentary notes on Col 4:10-14.

Subject Index[1]

[1]Index was prepared by Lanese Dockery.

Person Index

Scripture Index